The **Rough Guide** to

Copenhagen

written and researched by

Lone Mouritsen & Caroline Osborne

www.roughguides.com

Contents

◀◀ Christiania ◀ Tivoli

Introduction to Copenhagen

Small, compact and easily explored, Copenhagen (København) is a capital city on a human scale, with a skyline largely unchanged for centuries and an unhurried vibe – people rather than cars set the pace here, with a multitude of pedestrianized thoroughfares, cycle lanes and pavement cafés. And though, Little Mermaid aside, most people would be hard pressed to name a landmark building or monument, that's part of the city's understated charm – there's a cornucopia of historic royal palaces, museums, galleries, parks and beaches to be discovered, all within walking distance or a short bus ride of each other.

Confident, patriotic and looking to the future, Copenhagen is shaking off its parochial ways and striving for a more cosmopolitan, international feel: the vibrant harbourfront has seen three major cultural institutions built in the last decade; there's a renewed focus on environmental issues; and, at street level, the city boasts a range of chic hotels, an exciting culinary scene, revamped museums and fabulous shops showcasing the country's outstanding design talent. What's more, the lively nightlife belies the city's relatively modest size, with plenty of cosy bars, clubs and live music venues.

The new harbourfront development aside, architecturally, much of the city dates from the seventeenth and eighteenth centuries, a cultured ensemble of handsome Renaissance palaces, parks and merchant houses laid out around the waterways and canals that give the city, in places, a pronounced Dutch flavour. Successive Danish monarchs left their mark, but none more so than Christian IV, mastermind behind many of the city's most striking landmarks – including **Rosenborg Slot**, the **Rundetårn** and the district of

▲ Louisiana museum

Christianshavn – and Frederik V, who graced the capital with the palaces of **Amalienborg** and the grandiose **Marmorkirken**. These landmarks and the characteristic copper spires of the city's churches remain the highest points in a refreshingly low and undeveloped skyline.

Historically, Copenhagen owes its existence to its position on the narrow Øresund strait separating Denmark from Sweden and commanding the entrance to the Baltic – one of the great trading routes of medieval Europe and now the site of the region's grandest engineering feat, the massive **Øresunds Bridge**. It's this location, poised between Scandinavia and the rest of Europe, which continues to give Copenhagen its distinctive character. Compared to the relatively staid capitals further north, the city has a more European flavour; the freedom with which its most famous export, Carlsberg, flows in the city's hundreds of bars is in stark contrast to the puritanical licensing laws elsewhere in Scandinavia. Yet Copenhagen is also a flagship example of the Scandinavian commitment to liberal social values – exemplified by its attitudes to everything from gay marriage to pornography – and its continued (if precarious) respect for the unique "Free City" of **Christiania**.

Although, in common with most European capitals, increased immigration has led to a degree of racial tension and gang-related crime in some areas and an unpalatable, concomitant rise in the far right, on the whole this is a very tolerant and safe city. And if there's the occasional smugness – a tendency to think all things Danish are the best – this is only the result of a huge, and not unjustified, pride. As a visitor, you can be sure you'll be made to feel welcome wherever you go.

What to see

▲ Skuespilhus café

It takes just thirty minutes to walk across Copenhagen's compact centre, and the wealth of green spaces and pedestrianized areas make exploring a relaxed and thoroughly civilized experience. The historic core of the city is **Slotsholmen**, originally the site of the twelfth-century castle and now home to the huge royal and governmental complex of Christiansborg. Facing Slotsholmen over the Slotsholmen Kanal is the medieval maze of **Indre By**, the bustling heart of the city, traversed by Strøget, the world's longest pedestrianized street, and packed with great shops, cafés and bars, as well as an eclectic clutch of museums and churches. On the opposite side of Slotsholmen from Indre By, the island of **Christianshavn** is one of the inner city's most relaxed and bohemian areas, and home to the "Free City" of Christiania, Copenhagen's famous alternative-lifestyle community. Northeast of Indre By, the fairy-tale castle of **Rosenborg**, one of several royal residences in

Messing about on the water

You're never far from water in Copenhagen, be it the harbour, the sandy, suburban beaches, or the ring of canals and lakes that once formed the city's defensive moats and fortifications. Here are some pointers on how best to experience the city's waterways.

- View the harbour at duck's-eye level on an organized kayak trip. See p.25
- Join the Little Mermaid tourist trail on a canal-boat trip through the old city centre and out into the harbour. See p.25
- Knock back a beer and a plate of herring at one of the many restaurants along Nyhavn. See pp.147–152
- Load up on Danish pastries and coffee from *Lagkagehuset* (see p.152) and wander along pretty Christianshavns Kanal. See p.57
- Join the joggers on the harbourfront Larsens Plads for a bracing stroll past new and old architecture up to the Little Mermaid. See p.76
- Head for the beach at Amager Strandpark, Charlottenlund or Klampenborg. See p.110, p.104 & p.106
- Take a dip in the harbour in an open-air swimming pool. See p.194

the city, sits at the heart of the inner city's greenest area – Kongens Have and the lush gardens of Botanisk Have – and within striking distance of two excellent art museums. Abutting Kongens Have, **Frederikstad**, Frederik V's royal quarter, is dominated by the huge dome of the Marmorkirken and centred on the royal palaces of Amalienborg. South of Indre By, close to the town hall and main square, Rådhuspladsen, you'll find the delightful **Tivoli** amusement park, as well as the excellent **Nationalmuseet** and **Glyptotek** art and sculpture gallery.

▲ Royal jewels at Rosenborg Slot

A little out of the city to the west, exciting, multicultural **Vesterbro**, with its ethnic restaurants, funky shops and trendy nightlife, is one of the hottest spots in town; it rubs shoulders with the genteel, villa-lined streets of **Frederiksberg**, where you'll find the tranquil Frederiksberg Have, the zoo, and the Carlsberg Brewery visitor centre. North of the centre, the once working-class but increasingly gentrified district of **Nørrebro** is centred on the fashionable bars and restaurants of Sankt Hans Torv and Blågårdsgade; to its east, snooty **Østerbro** is home to Copenhagen's old money, as well as the city centre's largest open space, Fælledparken. East of the city lies the island suburb of **Amager** with its beaches, watersports and nature reserve.

▶ Bellevue beach

Copenhagen, as any Dane will tell you, is by no means an accurate reflection of Denmark itself – indeed, a greater contrast with the sleepy provincialism of the rest of the country would be hard to find. Thanks to rapid transport links that connect

▲ Nyboder

the capital with its surrounding countryside, however, you can enjoy all the pleasures of rural Zealand without being much more than an hour away from the capital. Among the many attractions that ring the city are the stunning modern art museums of **Arken** and **Louisiana**, and the great castles of **Kronborg** (the "Elsinore Castle" of Shakespeare's *Hamlet*) and Frederiksborg, while the ancient Danish capital of **Roskilde**, with its magnificent cathedral and museum of Viking ships, offers another enticing day-trip. You're also just a short train ride away from the **beaches** of the Øresund coast, and – with an overnight stop in **Helsingør** – the even more beautiful sandy stretches and pretty fishing villages of the North Zealand coast make for a very rewarding side-trip. Neither are you confined to Denmark for excursions – just across the Øresunds Bridge, **Malmö**, in southern Sweden, offers a historic centre along with good shops and restaurants.

▶ Relaxing by the water

A thoroughly green city

With just over a third of the city's population cycling to work on 300km of cycle paths, a harbour that's clean enough to swim in and nearly a quarter of all food consumed being organic, Copenhagen is way ahead of most of its European counterparts in the green stakes. It recycles more than any other European capital and has the lowest amount of rubbish going to landfill – three-quarters of its household waste is incinerated, producing energy to power the city. Setting itself the target of being the world's leading environmental capital by 2015, Copenhagen also plans to further reduce per capita carbon emissions, introduce electric buses and increase organic food consumption even further. Even the hotels are playing ball, becoming CO_2-neutral and environmentally sound; some even hire out electric cars to guests.

When to go

Copenhagen is on the same latitude as Edinburgh and Moscow, and winters, as you'd expect, are wet, windy and cold, with temperatures regularly falling below zero. With the freeze comes the chance to go skating on icy city lakes before retreating indoors for a comfortable glass of *gløgg*. The city is prettiest in spring, when the trees come into leaf and high-spirited locals emerge from their layers of winter clothing. Summer can be variable: rain is common, though when the sun appears the locals turn out in force, occupying every last corner of every park and pavement café, while the long summer evenings see the city at its liveliest. Autumn can be pleasant, with rainy periods interspersed with beautiful sunny days and stunning seasonal colours.

Average daily temperatures and average monthly rainfall

	Jan	Feb	Mar	Apr	May	Jun	Jul	Aug	Sep	Oct	Nov	Dec
Copenhagen												
Max/min (°C)	2/-2	2/-3	6/-1	10/3	16/8	19/11	22/14	21/14	18/11	12/7	7/3	4/1
Max/min (°F)	36/28	36/26	41/30	50/37	61/46	66/52	72/57	70/57	64/52	54/45	45/37	39/34
Rainfall (mm)	1.9	1.5	1.3	1.5	1.7	1.9	2.8	2.6	2.4	2.3	1.9	1.9

things not to miss

It's not possible to see everything that Copenhagen has to offer in one trip – and we don't suggest you try. What follows is a selective taste of the city's highlights, from atmospheric castles and superb museums to hippie hangouts and funky jazz dives. They're arranged in three colour-coded categories to help you find the very best things to see, do, eat and experience. All highlights have a page reference to take you straight into the Guide, where you can find out more.

01 **Nyhavn** Page **53** • Day or night, picture-postcard Nyhavn, with its canalside stretch of lively bars and cafés, is a great spot for a beer and a herring platter.

02 Kronborg Slot Page **116** • Tactically positioned on a sandy curl of land looking out over the Øresund, for centuries Kronborg collected the Sound tolls from passing ships, though it's more famous as the moody setting for Shakespeare's *Hamlet*.

03 Smørrebrød See ***Food and drink* colour section** • This delicious and quintessentially Danish lunch is best washed down with a snaps or a cold beer.

04 Nationalmuseet Page **84** • A treasure trove of the nation's history from Bronze Age skeletons to dazzling Viking silver to Christian IV's dagger, as well as fascinating ethnological collections.

05 Cycling Page **25** • Do as the locals do and hop on a bike to see the best of the city and its surroundings.

06 Tivoli Page **79** • The city's pleasure gardens still pull in punters by the thousands for the magical mix of funfair, food and music.

07 Glyptotek Page **82** • End your tour of ancient Mediterranean artefacts, Rodin sculptures and French Impressionists with lunch at the beautiful Winter Garden café.

08 Marmorkirken Page **71** • Built by Frederik V for his new royal quarter, Marmorkirken was northern Europe's answer to St Peter's in Rome.

09 Pølser Page **146** • The city's ubiquitous fast food of choice goes further than the average hot dog, with a wider range of sausages and sauces.

10 The Queen's Tapestries Page **35** • The royals may no longer live in Christiansborg Slot, but the modern tapestries there provide a stunning backdrop to royal functions.

11 Swimming in the harbour Page **194** • In summer, nothing beats a refreshing dip in one of the Copenhagen's open-air harbour swimming pools, with the city skyline as a backdrop.

12 Illums Bolighus Page **185** • Illums Bolighus offers the best in Danish design from Arne Jacobsen chairs to Bodum coffeeware.

13 Rosenborg Slot Page **66** • This wonderful castle, once home to Christian IV, now houses the crown jewels.

14 Exploring the waterways Page **25** • Cruise the city's waterways for a revealing glimpse of its merchant past and stunning views of its modern harbourfront.

15 Jazz Page **196** • You're never far from jazz in Copenhagen, from street buskers to world-class music venues.

16 The Little Mermaid Page **75** • The wistful mermaid is Copenhagen's most famous symbol, represented in all manner of postcards, gifts and souvenirs.

17 Outdoor cafés Page **164** • Considering its northern latitude, Copenhagen has an astounding number of outdoor cafés and bars, made cosy with blankets and heaters when it gets cold.

18 Christiania Page **58** • The hippie city within a city has its own funky restaurants, cafés, arts venues, shops and galleries, as well as colourful houses in a peaceful waterfront setting.

19 **Vikingeskibs Museet** Page **124** • On the banks of scenic Roskilde Fjord – once home of Viking settlements – this collection of wooden hulls provides an engrossing introduction to Viking boat-building and nautical skills.

20 **Danish pastries** See ***Food and drink* colour section** • Lighter, flakier and infinitely more delicious than the ones back home.

21 **Nightlife** Page **169** • Copenhagen has a plethora of late-night clubs and drinking holes, including some very swanky cocktail bars.

22 **Louisiana** Page **115** • An outstanding collection of modern art in spectacular surroundings, with a fabulous sculpture garden overlooking the Øresund.

Basics

Basics

Getting there

From the UK and Ireland, the cheapest and most convenient way of getting to Copenhagen is to fly. From North America, a handful of airlines fly direct, though it may be cheaper to route via London. Going via London or another European hub is the only option from Australia, New Zealand and South Africa.

Fares from the UK are not subject to seasonal changes to the extent that they are in North America, but as a rule of thumb you'll pay more from (roughly) early June to mid-September, when the weather is best; and less in the low season, November through to April (excluding Christmas and New Year). Flying on weekends is generally more expensive; price ranges quoted below assume midweek travel.

Flights from the UK and Ireland

Budget airline schedules and prices are especially vulnerable in a volatile economic climate, so the information below may be subject to change; you can check the latest on the Copenhagen airport website (Ⓦwww.cph.dk).

There are many direct services from **London's airports** to Copenhagen (roughly 2hr) with SAS, British Airways, Cimber Air, Norwegian Air Shuttle, easyJet and bmi. All operate at least one flight a day, though services may be reduced at weekends. Copenhagen is also served by regional UK airports, including **Aberdeen** (SAS), **Birmingham** (SAS, bmi), **Edinburgh** (Cimber Air, Norwegian Air Shuttle, bmi, SAS), **Glasgow** (SAS, bmi), **Manchester** (SAS, easyJet, bmi) and **Newcastle** (Cimber Air). Most of these carriers operate two to four flights a week.

Scheduled fares of the major airlines are pretty well matched; smaller carriers such as Cimber and bmi prove the cheapest (around £100 return). Low-cost carriers easyJet and Norwegian Air Shuttle offer the best deals (around £50 return), but are less flexible. Otherwise, you'll pay about £130 for a discounted return ticket bought directly from SAS or British Airways.

From Ireland you have twice-daily SAS flights from **Dublin** or thrice-weekly departures with Norwegian Air Shuttle. From **Cork** or **Shannon** your best bet is with Aer Lingus via London Heathrow or Ryanair via Stansted or London Gatwick. Official **fares** with SAS are around €200 for a midweek economy fare and €55 with Norwegian Air Shuttle for a non-refundable return. If you're flying from a regional airport, it may be cheaper to find one of the numerous special deals to London and then fly from there (see p.21).

There are no direct flights to Copenhagen from **Belfast**; your best bet is to fly via London, Glasgow or Edinburgh.

Flights from the US and Canada

The only direct **flights** are available from the US – from Chicago (SAS, United), Washington (SAS, United), Atlanta (Delta, Air France) and New York (Continental, SAS, United). All these airlines offer regular promotions which prove a good deal if you have flexibility.

Fares are similar whichever carrier you choose, though it's still worth shopping around. SAS and United's daily flights from **Newark** cost $2900–3300 for a fully flexible return and $500–800 for an economy fixed return, depending on the season. Tickets from **Chicago** and **Washington** go for $3000–3800 flexible/$660–900 fixed. Continental's four weekly direct flights from Newark cost around $3600/$600–800, while Delta's daily flight from Atlanta goes for $3200–3500 for a flexible fully refundable ticket in high season, and $650–750 for a fixed low-season return.

You could also consider flying to **London**, one of the cheapest European cities to get to, and taking a discount flight from there (see p.19).

Flights from Australia, New Zealand and South Africa

There are **no direct flights** from Australia, New Zealand or South Africa to Scandinavia; instead, you'll have to fly via a European or Asian gateway city – or both. Fares are pretty steep, so it's worth flying to London, Paris, Amsterdam or Frankfurt first and picking up a cheap flight from there. Fares to Europe vary significantly with the **season**: low season runs from mid-January to the end of February and during October and November; high season runs from mid-May to the end of August and from December to mid-January.

Airlines flying out of **Australia** and **New Zealand** often use SAS for connecting services on to Copenhagen and involve one stop en route. Other less direct routes involve a minimum of two stops, one Middle Eastern or Asian – Dubai, Singapore, Beijing or Bangkok – and one European – Frankfurt, Paris, Helsinki or London. Airlines such as Thai, British Airways, Finnair, Lufthansa, Emirates and Qantas ply these routes. For tickets from **Sydney**, **Melbourne**, **Perth** or **Auckland** expect to pay from Aus$1700/NZ$2100 in low season or from Aus$2500/NZ$3100 in high season. Flights from

Six steps to a better kind of travel

At Rough Guides we are passionately committed to travel. We feel strongly that only through travelling do we truly come to understand the world we live in and the people we share it with – plus tourism has brought a great deal of **benefit** to developing economies around the world over the last few decades. But the extraordinary growth in tourism has also damaged some places irreparably, and of course **climate change** is exacerbated by most forms of transport, especially flying. This means that now more than ever it's important to **travel thoughtfully** and **responsibly**, with respect for the cultures you're visiting – not only to derive the most benefit from your trip but also to preserve the best bits of the planet for everyone to enjoy. At Rough Guides we feel there are six main areas in which you can make a difference:

- Consider what you're contributing to the **local economy**, and how much the services you use do the same, whether it's through employing local workers and guides or sourcing locally grown produce and local services.
- Consider the **environment** on holiday as well as at home. Water is scarce in many developing destinations, and the biodiversity of local flora and fauna can be adversely affected by tourism. Try to patronize businesses that take account of this.
- Travel with a purpose, not just to tick off experiences. Consider **spending longer** in a place, and getting to know it and its people.
- Give thought to how often you **fly**. Try to avoid short hops by air and more harmful night flights.
- Consider **alternatives to flying**, travelling instead by bus, train, boat and even by bike or on foot where possible.
- Make your trips "**climate neutral**" via a reputable carbon offset scheme. All Rough Guide flights are offset, and every year we donate money to a variety of charities devoted to combating the effects of climate change.

Christchurch and **Wellington** tend to go via Sydney or Auckland and cost around NZ$150–300 more.

The best deals from **South Africa** are from **Johannesburg** with Swiss via Zurich, Air France via Paris, KLM via Amsterdam and British Airways via London. Prices hover around R8000 and R9000 depending on the season.

Trains

Taking a **train** is a relaxed, and climate-conscious, way of getting to Copenhagen from the UK. You can cross over to the continent by boat and pick up a train from there or take the Eurostar from St Pancras in London. Almost all ticketing for train travel within Europe is now handled by **Rail Europe** (see p.22), which provides the fastest and most convenient routings via Eurostar to Brussels and then on to Copenhagen via Cologne (20hr). The **cheapest fares** entail booking a round-trip fourteen days in advance with one Saturday night away – currently around £240 (more with a sleeper berth). **Rail Europe** also sells through-tickets from most UK starting points; check the site for special offers. Through-tickets for the train/cross-channel ferry are only available from a few agents and larger train stations. You could, with careful planning, organize your own train and ferry tickets – a cheaper, if more complicated, process.

Buses

Taking the **bus** to Copenhagen can be an endurance test, but it's an option if time (and occasionally, with air fares so cheap, money) is no object or you specifically do not want to fly.

Eurolines (see p.22) is the major UK operator of international bus routes; you can book online, through most major travel agents (see below), or through any Eurolines agent. They run six weekly services to **Copenhagen** either via Brussels (24hr) or Amsterdam (30hr). **Fares** start at £120 return – with discounts for the over-60s and those under 26 – and rise slightly in summer.

There are no through-services from anywhere in the UK outside London, but **National Express** buses from all over the British Isles connect with Eurolines in London.

Airlines, agents and operators

Airlines

Aer Lingus Ⓦwww.aerlingus.com
Air New Zealand Ⓦwww.airnz.co.nz
bmi Ⓦwww.flybmi.com
British Airways Ⓦwww.ba.com
Cimber Air Ⓦwww.cimber.com
Continental Airlines Ⓦwww.continental.com
Delta Ⓦwww.delta.com
easyJet Ⓦwww.easyjet.com
Emirates Ⓦwww.emirates.com
Finnair Ⓦwww.finnair.com
KLM (Royal Dutch Airlines) Ⓦwww.klm.com
Lufthansa Ⓦwww.lufthansa.com
Norwegian Air Shuttle Ⓦwww.norwegian.com
Qantas Airways Ⓦwww.qantas.com
Ryanair Ⓦwww.ryanair.com
SAS (Scandinavian Airlines) Ⓦwww.flysas.com
South African Airways Ⓦwww.flysaa.com
Swiss Ⓦwww.swiss.com
Thai Airways Ⓦwww.thaiair.com
United Airlines Ⓦwww.united.com

Agents and operators

North South Travel UK Ⓣ01245/608291, Ⓦwww.northsouthtravel.co.uk. Friendly, competitive travel agency, offering discounted fares worldwide. Profits are used to support projects in the developing world, especially the promotion of sustainable tourism.

Scantours UK Ⓣ020/7839 2927, Ⓦwww.scantoursuk.com, US Ⓣ1-800/223-7226, Ⓦwww.scantours.com. Package deals, hotel booking, customized itineraries and sightseeing tours.

STA Travel US Ⓣ1-800/781-4040, UK Ⓣ0871/230 0040, Australia Ⓣ134 782, New Zealand Ⓣ0800/474 400, South Africa Ⓣ0861/781 781; Ⓦwww.statravel.com. Worldwide specialists in independent travel; also student IDs, travel insurance, car rental, rail passes, and more. Good discounts for students and under-26s.

Trailfinders UK Ⓣ0845/058 5858, Ireland Ⓣ01/677 7888, Australia Ⓣ1300/780 212; Ⓦwww.trailfinders.com. One of the best-informed and most efficient agents for independent travellers.

Travel CUTS Canada Ⓣ1-866/246-9762, US Ⓣ1-800/592-2887; Ⓦwww.travelcuts.com. Canadian youth and student travel firm.

USIT Ireland Ⓣ01/602 1906, Northern Ireland Ⓣ028/9032 7111; Ⓦwww.usit.ie. Ireland's main student and youth travel specialists.

Rail contacts

Europrail International Canada ⓣ1-888/667-9734, ⓦwww.europrail.net
Eurostar UK ⓣ0870/518 6186, ⓦwww.eurostar.com
Rail Europe US ⓣ1-888/382-7245, Canada ⓣ1-800/361-7245, UK ⓣ0844/848 4064, Australia ⓣ03/9642 8644, South Africa ⓣ11/628 2319; ⓦwww.raileurope.com
ScanTours see p.21
STA Travel see p.21
Trailfinders see p.21

Bus contacts

Eurolines UK ⓣ0871/781 8181, ⓦwww.eurolines.com
STA Travel see p.21
Trailfinders see p.21

Arrival

However you arrive in Copenhagen you'll find yourself within easy reach of the city centre. Copenhagen airport is just a few kilometres to the southeast, on the edge of the island of Amager, while almost all trains and buses deposit you near the city's main transport hub, Central Station.

By air

Getting into the city from Copenhagen **airport** (ⓦwww.cph.dk), 11km from the city in the suburb of Kastrup, couldn't be easier: one of Europe's fastest airport-to-city rail lines runs directly to Central Station (every 10min during the day, hourly at 3min past the hour 1–4.30am; 10–13min; 31.50kr). Half of these trains continue north to the town of Helsingør (1hr; 94.50kr), calling at Nørreport (16min) and Østerport (18min) stations. In addition, a fast new metro links the airport with Christianshavn (12min), Kongens Nytorv (13min) and Nørreport (15min) stations (all 31.50kr) in the centre (every 4–6min during the day, every 15min midnight–7am). There's also a much slower city bus (#5A 31.50kr; #96N night bus, 63kr) to Rådhuspladsen and Nørreport station, which is only convenient if you want to get off on the way. A taxi to the centre costs about 180kr – there's a rank outside the arrivals hall.

You can pick up a copy of the English-language *Copenhagen This Week* and free maps of the city from a helpful **information desk** (daily: June–Aug 5am–midnight; Sept–May 6am–11pm) in the sleek arrivals hall at Terminal 3. They also offer an efficient **hotel-booking service** (70kr per reservation) and some good last-minute deals on accommodation. The airport also has two late-opening **banks** (daily 6am–10pm), lots of ATMs, a 7-Eleven with internet access (29kr for 1hr 30min), a number of wi-fi hubs, numerous car-rental agencies and a post office. The stylish *Hilton Hotel*, connected to the airport by a pedestrian walkway, is a good place to kill some time – their lobby bar is equipped with arrival and departure screens.

By bus and train

All buses and trains to Copenhagen arrive at or near the **Central Station** (in Danish, Hovedbanegården or København H), the city's main transport hub, from where there are excellent connections to virtually every part of the city via bus or local train – but note, not the new metro (see p.23). The station also has an array of shops, a foreign-exchange bureau (daily 8am–9pm), a bicycle-rental service (see p.25), places to eat and, downstairs, left-luggage lockers (see p.29). The national train company, DSB, has a travel agency and information centre just inside the main entrance off Vesterbrogade (daily 5.45am–11.30pm; ⓣ70 13 14 15, ⓦwww.dsb.dk).

Eurolines coaches (see p.22) from around Europe stop behind the station on Ingerslevgade, across from DGI-byen.

Getting around

The best way to explore Copenhagen is either to walk or cycle: the inner city is compact, much of the central area pedestrianized, and there's a comprehensive network of excellent bike paths. For travelling further afield, there's an integrated network of buses, metros, S-Tog and local trains.

Tickets

All city transport operates on an integrated **zonal system** extending far beyond the suburbs and encompassing S-Tog trains, the metro system, regional trains and buses. There are an astounding 99 zones (pick up a free leaflet from any S-Tog station); you may find it easiest at first simply to state your destination and you'll be sold the appropriate ticket. The city centre and immediate area, as you'd expect, are in zones 1 and 2. **Fares** are based on a combination of zones and time: the cheapest ticket (*billet*) costs 21kr and is valid for one hour's travel within any two zones, with unlimited transfers between buses and trains. Another option is the *klippekort*, a discount card containing ten stamps. The cheapest *klippekort* costs 130kr, with each stamp being valid for an hour's travel within any two zones; stamps on a 170kr *klippekort* are valid for one hour within any three zones – good value if you plan to travel outside the city centre – and are also valid to and from the airport. Unlimited transfers are allowed, and two or more people can use the same *klippekort* simultaneously, provided you clip the required number of stamps per person. There's also an excellent-value **24-hour ticket** (120kr), which is valid on all transport as far away as Helsingør and Roskilde, as well as night buses. Finally, a good option if you're staying on for a while is the seven-day **FlexCard** (205kr for 2 zones; 250kr for 3), which gives unlimited travel for seven days to whoever is carrying it, meaning that it can be shared as long as the people sharing aren't travelling at the same time. *Billets* can be bought on board buses or at train stations, while *klippekort*, 24-hour tickets and FlexCards are only available at bus or train stations and HT Kortsalg kiosks; *klippekort* should be stamped when boarding the bus or via machines on train-station platforms. Route maps can be picked up free at stations, and most free city maps include bus lines and a diagram of the S-Tog and metro network.

By train

The **S-Tog** train service (ⓦwww.s-tog.dk; see colour map at the back of the book; 5am–12.30am every 10–15min) is a metropolitan network laid out in a huge "U" shape and covering Copenhagen and the surrounding areas. Six of its seven lines stop at Central Station (in Danish, Hovedbanegården or København H), while the remaining line runs a circular route around the centre. Each line has a letter, from A to H (some letters are not used), and is also colour-coded on route maps. Stations are marked by red hexagonal signs with a yellow "S" inside them.

Copenhagen's fast and efficient underground **metro system** (ⓦwww.m.dk; departures every couple of minutes) circumvents the Central Station in a "U" shape, connecting the island of Amager and Copenhagen airport with west Copenhagen via Christianshavn and Kongens Nytorv. The metro's two lines – M1 and M2 – cross the S-Tog and regional trains at Nørreport, Flintholm and Vanløse. Stations are marked by a large red underlined "M" painted onto aluminium pillars.

Finally, a regional train network run by the **Danish State Railway** (DSB; Ⓦwww.dsb.dk) connects the city to Helsingør and Roskilde, calling at Østerport and Nørreport stations and some suburban destinations on the way; remember that the S-Tog, metros and the regional trains depart from different platforms at Nørreport station.

By bus

The city's **bus** network (Ⓦwww.moviatrafik.dk) is more comprehensive than the S-Tog system and can be a more convenient way to get around once you get the hang of finding the stops – marked by yellow placards on signposts – and as long as you avoid the rush hour (7–9am & 5–6pm). The excellent free city map produced by Copenhagen Right Now includes all bus routes in the centre. The bus terminal is a slick black building on Rådhuspladsen, a block from both Central Station and Tivoli; you can pick up route maps here, and get general information about the metropolitan transport system. Other useful buses leave from Central Station's Vesterbro side entrance, the Tivoli side entrance, and the bridge at the end of the tracks. Buses with an "S" suffix only make limited stops, offering a faster service – check they make the stop you require before you get on. Buses with an "A" suffix indicate that the bus runs frequently. All buses have a small electronic board above the driver's seat displaying both the zone you're currently in and the time – so there's no excuse for not having a valid ticket. A skeletal **night-bus** service runs once or twice an hour, when fares double. Night-bus numbers always end with "N".

Harbour buses

A cheaper way to experience Copenhagen from the waterfront than a canal tour (see box opposite), yellow **harbour "buses"** sail along the harbour between Nordre Toldbod (near the Little Mermaid) and the Royal Library, stopping six times and costing the same as a normal bus fare. Services (daily every 20min about 7am–7pm) are cancelled when the harbour is frozen.

Useful bus routes

#1A DGI-byen (near Kødbyen), Central Station, Tivoli, National Museum, Christiansborg, Kongens Nytorv (near Nyhavn), Bredgade (near Amalienborg) and Esplanaden (near Kastellet and the Little Mermaid)

#2A Central Station, Rådhuspladsen, Christiansborg and Christianshavns Torv (near Christiania)

#3A Trianglen (near Fælledparken), Sankt Hans Torv, Enghavevej (near Vega)

#5A Assistens Kirkegård, Nørrebrogade (near Skt Hans Torv and Blågårdsgade), Nørreport Station, Nørre Voldgade, Rådhuspladsen, Central Station, Copenhagen Airport

#6A Sortedams Dosseringen (the lakes), Statens Museum for Kunst (Royal Museum of Fine Arts), Nørreport Station, Gammel Torv-Nytorv, Rådhusstræde, Vester Voldgade, Rådhuspladsen, Vesterport Station, Vesterbrogade (City Museum), Roskildevej, Frederiksberg Slot and the City Zoo

#10 Rådhuspladsen, Hovedbanegården, Istedgade, Enghavevej (and Vega)

#26 Valby Langgade, Carlsberg Brewery, Pile Allé, Frederiksberg Allé, Vesterbrogade, Central Station, Rådhuspladsen, Vester Voldgade, Kongens Nytorv, Dronnings Tværgade, Øster Voldgade, Østerport Station, Indiakaj, Langelinieka

#40 Central Station, Christiansborg, Christianshavns Torv, Refshaleøen and Halvandet

#66 Åboulevard, Vesterport Station, Tivoli and Central Station, Christians Brygge on Slotsholmen, City Hostel, Christianshavns Torv, Christiania, Operaen

Guided tours

Bike Copenhagen with Mike ⓣ26 39 56 88, ⓦwww.bikecopenhagenwithmike.dk. Guided cyle tours from Central Station's Rewentlowsgade exit in front of the Københavns Cykler bike rental shop. Charismatic Mike guides the way past downtown Vesterbro, Amalienborg, the Little Mermaid, Christiania and much more, stopping to give you his colourful take on the city's history and its current trends. No booking required. Daily 10.30am; 3hr 30min; 165kr, plus 85kr for bike rental. Cash only.

Copenhagen Adventure Tours ⓣ40 50 40 06, ⓦwww.kajakole.dk. Original and challenging tours (April–Oct) using safe, easy-to-handle kayaks. Tours start from Christianshavns Kanal, Strandgade 50 in front of *Restaurant Kanalen*, and give a unique view of the city from its canals. Ninety-minute tours (185kr) take in Innerhavnen and the canals around Christianshavn; the 2 hour trip (295kr) includes the Holmen; and the arm-shattering 3hr trip crosses Innerhaven and circumnavigates Slotsholmen (345kr). The price includes a free drink in a canalside floating bar.

Copenhagen Sightseeing Tours ⓦwww.sightseeing.dk. A variety of bus tours (with multilingual headphone commentary) from Rådhuspladsen, including some that cover the rest of Zealand, taking in places such as Helsingør and Roskilde.

DFDS Canal Tours ⓣ32 96 30 00, ⓦwww.canaltours.dk. Two options (daily: April–Oct every 30min 10am–5pm; Nov & Dec hourly 10am–3pm; 1hr) start from Nyhavn or Gammel Strand and take in various city sights, including the Little Mermaid, Amalienborg Palace and the Operaen; at 60kr, however, you'll get more for your money with Netto-Bådene (see below). DFDS also run three hop-on hop-off **waterbus** routes (daily mid-May to Aug, roughly hourly 10am–5pm), one north to the Trekroner fort/island and stopping at Halvandet, one south to the Fisketorvet shopping complex, and one around the canals of Christianshavn. A two-day unlimited-use ticket, which includes open-top bus tours (see Copenhagen Sightseeing Tours above) costs 220kr, a one-day ticket 60kr, and a single trip 40kr.

Netto-Bådene ⓣ32 54 41 02, ⓦwww.havnerundfart.dk. Offering a combination of the two DFDS tours listed above, Netto-Bådene's one-hour trip for only 30kr is much better value. Tours start at Holmens Kirke across from Børsen, pass Nyhavn, Holmen, Nyholm, Amalienborg Palace and the Little Mermaid, and circumnavigate Slotsholmen before finishing back at Holmens Kirke. Daily: April to mid-Oct 2–5 times hourly 10am–5pm (July & Aug 10am–7pm).

Walking Tours The Copenhagen Right Now office on Berstorffsgade (see p.30) has a list of English-language walking tours. Most unusual is the "Watchman's Round" (ⓦwww.nattevaegterne.dk) starting at dusk (Thurs, Fri & Sat mid-July to mid-Sept 9pm; rest of the year 7pm; 75kr; 1hr 15min) from Gråbrødre Torv in front of *Peder Oxe* restaurant. The tour follows an "eighteenth-century watchman" on his round, while he tells tales (in English) of the old city.

By bike

If the weather's good, the best way to see Copenhagen is to do as the locals do and get on your bike. Cycling is also excellent for exploring the immediate countryside, as bikes can be taken on S-Togs (12kr) through any number of zones; you can also buy a special bicycle *klippekort* (valid for 10 journeys; 105kr). The superb, city-wide cycle lanes make cycling very safe; lights are a legal requirement at night (you'll be stopped and fined if the police catch you without them) and helmets are recommended at all times.

During the summer-only free **City Bike scheme** (ⓦwww.bycyklen.dk) two thousand free bikes (look for the ads painted onto their solid wheels) are scattered about the city at S-Tog stations and other busy locations. Leave a refundable 20kr deposit and relock the bike in a designated rack when you've finished, or just leave it out on a pavement, in which case someone else will happily return it and pocket the coin. Don't use your own lock and don't take a bike outside the city limits (marked by the old rampart lakes) or you risk a fine.

There are also a number of rental outlets in central Copenhagen: Københavns Cyklebørs, Gothersgade 157, Indre By (Mon–Fri 9am–5.30pm, Sat 10am–1.30pm; ⓣ33 14 07 17, ⓦwww.cykelboersen.dk; 75kr per day, 285kr per week, 300kr deposit); Østerport Cykler, Oslo Plads 9, next to Østerport Station (Mon–Fri 8am–6pm, Sat 9am–1pm; ⓣ33 33 85 13, ⓦwww.oesterport-cykler.dk; 85kr per day, 375kr per week, 500kr deposit), and Baisikeli, Turesensgade 10, Indre By (Mon–Fri 9am–5pm, Sat 10am–1pm; ⓣ26 70 02 29, ⓦwww.baisikeli.dk; 60kr per day, 250kr per week, 200kr deposit) which rents out used bikes and uses all profits to send refurbished bikes to Africa.

Taxis

Taxis are plentiful, but with a flat starting fare of 24kr, then 12.50kr per kilometre (13.50–16.80kr after 4pm and at weekends), they're only worth taking in a group. There's a handy rank outside Central Station; you can phone Taxamotor (ⓣ38 10 10 10); or you can hail one in the street – the green "*Fri*" sign on top shows it's available. Rickshaw-styled **cycle taxis** (April–Oct; ⓣ35 43 01 22, ⓦwww.rickshaw.dk), carrying a maximum of two people, operate a flat starting fare of 40kr if you flag them down on the street, then charge 4kr per minute.

The media

Overseas newspapers are sold at the Magasin du Nord and Illum department stores (see p.187 for both), the stall on the eastern side of Rådhuspladsen, newsagents along Strøget, and stalls in Central Station. Most UK and US weekday titles cost 25–40kr and are available the day after publication.

The **English-language** *Copenhagen Post* (20kr; downloadable at ⓦwww.copenhagenpost.dk) covers domestic issues and has an in-depth listings section; it comes out every Friday. If you can read Danish, your choices among the main daily **newspapers** (22–28kr) are *Politiken*, a reasonably impartial broadsheet with strong arts features; the conservative/centrist *Berlingske Tidende*; *Kristeligt Dagblad*, a Christian paper; *Jyllands-Posten*, a well-respected Jutland-based right-wing paper; and *Information*, left-wing and intellectual. The weekly *Weekendavisen*, published on Thursdays, has excellent background features. The best sports coverage can be found in the two tabloids: *BT*, which has a conservative bias, and *Ekstra Bladet*. You'll find excellent **entertainment listings** in *Politiken*, and every Thursday *Information* has a section devoted to listings, too. The free monthly **music** magazine, *Gaffa*, found in cafés and record shops, lists most of the bigger shows.

Television

Denmark has four national TV stations and a host of cable channels. The four nationals are the non-commercial DR1 and DR2, and the commercial TV2 and TV2 Zulu – though, apart from the advertising, you'll probably struggle to spot the difference between them. The cable channels, some of which are shared with Sweden and Norway, are all commercial and rich in American sitcoms and soaps (usually with Danish subtitles). If you're staying in a hotel, or a youth hostel with a TV room, you may also have the option of German and Swedish channels – plus a dozen cable and satellite stations.

Travel essentials

Crime and personal safety

Copenhagen is one of the most peaceful cities in Europe. Most public places are well lit and secure, the majority of people genuinely friendly and helpful, and street crime and hassle relatively rare. Like any capital city, it has its share of **petty crime**, but keep an eye on your cash and passport and you should have little reason to visit the **police**. If you do, you'll find them courteous, concerned and usually able to speak English. If you have something stolen, make sure you get a **police report** – essential if you are to make an insurance claim.

As for **offences** you might commit, **nude sunbathing** is universally accepted in all the major resorts (elsewhere, there'll be nobody around to care). Being **drunk** on the streets can get you arrested, and **drinking and driving** is treated especially rigorously. **Drug** offences, too, meet with the same strict attitude that prevails throughout the rest of Europe.

Culture and etiquette

There is no single word in the Danish language for "**please**". So when a Dane doesn't say "please" when speaking to you in English, it's not because they're rude – the word just doesn't come naturally. Danes are also renowned for being direct – if they want something they say "Give me..." – which can, incorrectly, be interpreted as impolite.

Service is included on all restaurant, hotel and taxi bills, so unless you feel you've been given exceptionally good service, tipping is not necessary.

Electricity

The Danish electricity supply runs at 220–240V, 50Hz AC; sockets generally require a two-pin plug. Visitors from the UK will need an adaptor; visitors from outside the EU may need a transformer.

Emergencies

Dial ⓣ112 for police, fire or ambulance. The central police station is at Polititorvet 14 (ⓣ33 14 88 88), with additional stations at Halmtorvet 20 (ⓣ33 14 14 48) and Nørrebrogade 88 (ⓣ35 21 53 20), as well as Central Station (ⓣ33 25 14 48). See also "Health", on p.28.

Entry requirements

European Union, US, Canadian, Australian and New Zealand citizens need only a valid **passport** to enter Denmark for up to three months. South African citizens must obtain **visas** from the embassy in Pretoria (see overleaf) before travelling. All other nationals should consult the relevant embassy about visa requirements.

For **longer stays**, EU nationals can apply for a residence permit while in the country, which, if it's granted, may be valid for up to five years. Non-EU nationals can only apply for residence permits before leaving home, and must be able to prove they can support themselves without working.

In spite of the lack of restrictions, **checks** are frequently made on travellers at the major points of entry. If you're young and are carrying a rucksack, be prepared to prove that you have enough money to support yourself during your stay. You may also be asked how long you intend to stay and why.

Danish embassies

The addresses given are for the embassy in that country. To find out if there is a consulate in a major city nearer to your home, contact the main embassy or check their website.

Australia and New Zealand 15 Hunter St, Yarralumla, Canberra ACT 2600 ⓣ061/26270 5333, ⓦwww.canberra.um.dk.

Canada 47 Clarence St, Suite 450, Ottawa, Ontario K1N 9K1 ⓣ613/562-1811, ⓦwww.ambottawa.um.dk.

Ireland 7th floor Block E Iveagh Court, Harcourt Rd, Dublin 2 ⓣ01/475 6404, ⓦwww.ambdublin.um.dk.

South Africa Parioli Office Park, Block B2, Ground Floor, 1166 Park St, Pretoria ⓣ012/430 9340, ⓦwww.ambpretoria.um.dk.
UK 55 Sloane St, London SW1X 9SR ⓣ020/7333 0200, ⓦwww.denmark.org.uk.
US 3200 Whitehaven St NW, Washington DC 20008 ⓣ202/234-4300, ⓦwww.denmarkemb.org.

Health

Most visitors to Copenhagen will, of course, enjoy a trouble-free trip, but should you require medical attention, then you can rest assured that health care in Denmark is superb. There are **emergency departments** at Amager Hospital, Italiensvej 1, Amager (ⓣ32 34 35 00); Bispebjerg Hospital, Bispebjerg Bakke 23 (ⓣ35 31 23 73) and Frederiksberg Hospital, Nordre Fasanvej 57, Frederiksberg (ⓣ38 16 35 22). They provide free treatment for EU and Scandinavian nationals, though citizens of other countries are unlikely to have to pay. For general **medical emergencies**, call ⓣ122.

If you need a **doctor**, call ⓣ33 15 46 00 (Mon–Fri 8am–4pm) and you'll be given the name of one in your area; outside these hours, call ⓣ70 13 00 41. Doctors' fees start at 250kr, to be paid in cash. If you're an EU citizen and you have a European Health Insurance Card (EHIC) – available from post offices in your home country – you can claim back doctors' fees and charges for medicine from the local health department. You'll need to produce the relevant receipts and card. For **dental emergencies**, contact Tandlægevagten, Oslo Plads 14 ⓣ35 38 02 51 (Mon–Fri 8–9.30pm, Sat & Sun 10am–noon), but be prepared to pay at least 200kr on the spot.

Copenhagen's two main 24-hour **pharmacies** are Steno Apotek, Vesterbrogade 6C in front of Central Station (ⓣ33 14 82 66) and Sønderbro Apotek, Amagerbrogade 158, Amager (ⓣ32 58 01 40).

Insurance

A typical travel insurance policy usually provides cover for the loss of baggage, tickets and – up to a certain limit – cash or cheques, as well as cancellation or curtailment of your journey. Before paying for a new policy, it's worth checking whether you are already covered. Some all-risks home insurance policies may cover your possessions when overseas, and many private medical schemes include cover when abroad. In Canada, provincial health plans usually provide partial cover for medical mishaps overseas, while holders of official student/teacher/youth cards in North America are entitled to meagre accident coverage and hospital in-patient benefits. Students will often find that their student health coverage extends during the vacations and for one term beyond the date of last enrolment.

Internet

Copenhagen has plenty of wireless hubs in cafés and bars and on board all trains. Most hotels and hostels – and even some campsites – offer wireless access (some for free) or some other form of internet access, and access is also available **free** at libraries (though not the Royal Library). Most central are Københavns Hovedbibliotek at Krystalgade 15, Indre By; Christianshavn Bibliotek at Dronningensgade 53; Blågårdens Bibliotek at Blågårdsplads 5, Nørrebro; and Østerbros Bibliotek, Dag Hammaskjölds

Allé 19. Opening hours are usually Mon–Fri 10am–7pm, Sat 10am–2pm. The main **internet café** is the huge Boomtown, Axeltorv 1–3 (daily 24hr; ⓦwww.boomtown.net).

Left luggage

The DSB Garderobe office downstairs in Central Station **stores luggage** for 30kr per item per day and has lockers (Mon–Sat 5.30am–1am, Sun 6am–1am; 35kr/45kr for 24hr). Copenhagen airport's left-luggage facility, in the walkway between Terminal 2 and Terminal 3, charges 40kr per day (max 1 month), and has small and large lockers for 30kr and 50kr per day respectively (max 3 days).

Lost property

The police department's **lost-property** office is at Slotsherrensvej 113, Vanløse ⓣ38 74 88 22. For items lost on a bus, contact the bus information office on ⓣ36 13 14 15; lost on a train or S-Tog, the central train information office on ⓣ70 13 14 15; lost on the metro, call ⓣ70 15 16 15; lost on a plane, contact the airline or Copenhagen airport on ⓣ32 47 47 25.

Mail

Like most of the country's public bodies, the Danish **post office** runs an exceedingly tight ship – within Denmark, anything you post is almost certain to arrive within two days. You can buy stamps from most newsagents and from post offices. The main post office is at Købmagergade 1 (Mon–Fri 10am–6pm, Sat 10am–2pm) and there's a late-opening one inside the Central Station (Mon–Fri 8am–9pm, Sat & Sun 10am–4pm). Mail under 50g costs 8kr to other parts of Europe, and 9kr to the rest of the world.

Maps

The best **city** maps are those produced by Kraks, either in booklet form at various scales, or as a folding map at 1:15,000; they're updated yearly. **Denmark c**ountry maps are produced by Kümmerley & Frey (1:300,000), Ravenstein (1:500,000), and Baedeker (1:400,000); make sure you check the date before you buy these as they quickly become outdated. The **provinces** of Denmark are covered by the 1:200,000 Kort og Matrikelstyren series.

Money and costs

The Danish currency is the **krone** (plural kroner), made up of 100 øre, and comes in notes of 1000kr, 500kr, 200kr, 100kr and 50kr, and coins of 20kr, 10kr, 5kr, 2kr, 1kr, 50øre and 25øre. At the time of writing, the exchange rate was approximately 8.30kr to the pound, 7.40kr to the euro and 5.05kr to the US dollar. For the latest rates, go to ⓦwww.xe.com.

Red Kontanten high-street cash machines (**ATMs**) give cash advances on credit cards and, if you've a Link, Cirrus or Maestro symbol on your ATM card, will allow you to withdraw funds from your own account in local currency (check with your home bank), which can work out cheaper than changing cash or traveller's cheques.

For the latter, **banks** (Mon–Wed & Fri 10am–4pm, Thurs 10am–6pm) charge 30kr commission per transaction, so change as much as is feasible in one go. A similar commission is charged at the late-opening exchange facilities at the airport and Central Station. **Forex** exchange bureaux, which charge 30kr to exchange cash and 20kr to exchange traveller's cheques, are much rarer; there's one at Central Station (daily 8am–9pm), one at Nørre Voldgade 90, near Nørreport Station (Mon–Fri 9am–7pm, Sat 10am–4pm), and another at Gothersgade 8, near Kongens Nytorv (Mon–Fri 10am–6pm, Sat 10.30am–3.30pm).

As for costs, Copenhagen is **expensive**. Staying in cheap hotels and moving around the city visiting museums, eating in a restaurant each day, buying a few snacks and going for a drink in the evening, you can expect to spend a minimum of £45–55/US$70–90 per day. A **Copenhagen Card** can help cut costs; see p.30. For details of sales tax, see p.30.

Phones

You should be able to use your **mobile phone** in Denmark if it's been connected via the GSM system common to the rest of Europe, Australia, New Zealand and South Africa. Check with your phone company, however, as some mobiles are barred from international use. The North American mobile network is not compatible with the GSM system, so you'll need a tri-band phone that will be able to switch from one band to the other. If you plan to make a lot of mobile calls while in Denmark, you could also invest in a Danish SIM card for use in your phone; these are available in all mobile phone shops. For 99kr, you'll get a Danish number plus about forty minutes of domestic calling time. The most commonly used network is TDC (the national landline network), but coverage with Telemore, Telia and others is just as good. Top-up cards can be bought in supermarkets, kiosks and phone shops.

Calling Denmark from abroad, the **international code** is ⓣ45. To make a **collect international call**, dial ⓣ80 30 40 00 for the operator and ask to be connected to the operator in your own country, who will then put through the collect call – full instructions for this "Country Direct" system are displayed in phone booths (in English), and you can dial ⓣ80 60 40 50 for free assistance. For directory enquiries within Denmark your best bet is to try a phone book (there should be one in all public phone booths), the national phone company's website (ⓦwww.tdc.dk), or the online (Danish-language) yellow pages (ⓦwww.degulesider.dk).

Public holidays

Danish public holidays, when most shops and businesses are closed and transport services are reduced, are New Year's Day; Maundy Thursday; Good Friday; Easter Sunday; Easter Monday; Common Prayer Day (fourth Friday after Easter); Ascension Day (fifth Thursday after Easter); Whit Sunday and Whit Monday (seven weeks after Easter); Constitution Day (June 5); Christmas (December 24–26).

Taxes

A sales tax, MOMS, of 25 percent is added to almost everything you buy – but it's always included in the price. Non-EU citizens can claim a refund at the airport, provided you ask for and fill out a Global Refund Cheque at the point of purchase.

Time

Denmark is one hour ahead of GMT, six hours ahead of US Eastern Standard Time, and nine ahead of US Pacific Standard Time.

Tourist information

The Copenhagen Right Now **tourist office** (May & June Mon–Sat 9am–6pm; July & Aug Mon–Sat 9am–8pm, Sun 10am–6pm; Sept Mon–Sat 9am–6pm, Oct–April Mon–Fri 9am–4pm, Sat 9am–2pm; telephone enquiries Mon–Fri 10am–4pm ⓣ70 22 24 42; ⓦwww.visitcopenhagen.dk), across the road from the Central Station at Vesterbrogade 4A, offers maps, general information, and accommodation reservations, along with free accommodation-booking terminals.

If you plan to do lots of sightseeing, either in Copenhagen or in nearby Helsingør and Roskilde, you might want to buy a **Copenhagen Card**. Valid for 24 or 72 hours (225kr/450kr), it covers transport on the entire metropolitan system (including Helsingør and Roskilde) and gives free (or discounted) entry to most museums in the area. If well used this can save a lot of money – especially since it also gets you twenty- to fifty-percent discounts on some car hire, ferry rides and theatre tickets. The cards are available from tourist offices, hotels and travel agents in the metropolitan region, and at train stations.

Travellers with disabilities

In many ways, Copenhagen is a model of awareness for travellers with disabilities: wheelchair access, facilities and help are generally available at hotels, hostels, museums and public places. To see whether a place caters for travellers with disabilities, check the useful tourist-office-financed website ⓦwww.godadgang.dk. Clicking the Practical Information tab at ⓦwww.visitcopenhagen.dk brings up a list of attractions with wheelchair access and information about disabled access to public transport.

The City

The City

1

Slotsholmen

The small island of **Slotsholmen** is the historical and geographical heart of Copenhagen. It was here, in 1167, that Bishop Absalon founded the castle, or *slot*, that became the nucleus of the future city, and it's been the seat of Danish rule ever since. Set imperiously apart from the bustling commercialism of Indre By, Slotsholmen is packed with historic buildings housing government and royal offices and a quirky collection of **museums** – even if you're choosy, it will take the best part of a day to explore.

The island is dominated by the massive Christiansborg complex, an absorbing, if sometimes confusing, collection of the surviving portions of the various palaces and castles that have occupied the site since Absalon put it on the map. At the heart of the complex, the austere grey bulk of **Christiansborg Slot**, built early last century, is home to the Danish parliament and the dazzling Kongelige Repræsentationslokaler. Behind it lies the elegant courtyard known as the **Ridebane**, all that remains of the original Baroque palace built by Christian VI in the early eighteenth century and still home to the Royal Stables and Royal Riding School, as well as a couple of minor, specialized museums.

On the northern side of the complex are the delightful **Christiansborg Slotskirke** of 1826, and **Thorvaldsens Museum**, a charming collection of the work of the nineteenth-century Danish sculptor, while several older buildings to the south date from the time when Slotsholmen was at the heart of Christian IV's drive for naval expansion – the most impressive is now home to the **Tøjhusmuseet** with its world-class collection of guns and cannons. Just beyond, a tranquil garden leads to the more refined collections of the **Det Kongelige Bibliotek** and its sleek modern extension, the **Den Sorte Diamant**, as well as the newest – and arguably best – of the area's bevy of museums, the **Dansk Jødisk Museum**.

Christiansborg Slot

The history of Christiansborg (see box, p.35) is inseparably linked to that of Copenhagen. Since the late twelfth century, there has been a castle of some sort on the site: the current **Christiansborg Slot** (Ⓦ www.ses.dk/christiansborg), a hefty granite-faced neo-Baroque building topped by an enormous copper-brown spire, was constructed between 1907 and 1928 using the remains of the previous palace destroyed by fire in 1884. Its illustrious occupants include the Folketing (Danish Parliament), Supreme Court, prime minister's office and the Royal Reception Rooms.

The **main entrance** is on the square of **Christiansborgs Slotsplads** – long-time favourite spot for demonstrations against king or parliament – adorned with Bissen's pompous equestrian statue of Frederik VII. For a more attractive

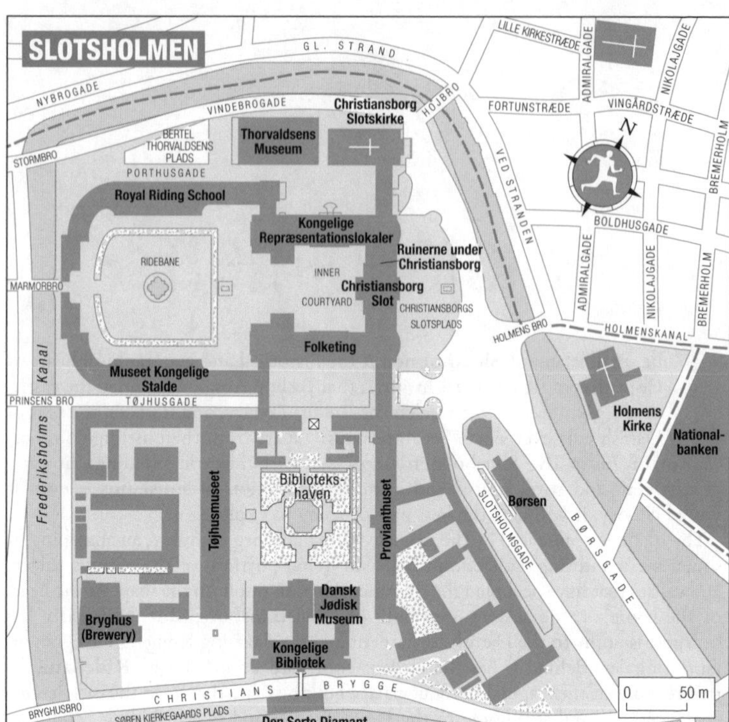

approach to the palace, head along Frederiksholms Kanal and across the eighteenth-century **Marmorbro** (Marble Bridge), the original entry point for Christian VI's castle, which leads you into the Ridebane and gives a fine view of the palace complex.

Folketing

Folketing (Ⓦwww.folketinget.dk), home to the Danish Parliament, is located in Christiansborg Slot's south wing – facing the palace from Christiansborgs Slotsplads, walk left around the outside of the building to reach the entrance. You can visit the main parliamentary chamber, the **Folketingssal**, and watch from the public galleries at any time during the surprisingly informal parliamentary sittings (usually from 1pm on Tues & Wed, and from 10am Thurs & Fri; no sessions June–Sept) and see Danish democracy at work, but you'll get a much better impression of it all by taking one of the free guided tours in English (July to mid-Aug Mon–Fri & Sun 2pm; Oct–May Sun 2pm). Well-informed guides lead you up the magnificent staircase to the seemingly endless **Vandrehal** (Hall of Wandering), where the original Danish constitution from 1849 is exhibited in a silver chest, along with other important historical documents. They'll also explain who sits where – briefly, the 179 members sit grouped in their political parties, with the Cabinet occupying the front seats on the right side of the chamber; on the left side are special galleries reserved for the royal family and representatives of the Supreme Court, who attend the opening debate of the Folketing on the first Tuesday in October.

De Kongelige Repræsentationslokaler

The royal presence at Christiansborg is today limited, for the most part, to **De Kongelige Repræsentationslokaler** (Royal Reception Rooms; May–Sept daily 10am–4pm, Oct–April Tues–Sun 10am–4pm; 70kr), in the palace's north wing – go through the main entrance into the Inner Courtyard and they're on your right, marked by the red sentry box. The rooms are mainly for the royal family to wow important visitors, though given the Danish royals' easy-going attitude, the formality and opulence of these meticulously kept chambers can come as a surprise. It's worth joining one of the entertaining guided tours (in English at 3pm), which keep things lively with a sprinkling of royal anecdotes and gossip.

Particularly noteworthy are the **Throne Room**, with its marble walls covered in richly decorated silk from Lyon, and the Alexander Hall, encircled by Bertel Thorvaldsen's magnificent frieze depicting Alexander the Great's arrival into Babylon. The real highlight, though, is the **Great Hall**, adorned with Bjørn Nørgaard's wonderfully vibrant **tapestries** (a fiftieth birthday gift to the queen from the Danish business community), woven in the famous Gobelin workshops

Christiansborg through the ages

In 1167, **Bishop Absalon** of Roskilde was granted the small village of Havn (on the site of modern Indre By) by his foster brother, King Valdemar the Great. Absalon set about constructing a castle to protect herring traders in the village from Wendish pirates, and the castle's strategic placement subsequently ensured Danish domination of Øresund and a large part of the Baltic, until in 1369 a strong Hanseatic fleet finally succeeded in occupying the town and set about methodically dismantling the castle to ensure that it would never be rebuilt.

A new castle, **Københavns Slot**, constructed by the church to replace Absalon's castle, was completed in 1417, and promptly confiscated by the Danish king, Erik of Pomerania, who made it the seat of Danish rule and residence of the royal family. Over the years, the *slot* was extended and modernized innumerable times – Christian IV completely refurbished it, adding a spire to the infamous Blue Tower (see p.37). Over the years, foreign visitors and dignitaries became increasingly amused by the *slot*'s mishmash of architectural styles, until, to avoid further ridicule, the newly crowned Christian VI decided in 1730 to have the castle demolished and a much grander palace, inspired by the Rococo palaces of France's Louis XIV, erected in its place. Architects from all over Europe were called in to furnish **Christiansborg**, as it became known, with some of the finest art and decoration of the period. Christian VI died long before the palace was completed in 1766, and only 28 years later, in 1794, it burnt down in all its splendour – the Ridebane with its two low, Baroque wings (which now house the Royal Stables, the Royal Riding School and the small Theatre Museum) are all that remain.

The building of a **second Christiansborg** was delayed by the country's dire position following the war with England and the bombardment of Copenhagen in 1807. The palace square and its ruins were used as emergency housing for homeless Copenhageners, and when construction finally began, the walls of the ruins were incorporated into the new palace to save money. By 1828, a new Romanesque-style palace had arisen, but its lifetime was short: in 1884 it, too, burnt to the ground. The chapel – the present Christiansborg Slotskirke – is all that remains from this second Christiansborg.

Today's Christiansborg Slot, the **third Christiansborg**, took 21 years to complete, since the three parties it was to house – the royal family, the parliament and the Supreme Court – couldn't agree on a suitable style. In the end, the royal family decided to stay at Amalienborg (see p.72), leaving the building, for the most part, to the other two pillars of Danish society: the parliament and the Supreme Court.

The Danish monarchy

The Danish monarchy is one of the oldest in the world, but the royal line of the current monarchy, the **House of Glücksborg**, only dates back to 1853 and the reign of Christian IX, who was nicknamed the "Father-in-law of Europe" as a result of having married off his female progeny to various European royals (including Alexandra, who married Edward VII of England). There's a portrait of his vast family in Fredensborgsalen at De Kongelige Repræsentationslokaler. Denmark's rulers were always men, until Denmark's first and current queen, **Margrethe II** (1940–), came to the throne in 1972. The head of the current royal family is highly educated and independent, with her own interests and work (as a stage designer and translator). Together with her French husband, the **Prince Consort, Henrik II**, she has done much to make the monarchy more approachable and human, although one aspect of her relaxed public demeanour – her chain-smoking – has been criticized in some quarters. Her husband, never as popular a figure, also recently came under public scrutiny for his penchant for dog meat, a habit from his childhood in Vietnam, and one that he maintains – despite being such an avowed dog-lover that he has published a book of poems eulogizing his pet dachshunds. The heir to the throne, **Crown Prince Frederik**, is currently riding a wave of popularity; the seemingly eternal bachelor, once a regular face in the trendy bar scene around Skt Hans Torv, married his Tasmanian wife, Crown Princess Mary, in 2005, and they now have a son, Christian, and a daughter, Isabella. In 2008 his younger brother, **Prince Joachim**, married the French Princess Marie after having divorced his Hong Kong-born wife, Countess Alexandra – with whom he has two young sons, Prince Nikolai and Prince Felix – in 2005.

Like their British counterparts, the Danish monarchy has been pretty much stripped of any real power, but is for the most part respected by ordinary Danes – a proudly patriotic lot, on the whole, who see their royal family as a living manifestation of the country's history and tradition. You'll encounter little cynicism towards them and their burden to the taxpayer, not least because they have reduced the pomp to a minimum. Not that they live the simple life – in addition to the largely ceremonial splendour of De Kongelige Repræsentationslokaler (see p.35), they have several palaces, including their principal home, **Amalienborg** (see p.72); a summer residence at Fredensborg (see p.122); and, for visits to Jutland, the Marselisborg and Gråsten palaces.

in Paris and depicting the history of Denmark in a refreshingly modern and colourful fashion that somehow fits perfectly in the otherwise classical room. The rather unflattering portrayal of the queen with long arms, huge hands and high forehead was skilfully explained away by Nørgaard as symbolic of her intelligence and ability to embrace the people; similarly, Prince Frederik's pink flush represents his being next in line to the royal "red" throne. On the central benches in the Great Hall you will find keys to the many cameo appearances on the tapestries from The Beatles, Bob Dylan, Mao Tse-tung, and Hitler, among others.

Ruinerne under Christiansborg

In 1907, during the digging of the extraordinarily deep foundations necessary for Christiansborg's soaring new spire, the foundations from previous castles – **Absalon's castle** and **Københavns Slot** (see box, p.35) – were discovered. Prior to this, nobody had known what Absalon's castle had looked like – or, indeed, whether it was just a myth – so massive effort went into the excavation. The inconspicuous entrance to the **ruins** (Ruinerne under Christiansborg; May–Sept daily 10am–4pm, Oct–April Tues–Sun 10am–4pm; 40kr) is via a staircase on the right as you pass through the *slot*'s main entrance. From here you head down into two massive subterranean rooms, connected by an archway, which follow the circumference of Absalon's castle. Diagrams and explanations in English help decipher the stone and brick jumble of ring walls, foundations, drains and wells, indicating which bits belong to which castle, and though it's still fairly easy to lose the plot, it's all surprisingly absorbing. There's also the odd juicy historical footnote: the second room contains the foundations of the **Blue Tower**, the notorious prison of Københavns Slot where Princess Leonora Christina, daughter of Christian IV, was held captive from 1663 to 1685 by her father's successor, Frederik III, officially for treason, unofficially on the orders of the queen, who was jealous of her beauty.

You'll find more detailed information (including a useful short film) relating to the succession of castles – and the fires that have ravaged them – in the **exhibition** in the archway linking the two sections, including astonishingly intricate pieces of carved granite and sandstone discovered during excavations – it's thought they formed part of Absalon's chapel and were dumped here by the Hanseatic fleet while the castle was being dismantled in 1369.

Ridebane

Walk through Christiansborg Slot's main entrance and the Inner Courtyard to reach the **Ridebane** (Royal Riding Ground) whose buildings, sole survivors from the original Baroque Christiansborg that burnt down in 1794, still largely serve their original function as home and training ground for the royal horses. The peaceful courtyard, overlooked by an equestrian statue of Christian IX and flanked by two long, low wings that curve around to meet at the Marmorbro, offers a fine view of the palace as a whole. If you're lucky, you may see the queen's horses being exercised here in the morning; alternatively, look in at the magnificent Royal Riding School, housed in the north wing of the courtyard and open most days until 4pm. This exquisite, light-filled indoor riding arena, flanked by delicate arches and a balcony running into a royal box at the far end, is considered Denmark's most important piece of eighteenth-century architecture and gives a clear indication of how highly equestrian skills were valued.

Museet Kongelige Stalde og Kareter

In the south wing of the Ridebane is all that remains of the **Museet Kongelige Stalde og Kareter** (Royal Stables & Coach Museum; May–Sept Fri–Sun 2–4pm; Oct–April Sat & Sun 2–4pm; 20kr), which once occupied both wings and housed the royal family's retinue of two hundred horses (there are now just twenty). Even if you're not interested in horses, the stables are worth seeing for their unexpectedly lavish interiors, with pillars, vaulted ceilings, and walls and cribs of Tuscan marble – apparently, not even the king's own chambers were this extravagantly decorated. To the right, as you enter, the **Harness Room** contains a motley collection of old riding uniforms, harnesses and horse portraits – which shouldn't keep you long. Further on, through the stables, the **Coach Museum** displays the royal family's collection of coaches and carriages (some of them still in use), ranging from Dowager Queen Juliane Marie's state coach from 1778 – the collection's oldest and most elaborately decorated carriage – to Frederik IX's black Bentley T, left here since his death in 1972.

Teatermuseet I Hofteatret

Incongruously situated above the Royal Stables, the **Teatermuseet i Hofteatret** (Theatre Museum in the Court Theatre; Tues & Thurs 11am–3pm, Wed 11am–5pm, Sat & Sun 1–4pm; 40kr; ⓦwww.teatermuseet.dk) occupies the charming former

Court Theatre of 1767. When Christian VII came to the throne in 1766, he immediately set French architect Nicolas-Henri Jardin the task of turning a tack room into a small Italian-style theatre (the first Christiansborg lacked a theatre, thanks to the pietistic Christian VI, who prohibited theatre performances throughout Denmark). It remained in use until the fire authorities closed it in 1881, fearing a repeat of the disastrous theatre fire that occurred earlier that year in Vienna.

The building reopened as the Theatre Museum in 1922; each of its rooms explores a particular theme of Danish theatrical history – opera, pantomime, ballet and drama – from the seventeenth century to the present day with the aid of photographs, prints, paintings, video and assorted memorabilia. There are few labels in English, so the free 30 minutes guided tours at 2.30pm on Wednesdays are a must if you want a full introduction to the place. The auditorium itself is an unexpected gem, its deep, sloping stage, plush velvet upholstery, elegant royal boxes and beautifully decorated oriental ceiling (painted for a royal masquerade in 1857) best experienced during one of the plays and concerts occasionally held here.

Around Christiansborgs Slotsplads

The graceful, white-domed building tacked on the northwest end of the palace is **Christiansborg Slotskirke** (Palace Chapel; Easter, July and third week of Oct daily noon–4pm, at other times Sun noon–4pm; free; Ⓦwww.ses.dk/christiansborg), all that remains of the second Christiansborg, which burnt down in 1884. Consecrated in 1826, the chapel – designed by C.F. Hansen, one of the most important Danish Golden Age architects – is a beautiful example of the simple Neoclassical architecture typical of the period. Ironically, having escaped the fire of 1884, the chapel went up in flames in 1992 when a flare from a passing boat landed on its roof during Copenhagen's Lent carnival – the dome collapsed and the inside was seriously damaged. The lavish custard-and-cream-coloured marble stucco interior has since been returned to its original state, with Thorvaldsen's magnificent angel frieze encircling the dome and Bissen's four angel reliefs seeming to float from the walls beneath. Originally the parish church of the royal family, it was demoted in 1926 and now

▲ Thorvaldsens Museum

only hosts the occasional christening and lying in state. Services are no longer held here (with the exception of the annual opening of parliament), and the chapel is mainly used by the Royal Danish Music Conservatory for organ lessons. Check with the tourist office (see p.30) for details of occasional concerts.

Thorvaldsens Museum

Tucked behind Christiansborg Slotskirke, **Thorvaldsens Museum** (Tues–Sun 10am–5pm; July & Aug guided tours in English Sun 3pm; 20kr, free on Wed; Ⓦwww.thorvaldsensmuseum.dk) is a refreshing antidote to the power and pomp of Slotsholmen's historical heavyweights. The striking Neoclassical building, with its ochre facade and eye-catching frieze, was purpose-built in 1839 to house the enormous collection of works and personal possessions (and the body) of Denmark's only sculptor of note – **Bertel Thorvaldsen** (see box below). Though the name is unlikely to ring any bells, in his time Thorvaldsen enjoyed international renown as sculptor to Europe's elite, and while none of the pieces is famous in its own right, it makes for a pleasant wander amid the roll call of famous and infamous gods and mortals – Byron, Christian IV, Napoleon and Hercules among others – set off beautifully by the richly coloured walls, mosaic floors and finely painted ceilings. Excellent, free audioguides give useful background.

On the **ground floor**, the hall to the left of the entrance is stuffed with the plaster models of some of his most important commissions – hulking homages to the likes of Pope Pius VII and Maximilian I – but the numerous small rooms surrounding the inner courtyard where the sculptor is buried are far more rewarding, housing a succession of more delicate works that reflect his love for classical antiquity. Highlights include the enchanting *Cupid and Psyche* (room 2), the masculine *Jason with the Golden Fleece* (room 5), and *Mars and Cupid* (room 7), depicting the eternal tussle of love and war. Further along, in the **Christ Hall**, are the huge, grubby casts (left uncleaned for fear of erasing the sculptor's original marks) of the statues of Christ and the Apostles that cut such a dash in Vor Frue Kirke (see p.46). Look out, too, for the debonair and self-congratulatory sculpture of the man himself in room 20.

Bertel Thorvaldsen

Born into a poor family, **Bertel Thorvaldsen** (1770–1844) had negligible schooling but plenty of talent, and at the age of 11 drew his way into the Danish Academy of Fine Arts. However, with Neoclassicism in full swing, **Rome** beckoned, and when he got the chance to visit the city in 1797, he found his spiritual home, staying on for forty years. Of his early days in Rome, he said, "Every day I hurried to the Vatican and devoured as much as I could of the works of Antiquity". Inspired by the wealth of classical tradition around him, he began to perfect his own trademark heroic, classical sculptures – well-proportioned, graceful figures with contemplative, absorbed expressions. Before long he was fulfilling prestigious commissions for Europe's most powerful players – chief among them the Alexander frieze for the Palazzo del Quirinale to commemorate Napoleon's entry into Rome, and Pope Pius VII's tomb for the basilica in St Peter's. But Thorvaldsen never forgot his native city and played his part in the cultural and artistic rejuvenation of a Copenhagen half destroyed by fires and British bombs, with several important commissions, including the Christ and Apostles for Vor Frue Kirke and the frieze in Christiansborg Slotskirke. He eventually **returned to Denmark** in 1838 to a hero's welcome, and died six years later, leaving his sculptures and private collections to the nation. Thorvaldsen was something of a wit, too. Asked by the Swedish artist J.T. Sergel how he managed to make such beautiful figures, he held up the scraper with which he was working and replied, "With this".

The **first floor** displays Thorvaldsen's considerable, but unexceptional, collection of **antiquities** – ancient Egyptian artefacts, greek coins and pottery and Etruscan gold jewellery – as well as some of his furniture and paintings, including numerous self-portraits. The **lower ground floor** has the inevitable film on his life and art, as well as several rough cuts of the finished models upstairs, and a display on how a sculpture is made. After you exit, walk around the building to see the magnificent painted frieze by Jørgen Sonne, which shows hat-doffing citizens lining up to welcome the sculptor home after his many years in Rome.

Børsen, Holmens Kirke and Nationalbanken

At the eastern end of Christiansborgs Slotsplads, the flamboyant red-brick building with the distinctive gabled green copper roof and fanciful spire formed out of four entwined dragons' tails is the seventeenth-century **Børsen** (Stock Exchange) – centrepiece of Christian IV's plan to make Copenhagen the centre of trade in the Baltic region. The building served as a stock exchange before money traders and bankers began moving in during the eighteenth century. It's now owned by the Chamber of Commerce and is not open to the public.

Just across the canal, **Holmens Kirke** (Mon–Fri 9am–2pm, Sat 9am–noon; ⓦwww.holmenskirke.dk) also caught the eye of the ambitious king. Originally built as an anchor forge for the naval dockyard in 1562, it was converted into a church for naval personnel from Bremerholmen (the naval yard) and Slotsholmen in 1619, and it has changed little since. The long chapel by the canal (go through the door to the left of the altar), added in the early eighteenth century, is dedicated to Denmark's seafaring heroes, several of whom are buried here. Just east of the church, occupying the entire block between waterfront Havnegade and Holmenskanal, is the subdued, black presence of **Nationalbanken** (National Bank), the final project of Denmark's revered architect and designer, Arne Jacobsen, who died before it could be completed. Ever mindful of the bigger picture, Jacobsen designed the part of the bank nearest to Holmens Kirke on one level so as not to compete with the church and Børsen.

South of Christiansborg

The buildings in the area **south of Christiansborg** are mostly much older than those of Christiansborg and are connected to the expansionist Christian IV (1577–1648) and the period when Slotsholmen was home to the Danish Royal Navy. With military domination of the Baltic in mind and relations with Sweden permanently on a war footing, Christian IV transformed the area south of the then Københavns Slot into a dock and supply depot capable of feeding his ever-expanding naval fleet – hence the predominance of large, functional red-brick constructions capped by massive tiled roofs. Today these historic buildings house the **Tøjhusmuseet** and the excellent Libeskind-designed **Dansk Jødisk Museum**. Modern architecture gets a look-in with the impressive **Den Sorte Diamant**, occupying a peaceful waterfront location and the perfect spot for a coffee or lunch break.

Tøjhusmuseet

The exhaustive **Tøjhusmuseet** (Royal Danish Arsenal Museum; July daily noon–4pm, rest of the year Tues–Sun noon–4pm; 30kr; free Wed; ⓦwww.thm.dk) is appropriately housed in the old Tøjhus (Arms House), a huge armoury built in 1604 to supply Christian IV's navy with cannons, guns, ammunition and gunpowder. Ships docked at the adjacent naval basin (now the Bibliotekshaven, see opposite), to be loaded with arms from the Tøjhus, and clothes, food and drink from the **Provianthuset** (Victuallers' Building), on the eastern side of the basin. Eighty years later, the royal naval base moved to Nyholm on Christianshavn (see p.62) and the Tøjhus and Provianthuset fell into disuse (the latter now houses parliamentary offices and isn't open to the public).

Though the sheer scope of the paraphernalia on display is undeniably impressive, the collections are unlikely to excite unless you're into displays of military hardware, and it doesn't help that most of the signs are in Danish only – although refurbishments started in 2009 should remedy this. On the ground floor, cannons (some dating back to the fifteenth century), tanks and artillery line both sides of the enormous **Cannon Hall** – at 156m the longest arched room in Europe, and a handsome sight in itself with its succession of whitewashed arches and expanse of cobbled floor. On the first floor, the even longer **Armoury Hall** displays endless rows of swords and firearms in chronological order starting with a prototype gun from around 1400, with just the odd suit of armour for relief – look out for Christian IV's breastplate and guns halfway along. Needless to say, the glorification of weaponry can get overwhelming, though the friendly guides do their best to humanize the experience with insights into the exhibits.

Det Kongelige Bibliotek and Den Sorte Diamant

The basin in which ships would dock while being provisioned at the Tøjhus and Provianthuset was filled in during the 1860s and is now the **Bibliotekshaven** (Royal Library Garden; entrance on Tøjhusgade) – a peaceful spot for a picnic, with shady lawns, a fountain and fishpond, and assorted statues, including one of a lovesick Søren Kierkegaard looking over to where his fiancée, Regine Olsen, used to live. At the far end of the garden stands **Det Kongelige Bibliotek** (Royal Library), a romantic, Venetian-inspired building with large, curved windows and slim pillars, built in 1906 to house the extensive collections begun by Frederik III over two and a half centuries earlier. You can't actually get in here – walk around the right side of the building to the stunning black-granite and glass extension known as **Den Sorte Diamant** (Black Diamond; building Mon–Fri 8am–9pm, Sat 8am–5pm, free; library & exhibitions Mon–Sat 10am–7pm, 40kr; Ⓦwww.kb.dk; to arrange guided tours in English contact Ⓣ33 47 48 80 or Ⓔbooking@kb.dk). Connected to the original library by a glass walkway above the road, the Diamond tilts elegantly on its glass base to the edge of the harbour, dominating the waterfront and dwarfing all around it. Inside, the glass-walled foyer with harbour views and soaring, light-filled atrium create an exciting public space that includes a concert hall, bookshop (with a decent English paperbacks section), café, and the expensive *Søren K* restaurant (the only restaurant on Slotsholmen). The lower ground floor is given over to temporary exhibitions (40kr) drawing on the library's collections of books, prints and music, as well as changing selections from the archives of the **National Museum of Photography**, which also has its home here. The information desk can give you a free floorplan, but you'll get a better impression of the building as a whole by heading up the travelator onto the glass walkway, with its ceiling mural by Danish expressionist painter Per Kirkeby. You're free to wander across to the old library, but the reading rooms and collections, which include manuscripts by Hans Christian Andersen, Karen Blixen and Søren Kierkegaard, are for members only.

Dansk Jødisk Museum

Designed by Daniel Libeskind, architect of the Jewish Museum in Berlin and the Ground Zero memorial in New York, the **Dansk Jødisk Museum** (Danish Jewish Museum; June–Aug Tues–Sun 10am–5pm; Sept–May Tues–Fri 1–4pm, Sat & Sun noon–5pm; 40kr) recounts the largely peaceful coexistence of Jews and Danes in Denmark for over four centuries. The concept of *Mitzvah*, or "good deed", runs through the museum, Libeskind taking as his inspiration one of the few Jewish

Flight to Sweden

Exploiting the Nazis' desire for collaboration, the Danish government had, for the first few years of **occupation**, managed to keep their Jewish population safe from persecution, refusing to enforce the special laws applied to Jews in other occupied countries, such as the wearing of the Star of David. This **protected status** couldn't last forever, though, and in September 1943, the issue of the Danish Jews was brought to the attention of Hitler himself by Werner Best, the ambitious head of the German Legation in Denmark. The Führer's subsequent order that **Endlösung** (the "Final Solution") should now be extended to Danish Jews disgruntled many prominent Nazis, who were mindful of disrupting the so-far peaceful occupation and beginnings of collaboration. Their reservations were ignored, and desperate to avoid the impending confrontation with the Danish government and political fallout for his ally and boss, **C.F. Duckwitz**, a high-ranking official at the German Legation, embarked on a frantic and secret round of meetings (probably sanctioned by a now-anxious Best) with Swedish ministers, who proposed to Berlin that Sweden give safe haven to all Danish Jews. Again, their suggestions fell on deaf ears, and Best was told to proceed – the date was set for October 2 that year. Having exhausted all diplomatic routes and with just four days to go, Duckwitz leaked the information to the Danish authorities – a message that was quickly disseminated via the congregation at the Copenhagen synagogue to every Jew in Denmark. By the time the Gestapo began knocking on doors, most Jews had already fled their homes and were either escaping across the Ønesund Sound or lying low in hiding places up and down the coast.

The **Danish population** played a crucial role in helping their Jewish compatriots to escape – offering them shelter, raising funds, volunteering their boats as the Danish Resistance found their traditional escape routes swamped under the volume of refugees. In small fishing towns along the Zealand coast, inhabitants improvised **escape routes**; 1800 Jews fled from Gilleleje alone, the town's fishermen ferrying the waiting escapees out night after night to a larger vessel on its return journey from delivering potatoes. All but a few hundred of Denmark's 7500 Jews made it safely across to Sweden – some were discovered by the Gestapo (including 80 who had been hiding in the attic of Gilleleje church), others were too old or sick to flee. Those captured were sent to a concentration camp in Czechoslovakia, where, as a final, happy endnote to this remarkable story, most survived the war. An insight into Denmark's position in World War II can be had at the Frihedsmuseet (see p.74).

success stories of World War II – the escape from imminent deportation to concentration camps of 7000 Jews, helped across the Øresund to safety in neutral Sweden by the Danish Resistance, the Danish people and reputedly several German officers who turned a blind eye (see box above). It's a fitting and, at times, moving memorial to this proud period in Denmark's history and the tolerance of the Danes themselves, moving deftly from the events of 1943 to broader themes such as the history of Jewish immigration to Denmark, what it means to be Jewish, and the concept of "homeland", all illuminated by personal histories and possessions, and a beautiful array of paraphernalia used in Jewish rituals – prayer shawls, Torah bells and shields, and an exquisitely illustrated eighteenth-century copy of the *Haggadah* (the story of the Exodus from Egypt). The displays are perfectly set off by the striking architecture: a series of sloping corridors – all jutting angles and rods of light – whose layout corresponds to the interlaced Hebrew letters of the word "*Mitzvah*". The brick, vaulted ceiling is the only visible reminder that the museum is housed in Christian IV's old royal boathouse, a fitting location as it was Christian who first invited wealthy merchant Jews to settle in Denmark in 1616, enticing them with the privilege of a tax-free status for 25 years.

2

Indre By

Compared to the monumental edifices of Christiansborg across the Slotsholmen canal, the district of **Indre By** presents Copenhagen on a more human scale. The heart of both medieval and modern cities, Indre By (Inner City) is where it all began – the site of the small and marshy fishing village of Havn, whose fortunes were transformed by the arrival of Bishop Absalon in 1167 (see box, p.35). Whilst Absalon and his successors raised their castles on the island of Slotsholmen, the settlement of Havn prospered through tax and trade, acquiring the name of København (Merchant's Harbour) and becoming capital of Denmark in 1445. Within its fortifications – which endure as a ring of parks, lakes and green areas – Copenhagen grew rapidly. Although it was subsequently ravaged by a series of major fires, and bombarded by first the Swedish and then the British, the medieval town's tangle of tiny streets, squares and ancient churches survived and is still very much in evidence, forming a sharp contrast to the relatively modern areas outside the old fortifications, where permanent settlement only started after 1851.

Indre By is very much the public face of Copenhagen; the hub of the city's day-to-day activity and its main shopping district, it's a maze of lively, attractive streets and squares perfectly suited to idle ambling (or serious shopping). It's all the more enjoyable for the fact that its two main thoroughfares are pedestrianized and wide enough to accommodate the inevitable hordes of shoppers. The first is **Strøget**, the colloquial name (it's not on any street signs) given to the series of connecting streets (Frederiksberggade, Nygade, Vimmelskaftet, Amagertorv and Østergade) that run across Indre By from Rådhuspladsen in the west to Kongens Nytorv in the east. The other main street, **Købmagergade**, leaves Strøget at Højbro Plads, heading northwest towards Nørreport Station. You won't find much beyond mainstream chain stores on either, but a detour into the side streets anywhere along their length reveals an enticing array of more individual Danish designer shops. See the "Shopping" chapter for more on the best places to shop in Indre By.

Indre By also has a number of historic buildings, churches and museums. Foremost among these is Christian IV's wonderfully quirky **Rundetårn**, which offers a fantastic view over the city, while, close by, are the eclectic collections of the **Musikhistorisk Museum**, **Arbejdermuseet** and **Post & Tele Museum**. At some point be sure to make it to **Nyhavn** – a picture-postcard canalside street lined with colourful old merchants' houses now home to crowded restaurants and bars that spill out onto the cobbled pavements.

Indre By is served by two metro stations: Nørreport (also an S-Tog stop) on its northwestern side, at the top of Købmagergade, and Kongens Nytorv on the eastern side. Given the narrow, largely pedestrianized streets, bus access is limited to the encircling main roads.

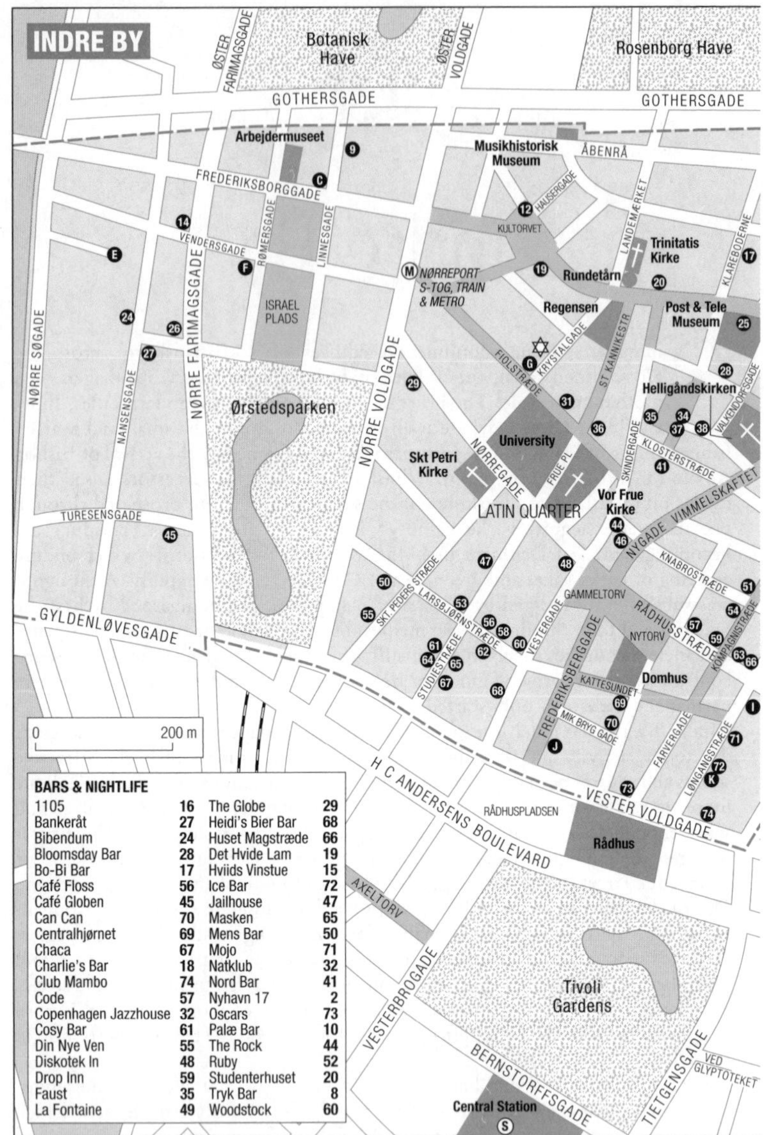

BARS & NIGHTLIFE

1105	16	The Globe	29
Bankeråt	27	Heidi's Bier Bar	68
Bibendum	24	Huset Magstræde	66
Bloomsday Bar	28	Det Hvide Lam	19
Bo-Bi Bar	17	Hviids Vinstue	15
Café Floss	56	Ice Bar	72
Café Globen	45	Jailhouse	47
Can Can	70	Masken	65
Centralhjørnet	69	Mens Bar	50
Chaca	67	Mojo	71
Charlie's Bar	18	Natklub	32
Club Mambo	74	Nord Bar	41
Code	57	Nyhavn 17	2
Copenhagen Jazzhouse	32	Oscars	73
Cosy Bar	61	Palæ Bar	10
Din Nye Ven	55	The Rock	44
Diskotek In	48	Ruby	52
Drop Inn	59	Studenterhuset	20
Faust	35	Tryk Bar	8
La Fontaine	49	Woodstock	60

Along Frederiksberggade to the Latin Quarter

Frederiksberggade is the first – and tackiest – of the series of streets that make up **Strøget**. The fast-food joints, souvenir shops and touristy pubs aren't the best introduction to the area, but the side street of Kattesundet leads to the altogether

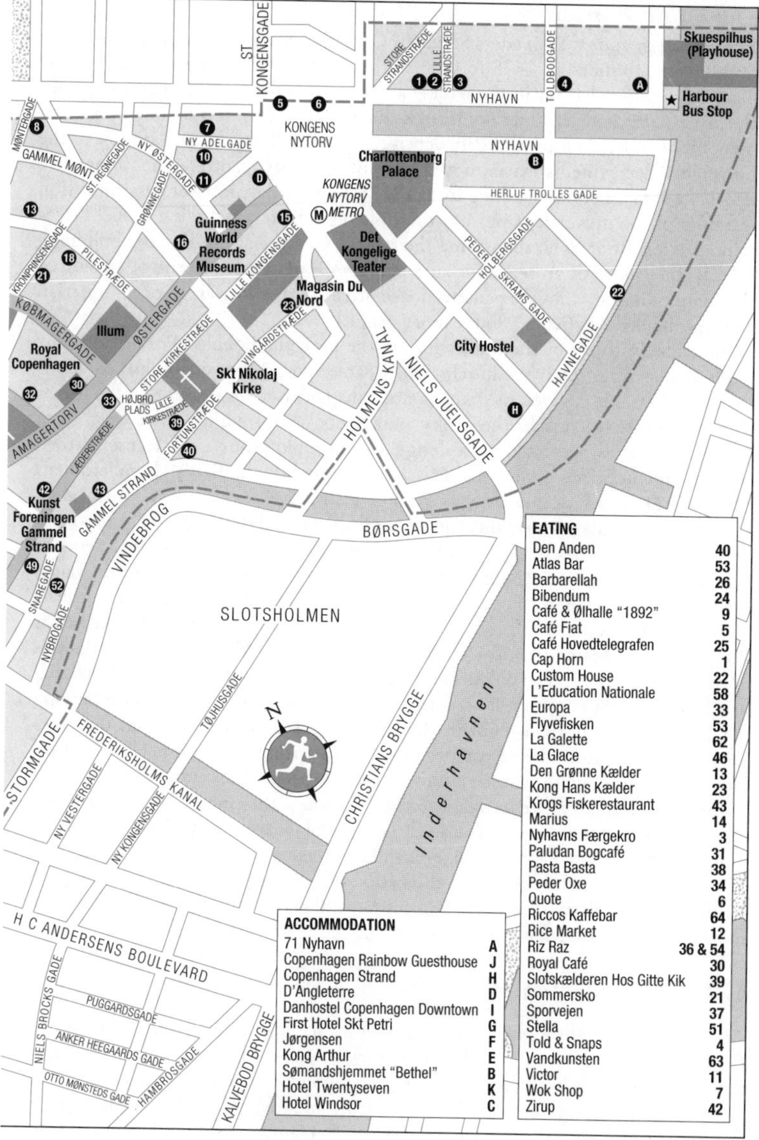

trendier area centred on **Larsbjørnstræde**, one of the liveliest streets in the city, crammed with new and used clothes shops, independent music stores, second-hand bookshops and funky cafés; it also has a buzzing nightlife including much of the city's gay scene. The quieter streets crossing Larsbjørnstræde – **Studiestræde** and **Skt Peders Stræde** – are also worth exploring whether you want to kit yourself out in vintage denim or leather bondage gear.

The Latin Quarter

At the eastern end of Skt Peders Stræde is Copenhagen's **University**, the oldest in Scandinavia, founded in 1475 to train Catholic priests. The university sits at the heart of the so-called **Latin Quarter** – a reference to the fact that Latin was once the *lingua franca* here. It's a far cry from its lively Parisian namesake, however – this quiet bit of Indre By is now largely deprived of its intellectual buzz, as most of the university departments have moved out of the city centre. The impressive neo-Gothic main building dating from 1836 is now used mainly for administration – statues of the university's most distinguished graduates, including Nobel Prize-winner Niels Bohr, who discovered the structure of the atom, line the building's side. Rather more of an academic aura pervades **Fiolstræde**, on the other side of the main building, a lovely pedestrianized street with a fine array of antiquarian and new bookshops (see p.186 for more details).

Immediately south of the university, on the peaceful, cobbled Frue Plads, **Vor Frue Kirke** (Our Lady's Church; daily 8am–5pm; Ⓦwww.domkirken.dk) is surprisingly modest, given its status as Copenhagen's cathedral. Built on the site of a twelfth-century church, the dusky pink Neoclassical edifice dates only from 1829, when it was erected to a design by the ubiquitous C.F. Hansen, town planner and architect, amidst the devastation caused by the British bombardment of 1807. Hansen's simple designs were a distinctive feature of Copenhagen's Golden Age. Inside, the weighty figure of Christ behind the altar merits a look, as do the solemn statues of the apostles – some crafted by Bertel Thorvaldsen (see box, p.39), others by his pupils – that line the nave. Copenhagen Royal Chapel boys' choir is based at Vor Frue; check the cathedral website for details of concerts.

Across from the university on the other side of Nørregade, **Skt Petri Kirke** (St Peter's Church; March to mid-Oct Tues–Sat 11am–3pm; Ⓦwww.sankt-petri.dk) is one of the city's best-preserved medieval buildings. Built as a Roman Catholic church in the mid-fifteenth century, it became the king's cannon and bell foundry following the Reformation in 1536, until its donation by Frederik II in 1585 to the city's substantial German Lutheran congregation. Some sermons are still held in German (Sun 11am), although the church is now Danish Lutheran. The central nave and choir of the present building are its oldest sections, although the church's most interesting feature is the atmospheric Italian-style sepulchral chapel from 1683 (25kr); its numerous tombs and crypts are the resting place of many prominent Danish members of court and political figures from the period of absolute monarchy, including the architect Nikolai Eigtved. The cannonballs suspended from the chapel ceiling are just some of the 150 that fell on the church during the 1807 British bombardment.

Gammeltorv and Nytorv

At the junction with Nørregade, Strøget is flanked by the busy squares of **Gammeltorv** and **Nytorv** ("old" and "new" squares), two large ancient spaces that mark the site of the first marketplace in Havn when it was still a fishing village – a tradition kept alive today by a few fruit-and-veg stalls. The wide, gently sloping expanse and presence of the city's C.F. Hansen-designed **Domhus** (Law Courts), with its suitably forbidding row of Neoclassical columns, lend a faintly Roman whiff to Nytorv, and it's a refreshingly open spot to sit with a drink from one of the square's kiosks and watch the stream of shoppers passing along Strøget. Gammeltorv's most striking feature is the **Caritas Fountain**, by Statius Otto, dating from 1608. Ten years older than the similarly risqué – but much more famous – Manneken Pis in Brussels, the fountain's water flows from Caritas's breasts and from the little boy at her feet taking a leak (the three holes were sealed with lead during the puritanical nineteenth century). The fountain supposedly symbolizes Christian IV's compassion for his people: the well on top of which it stands was Copenhagen's first external water supply, linked by lead piping to a source 6km north of the city.

A short detour south from Nytorv down Rådhusstræde brings you to lively **Kompagnistræde**, a great hunting ground for antiques from Persian carpets and oak furniture to silver candlestick holders, antique plates, delicate crystal glassware and collectable children's toys. Other small, one-off shops line the street as it leads into Læderstræde – all along this stretch you'll find plenty of cafés and it's a great place to linger over coffee, beer or lunch, away from the main throng.

Helligåndskirken Gråbrødretorv and Amagertorv

On Vimmelskaftet, **Helligåndskirken** (Church of the Holy Ghost; Mon–Fri noon–4pm), founded in 1296 as part of a Catholic monastery of the same name, is one of the oldest churches in the city. The monastery was dissolved during the Reformation, but the building survived as a Lutheran parish church until being completely gutted by the Great Fire of 1728; it has been largely rebuilt since. Entrance is through a beautifully carved sandstone portal, dating back to 1620, which was originally intended for the old stock exchange (Børsen) on Slotsholmen; inside, look out for an impressive altarpiece donated by Christian VI depicting the ascension of Christ. Also dating from 1296, **Helligåndshuset** (entered from the church close, left of the main church entrance), the west wing of the original monastery, survived the fire and is today the only completely preserved medieval building in Copenhagen. It's now used for book fairs, art shows and exhibitions, and is worth a look for the formidable vaulted ceiling and slender granite columns.

Adjacent to Helligåndskirken, cobbled Valkendorfsgade leads to Kringlegangen – a pedestrian passageway that takes you on a little detour through no.17 to **Gråbrødretorv**, a charming, enclosed square with several good cafés and restaurants. The square dates back to 1238 when Franciscan monks started the city's first monastery here – the name (Grey Brothers' Square) is a reference to their habits. The monks left Copenhagen shortly before the Reformation, and today the square is a gathering place for locals in the know, who come in good weather to eat outside or just sit by the fountain and enjoy a cold *høker* beer. Concerts and buskers provide entertainment during the summer.

Back at Helligåndskirken, Strøget gets broader and lighter as you head into the Amagertorv stretch of Strøget, accentuated by the beautiful mosaics of Danish artist **Bjørn Nørgaard** (famous for the Queen's Tapestries; see p.35) that in 1994 replaced the street's old cobbled stones. On the north side of Amagertorv, you'll find three of the torchbearers of classic Danish design: Georg Jensen's Silverware, Royal Copenhagen Porcelain and the furniture and household design store Illums Bolighus (see p.185). This is all classy, beautifully crafted stuff and makes for an aspirational browse. Georg Jensen became famous in the early twentieth century for his Art Nouveau silverware ranging from jewellery to cutlery; a small museum in the shop has some beautiful examples of his early work. Next door, Royal Copenhagen Porcelain, founded in 1775, is housed in one of Copenhagen's oldest buildings (dating from 1616); the exquisite porcelain is still handpainted with brushes made from hair from the tips of cows' ears.

Højbro Plads and Gammel Strand

Højbro Plads, at the busy junction of Amagertorv and Købmagergade, is a natural spot for a break – its centrepiece, the eye-catching **Storkespringvandet**

▲ Strøget

(Stork Fountain, though the birds which adorn it are actually herons), is usually surrounded by weary shoppers. The two perennially popular cafés *Europa* (see p.148) and *Norden*, and occasional street entertainers and buskers, guarantee a lively atmosphere, while in summer there's usually a small jazz band playing.

The southern end of the square is dominated by an equestrian statue of the founder of Copenhagen, Bishop Absalon, positioned on the spot where he is presumed to have first sighted Slotsholmen, site of his future castle. The statue, by Wilhelm Bissen, dating from 1901, was criticized for its aggressive portrayal of Absalon – perched on a rearing charger, he looks more like a warrior than a man of the church – though the plinth, by Martin Nyrop (also architect of the town hall, see p.77), was much praised; some critics even suggested that horse and rider be removed, leaving the plinth alone to stand as a more worthy memorial to the bishop. At the bridge, Højbro, peer down into the canal on the left to see the enchanting underwater sculpture of *The Merman and his Seven Sons*.

To the right of Absalon's statue on Højbro Plads is the delightful canalside stretch of **Gammel Strand** (Old Beach), home to another, more earthy statue, *The Fisher Woman*, commemorating the tough women who used to line up along the beachfront here, selling the fish their husbands had caught. Keeping tradition alive, there's usually a fish stall here in summer trading all manner of seafood to tourists hanging around for the next DFDS boat (see p.25 for more details). From Gammel Strand, there's a fine view across the canal to Slotsholmen and the brightly coloured Thorvaldsens Museum, best appreciated during spring and summer from the outside tables of the row of cafés and restaurants.

Squeezed in between the cafés and restaurants, at no. 48, is a fine building housing the city's oldest art gallery **Kunstforeningen Gammel Strand** (Tues & Fri–Sun 11am–5pm, Wed & Thurs 11am–8pm; 55kr; Ⓦwww.glstrand.dk), where, over three floors with striking views of the city, you can catch temporary exhibitions of modern and contemporary art. The **Fotografisk Center** (Tues–Sun 11am–5pm; 25kr; Ⓦwww.photography.dk), in the same building, has temporary exhibitions of the work of renowned local and international photographers.

In summer, there's also a good **flea market** here on Fridays and Saturdays (see p.189) – a chance to pick up, among other things, a piece of Royal Copenhagen Porcelain at a price approaching affordable.

North along Købmagergade

Indre By's other main shopping street, **Købmagergade** now rivals Strøget for mainstream shops and chain stores, though for something different, you need only dive off into the smaller streets – in particular the hyper-trendy knot of lanes centred on **Kronprinsensgade**, Pilestræde, Store Regnegade, Ny Østergade and Grønnegade, where a number of independent Danish fashion designers have outlets. On the corner of Købmagergade and Strøget is the enticing **Illum** department store (see p.187).

Post & Tele Museum

At Købmagergade 37, the **Post & Tele Museum** (Tues & Thurs–Sat 10am–5pm, Wed 10am–8pm, Sun noon–4pm; 50kr, free on Wed; Ⓦwww.ptt-museum.dk) charts the history of communication in Denmark from Christian IV's 1624 decree establishing the Danish Royal Post Office to the arrival of mobile phones and the internet. Head up to the third floor where the permanent exhibitions do a pretty good job of bringing the somewhat dry subject matter to life with a well-displayed collection of old telephones and telephone boxes from various eras, radio and morse-code equipment, a mock-up of a nineteenth-century post office, philatelic displays and historical artefacts such as Denmark's first mail coach, its egg-shaped mail drum designed to minimize air resistance and prevent the coachman from taking along passengers. It's an exhibition about changing design through the ages as much as anything – you can get a taste of what's to come in the screening room where videos (in English and Danish) map out the future of communications. There's also a kids' section (Sat & Sun only; see p.201). The museum's real highlight, however, is its rooftop café *Hovedtelegrafen* (see p.148), which offers delicious food and a fine view; it gets packed at lunchtime so head up early or book ahead.

Rundetårn

Copenhagen's most unusual historic landmark, and one of the city's most intriguing sights, the 42-metre-high **Rundetårn** (Round Tower; daily: mid-May to mid-Sept 10am–8pm; mid-Sept to mid-May 10am–5pm; 25kr; mid-Oct to mid-March also Tues & Wed 7–10pm; Ⓦwww.rundetaarn.dk) stands on Købmagergade as an

Christian IV: The architect king

The layout of present-day Copenhagen is largely thanks to **Christian IV** (1588–1648), despite the fact that he was broke for most of his reign. Not only did he extend the city northwards, to include Rosenborg and Frederikstad, but he also fortified its defences, building Kastellet to the north, creating a ring of moats and ramparts (today's Tivoli, Ørstedsparken, Botanisk Have and Østre Anlæg) to the west, and reclaiming the Christianshavn area, in the east, from the sea – a series of sweeping changes that earned him the moniker "the architect king".

The list of his architectural achievements is long. Shortly after taking over the country's reins (his father Frederik II died when Christian was 10) he instigated the construction of a naval yard and supply depot, a brewery – for the navy – and an arsenal (today's **Tøjhusmuseet**; see p.40) next to his castle on Slotsholmen, **Københavns Slot**. Of these, only Københavns Slot is gone; apparently, Christian made such a mess of its refurbishment that future kings were too embarrassed to have visitors here and decided to tear the whole thing down and start afresh, replacing it with the grander Christiansborg Slot. Christian returned to form with **Rosenborg Slot** (p.66), which he gradually built up from a mere summer-chalet to the romantic Dutch-Renaissance palace that rises over Kongens Have today.

Of his more unusual feats, the **Trinitatis** complex (see below) is arguably his greatest – a combined church, university library and astronomical observatory, whose church tower, **Rundetårn** (see p.49), with its spiral cobbled ramp leading all the way up to the still-functioning observatory, is one of the best places from which to view the city's skyline (and may well have been built for that reason). Looking southwest from here you can see another of Christian's quirky mementos, the **Caritas Fountain** (p.46) on Gammeltorv.

enduring testament to a king's vision. It was built by Christian IV as part of the **Trinitatis** complex, which combined three important facilities for seventeenth-century scholars and students: an astronomical observatory, a church and a university library. The tower functioned both as observatory lookout and as the Trinitatis church tower – and perhaps also as a vantage point from which Copenhagen's citizens could admire Christian's additions to the city. It's still a functioning **observatory** – the oldest in Europe – and you can view the winter night sky through the astronomical telescope (mid-Oct to mid-March Tues & Wed 7–10pm). Inside the tower a wide, cobbled ramp (no lifts) spirals its way to the top for a wonderful view of the hive of medieval streets below and the city beyond. Legend has it that Peter the Great sped to the top on horseback in 1715, pursued by the tsarina in a six-horse carriage.

Midway up the ramp, the **Library Hall** housed the university's book collections until 1861; left unused for many years it's now a gallery featuring changing artistic, cultural and historical exhibitions and also hosts regular classical music concerts (see p.175). Look out for the original privy, recently restored and reopened – it hasn't been used since the late 1800s but you can sit on it and look up at the ceiling, as in all likelihood luminaries such as Hans Christian Andersen did when caught short visiting the library. Above the library, the impressive, timbered Bell Loft houses the church bells as well as a small exhibition of curios related to the tower's history. It's also worth peeping into the **church** itself (Mon–Sat 9.30am–4.30pm); rebuilt in restrained Baroque style following the Great Fire of 1728 and dominated by a giant organ, it is still affiliated to the university's student congregation.

Musikhistorisk Museum

North of Kultorvet, at Åbenrå 30, the charming **Musikhistorisk Museum** (Musical History Museum; May–Sept Tues–Sun 1–3.50pm; Oct–April Tues, Wed,

Sat & Sun 1–3.50pm; free; Ⓦwww.natmus.dk), set in three lovely eighteenth-century houses, has an impressive collection of instruments spanning the globe and the last thousand years. The antique musical manuscripts, photos showing how various instruments are made, and cabinets of beautifully crafted, often unfamiliar, pieces – everything from a conch shell with brass mouthpiece to ornately painted klavichords – are captivating, and there are some real treasures, not least the original Elizabethan Orpharion, a lute-like, stringed instrument from England dating from 1617 and one of only three in the world. Look out too for the reconstructions of wind instruments from the Middle Ages (room 15) that look like primitive bagpipes. There are recordings of most of the instruments to listen to (helpful with some of the odder ones, where it's a mystery even which end the sound comes out) and a room where children can try out all sorts of percussion instruments. Jazz and classical concerts are occasionally held in the small concert hall – check the website for details.

Around Nørreport

Cars hurtle along **Nørre Voldgade**, north of Kultorvet, which marks the position of the former ramparts and the end of the pedestrianized streets of the old city. The site of the Nørreport city gate is now occupied by the busy **Nørreport Station**. No construction was allowed in the area outside the old ramparts until 1851, which is why most developments in the area north of Nørre Voldgade up to the lakes are relatively new.

Israels Plads and Ørstedsparken

Israels Plads is a fairly unexciting expanse only notable for its fruit and vegetable market, and, on Saturdays, the **flea market** on the playground behind (see p.189). Just west of Israels Plads, the pretty **Ørstedsparken**, one of the city's most popular gay cruising grounds, is named after the famous Danish physicist, H.C. Ørsted, who discovered electromagnetism. It's one of the few areas where the layout of the old ramparts has been preserved – the lakes here (part of the old defence system) follow the shape of the former battlements. In summer, you can get refreshments at the park café in the centre and watch the world go by. Just north of here, Nansensgade is an up-and-coming little street with a bevy of good delis, quirky clothes shops and bars.

Arbejdermuseet

On the far side of Nørre Voldgade, at Rømersgade 22, is the **Arbejdermuseet** (Workers' Museum; daily 10am–4pm; 50kr; Ⓦwww.arbejdermuseet.dk), housed in the former Workers' Hall (still used for occasional union meetings). Not an obvious port of call but, nevertheless, a reasonably engaging (if rather earnest) guide to working-class life in Copenhagen from the 1870s onwards and worth a look for some background on the city's more recent history.

It's best to begin on the third floor with the history of the **labour movement** in Denmark and around the world – look out for the original copy of the 1899 "September Accord" that gave workers the right to organize into unions. The rest of the permanent exhibition relies heavily on reconstructed scenes chronicling the workers' living and working conditions, starting on the second floor with an apartment that housed generations of a working-class family from 1885 to 1990, and continuing on the more absorbing first floor with a Copenhagen street of the 1950s, complete with shop windows hawking the consumer durables of the day and the Fifties-style museum coffee-shop where you can buy a cup of an old-fashioned coffee and chicory blend. Further on, a drab house interior, complete with suitably wretched-looking mannequins, evokes the life of a working-class Nørrebro family during the **1930s depression**; the apartment of the **1950s** with family photos, newspapers and TVs showing newsreels of the time is a far brighter affair, its occupants clearly benefiting from the influx of Marshall Plan American funding to a battered postwar Europe.

The ground floor and basement are given over to the shop and temporary exhibitions. Look out for the copy of the Saint Petersburg statue of **Lenin** demoted to a small, dark back yard. Sculpted in 1985 for one of the few communist unions in Denmark, the Danish Seaman's Union, it was donated to the museum following the fall of communism. It created a massive stir: critics demanded that, if the statue was to be displayed at all, then Lenin should be depicted as an executioner and mass murderer; the museum insisted it be exhibited for his visit to Copenhagen – and this building – during the Socialist World Congress in 1910, seven years prior to the October Revolution, and for his efforts to promote international socialism throughout the world.

In the street-front section of the basement, the cosy **restaurant** *Café & Ølhalle* (see p.147) has been restored to its 1892 state and serves traditional Danish food.

East to Kongens Nytorv and Nyhavn

Although one of the oldest churches in Copenhagen, and mother church of the Danish Reformation in 1536, **Skt Nikolaj Kirke**, east of Højbro Plads, hasn't been used for ecclesiastical purposes since 1795, when the city's second great fire destroyed everything except the tower. The massive red-brick church wasn't rebuilt until early in the twentieth century, and now, as the deconsecrated **Kunsthallen Nikolaj** (Tues–Sun noon–5pm, Thurs open till 9pm; 20kr, Wed free; Ⓦwww.kunsthallennikolaj.dk), houses temporary exhibitions of contemporary art.

Heading east along the final section of Strøget – here called **Østergade**, and undoubtedly the most exclusive section of the entire thoroughfare – you'll pass the likes of Louis Vuitton, Hermes and Mulberry and, on the left, the alleyway and courtyard of **Pistolstræde** with its quaint timbered buildings and quirky magpie fountain, home to a handful of super-cool Danish design shops.

Kongens Nytorv

For most Copenhageners, Strøget ends, rather than begins, at **Kongens Nytorv**. In summer, tired shoppers head for the outdoor seats of the square's many high-ceilinged, glass-fronted cafés; in winter, for the cosy dens selling *gløgg* and *æbleskiver* (warm, mulled wine with nuts, raisins and spices, served with round dough balls).

At the centre of Kongens Nytorv is an equestrian statue of Christian V, who completed the square by ordering the owners of land bordering it to erect houses of a certain regal standard or sell up, which is why the square is entirely surrounded by pompous-looking buildings from the seventeenth century, such as the swish *Hôtel d'Angleterre* (see p.136). In winter, the square is transformed into a free open-air ice-skating rink; a stall nearby rents out skates. On the right, as you leave Strøget, is the classy **Magasin du Nord** – the city's oldest and largest department store (see "Shopping" p.187).

The southern end of the square is dominated by the grand, late nineteenth-century **Det Kongelige Teater** (Royal Theatre; guided tours in Danish every Sun 11am; 75kr; tickets must be bought in advance from BilletNet [see p.169] or the theatre box office [see p.174]; Ⓦwww.kgl-teater.dk). Hans Christian Andersen supposedly tried his luck here as a ballet dancer while attempting to court the prima ballerina. Until recently, the theatre was one of the few in the world where ballet, opera and drama were performed under one roof. However, conditions became too cramped, and in 2005 opera moved to Operæn (see p.61), while the flashy new Skuespilhus (Playhouse, see p.53) takes care of theatre, leaving only ballet to be performed on the old regal stage. An extension to the theatre was added in 1931, **Stærekassen**, in Danish Art Deco style, its plain surfaces and clean decoration in sharp contrast to the Italianate "old stage", as the main building is now called. For details of performances at Det Kongelige Teater, see p.175 and p.176.

Next door, **Charlottenborg Palace**, the oldest building on the square, was built in Dutch Baroque style by an illegitimate son of Frederik III in 1677. It was handed over to the Royal Academy of Fine Arts in 1754, since when many prominent artists, including Thorvaldsen (see box, p.39), have lived here. It's still home to the Royal Academy, and though there are no specific public displays, it's worth dropping in just to glimpse the palace's elegant interior. The spacious, light rooms of the **Kunsthal Charlottenborg** (exhibition hall; Tues–Sun noon–5pm; 60kr; Ⓦwww.kunsthalcharlottenborg.dk) at the back, in a separate building from 1883, provide a perfect setting for eclectic Danish and international temporary exhibitions of contemporary art, architecture and decorative art.

Nyhavn

Just round the corner from Charlottenborg Palace, **Nyhavn** (New Harbour) – created in 1671 as a canal leading from the city's main port to Kongens Nytorv – is one of the most picturesque and lively spots in the city, with DFDS tour boats (see p.25) coming and going to and from the harbour and hordes of tourists and locals hanging out in the seemingly endless row of bars, cafés and restaurants occupying the brightly coloured, gabled houses. Some of the buildings date back to 1681 and can boast famous occupants – Hans Christian Andersen was a resident at no. 67 from 1845 to 1864 – and this cobbled promenade is now one of the trendiest places to live in the city, a complete turnaround from its seedy past as a disreputable sailors' haunt and red-light district, traces of which linger in the odd tattoo parlour and seedy bar.

In summer, it's packed with locals drinking away the afternoon on the quayside with their six-packs of Carlsberg and tourists sitting outside at the cafés – on a sunny day here, drinking beer and snaps and eating plates of herring is about as good as it gets in Copenhagen. Or you can just grab an ice cream or hot-dog and wander along to the end of Nyhavn for a look at the new playhouse (see below) and the fine harbour views across to the opera house.

Skuespilhus

Turning the corner at the harbour end of Nyhavn you're quickly reminded of the city's modern aspirations in the form of the new **Skuespilhus** (Playhouse; Mon–Sat 8am–11.30pm, Sun 8am–3pm; Ⓦwww.skuespilhus.dk), latest offshoot of Det Kongelige Teater (see opposite). Its Danish architects avoided competing with the glamour of the opera house just across the harbour, opting instead for a more unassuming, low-rise building of geometric simplicity and sober materials – by day it's more library than centre for the dramatic arts – that fits humbly into its historic and regal surroundings. By night, though, it's a different matter, and the building assumes a more monumental presence – the Danish talent for lighting illuminating the long glass-walled foyer and upper floor beautifully and casting a gentle glow on the looming copper-clad tower. It's worth popping in to the foyer café – its stunning views over the harbour make it a scenic place to have a coffee. For details on performances at Skuespilhus see p.177.

Christianshavn

Facing Indre By and Slotsholmen across the waters of Inderhavnen, and linked to them by Knippelsbro, is the charming island of **Christianshavn**. Nicknamed "Little Amsterdam" on account of its pretty canals, cobbled streets and old Dutch-style houses with brightly painted facades, it's a laid-back area with a cosy, neighbourhood feel and a pleasant spot to hang out with a *høker* beer while watching the boats meander up and down the canals.

Until the seventeenth century, however, Christianshavn didn't even exist. The area was under water, creating a breach in Copenhagen's defences that left the city vulnerable to attack from the sea, until **Christian IV** reclaimed an arc of land in the early 1600s and built a ring of defensive fortifications on it. An autonomous borough was created to house Dutch merchants, with a Dutch architect, Johan Semp, employed to plan the new district. The Dutch merchants never arrived and the island was instead distributed between rich Danish merchants and aristocrats, who moved into the elegant dwellings along the waterfront and Christianhavns Kanal, and the workers, who were assigned the dark and dingy areas in between. For much of the next three hundred years Christianshavn prospered from the trade created by the huge naval base on the adjacent islands of **Holmen**, and from the late 1800s to mid-1900s, with the large commercial shipbuilding yards of Burmeister & Wain. Today, many of Christianhavn's and Holmen's waterfront warehouses and fine naval buildings have been transformed into offices, cultural centres, educational institutions and expensive housing developments, while the Operaen, the new opera house, has placed the area firmly at the forefront of the city's cultural scene.

Christianshavn's ordered grid of streets, pretty canals and moatside paths – along with its well-placed cafés and restaurants – make it perfectly suited to idle exploration. The sights are, for the most part, low-key, but you won't want to miss **Vor Frelsers Kirke**, with its magnificent spire; the attention-grabbing **Operaen**; or the "Free City" of **Christiania**, whose improvised dwellings and alternative, independently run community has long been one of Copenhagen's major tourist attractions, not least because of its famous street of hash stalls. **Christianhavns Torv**, halfway along the busy main thoroughfare of **Torvegade**, is the district's hub and a natural starting point – the metro station is here, as are stops for all buses crossing Christianshavn.

Along Strandgade

The eastern side of **Strandgade** is home to some of the island's oldest houses. As interesting as its few rather specialized sights is the chance to head off the street's western side to explore Christianshavn's peaceful and much-renovated harbour front, whose gigantic converted warehouses offer a glimpse of the island's trading past.

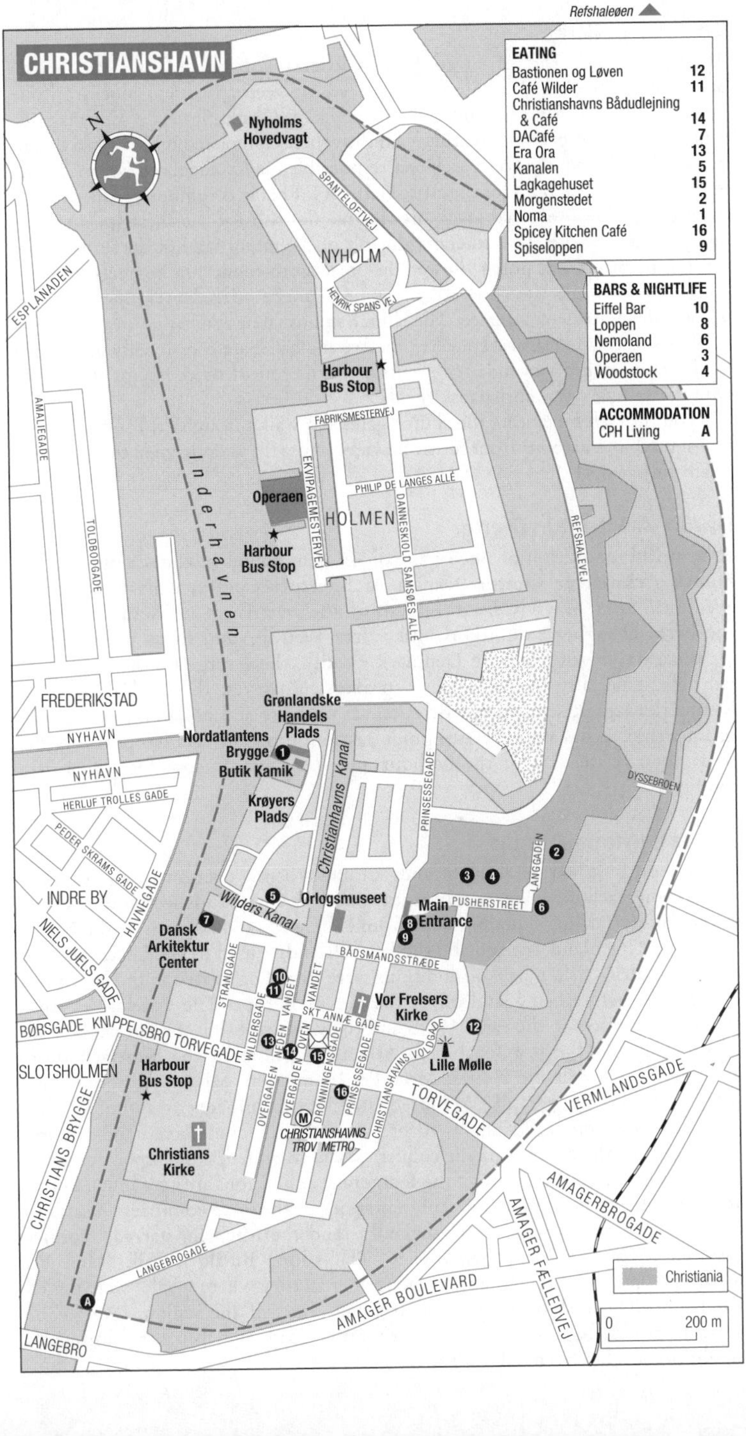

Refshaleøen

CHRISTIANSHAVN

EATING	
Bastionen og Løven	12
Café Wilder	11
Christianshavns Bådudlejning & Café	14
DACafé	7
Era Ora	13
Kanalen	5
Lagkagehuset	15
Morgenstedet	2
Noma	1
Spicey Kitchen Café	16
Spiseloppen	9

BARS & NIGHTLIFE	
Eiffel Bar	10
Loppen	8
Nemoland	6
Operaen	3
Woodstock	4

ACCOMMODATION	
CPH Living	A

Nyholms Hovedvagt
SPANTELOFTVEJ
NYHOLM
HENRIK SPANS VEJ
ESPLANADEN
Harbour Bus Stop
FABRIKSMESTERVEJ
AMALIEGADE
Inderhavnen
EKVIPAGEMESTERVEJ
PHILIP DE LANGES ALLÉ
Operaen
HOLMEN
DANNESKIOLD SAMSØES ALLÉ
REFSHALEVEJ
Harbour Bus Stop
TOLDBODGADE
FREDERIKSTAD
Grønlandske Handels Plads
NYHAVN
Nordatlantens Brygge
Butik Kamik
NYHAVN
Christianshavns Kanal
PRINSESSEGADE
DYSSEBROEN
HERLUF TROLLES GADE
Krøyers Plads
PEDER SKRAMS GADE
LANGGADEN
HAVNEGADE
INDRE BY
Wilders Kanal
Orlogsmuseet
Main Entrance
PUSHERSTREET
NIELS JUELS GADE
Dansk Arkitektur Center
BÅDSMANDSSTRÆDE
STRANDGADE
VANDET
Vor Frelsers Kirke
WILDERSGADE
NEDEN VANDET
OVEN
SKT ANNÆ GADE
BØRSGADE
KNIPPELSBRO
TORVEGADE
Lille Mølle
CHRISTIANSHAVNS VOLDGADE
SLOTSHOLMEN
Harbour Bus Stop
OVERGADEN
OVERGADEN
DRONNINGENSGADE
PRINSESSEGADE
TORVEGADE
VERMLANDSGADE
CHRISTIANSHAVNS TROV METRO
CHRISTIANS BRYGGE
Christians Kirke
AMAGERBROGADE
AMAGER FÆLLEDVEJ
LANGEBROGADE
Christiania
AMAGER BOULEVARD
0 200 m
LANGEBRO

Christians Kirke

At the southern end of Strandgade, **Christians Kirke** (daily: March–Oct 8am–6pm; Nov–Feb 8am–5pm) is squeezed between apartment blocks on one side and the waterfront headquarters of the Danish bank Nordea – four magnificent rectangles of glass and marble – on the other. Completed in 1759 to a design by Nicolai Eigtved, the court architect responsible for Amalienborg (see p.72), the Rococo church was built for the city's German Lutheran community. The exterior is unremarkable – Eigtved saved his creative flourish for the theatrical interior, designed in line with the Lutheran principle of the importance of the sermon: the central and prominent pulpit allowed the preacher to connect more freely with the congregation while the three-storey arched gallery offered everyone the same visual and auditory experience. The church's unusual design has given it excellent acoustics: rock and classical concerts, theatre and ballet are occasionally performed here – you can get a calendar of events from the tourist office (see p.30) and the church itself (Ⓦwww.christianskirke.dk).

If you turn left on exiting the church gates and walk through the bank complex, you'll reach the harbour front for a fine view across the Inderhavnen to Den Sorte Diamant (see p.41).

Dansk Arkitektur Center

A beautiful renovation of one of the oldest warehouses in Christianshavn, the **Dansk Arkitektur Center** (Danish Architecture Centre; daily 10am–5pm, Wed until 9pm; Ⓦwww.dac.dk) stands on the waterfront at Gammel Dok. At the back, changing exhibitions (40kr, free Wed 5–9pm) focus primarily on architectural development in Denmark – sadly, these verge on the incomprehensible, especially to non-Danish speakers. However, the bookshop stocks Denmark's largest selection of titles on architecture and design (most of them in English) and has a good travel guide section, too. The café has probably the best views in the city of the harbour and is a fantastic spot for coffee or a sandwich.

Nordatlantens Brygge

Pushing on a bit further along Strandgade and crossing over onto another small island, you reach the wide, windswept expanse of **Grønlandske Handels Plads** (Greenlandic Trading Square). Ships from Denmark's old colonies in the North Atlantic – Greenland, Iceland and the Faroe Islands – used to dock here, and the cargoes of dried fish, whale oil and skins were stored or treated in the enormous warehouses before being sold off to the rest of Europe. The warehouses were turned into offices in the early 1980s and the whiff of fish is long gone, but the square still flies the flag for North Atlantic relations in the **Nordatlantens Brygge** (North Atlantic House; Mon–Fri 10am–5pm, Sat & Sun noon–5pm; 40kr; Ⓦwww.bryggen.dk). Housed in the magnificent warehouse that dominates the square, its aim is to promote artistic, commercial and cultural links between the North Atlantic countries, and to present contemporary North Atlantic art and culture, though the temporary exhibitions are a bit hit and miss. It's also home to the diplomatic representations of the three countries – useful to know if you need a visa for Greenland – and the Michelin-starred, Nordic-inspired restaurant *Noma* (see p.152). The **shop**, **Butik Kamik** (Mon–Fri 10am–5.30pm, Sat 11am–3pm), in the former factory where whales were boiled for lamp oil, is a showcase for the arts and crafts of the region, though the seal-fur gloves, bags and hats, racks of mink coats and fish-skin lampshades might prove a bit too much for some.

Christianshavns Kanal and Orlogsmuseet

Lapping the eastern side of Grønlandske Handels Plads and running north–south down the centre of the island, the delightful **Christianshavns Kanal** – Christianshavn at its most Dutch – bristles and tinkles with the bobbing masts and halyards of its many sailing boats, especially thick around the small marina at its north-western end. The lively cobbled streets of Overgaden Oven Vandet and Overgaden Neden Vandet flank its length, and though they harbour no compelling tourist sights, a stroll along the banks taking in the grand and colourful old buildings, cafés and locals pottering about on their boats is one of the island's highlights.

The nautical theme continues on the corner of Bådsmandsstræde (Boatswain's Alley) and Overgaden Oven Vandet in the cheery yellow Naval Hospital of 1780, now home to the **Orlogsmuseet** (Royal Danish Naval Museum; Tues–Sun noon–4pm; 40kr, free on Wed; Ⓦwww.orlogsmuseet.dk). Devoted to the illustrious history of the Danish Navy, the museum's pride and joy is its collection of four hundred intricate **ship models** – some dating back to the sixteenth century. Ships' equipment, uniforms, weapons, nautical instruments, maritime art and minutely detailed models of the many sea battles the Danish Navy has fought (they even include cotton-wool smoke clouds from the cannons) make up the rest of the collection. You can also go aboard the *Spækhuggeren* (Killer Whale) submarine – radio broadcasts help you to relive the moment it narrowly escaped the Germans during World War II – or clamber up onto the bridge of a torpedo boat. There's an eating area downstairs where you can tuck into your packed lunch in the company of a selection of cannons, and a **children's museum** where kids can scramble around on bits of ships.

Vor Frelsers Kirke and Lille Mølle

Just south of the Orlogsmuseet, soaring skywards through the trees on Skt Annæ Gade, is the unmistakable copper-and-gold spire of Christianshavn's famous landmark, **Vor Frelsers Kirke** (April–Aug Mon–Sat 11am–4.30pm, Sun noon–4.30pm; Sept–March Mon–Sat 11am–3.30pm, Sun noon–3.30pm; Ⓦwww.vorfrelserskirke.dk). Completed in 1696 in Dutch Baroque style, it was the first church to be built following the 1660 declaration of absolute monarchy, and Christian V certainly rammed the point home with a generous sprinkling of his initials and symbols.

The lavish **spire**, with its spiralling exterior staircase and large golden globe carrying a three-metre-high Jesus waving a flag, was added to the otherwise plain

Walking the bastions

One of the highlights of a visit to Christianshavn is a walk along the picturesque moat on the eastern side of the island. **Lille Mølle** (see above) makes a good starting point, from where you can head north through **Christiania** (see p.58), either along the top of the bastions themselves for fine views over the moat and Free City, or along the narrow path that winds its way along the water's edge through Christiania and continues by way of a minor road up to **Nyholm** (see p.62). The latter is a pretty walk, negotiating the rambling track through Christiania's waterside homes with just the wind in the reeds and the cries of waterfowl to break the silence. Alternatively, you can head **south** from Lille Mølle, crossing over Torvegade and following the line of the moat until you reach Langebro, from where you can cross back into the city proper. This stretch is noisier and more built up, and is also a popular jogging path, but it offers a scenic route back into town if you have time (45min walk).

exterior in the mid-eighteenth century, instantly becoming one of the city skyline's most recognizable features – it's said to have been used as a target by Nelson during the 1807 bombardment, though fortunately he only managed to hit a leg. To ascend the spire (11am–4pm, 25kr; closed Nov–March and on wet and windy days) you'll have to climb a total of 400 steps, 150 of them outside, slanted and slippery (especially after rain), and gradually becoming smaller and smaller. The reward for reaching the top, however, is a great **view** of Copenhagen and beyond.

Inside, the Baroque extravagance reaches its peak in the showy **altar**, depicting a gilded sun (representing God) breaking through black clouds to shine on frolicking cherubs and archangels. To the left of the altar, the white marble font surrounded by menacing marble toddlers was intended as a fertility charm for the childless wife of Frederik IV. The two stucco elephants appearing to hold up the gigantic **organ** were included due to their association with the king – the animal became the symbol of the nation's highest order, the Order of the Elephant, started by Christian V and still in existence today. If you want to hear the magnificent organ, join services held every Sunday at noon from May to September.

Continue to the end of Skt Annæ Gade and head up onto the ramparts to **Lille Mølle** (guided tours in Danish only June–Sept Sat & Sun 1pm, 2pm & 3pm; 50kr; tickets from *Bastionen og Løven* (see below) on same day; for English tours call ⓣ 33 47 38 38), the only surviving example of the many windmills that formerly stood on the Christianshavn ramparts. Built in 1783 to a Dutch design, the windmill ground wheat for the ever-increasing numbers of Copenhageners until being converted into a private home at the beginning of the twentieth century. In 1973 it was given to the National Museum by its flamboyant owners, and today it bears witness to their lavish lifestyle, with many odd rooms furnished in a mixture of styles from quaintly Germanic to romantic British. Next door, in the miller's old domicile, is *Bastionen og Løven*, a fine restaurant (p.152) with outdoor seating on the edge of the ramparts.

Christiania

Stretching for almost 1km along either side of the moat north of Lille Mølle, the remarkable "Free City" of **Christiania** (ⓦ www.christiania.org) is living proof of Copenhagen's liberal social traditions. Ever since a group of young and homeless people colonized the complex of disused military barracks in the spring of 1971, the area has excited controversy, sympathy and admiration in equal measure. Declared a "Free City" by its residents later that year – with the aim of operating autonomously from Copenhagen proper and pursuing more egalitarian and environmentally friendly lifestyles – it inevitably became best known outside Denmark for its open selling of hash on "Pusherstreet", while its continued existence on some of Copenhagen's finest real estate has fuelled one of the longest-running debates in Danish society.

Initially categorized and tolerated by those in power as a "social experiment" (a term dismissed by Christianites themselves), Christiania has had a rollercoaster ride at the hands of successive governments, who either largely left the community alone or tried to bring it under the city's municipal machinery. Time after time Christiania has mobilized itself, mustering popular, political and legal support to repel any attempts to curtail its freedoms, no doubt helped by the fact that, when push came to shove, politicians proved too wary of potential electoral damage at the hands of the Free City's broader public support. Not that Christiania is a hippie paradise – an inevitable by-product of its idealism and freedoms is that it has, at times, been a refuge for petty criminals and undesirable characters. But the problems have been overplayed by its critics, and though there have been sporadic raids and police crackdowns on drugs the authorities have mostly proved tolerant of the open trade in hash (though use and possession is illegal in Denmark), in the knowledge that Christiania has enforced, as far as possible, its own ban on hard drugs imposed in the late 1970s following problems caused by an influx of heroin.

However, Christiania's **future** hangs in the balance under the current right-wing government, which has been strident in its disapproval of the rebel in its midst. In 2004, faced with imminent police action, Christiania made a pre-emptive strike by removing the biggest stick the government had to beat it with: the hash booths on Pusherstreet. The booths have since gradually re-emerged – one, considered a cultural artefact, has even been moved into the national museum (see p.84) – and, despite the almost daily police raids, the street continues to pull in almost one million visitors a year. Whether Christiania can survive in its present form, however, remains to be seen, particularly in the light of proposed new property laws that would enforce private ownership of homes and render Christiana's policy of collective use – no one owns their own home – illegal, thus opening the door for property developers. The Free City has to mobilize itself yet again in the face of what it sees as inevitable gentrification but, for the time being at least, its one thousand inhabitants continue to make an economic, social and environmental success of their long-running "experiment" (see below).

Walking around Christiania

Christiania has a few entrances along the bastions but it's best to head for the **main entrance** on Prinsessegade (or the former main entrance on the corner of Prinsessegade and Bådsmandsstræde), which leads you straight into the heart of the Free City. The long, narrow yellow-brick loppebygningen on your right houses **Infocaféen** (daily noon–6pm), where you can pick up the excellent *Christiania Guide* (10kr), which gives the lowdown on the area's turbulent history and includes a map locating all the places of interest; you can also buy a

Anarchy rules

A colony of hippies it may be, but given its low budget – 18 million kroner per year raised through residential rents, business revenue and metered utilities – Christiania is a pretty well-organized community. From this **common purse** it has to pay municipal taxes, electricity and water bills, rubbish-collection fees and for the maintenance and running of all of its buildings and services, such as the post office, youth clubs and playgrounds. Christianites aren't all sitting around smoking pot either: eighty percent of the community is in **work**, half with "straight" jobs in the city, the rest employed within Christiania itself.

Adhering to anarchist principles of a social system based on voluntary cooperation not government, there's no hierarchy of rule, and community-related decisions are reached by **consensus** not votes, with a representative of each of the fourteen area committees regularly attending the **Common Meeting**, which makes Christiania-wide decisions, sets the annual budget, negotiates with outside authorities and, when necessary, acts as a kind of court, settling private disagreements that can't be resolved at the Area Meetings. Increasingly severe building restrictions imposed by the city council have meant that planning permission to build a new home is rarely, if ever, granted, so property only becomes available as people leave or die; should you be taken with the idea of living in the Free City, you'll have to wait for an advertisement in Christiania's weekly gazette, *Ugespejlet*, and put your case to an interview panel.

T-shirt or car sticker to help the cause. Don't be intimidated by the idea of wandering around by yourself: naturally, the area has a grungy, offbeat feel and you'll still get more than the odd whiff of dope, but the atmosphere is welcoming and relaxed (cars aren't allowed). Moreover, Christianites are used to the constant influx of the curious and sympathetic, although residents ask tourists, reasonably enough, not to enter their gardens or photograph them without asking first. It's worth joining one of the **guided tours** (July & Aug daily 3pm; Sept–June Sat & Sun 3pm; 1hr 30min; 30kr) that leave from the main entrance. Conducted by residents, they're a good introduction to the workings of this rather complex community.

Covering almost 85 acres, Christiania spreads out in a loose network of unpaved paths and small green open spaces on both sides of Christian IV's old moat between Christianshavn and Amager (a bridge, Dyssebroen, connects the two sides), many of its ramshackle homes hugging the reedy water's edge in a picture of rural charm. As you'd expect given its military past, its buildings are a peculiar mix of magnificent old barracks and warehouses – livened up with a generous splattering of vivid murals and now housing workshops, art centres and crèches – and small, decorative homes cluttered with flowerpots. There's also a good smattering of cafés and shops selling locally made goods.

The best place to start your wanderings is at loppebygningen (see p.59) – whose music venue *Loppen* (see p.170) and highly rated restaurant *Spiseloppen* (see p.153) have ensured its fame beyond the Free City's walls. It also houses **Gallopperiet**, Christiania's art gallery (Tues–Sun noon–5pm). Continuing straight ahead you soon come to the city's hub, where you'll find most of its bars, cafés and nightlife as well as the closest Christiania gets to a commercial centre – Carl Madsens Plads – a small square lined with stalls selling snacks, cheap clothing, CDs, jewellery, incense and the like. The square marks the start of the infamous **Pusherstreet**, where lines of stalls sell pre-rolled joints and an international selection of grass – wildly popular with tourists in summer. The Sunshine Bakery is a good spot to pick up a picnic lunch, while the large building on the left, **Operaen**, acts as a music venue (see p.170), community centre and children's theatre. Push on to the small square on the right, crowded in summer with the chilled-out clientele of *Nemoland* (see p.164), Christiania's most popular bar. Pusherstreet ends at the huge ex-military riding hall, **Den Grønne Hal** (Green Hall), a one-stop new and secondhand shop, piled high with everything from building materials to fuel to clothes. From here, head left along **Langgaden** (Long Street), a quiet, mostly residential street that runs parallel to the moat and from where narrow paths lead up on to the bastions. The path leading up from the Buddhist stupa at the entrance to the residential quarter known as Mælkebøtten will take you down to the water's edge at the Dyssebroen, from where you can either cross the bridge to an even quieter, greener area of the Free City, or continue your ramble in either direction along the waterside path (very muddy in winter) for a look at some more of Christiania's alternative dwellings.

Holmen

North of Christiania, the area of **Holmen** – five reclaimed islands, formerly home to the old naval station founded by Frederik III – is linked to the Refshaleøen area of Amager by a bridge to the north. The base of the Danish fleet from the middle of the seventeenth century, it was a small town in its own right, with all manner of factories and workshops attending to the navy, and its own schools, churches, courts and hospitals catering to the huge workforces stationed there. Most of the base was moved elsewhere in the early 1990s, and the area, home to several prestigious **art schools**, is now busy producing Denmark's next generation of architects, movie directors, musicians and actors. There's nothing much to do, but the atmospheric, listed buildings (the navy employed only the best architects) and laid-back campus-feel make it an enjoyable area to wander around.

Operaen

Occupying a prime waterfront spot at the western edge of Holmen, Copenhagen's state-of-the-art **Operaen** opened in 2005 – funded by Denmark's richest man, the 91-year-old shipping magnate Maersk Mc-Kinney Møller. The work of the country's leading architect, Henning Larsen, the opera house is an undeniably bold and original, if not immediately appealing, building, completely dominated by the immense slab of the 158-metre-long **"floating" roof**, which extends 32m beyond the orb-like foyer and stepped entrance plaza out to the water's edge like a giant diving board. A generous gift and significant boost to the city's cultural life it may be, but the project hasn't escaped criticism: the press sniped at Møller's insistence on total control over what was a public project, while the building's critics have likened the glass and metal facade of the foyer to the grille of a 1955 Pontiac, called the auditorium's gold-leaf ceiling vulgar and questioned the location, suggesting that the building reduces the dome of the royal palace of Amalienborg across the harbour to a bit-part player in the city's skyline. However, it's a hit with the public, with many performances selling out way in advance, and the acoustics are world class. Should you want to see the inside of the building, you'll have to get tickets for a **performance** (see p.175) or join a **guided tour** (July daily at 4pm in English, rest of the year Sat & Sun 9.30am & 4.30pm primarily in Danish – although the guide will provide some English translation; 100kr).

The building is at its most striking by night, but at any time, it's worth visiting the wonderful light-filled **foyer** to admire the three stunning multi-faceted glass lighting globes suspended from the ceiling – designed by world famous Danish-Icelandic artist Olafur Eliasson – and the sumptuously rich maplewood shell that

▲ Operaen

encases the auditorium as though it were a giant musical instrument. Look out also for the many hundred beautiful fossils hidden in the South German Jura Gelb sandstone, visible both inside and outside the building. Access to Operaen is somewhat limited – the harbour bus being the most frequent means of getting here – which means, sadly, that the outstanding café/restaurant is only open when there are performances. A pedestrian bridge across Inderhavnen may, however, be in the pipeline – if Møller agrees to pay.

Nyholm

The island of **Nyholm** (daily 8am–sunset) is worth a look with its naval station and a few gems of naval architecture. At its northern edge stands Nyholms Hovedvagt; the former main gate dates from 1745 and is one of Holmen's oldest buildings, with a slightly out-of-proportion tower capped by a huge crown – the Danish flag is still raised and lowered here by the navy every sunrise and sunset. Next door is the Elephanten Dock, constructed on an old ship that was deliberately sunk to establish the foundations of the dock. There's a line of old cannons nearby, and you can walk along the top of the fortifications overlooking Inderhavnen – on a sunny day, the view from here over to mainland Copenhagen and the spires and domes of Frederikstad is incomparable.

Just east of Nyholm, crossing a short bridge across the bastion lakes on Refshalevej, leads you on to the old industrial island of Refshaleøen, home to some superb watersports venues.

4

Rosenborg, Frederikstad and Kastellet

There's quite a contrast between the narrow streets of Indre By and the open parks and boulevards of the northeastern side of the city centre. This part of Copenhagen owes its character to the grand plans of two royal builders, Christian IV – creator of the fanciful palace of **Rosenborg Slot** and the fortress of **Kastellet** – and Frederik V, whose name is preserved in the district he created, **Frederikstad**, a somewhat pompous quarter boasting proud aristocratic monuments such as the **Marmorkirken** and **Amalienborg** – residence of the royal family. A moneyed air pervades the streets – antique dealers, furniture shops and art galleries vie for attention along the main thoroughfares of Store Kongensgade and Bredgade. Royal attractions aside, two of the city's best **art museums** are also here – the Statens Museum for Kunst and the Hirschsprungske Samling – as well as the excellent Kunstindustrimuseet, a must-see if you're interested in Danish design, not to mention several other smaller, more eclectic museums. There are also some glorious **parks and gardens**, while a walk along the revamped **harbourfront** takes you to the area's star attraction – **the Little Mermaid**.

Rosenborg and around

Immediately north of Gothersgade, the medieval streets of Indre By give way to regal boulevards surrounding **Rosenborg Slot**, once protected to the west by the old city ramparts, which have since been converted into parks and now house the lovely open spaces of the **Botanisk Have** and Østre Anlæg. In the parklands are the impressive artworks of the **Statens Museum for Kunst** and the **Hirschsprungske Samling**, as well as the rather less compelling offerings of the **Geologisk Museum** and **Den Frie Udstilling** exhibition hall. The primarily residential area immediately east of Rosenborg Slot is worth seeking out for the **Davids Samling**, with its fine Islamic collection, and the rows of quaint old sailor cottages at **Nyboder**, while, for film buffs, **Cinemateket**, to the south, on Gothersgade, is devoted to the silver screen. Note that, apart from museum cafés, places to eat are thin on the ground in this area.

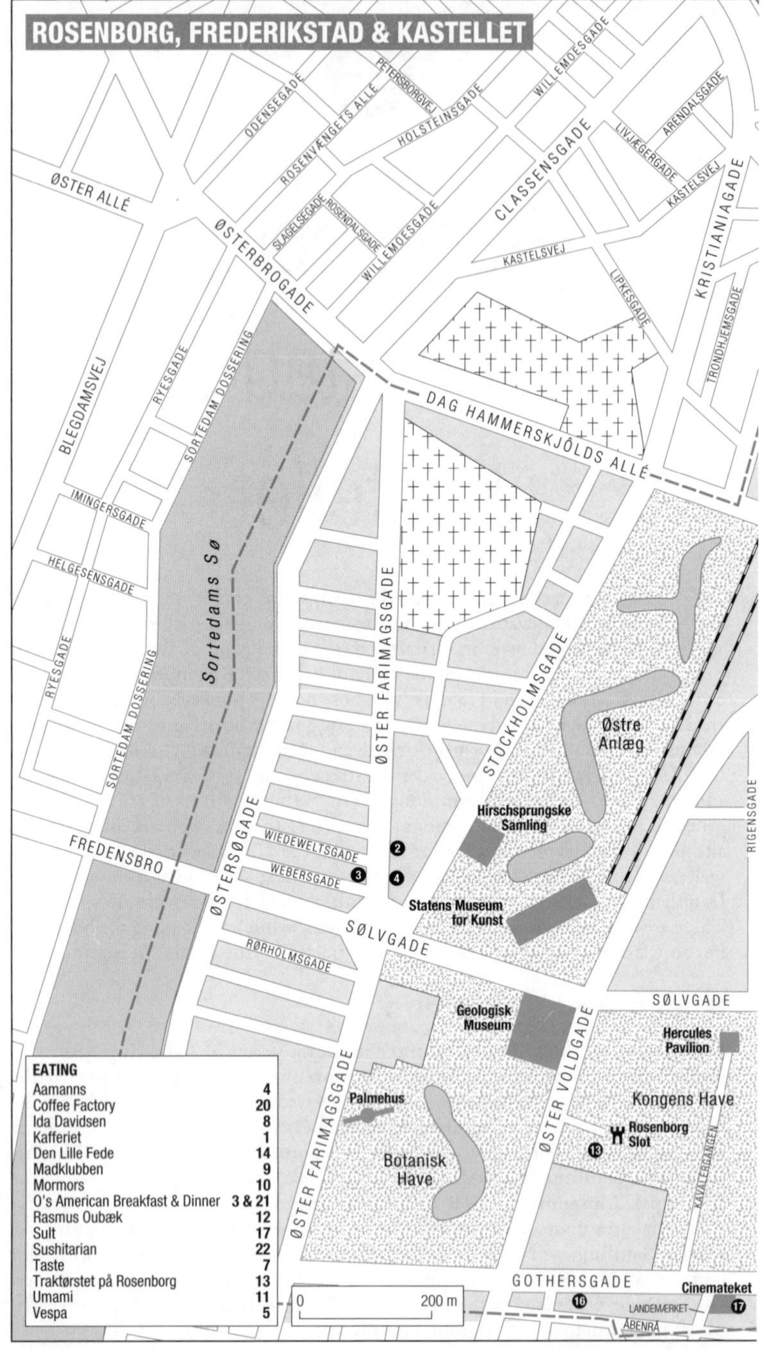
ROSENBORG, FREDERIKSTAD & KASTELLET
ØSTER ALLÉ
ODENSEGADE
ROSENVÆNGETS ALLÉ
PETERSBORGVEJ
HOLSTEINSGADE
WILLEMOESGADE
CLASSENSGADE
LIVJÆGERGADE
ARENDALSGADE
KASTELSVEJ
KRISTIANIAGADE
ØSTERBROGADE
SLAGELSEGADE
ROSENDALSGADE
WILLEMOESGADE
KASTELSVEJ
LIPKESGADE
TRONDHJEMSGADE
BLEGDAMSVEJ
RYESGADE
SORTEDAM DOSSERING
DAG HAMMERSKJÖLDS ALLÉ
IMINGERSGADE
HELGESENSGADE
Sortedams Sø
ØSTER FARIMAGSGADE
STOCKHOLMSGADE
Østre Anlæg
RYESGADE
SORTEDAM DOSSERING
RIGENSGADE
Hirschsprungske Samling
FREDENSBRO
ØSTERSØGADE
WIEDEWELTSGADE
WEBERSGADE
Statens Museum for Kunst
SØLVGADE
RØRHOLMSGADE
SØLVGADE
Geologisk Museum
Hercules Pavilion
ØSTER VOLDGADE
ØSTER FARIMAGSGADE
Palmehus
Kongens Have
Rosenborg Slot
Botanisk Have
KAVALERGANGEN
GOTHERSGADE
Cinemateket
LANDEMÆRKET
ÅBENRÅ
0 200 m
EATING
Aamanns 4
Coffee Factory 20
Ida Davidsen 8
Kafferiet 1
Den Lille Fede 14
Madklubben 9
Mormors 10
O's American Breakfast & Dinner 3 & 21
Rasmus Oubæk 12
Sult 17
Sushitarian 22
Taste 7
Traktørstet på Rosenborg 13
Umami 11
Vespa 5

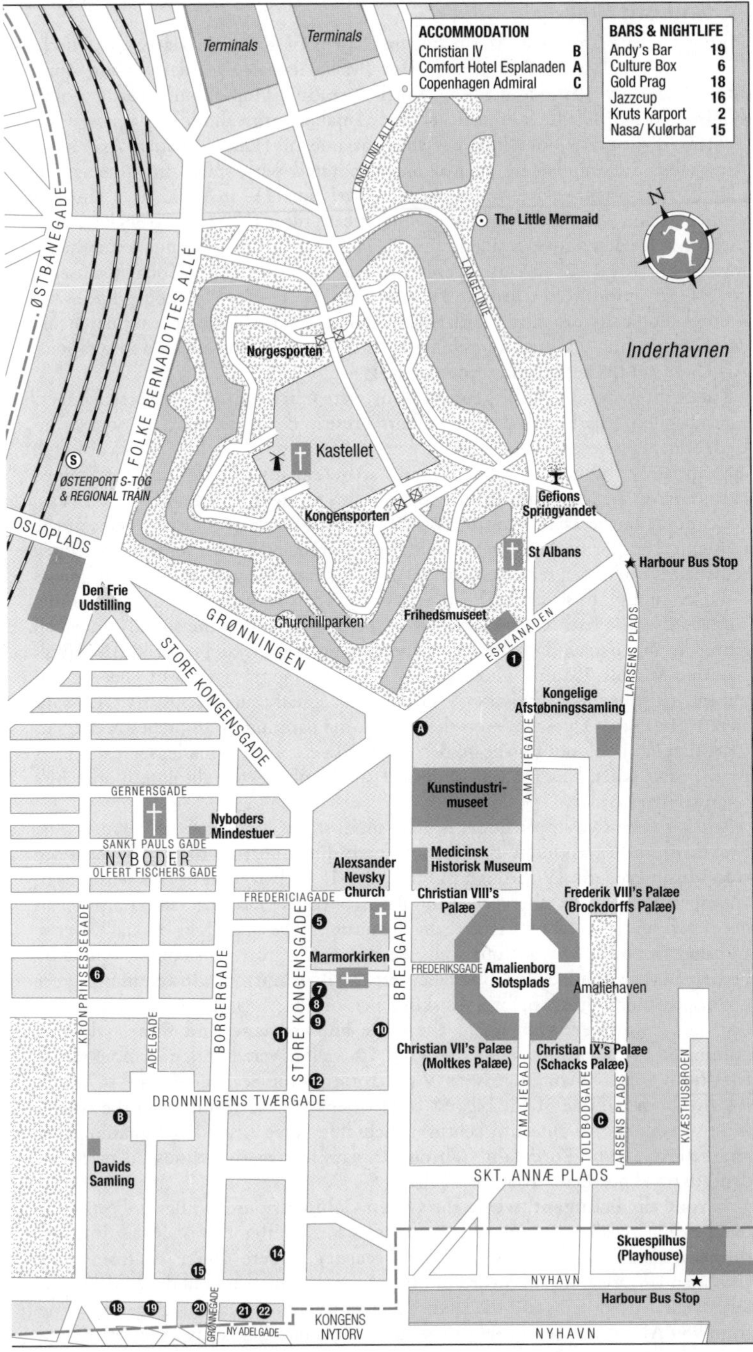
ACCOMMODATION
Christian IV B
Comfort Hotel Esplanaden A
Copenhagen Admiral C
BARS & NIGHTLIFE
Andy's Bar 19
Culture Box 6
Gold Prag 18
Jazzcup 16
Kruts Karport 2
Nasa/ Kulørbar 15
Terminals
Terminals
LANGELINIE ALLÉ
The Little Mermaid
LANGELINIE
Inderhavnen
ØSTBANEGADE
FOLKE BERNADOTTES ALLÉ
Norgesporten
Kastellet
Kongensporten
Gefions Springvandet
St Albans
Harbour Bus Stop
ØSTERPORT S-TOG & REGIONAL TRAIN
OSLOPLADS
Den Frie Udstilling
GRØNNINGEN
Churchillparken
Frihedsmuseet
ESPLANADEN
STORE KONGENSGADE
LARSENS PLADS
Kongelige Afstøbningssamling
AMALIEGADE
Kunstindustri-museet
GERNERSGADE
Nyboders Mindestuer
SANKT PAULS GADE
NYBODER
OLFERT FISCHERS GADE
Medicinsk Historisk Museum
Alexsander Nevsky Church
Christian VIII's Palæe
Frederik VIII's Palæe (Brockdorffs Palæe)
FREDERICIAGADE
KRONPRINSESSEGADE
BORGERGADE
STORE KONGENSGADE
BREDGADE
Marmorkirken
FREDERIKSGADE
Amalienborg Slotsplads
Amaliehaven
ADELGADE
Christian VII's Palæe (Moltkes Palæe)
Christian IX's Palæe (Schacks Palæe)
DRONNINGENS TVÆRGADE
TOLDBODGADE
LARSENS PLADS
KVÆSTHUSBROEN
AMALIEGADE
Davids Samling
SKT. ANNÆ PLADS
Skuespilhus (Playhouse)
NYHAVN
Harbour Bus Stop
GRØNNEGADE
NY ADELGADE
KONGENS NYTORV
NYHAVN

Rosenborg Slot

Rising enchantingly from the manicured lawns of Kongens Have, the Dutch-Renaissance palace of **Rosenborg Slot** (May, Sept & Oct daily 10am–4pm; June–Aug daily 10am–5pm; Nov–April Tues–Sun 11am–2pm, Treasury open till 4pm; 70kr, 90kr for a joint ticket with Amalienborg valid for 2 days; Ⓦwww.rosenborg-slot.dk) looks like a setting for one of Hans Christian Andersen's fairy-tales. Surrounded by a moat and decorated with spires and towers, the playful, red-brick palace was built by **Christian IV** in 1606 as a summer residence, and was where he drew his final breath more than forty years later. The castle was used as a royal residence until 1710 after which it became a storehouse for various royal collections, opening to the public in 1833. Today's museum covers the period from Christian IV to Frederik VII – the Oldenburg line – and is chronologically organized with each room devoted to a different monarch and displaying a fabulous array of paintings, furniture, personal effects and weapons. Also here are the spectacular **crown jewels**.

The first few rooms of the **ground floor** were **Christian IV**'s private chambers – atmospheric, dark, oak-panelled affairs preserved largely intact. Room 3, his **bedroom**, is where he died; several personal belongings include his sword and, appropriately, his nightcap and slippers. Also on display are his bloodstained clothes from a naval battle against the Swedish in 1644 in which he lost an eye. Next door, in the **Dark Room**, you'll find one of several bizarre objects in the museum that glorify the power of the absolute monarchs – a seventeenth-century armchair with hidden tentacles in the armrests that would grab the wrists of guests unlucky enough to sit in it. The victim would then be soaked with water from a container in the back of the chair before being released to the sound of a small trumpet. Further along, the dark panelling gives way to Frederik III's lavish Baroque **Marble Room**, whose ceiling is a stucco extravaganza of cherubs and nymphs. Just beyond, **Christian V**'s room is an equally sumptuous affair, its walls covered in Dutch tapestries – on the ceiling, the painting of an orchestra dates to Christian IV. Look out for the golden chair with elephant trunk legs – it was used by the king when handing out Orders of the Elephant, the absolute monarchy's finest military order.

Access to the two upper floors is via a spiral stone staircase from room 7. The **first floor**, rather less interesting than the preceding one, runs through seven more rulers from Frederik IV through to Frederik VII – a labyrinth of ornate rooms in appropriate styles of the day from Rococo to Neoclassical and Empire, all decorated with suitably extravagant furniture. The highlight is the **Mirror Cabinet** (room 13A) – all four walls are covered in mirrors – commissioned by Frederik IV to indulge his erotic fantasies: the floor mirrors allowed him to peer up his partner's dress, before whisking her off down a spiral staircase to his bedroom below. Press on up to the more impressive **second floor**, which is dominated by the magnificent **Long Hall**, its walls covered with enormous tapestries from 1690 showing Christian V's victories in the Scanian War of 1675–79. It's also home to one of the biggest collections of silver furniture in the world, mostly from the seventeenth century, including three silver lions guarding the king's throne. The **Porcelain Cabinet** displays almost two thousand pieces of delicate royal porcelain from the 1790s.

Beyond the **basement**, where the **Green Cabinet** houses a huge collection of royal riding regalia, armour and weapons, a further flight of stairs leads down through massive steel doors into the **Treasury**, where you're confronted by Christian III's magnificent Sword of State, beyond which are hundreds of incredibly detailed gold items and the fabulous silver Oldenburg Horn, allegedly dating from 989 AD. A few steps lead further down to a dazzling array of jewellery and royal treasures, including the surprisingly restrained **crown of Christian IV** – an exquisite latticework of gold, pearls and minuscule enamel figurines. In the final section are two cases containing the present queen's **crown jewels**. The largest piece, the Crown of the Absolute Monarchs, weighs in at more than 2kg and includes a sapphire weighing over an ounce.

Kongens Have

Central Copenhagen's oldest and prettiest park, **Kongens Have** (Royal Gardens; daily 7am–sunset; free) was established in 1606 by Christian IV to provide the castle with a place in which the royal family could grow vegetables and flowers. The gardens still preserve much of their original layout, with a grid of wide tree-lined lanes and narrower pathways cutting through lawns perfect for a picnic. From the palace, it's a short stroll down to the park's southern entrance on Gothersgade, where two large plinths, topped with gold domes, neatly frame Kavalergangen (Squire's Lane), originally used as a jousting run. Walk down to the **Hercules Pavilion** – there's a small café here open in summer and a children's play area complete with large wooden dragons for clambering on. During summer months, the garden hosts live music and theatre performances, and jugglers from around the world gather to share tricks of the trade. The **puppet theatre** (June–Aug Tues–Sun 2pm & 3pm; free) along the outer wall of Kronprinsessegade is a hit with the kids.

Cinemateket

Opposite the Kongens Have on Gothersgade, **Cinemateket** (Film House; Tues–Fri 9.30am–10pm, Sat & Sun noon–10pm; free; Ⓦwww.cinemateket.dk) is a state-of-the-art complex dedicated to all things connected to the big screen. Occupying a restructured office block, the curious interior contains a large black sarcophagus-like edifice, which encloses two of Cinemateket's screens (see p.178). Other parts of the building are sometimes used as a gallery – expect to see cutting-edge, if not always interesting, Danish art. There's also a book and DVD shop, and a trendy café-restaurant (see p.154), but the main attraction is **Videotek** (Tues–Fri 2–10pm, Sat & Sun 2–8pm) with over 3000 films to choose from and free viewing facilities in the basement.

Davids Samling

Housed in an eighteenth-century building on Kronprinsessegade, east of Kongens Have, the **Davids Samling** (David Collection; Tues, Fri, Sat & Sun 1–5pm, Wed & Thurs 10am–5pm; free; Ⓦwww.davidmus.dk) is an Aladdin's cave of Persian, Arabian and Indian antiques dating back to the sixth century (it also houses a less noteworthy collection of eighteenth-century European painting, furniture and porcelain and Danish early modern art, including a room devoted to paintings by Vilhelm Hammershøi). Bequeathed to the state in 1960 by wealthy lawyer C.L. David and displayed in what was his home, it is one of the most important collections of Islamic art in the West. The house provides a suitably elegant backdrop to the beautifully displayed collections, which include everything from delicate embroidered silks to savage-looking daggers; there's also an extensive assortment of exquisite miniatures and illuminated manuscripts and Korans, dating back to the thirteenth century, from all over the Islamic world.

Nyboder

Christian IV built the **Nyboder district**, north of Sølvgade and east of Kronprinsessegade, to provide free housing for his sailors. The open, grid-like pattern of terraces was highly sophisticated, and Nyboder is still a highly desirable place to live. The striking cobbled streets, lined with quaint ochre terraces, make for a pleasant wander, even if it does all look a little bit too perfect to be true – in fact, all but one of the rows of buildings here are eighteenth-century two-storey versions of the originals. The solitary original row that does survive, dating from the 1630s, runs along Sankt Pauls Gade and now houses, at no. 24, the small and reasonably interesting **Nyboders Mindestuer** museum (Sun 11am–2pm; 15kr; Ⓦwww.nybodersmindestuer.dk), containing a collection of furniture and domestic objects, as well as a reconstructed schoolroom, reflecting the lives of Nyboder families in the late nineteenth century.

Botanisk Have

Established on their present site in 1874, the **Botanisk Have** (Botanical Gardens; May–Sept daily 8.30am–6pm; Oct–April Tues–Sun 8.30am–4pm; free; Ⓦwww.botanic-garden.ku.dk; entrances on Øster Farimagsgade and the corner of Gothersgade and Øster Voldgade) are the perfect spot to unwind after hitting the museums nearby. The gardens boast a small coniferous forest, rock gardens, ponds and waterfalls populated by herons, ducks and freshwater terrapins, while a handsome nineteenth-century greenhouse perched on a terrace overlooking the gardens holds wonderful collections of exotic plants and trees. The largest is the circular **Palmehus** (daily 10am–3pm), where massive palms hang lazily in the steamy atmosphere over ponds crowded with water lilies – a walkway runs around the top of the interior. Next to the Palmehus, the **Kaktushus** (Wed, Sat & Sun 1–2pm) contains around a thousand species of cacti and succulents, while at the **Orkidehuset** (Wed, Sat & Sun 2–3pm) the fragrance of more than six hundred types of orchids permeates the air. There's a pleasant café next to the Palmehus.

Geologisk Museum

At the northeastern corner of Botanisk Have, by the junction of Sølvgade and Øster Voldgade, the **Geologisk Museum** (Geological Museum; Tues–Sun 1–4pm; 40kr; Ⓦwww.geologisk-museum.dk) is housed in a grand old university building. As you'd expect there are exhibitions on volcanoes, earthquakes and continental drift, as well as a vast collection of minerals. The Solar System display features a startling collection of **meteorites** from a major fall thousands of years ago in Cape York, Greenland – some have been cut into enormous slices, creating strange, mirror-like effects. You'll also find exhibitions on the evolution of man and a kid-pleasing section devoted to prehistoric vertebrates.

Statens Museum for Kunst

In the southeastern corner of Østre Anlæg, the huge **Statens Museum for Kunst** (Royal Museum of Fine Arts; Tues & Thurs–Sun 10am–5pm, Wed 10am–8pm; free; Ⓦwww.smk.dk) spans the last seven centuries of art. It is well worth visiting, not only for its fine collections of Danish art from 1750 but also for its foreign collections – where the lack of exceptional works is made up for by inventive staging. The original redbrick Dahlerup-designed building from 1896 contains the Danish and Modern art while the gleaming white modern wing behind holds foreign art from 1300 to 1800.

The main body of works is on the **second floor** – head up the main stairs of the old building (the other two gallery floors are given over to temporary exhibitions and a children's museum, see p.201). **Danish art from 1750 to 1900** revolves around the central room, which offers a chronological sampler of what's to come: portraits of Danish (and other) royals rub shoulders with works by eighteenth-century artists including the accomplished Jens Juel and the more fanciful Nicolas Abildgaard, and a selection of Golden Age (see p.211) works featuring views of Rome by C.W. Eckersberg, bucolic landscapes by P.C. Skovgaard and portraits and views of Copenhagen by Christian Købke. Later works include Michael Ancher's *The Sick Girl*, L.A. Ring's early twentieth-century hyper-realistic and oddly anachronistic works, and Joachim Skovgaard's disturbing and zealously religious *Christ in the Realm of the Dead* standing in stark contrast to Vilhelm Hammershøi's typically calm, monotone *Female Model* from 1916. You might think this enough of a taste of Danish painting, but the rooms around repay some attention, exploring certain artists and themes in more depth – there's more Golden Age painting, works by the Skagen painters, particularly P.S. Krøyer and Michael and Anna Ancher, as well as an impressive room dominated by the distinctive and powerful work of Hammershøi – a mixture of empty, almost photographic scenes of Copenhagen buildings, and haunting portraits and nudes.

The **modern art** collections, to the right of the main stairs, highlight most of the major movements of the twentieth century. One huge room displays Danish painting and sculpture after 1960, with colourful canvases by Per Kirkeby and dramatic pieces by Asger Jorn, a member of the CoBrA movement (made up of mid-twentieth-century artists from *C*openhagen, *B*russels and *A*msterdam), sharing space with other internationally less well-known artists. Next door, another central gallery focuses on Danish work from 1900 to 1960, with pieces by fauvist Edvard Weie, expressionist Jens Sondergaard and surrealist Wilhelm Freddie. The rooms around concentrate, roughly chronologically, on 1900 to the present day with a great selection of paintings by Matisse – the equivalent of many larger museums – alongside works by his contemporary, German expressionist Emil Nolde. Here too is work by Andre Derain – the cheeky *Woman in a Chaise* – Braque, Dufy, Léger, Picasso and Gris, as well a couple of Modiglianis. Other rooms focus on Denmark and the post-war minimalism and abstraction of Albert Mertz, Richard Mortensen and Egil Jacobsen, whose *Accumulation* is a seminal painting of modern Danish art, and very modern for its time – 1938; exhibiting more in common with Asger Jorn's CoBrA-era work, which hangs nearby.

In the modern wing, **foreign art from 1300 to 1800** (mostly from Europe) offers up a taster of Italian, Dutch and Flemish masters with some lesser-known Tintorettos, Brueghels, Rembrandts and Van Dycks. The paintings are generally arranged thematically, with countries and artists jumbled up, and it's often impressive and powerful to see works from different places hung together, though there's a strong Dutch contingent – the Mythology and History gallery has paintings by Abraham Bloemaert, Rembrandt's student Ferdinand Bol, and Caravaggio-follower Henrik Terbrugghen sharing wall space with the Neapolitan Salvator Rosa. Look out too for Cornelisz van Haarlem's fleshy and horrific *Fall of the Titans*. There is the odd room devoted to single artists or movements: some impressive works by Lucas Cranach the Elder, including several portraits, the enigmatic *Melancholy* and a more characteristic *Venus with Cupid Stealing Honey*; another given over to Rembrandt and his workshop; one to large paintings by Rubens and Jacob Jordaens; another to portraits with works by Frans Hals among others; and finally another to the Italian Renaissance with works by Mantegna and Fra Filippo Lippi. The huge central room pulls all the themes together with paintings crammed floor to ceiling, old-style, and grouped by genre – still lifes, seascapes, portraits and landscapes.

Hirschsprungske Samling

Across Østre Anlæg from the Statens Museum for Kunst, with its main entrance on Stockholmsgade, is the Greek-inspired Neoclassical pavilion that houses the delightful and far more intimate **Hirschsprungske Samling** (Hirschsprung Collection; Mon & Wed–Sun 11am–4pm; 50kr, Wed free; Ⓦwww.hirschsprung.dk), by far the finest collection of nineteenth-century Danish art in the city. The collection was donated to the state in 1902 by second-generation German-Jewish immigrant and tobacco magnate Heinrich Hirschsprung – there's a large portrait of him smoking a cigar in the entrance hall.

Following the collection clockwise takes you through the major periods of nineteenth-century Danish art – the **Golden Age** (roughly 1810–40; see p.211) is particularly well represented. There are several C.W. Eckersbergs (one of Denmark's first professional artists), whose work was rooted firmly in romantic and idealistic traditions. *Woman Before a Mirror* is typical, with a poetic picture of a flesh-and-blood Venus de Milo, while his studies of seafaring folk such as *A View of the Gangway of a Corvette* and pastoral Danish landscapes and seascapes exhibit the typical Golden Age preoccupations with patriotic scenes of everyday life and the beauty of nature. His students, including Christen Købke and William Bendz, are also well represented with plenty of idyllic landscapes, while the collection of Marstrands in room 3 shows the influence of his travels in Italy with portraits and scenes from Neapolitan peasant life and the cheeky *Travellers in Venice* depicting an overweight tourist slumped in a gondola being nagged by his wife. The collection continues through several more rooms of pastoral scenes – gentle landscapes and milkmaids by P.C. Skovgaard, vignettes of farming life and livestock by Lundbye, and earthy interiors of barns, workshops and fishermen's bedrooms by Christen Dalsgaard.

In **room 13** are the remarkable historical paintings of Kristian Zahrtmann, a late nineteenth-century artist known for his colourful portrayals of eighteenth-century royal scandals, such as the ill-starred liaison between Princess Caroline Mathilde, the English wife of the particularly mad Christian VII, and Prime Minister Count Struensee (Caroline Mathilde was sent into exile in Germany; Struensee was beheaded for treason). Hirschsprung also supported the more rebellious figures in art and there are haunting works on display from the **Symbolists** of the 1890s, who rebelled against the artistic establishment, in particular Vilhelm Hammershøi whose solitary dark-clad figures (often with their backs to the viewer) occupy stark interiors, and Ejnar Nielsen, whose *The Blind Girl* is particularly melancholy. **Room 21** contains a wonderful collection of works by **the Skagen Painters** – artists from a town on the northernmost tip of the country renowned for its bewitching light – some of whom Hirschsprung personally supported. P.S. Krøyer's depictions of the beaches around Skagen give a real feel for the qualities of its strange light, in particular the well-known *Self-portrait with Wife* (1899) and the enchanting *Summer's Day on South Beach at Skagen* (1884). Skagen painters, husband and wife Michael and Anna Ancher, are also on display; the former's depictions of local fishermen beginning to exhibit the naturalistic portrayal of everyday life shown in his wife's paintings of Skagen fishermen and their wives, such as *Girl in the Kitchen* (1883), whose mastery of colour and light gives it an almost Vermeer-like quality.

Den Frie Udstilling

A rather strange-looking wooden building directly opposite Østerport station, at the northeastern tip of Østre Anlæg, **Den Frie Udstillingsbygning** (The Free Exhibition of Contemporary Art; Mon–Fri 10am–5pm, Thurs 10am–9pm; 45kr; Ⓦwww.denfrie.dk) is the place to check out Denmark's budding young artists – note, though, that it's "free" as in free space rather than free entry. The exhibition hall was built in 1898 by an artists' collective looking for a place to exhibit and sell their work, and the same collective still runs the hall today. Many of the big names of Danish art, such as Asger Jorn and Christian Lemmerz, have shown work here at various times, but the exhibitions, as you might expect, can vary dramatically in quality.

Frederikstad

Bordered by the Inderhavnen harbourfront to the east and cut in two by the broad sweep of Bredgade, the **Frederikstad** district was commissioned by Frederik V and designed by Danish architect Nicolai Eigtved, as a royal quarter fit for a noble elite. Containing the residence of Danish royalty, **Amalienborg**, and the grandest place of worship in the city, **Marmorkirken**, Frederikstad raised Copenhagen to new levels of urban elegance.

Marmorkirken

Easy to spot at the end of Frederiksgade, topped by a large green dome modelled on – and intended to rival – St Peter's in Rome, the grandiose **Marmorkirken** (Marble Church, officially called Frederikskirken; Mon–Thurs & Sat 10am–5pm, Wed 10am–6.30pm, Fri & Sun noon–5pm; free; Ⓦwww.marmorkirken.dk) was commissioned by Frederik V to be a splendid centre of worship befitting his new royal quarter. Originally designed by Eigtved, Frederik V himself laid the church's first stone in a grand ceremony in 1749. After Eigtved's death in 1754, however, the scheme ran into difficulties, and in 1770 the exorbitant cost of the Norwegian marble being used in the church's construction forced Count Struensee to abandon the project. The building was then left in disarray for a century, while various plans were mooted as to what to do with it – one proposed turning it into a gasworks – until N.F.S. Grundtvig (see p.108) finally had it completed using cheaper Danish marble (there's a portrait of him in the church, unmissable with flowing white beard and bald head, and a statue of him outside). The church was consecrated in 1894, 145 years after the foundation stone was laid.

The **interior** is grandly proportioned, if a bit drab – if you look at the walls, you can see the materials change from expensive Norwegian to cheaper Danish marble about a quarter of the way up. The best reason to visit, however, is to climb the steep, twisting steps, all 260 of them, to the top of the **bell tower** (mid-June to Aug daily 1 & 3pm; Sept to mid-June Sat & Sun 1 & 3pm; 25kr; they are very precise about these times). A guide will take you through the passages and staircases that lead to the summit, where the grand vista of Copenhagen is laid before you. The ascent involves entering the space between the inner and outer domes before climbing through a trap door and out into the elements. On a clear day, you can see out to Malmö, Helsingør and across the city to Roskilde – look for the arrows on the bell tower. The Marmorkirken stages concerts, normally on Wednesdays at 4.30pm and usually free – pick up a full programme at the church or check Ⓦwww.marmorkirken.dk/koncert.html.

Next door are the somewhat incongruous gilded onion domes of the **Alexander Nevsky Church** (Tues–Thurs 11.30am–1.30pm), Denmark's only functioning Russian Orthodox Church. The church was a gift from Tsar Alexander III to his Danish wife, Maria Feodorovna, formerly Princess Dagmar, second daughter of Christian IX, who was particularly adept at marrying off his daughters to foreign rulers. Maria converted to Orthodoxy on her marriage and worshipped here on trips home. Inside, look for the "weeping" icon behind the postcard pavilion, *Jerusalem Mother of Christ*, which from time to time – last on March 10, 1996, according to the caretaker – allegedly sheds miraculous tears.

Amalienborg

Across from Marmorkirken, along Frederiksgade, you cross Bredgade to reach Amalienborg Slotsplads, a square surrounded by the four palaces of **Amalienborg**, the centrepiece of Frederikstad and the home of the Danish royal family since 1794 when their former residence, Christiansborg, burnt down. Originally site of Queen Sophie Amalie's (wife of Frederik III) summer residence, which, in 1689, had also burnt down, killing almost two hundred party-goers in the process, the square was left vacant for more than sixty years until the newly crowned Frederik V decided to build a Louis XV-inspired model town (styled on Paris's Place de la Concorde) in the area. Designed by Eigtved, the four almost identical palaces (completed in 1760) are functional rather than sumptuous, and the whole ensemble is striking for its accessibility and openness rather than its grandeur – you're free to wander around the Slotsplads, though you'll be challenged by the bearskin-hatted **Livgarden** (Life Guards) if you get too close to the palaces.

The first palace to the left of Frederiksgade – Christian VIII's Palace – houses the **Danske Kongers Kronologiske Samling** (Royal Danish Collection; May–Oct daily 10am–4pm; Nov–April Tues–Sun 11am–4pm; 55kr, joint ticket with Rosenborg Slot 90kr; ⓦwww.amalienborgmuseet.dk), which includes a section of the royal family's living quarters that have been turned into what is basically a shrine to the monarchy, taking over where the Rosenborg collections (see p.66) left off and starting with Christian IX (1863–1906) and the beginning of the current royal line, the House of Glücksborg. The museum is a mishmash of royal paraphernalia – family mementos, jewellery, costumes, medals and paintings – and a series of carefully preserved rooms shielded from the hoi polloi behind glass screens. The rooms of former kings reveal something of their character – **Frederik IX**'s study (the father of the present queen) is cosy and homely with plenty of family photos and racks full of his pipes; Christian X's is a more macho affair festooned with swords, guns and assorted military gear; Christian IX's study, meanwhile, reflects his fascination with the new art of photography, every surface cluttered with framed photos.

▲ Changing of the guard at Amalienborg

Diagonally across the Slotsplads, past the enormous **equestrian statue** of Frederik V – which reputedly cost more than the four palaces combined, thanks to sculptor Jacques Saly, who, invited to Copenhagen to create the work, spent thirty years in the city living it up at the court's expense – is the queen's current residence in Christian IX's Palace, or Schack's Palace; for obvious reasons off limits to the public. Left of here, when facing the statue, Christian VII's Palace (also known as Moltke's Palace) is the royal guesthouse and occasionally houses exhibitions related to royal Copenhagen. To the right, Frederik VIII's Palace (or Brockdorff's Palace) is home to the crown prince and his young family.

Every day at noon, the Livgarden perform a **changing of the guard**, after which they march back to their barracks beside Rosenborg Slot. Exiting the eastern side of the palace complex and crossing Toldbodgade, you come to the landscaped gardens and fountains of **Amaliehavn** and the harbourfront beyond.

Medicinsk-Historisk Museum

The grisly **Medicinsk-Historisk Museum** at Bredgade 62 (Medical History Museum; guided tours only: in English July & Aug Wed–Fri & Sun 2.30pm; rest of the year only in Danish Wed–Fri & Sun 1.30pm, 2.30pm & 3.30pm; 50kr; Ⓦwww.mhm.ku.dk) is situated in a wing of what was originally the Danish Academy of Surgery, designed by Peter Meyn in 1787. The museum recounts the past three hundred years or so of Denmark's medical history in various fields from surgery to psychiatry and dentistry with the help of old medical equipment, a pharmacy from the eighteenth century, photos and a macabre supporting cast of aborted foetuses, syphilis treatments, amputated feet and a dissected head, along with the original dissection auditorium around which the pioneers of Danish surgery learnt their trade. A couple of early and late eighteenth-century dental surgeries, complete with hand-drills and sinks using recycled and often bloody water, finish off the exhibition.

Kunstindustrimuseet

Housed in the former Royal Frederiks Hospital, a sumptuous Rococo building from 1757, the charming **Kunstindustrimuseet** (Danish Museum of Art and Design; Tues–Sun 11am–5pm; 50kr; Ⓦwww.kunstindustrimuseet.dk), Bredgade 68, spreads itself through four wings enclosing a beautiful, tree-lined garden. Tracing the development of European (and particularly Danish) design from 1400 to the present day through its collections of furniture, ceramics, arts and crafts, it also examines the influence of Eastern styles on Western design.

Its notable **Oriental exhibits** include early Japanese porcelains and sword-hilt *tsuba* decorations, along with Chinese Ming vases, all displaying styles from which Europeans were to derive later designs. Early examples of styles borrowed from the East are shown through decorative work on Baroque furniture, while a section devoted to British design displays copies of Chinese lacquerware, Chippendale furniture and a velvet-lined trunk containing a spectacular silver toiletry set given to the unfortunate Princess Caroline Mathilde by George III when she left England for Denmark (see p.70). **The Study Collection** upstairs focuses on the development of European porcelain from its beginnings in the early eighteenth century, with pieces such as the first glazed European porcelain from Meissen, Germany, up until the late nineteenth century, with emphasis on Danish porcelain production in the district of Amager. Look out for the ceramic pieces produced by Gauguin – who was married to a Dane – including a unique ceramic self-portrait.

The last part of the collection heads through Arts and Crafts, featuring some lovely Art Nouveau pieces, to the **twentieth-century design** wing. This is the place to see why Danish design is renowned throughout the world and how it all came about; there's plenty on the history and philosophy behind the work of the founding fathers – Kaare Klint, Hans Wegner, Arne Jacobsen and Poul Henningsen – and several rooms devoted to their iconic, still effortlessly stylish creations.

The museum's excellent **café** serves homemade bread and cakes and light lunches; in the summer, there's outdoor service in the lovely gardens, also home to an open-air theatre.

Kastellet and around

At the far end of Bredgade, the straight streets of Eigtved's Frederikstad are replaced by the green open spaces of Churchillparken and **Kastellet**. There's a distinct military feel to this part of the city, with both the **Frihedsmuseet**, detailing Denmark's struggles against the Nazis during World War II, and Kastellet, Europe's oldest working fort, situated here. Nearby is that enduring symbol of the city, the **Little Mermaid**.

Frihedsmuseet

Situated within Churchillparken – a small park named after the British wartime leader – the engaging **Frihedsmuseet** (Museum of Danish Resistance; May–Sept Tues–Sun 10am–5pm; Oct–April Tues–Sun 10am–3pm; free; free guided tours in English May–Sept Tues, Thurs & Sun 2pm; Ⓦ www.natmus.dk) offers a comprehensive account of Denmark's role in World War II – its occupation, resistance and liberation. The museum grasps the thorny issue of the Danish government's **collusion** with German rule. Denmark, uniquely amongst the countries invaded by the Nazis, was afforded a kind of independence. The price was a large degree of collaboration: the Danish government was convinced that a Europe-wide Nazi victory was inevitable, and displays show the signed agreements between the two countries, while uniforms of the Danish Freikorps – volunteers who joined the German army – bear witness to the degree to which some Danes aligned themselves with the invaders.

Initially slow to offer armed resistance, the first Danish acts of sabotage were carried out in April 1942 by a remarkable group of teenage boys from Aalborg called the **Churchill Club**. These acts of sabotage gave impetus to other groups, largely made up of illegal Danish communists, and the period of collusion ended with a number of uprisings in 1943, which led to the Germans – as a direct order from Hitler – imposing martial law. A reign of terror by the Gestapo ensued in which hundreds were imprisoned and acts of terror were carried out against the Danish population. There are some dramatic photographs (and mundane police reports) of these first acts of sabotage, along with home-made printing devices, machine guns and bombs. Another act that infuriated the Nazis was the mass evacuation of Denmark's **Jewish population** (see box, p.42). Personal accounts, video interviews and original maps showing the escape routes attest to the courage shown during this episode of the war.

Unsurprisingly, the museum contains some extremely moving exhibits – including numerous objects made by prisoners in concentration camps from the meagre scraps available to them, like an address book made from leather meant for making oxygen masks. Perhaps the most moving, however, is just in front of the large stained-glass windows in a section called **"The Dead"**, showing the original wooden posts to which arrested resistance fighters were tied and shot, along with last letters to loved ones from those sentenced to death.

Gefion Fountain

At the eastern edge of Kastellet, beside the incongruous British St Alban's Church, the dramatic **Gefion Fountain** is based on the story of the goddess Gefion who, according to legend, was promised as much land as she could plough in a single night. She promptly turned her four sons into oxen and ploughed out a chunk of Sweden (creating Lake Vänern), then picked it up and tossed it into the sea – where it became the Danish island of Zealand. Created in 1908 by Anders Bundgaard, the fountain is one of the largest public monuments in Copenhagen, depicting an enormous bronze Gefion with her four oxen pulling a plough, water coming out as mist from their nostrils and cascading down from behind the plough in a series of steps from which huge snakes coil out of the bubbling water.

Kastellet

Behind Churchillparken are the unmistakable ramparts and moats of **Kastellet** (The Citadel; daily 6am–10pm; free). Conceived by Christian IV as the key element in the city's defences, the fortress has been occupied by troops since 1660, making it the oldest functioning military base in Europe, and it remains the only part of the city's ancient defence system still in use. The star-shaped fortress is formed by five grass-covered bastions surrounded by a series of moats; it can be entered via one of two gates – Kongensporten, near Churchillparken to the south, and Norgesporten, at the opposite end near the Little Mermaid – which are linked by a thoroughfare flanked by quaint red, timbered barracks (still in use) and storehouses. Kastellet was also used as a prison – the windows in the west wall of the **church** were bricked up so that those attending services did not have to look at the detainees in the prison building in front, although small holes were cut through, allowing prisoners to hear the words of the Lord. Count Struensee was held here after he was caught having an affair with Princess Caroline Mathilde (see p.70).

Kastellet's principal attraction has for generations been the chance it offers for a leisurely stroll around its bastions and ramparts. In the late 1990s, extensive restoration works were carried out and the entire area now stands pretty much as it did in the nineteenth century, complete with a windmill. Remember that in part this is still a working military complex – albeit mainly with administrative duties – and some areas are off limits: keep an eye out for the *Adgang Forbudt* ("No Entry") signs. Kastellet's church sometimes holds free classical concerts on Sundays.

The Little Mermaid

A stone's throw from Kastellet (take Norgesporten gate) on the stretch of coastline called Langelinie, and poised on a pile of carefully positioned rocks by the harbour's edge, is Copenhagen's most famous symbol, the **Little Mermaid** (Den Lille Havfrue). Created in 1913 by Edvard Eriksen, this rather plain bronze figure has become the city's de facto emblem despite its modest dimensions, and continues to hold a powerful sway over the imagination of Danes and visitors alike, conjuring up a period when Copenhagen was the fairy-tale capital of the world. Tour buses and boats arrive here in a steady stream throughout the summer with hordes eager to photograph themselves with the mermaid whilst trying to avoid the less scenic industrial harbour in the background.

Inspired by the 1837 Hans Christian Andersen story of the same name, the statue was commissioned by Carlsberg brewery boss and art lover Carl Jacobsen after he had seen a performance of a ballet based on the *Little Mermaid* story at the Royal Theatre. The prima ballerina in that production, Ellen Price, was to have been the model for the statue, but her reluctance to pose nude for Eriksen forced him to use his wife as a model for the mermaid's body – only the face is Price's. Jacobsen originally wanted the mermaid to have the traditional fish's tail, but Eriksen noted that in Andersen's story the mermaid exchanges her golden hair and beautiful voice for legs – hence the final statue, with the outline of a mermaid's tail between two human limbs.

North along Langelinie

Continuing north on **Langelinie** towards Nordhavnen and Østerbro (see p.102) will take you along one of Copenhagen's most popular Sunday destinations. On a sunny day, this scenic stretch of coast – with its numerous hot-dog stands and ice cream booths – is crowded with a happy mix of rollerbladers, joggers and dog walkers all enjoying the wonderful views out to sea to the **Trekroner Bastion** and the Swedish coast beyond. This harbour fortification dates to 1787 and was one of several that protected the city against seaborne attack. It saw action in the battles against the British in 1801 and 1807 and was used as a barracks by the Germans during World War II, after which it was given to the harbour authorities; you can visit the fort on a DFDS tour from Nyhavn (see p.53). At the end of Langelinie, along Langelinie Allé, there's a **cruise-ship terminal** with numerous designer shops catering to those disembarking for the day.

South along Larsens Plads to Nyhavn

Just south of Langelinie and the Gefion Fountain, the pedestrianized **Larsens Plads** runs along the scenic Frederikstad waterfront back to Nyhavn, its length lined with robust red-brick warehouses stemming from Copenhagen's maritime trading days but now housing converted flats – some of Copenhagen's most sought after residences.

Roughly halfway along, housed in the former Vestindisk Pakus (West Indian warehouse), **Den Kongelige Afstøbningssamling** (Royal Cast Collection; Wed 2–8pm, Sun 2–5pm; free; Ⓦwww.smk.dk) is an enormous collection of plaster casts of the oldest, largest and most important statues and reliefs from temples, churches and public places throughout the world, from Egyptian pharaohs to modern works by Danish artist Bjørn Nørgaard (see p.47). After a century or so of use, the collection, begun in the mid-eighteenth century by the Royal Academy of Art for students to practise their drawing skills, spent decades hidden away in this warehouse while painting took the museum's centre stage; it opened to the public in the late twentieth century. There's more than 2600 pieces here and it's undeniably astounding, albeit a bit overwhelming. Root around for a while and you'll see the *Venus de Milo* (no. 434), and pretty much all of Michelangelo's works. Donatello's complete works are also here, the most famous of which is *Erasmo da Narni* (no. 1170), a horse-and-rider statue that, not surprisingly, took six years to complete.

Just beyond, towards Nyhavn, is the stylistic **Amaliehaven park** and the eye-catching new playhouse (see p.53), vying for attention with the equally monumental old granary now housing the *Copenhagen Admiral* hotel (see p.138).

Rådhuspladsen and around

Sandwiched between Indre By to the east and Vesterbro to the west, the area around the town hall square, **Rådhuspladsen**, is Copenhagen at its most frivolous and touristy – above all in the **pleasure gardens of Tivoli**, the country's top tourist attraction and Copenhagen at its most innocently enjoyable. Tagging along for the ride are plenty of other popular amusements including the **Tycho Brahe Planetarium** and the family attractions, entertainment complexes and games arcades on and around Rådhuspladsen and Axeltorv. That said, the area is far more than an enormous fairground. Just south of the Rådhuspladsen lurk a few of the city's cultural heavyweights: the **Ny Carlsberg Glyptotek** with its soothing sculpture, paintings and Greek, Roman and Etruscan collections; the **Nationalmuseet**, home to many of Denmark's historic treasures; and the **Dansk Design Center**, slick temple to urban cool.

Rådhuspladsen

Flanked by two busy roads, the oblong, pedestrianized expanse of **Rådhuspladsen** (City Hall Square) is central Copenhagen's principal square, though you're more likely to come across it by accident than design, en route to Tivoli or the shops of Indre By. The striking Rådhus (City Hall) aside, it's not the most scenic of Copenhagen's squares – part transport hub (the city's main bus terminal is at one end), part tourist trap, with its fair share of fast-food joints and family amusements – but it's always lively with *pølser* stands and assorted street vendors and buskers. Once a lowly hay market, it was elevated to its present status after 1851 when the old city ramparts were demolished and it was decided to build a new city hall here, on what was then the largest available central space. The resulting Rådhus is an impressive building worth a little exploration; look out for the statue of Hans Christian Andersen on its southern side, his head turned towards the screams emanating from Tivoli's rollercoaster.

Rådhus

Occupying as much space as the square itself, the monumental red-brick **Rådhus** (Mon–Fri 10am–4pm, free; guided tours Mon–Fri 3pm, Sat 10am & 11am; 30kr; Ⓦ www.copenhagencity.dk), topped with an impressive bell tower, was designed by Danish architect Martin Nyrop and completed in 1905. The gold figure above

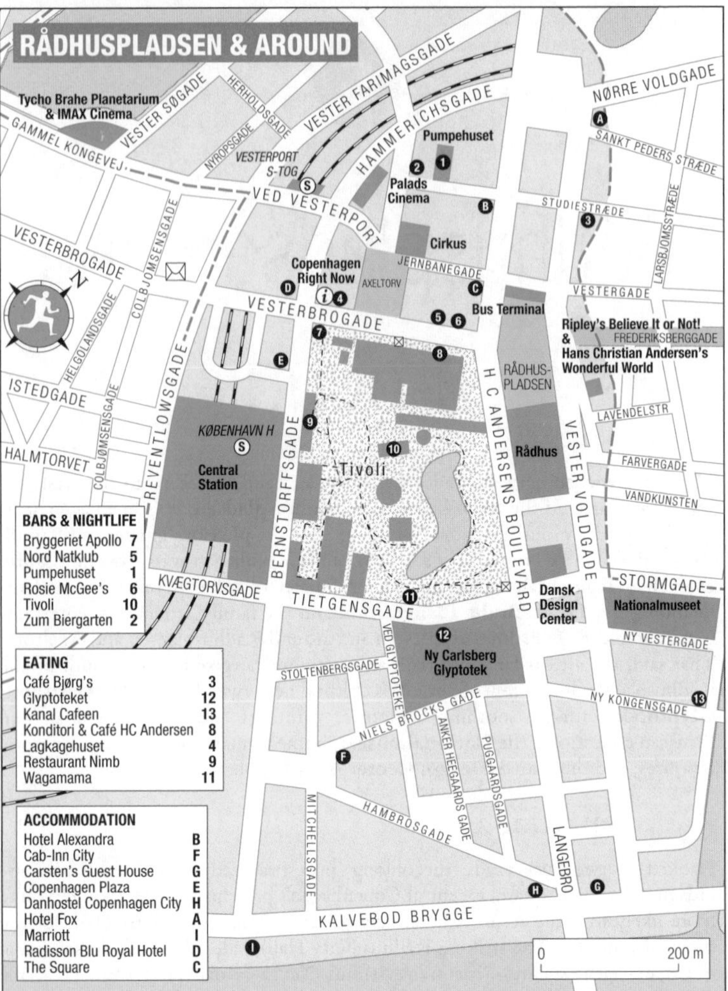

the main entrance is Bishop Absalon (see p.35), founder of the city. You're free to wander around the public areas during working hours, though given the building's size, it's worth joining a guided tour. Beyond the impressive entrance, the spacious and elegant main hall has retained most of its original features, such as the Italianate wall decorations – Nyrop was heavily influenced by Tuscan architecture – and the sculpted oak banisters heading up from the ground floor. Guided tours take you behind locked doors to a series of impressive wood-panelled rooms, including the council Meeting Hall and the Banqueting Hall, lined with the coats of arms of Denmark's merchant towns.

At 106m, the city-hall **tower** (guided tours Mon–Fri 11am & 2pm, Sat noon; 20kr) is Denmark's highest. It's about three hundred steps up to the balcony (no lifts), and a further fifty through a narrow passageway to the spire, past the bells

used as Danish Radio's hourly chime, but you'll be rewarded w
city and northeast down the length of Strøget all the way to Ko

In a side room opposite the ticket office, what looks like a m
dials is in fact the astronomical timepiece of **Jens Olsen's World**
8.30am–4.30pm, Sat 10am–1pm; 10kr). Set going in 1955, th
570,000-year calendar plotting eclipses of the moon and sun, sol
and various planetary orbits – all with incredible accuracy.
watch, too, as hundreds of ticking dials track the movements of

Tivoli

Across HC Andersens Boulevard from the Rådhus, with its main entrance at Vesterbrogade 3, is Denmark's most popular tourist attraction. Ninety percent of all foreign visitors to the city head for **Tivoli** (Ⓦwww.tivoli.dk) each summer, and though there are few rides here to compete with the white-knuckle thrills of modern theme parks, its popularity shows no signs of fading, and to the Danes it's nothing short of a national treasure. The opening of Tivoli for the new season in April is one of Copenhagen's major annual celebrations, and anyone who is anyone will have booked tables at one of the garden's posh restaurants.

Opened in 1843, Tivoli was the brainchild of architect/publisher/entertainment guru George Carstensen, who was inspired by the pleasure gardens of Europe, in particular London's Vauxhall Gardens. Though the number of rides has grown over the years from two to around twenty-five, it has stayed faithful to its creator's ideal – the pretty flower-lined paths, boating lake, fairground stalls, restaurants, bandstands, theatres and concert halls as much a part of the experience as the rides. It's an expensive day out, but a few hours spent wandering among the revellers of all ages, with the squeals from the rides echoing round the park, is all good, old-fashioned fun, while at night with the twinkling illuminations (no neon here) and music drifting through the gardens, it's positively magical.

As one of the few still-functioning nineteenth-century pleasure gardens, Tivoli has its historical aspect, too, with a number of playful and well-maintained period buildings, notably the Chinese-style, open-air **Pantomime Theatre**. Built in 1874, this now hosts the world's only regular performances of classical pantomime, a delicate art form somewhere between ballet and mime – with an element of farce – derived from Italian *commedia dell'arte*. Look out, too, for the beautiful 1940s Poul Henningsen-designed Glass Hall Theatre, the recently refurbished *Nimb* restaurant/hotel/deli/vinotek/bar complex housed in a fairy-tale white wood-and-plaster confection built in Moorish style, and the Chinese pagoda by the boating lake. Some of the fairground **rides** are also pretty old, like the rickety wooden Mountain Roller Coaster, dating from 1914, and the tiny Ferris wheel nearby. If this all sounds too tame, head for the newer rides: the Star Flyer, an eighty-metre-high swing-carousel, the Demon, a stomach-churning three-loop roller coaster, and the latest attraction, Vertigo – an interactive four-seater aeroplane where you are the pilot. There's also a great saltwater **aquarium** in the basement of the Concert Hall.

Music, some of it free, plays a large part in Tivoli. The two main arenas are ticket only (see p.171): the renowned **Concert Hall** (see p.176) has a summer programme of classical concerts (Tivoli has its own symphony orchestra) and also hosts famous names from the rock and jazz world, while the **Glass Hall theatre** offers jazz, rock, variety and kids' shows. You'll also find plenty of free music at numerous smaller venues; there's usually some jazz or blues on the bandstands, while the open-air stage **Plænen**, generally given over to displays of acrobatics and dance, hosts big-name Danish and international pop and rock bands, free with general admission charge, every Friday at 10pm.

...practicalities

Opening times and tickets

The Tivoli **summer season** runs from mid-April to the third week of September. **Opening hours** are: Mon–Thurs & Sun 11am–11pm, Fri 11am–12.30am, Sat 11am–midnight (slightly later mid-June to mid-Aug), with most rides opening at 11.30am, though be warned that some don't open till 2pm. Entrance **tickets** cost 85kr for adults, 45kr for children (ages 3–11); on top of that you'll be paying 20 to 80kr (depending on thrill factor) per ride, so if you're planning on riding several, it's well worth investing in a **multi-ride ticket** (200kr adults, 160kr children). The **Christmas season** begins the fourth week of November (check the website for the exact date), ending on December 23. If you want to **leave and re-enter Tivoli** – to get a cheaper lunch outside, or stagger your visit throughout the same day to make the most of the variety of entertainment on offer – get your hand stamped on exit.

Eating in Tivoli

Eating in Tivoli is all part of the experience, but be warned that prices are around twenty percent higher than in the outside world, while the cost of alcoholic drinks is a white-knuckle ride in itself. But there's something for everyone here, be it a slice of pizza, hot-dog, classic smørrebrød or gourmet cuisine. The following is a small selection of sit-down options to cover all budgets.

Grøften ⓣ33 75 06 75. Next to the pantomime theatre, this country-cabin-style restaurant with red-and-white check tablecloths is justifiably one of the oldest and most popular places to eat in the gardens, serving mouthwatering traditional Danish food. It boasts an extensive smørrebrød selection (around 55kr upwards), as well as main meat and fish dishes – the tiny fjord shrimp are delicious. Booking advisable.

Café Ketchup ⓦwww.cafeketchup.dk. Despite the name, this relaxed restaurant with veranda seating isn't a burger joint but a fusion restaurant offering a limited but good Danish/Asian lunch menu – sushi, fish or meat dishes for around 145kr. In the evening it changes to mix 'n' match Italian/Asian/French/Scandinavian food. Starters are around 99kr, mains from 195kr.

Logismose ⓦwww.nimb.dk. Located in the Nimb complex, the Logismose deli/dairy/chocolate shop outlet also has a hot-dog stand serving up gourmet versions that put the rest of the park's bangers to shame. While here, you can stock up on Danish delicacies to take home.

Mamma Mokka Terrace café around the side of the Concert Hall serving great coffee and cakes as well as light lunches and sandwiches for around 100kr and with a lovely view of the gardens and rides below.

The Paul ⓣ33 75 07 75, ⓦwww.thepaul.dk. The most glamorous dining spot in Tivoli and with a Michelin star to boot, *The Paul* occupies part of the lovely Poul Henningsen-designed "Glassalen" glass-dome building. Presided over by English chef Paul Cunningham, the menu is modern European with strong Scandinavian influences. Naturally, it comes at a price, but the food, location and atmosphere can't be beaten. The "Ma's Cuisine" three-course menu costs a cool 700kr for three courses (wine extra); there's also a seven-course taster menu for 850kr. If you just want a flavour of the Paul experience, go for the light lunch option of three small dishes with a glass of wine for 375kr (noon–2pm).

Restaurant Nimb ⓣ88 70 00 10; ⓦww.nimb.dk. This laid-back brasserie in the Nimb complex has an open kitchen. Lunch (11.30am–2pm) is classic, delicious Danish – herring, roast beef on rye bread, fish fillet or beef from 79kr to170kr. In the evening starters such as oysters or smoked salmon are followed by fish and meat mains; expect to pay around 450kr for a three-course meal. The Sunday brunch buffet (10.30am–2pm) is great value at 195kr, featuring goodies from the on-site Logismose dairy (see above), home-made butter and marmalade, and all the sausages, pancakes, eggs and fruit you can eat. Booking recommended.

▲ Tivoli

Tivoli is also open during Danish half-term in October for a **Halloween**-themed extravaganza, and the weeks around **Christmas**, when the festive spirit is cranked up with even more spectacular lighting displays, a "Christmas Market", and all sorts of cheery festivities – the braziers and torches help keep the worst of the chill at bay. Note, though, that around twenty percent of the rides are closed during the winter.

Axeltorv

Directly opposite the main entrance to Tivoli is the rather unattractive square of **Axeltorv**, bordered on one side by the empty, run-down Scala centre (set to become a hotel in the near future), and on the other by bowling alleys, games arcades and the Axelborg entertainment centre. The eye is drawn to the end of the square and the multi-coloured eyesore of the **Palads Cinema**. Built in 1917 to replace the old central station, Palads acquired its distinctive decor in 1987, when artist Poul Gernes was brought in to redesign the exterior. The most interesting building on Axeltorv is **Cirkus**, a circular, domed, pseudo-Roman auditorium with seating for two thousand people. Built in 1905, it was used as a proper circus until the 1960s, since when it has hosted everything from boxing matches to a talk by the Dalai Lama – it's now the venue of the nightly Wallman's cabaret show.

Just to the west, on the corner of Vesterbrogade and Hammerichsgade, the *Radisson Blu Royal Hotel* (see p.139), Denmark's first skyscraper, brought a taste of American glamour and hotel chic to the city when it was built in the 1960s. The renowned architect, Arne Jacobsen, designed everything from the furniture to the door handles and cutlery; pop into the sleek retro lobby for a look at his work.

Tycho Brahe Planetarium

At Gammel Kongevej 10, pleasantly situated at the southeastern corner of Skt Jørgens Sø (the southernmost of the lakes that enclose central Copenhagen), is the striking brick cylinder of the **Tycho Brahe Planetarium** (Tues–Sun 10.30am–9pm, Mon 1–9pm; 130kr including exhibition, IMAX or 3D film;

Ⓦwww.tycho.dk). It's named after the famous sixteenth-century Danish astronomer whose data on the movement of stars and planets, unparalleled in accuracy for its time, was used by subsequent astronomers to prove that the earth moved round the sun and not vice versa. Tycho is also famous for having lost part of his nose in a duel and wearing a prosthetic metal replacement. There's a rather uninspiring exhibition on the stars, planets and space travel, with the obligatory lump of moon rock, so the only real reason to visit is the **IMAX cinema**, which shows hourly IMAX and 3D films (you'll need to hire headphones with English translations; 20kr), though they're more likely to be about ancient Egypt, deep-sea exploration or dinosaurs than anything astronomical.

Dansk Design Center

A few minutes' walk southeast of Tivoli and the Rådhus, at HC Andersens Blvd 27, the Henning Larsen-designed, glass-fronted **Dansk Design Center** (Mon, Tues, Thurs & Fri 10am–5pm, Wed 10am–9pm, Sat & Sun 11am–4pm; 50kr, free on Wed from 5pm; Ⓦwww.ddc.dk) is a research facility and showcase for the country's outstanding design industry. While the Kunstindustrimuseet (see p.73) concentrates on the history of Danish design, the DDC focuses on the here and now, its galleries largely given over to cutting-edge temporary exhibitions so you'll have to be pretty keen on design to get the most out of it. There's a tiny permanent exhibition in the basement but it only takes a few minutes to peruse the small selection of design icons ranging from Zippo lighters to chairs. The café is a relaxing spot for a coffee or light lunch and there's a great **shop** with an excellent range of English-language books on design and architecture, plus lots of designer trinkets.

Ny Carlsberg Glyptotek

Copenhagen's finest art gallery, the **Ny Carlsberg Glyptotek** (Tues–Sun 11am–5pm; 60kr, Sun free; Ⓦwww.glyptoteket.com), Dantes Plads 7, was opened in 1897 by the philanthropic Carlsberg brewing magnate Carl Jacobsen (see p.75) as a place where ordinary people could see the collection of classical and modern art that he had generously donated to the state. Its focal point is the delightful glass-domed **Vinter Have** (Winter Garden), filled with soaring palm trees, a fountain and statues – Jacobsen correctly guessed that the warmth and tropical plantlife here would lure visitors who wouldn't be interested by the works of art alone. Nowadays, it has the added attraction of the gallery's highly rated **café** (see p.155).

The building itself is in three sections centred on the Vinter Have. The entrance is through the long, low facade of the **Dahlerup building**, completed in 1897 and largely given over to French and Danish sculpture and Danish painting. From here you pass through into the **Kampmann building**, added to the original Glyptotek in 1906 to house the antiquities collection. Off to the left is the stunning modern **French Wing**, housing the wonderful collection of French painting. At a push, you can see everything in a few hours; if time is limited, prioritize the Rodin collection, the Ancient Mediterranean galleries and the French Wing. Be sure to grab a free **floor plan** as the layout can be confusing.

French and Danish sculpture and Danish Golden Age painting

The entrance hall leads you into the Dahlerup building, where, spread over two floors, you'll find French and Danish sculpture and painting. Off to the right, the **French sculpture** collection is dominated by a particularly fine haul of **Rodins** – the largest outside France. There's a version of *The Kiss* and an agonized *Jeanne D'Arc* whose tortured face seems to emerge from the marble, as well as some lesser known marble and bronze busts. But it's the larger-than-life bronze cast of the powerful *Burghers of Calais* that draws the eye – commissioned by the mayor of Calais to commemorate an incident during the Hundred Years War in which the city, under siege for over a year and close to starvation, was spared by the surrender to the English of six of its highest-ranking officials. There is no hint here, though, of the heroism usually displayed in such public monuments; Rodin's figures seem to shamble despairingly in their defeat and it is a feeling of subdued sacrifice that dominates. Other sculptural highlights include a dramatic collection of white marbles – Marqueste's theatrical *Perseus Slaying Medusa* set amid a raft of huge, full-bodied women and muscular men by various other artists, and a series of ornate busts by Carpeaux.

The **Danish sculpture and painting** is, unsurprisingly, rather less stimulating, though it does provide a good reflection of Golden Age painting with some idealized landscapes by C.W. Eckersberg, some more naturalistic paintings depicting the travails of Danish peasants by Marstrand and a few decorative frescoes by Herman Freund, a close colleague of Bertel Thorvaldsen (see p.39), whose sensual relief *The Three Graces* is on display.

Antiquities collection

Just beyond the Vinter Have, the Kampmann building houses the collections of Ancient art split into two areas and best tackled in the order given here. Off to the left, rooms 19–25 have been revamped as **The Ancient Mediterranean** – more museum than art gallery, using the Glyptotek's substantial Egyptian, Greek, Etruscan and Roman collections to tell the history of the various civilizations that grew, flourished and declined around the Mediterranean from 6000 BC up to the Roman Empire. Straight ahead, up the steps, rooms 1–17 contain Egyptian, Greek and Roman sculpture displayed in traditional style.

The Ancient Mediterranean emphasizes how the Ancient Greeks, Phoenicians, Etruscans and Romans influenced each other; artefacts from different civilizations are displayed together to highlight common threads and cross-cultural influences. It's pretty exhaustive with thousands of exhibits ranging from clay unguent bottles and sacrificial drinking cups found in Greek burial tombs to Etruscan sarcophagi to Roman coins – and explores topics such as the Empires of the Middle East, the rise of the Greek city state and the role of the seafaring Phoenicians in trade and the spread of culture. There are some real treasures here – glazed tile facades depicting dragons, bulls and lions from the Ishtar Gate that led to the fabled Tower of Babylon, a fifth-century BC Greek vessel depicting scenes from the battle of Troy, and Etruscan pots and vases whose muscular figures painted in black were direct copies of much coveted Greek pottery but which clearly lack Greek artistry and finesse.

In fact it's the large and diverse haul of **Etruscan** works (rooms 20E to 22) that really stands out. This distinct civilization from central Italy, whose origins date back to around 700 BC, was eventually incorporated into the Roman world around the first century BC, but Etruscan culture heavily influenced that of the Romans and therefore persisted. The exhibition explores the development of Etruscan culture, religion and society through its impressive array of artefacts – the votive offerings, sculptures, figurines, funerary items and jewellery providing ample evidence of the Etruscans' mastery of gold, bronze, terracotta and stone, while their characteristic sarcophagi topped with the reclining, contented-looking statues of their owners offer some insight into the reverence they had for their dead and the ancestor cults that grew up as a result.

Time permitting, finish off your classical tour with a stroll through the sculpture galleries, which kick off in rooms 1–4 with a small but excellent collection of **Egyptian** artefacts – statuary, stelae, tomb models, reliefs and the obligatory handful of mummies. From then on it's a seemingly endless procession of busts and statues of famous Greeks and Romans – the portrait of Caligula, which still retains some of its original paint, and the large Alexander the Great are particularly striking, but equally entertaining are the surprisingly warts-and-all private portraits of rich commoners.

French Wing

The modern Henning Larsen-designed **French Wing** (rooms 56–66; access from the Vinter Have) houses the museum's fine collection of nineteenth- and twentieth-century French painting from David to Gauguin. A huge, light-filled white vault in the most minimalist of contemporary architectural styles, it's an architectural triumph, blending extraordinarily well into its classical context. On the lower ground floor (rooms 56–60), precursors of the Impressionists and artists from the Barbizon school are well represented with works by Corot, Delacroix, Courbet and Manet, including a version of the latter's well-known *Execution of Emperor Maximilian* and *The Absinthe Drinker*. The ground floor is given over to the **Impressionists** (rooms 61 & 62), with some exquisite Monets – notably *The Lemon Grove*, a wonderful play of colour and technique – a few lesser-known Renoirs and a complete set of charming Degas bronze figurines, including the exquisite *Little 14-year-old Dancer*. The exhibition continues upstairs with the **Post Impressionists** (rooms 63–66), including works by Toulouse-Lautrec, Pissarro, Bonnard and Van Gogh – look out for his luscious *Pink Roses*, a wonderful example of his ability to bring nature to life on canvas. Gauguin is particularly well represented, with over thirty paintings. *Tahitian Woman with a Flower* emphasizes his influential "primitive" style, melding bright primary colours, flat shapes and heavy contours. His more traditional *Skaters in Frederiksberg Gardens* dates from 1884, the year he spent as a stockbroker in Copenhagen with his Danish wife and their five children before returning to Paris to paint full time.

Nationalmuseet

To the east of Rådhuspladsen, on Ny Vestergade, the excellent **Nationalmuseet** (National Museum; Tues–Sun 10am–5pm; free; free guided tours in English June–Sept Tues, Thurs & Sun; Ⓦwww.natmus.dk), housed partly in an elegant eighteenth-century royal palace, is home to the country's finest collection of Danish artefacts from the Ice Age to the present day. The Danish prehistory collections alone are unmissable, but there's also a fantastic ethnographic collection including one of the world's largest and best displays of Inuit culture, a modest exhibit of Egyptian and classical antiquities, the Royal Coin Collection and an excellent **children's museum** (see p.200).

Danish Prehistory and the Viking Age

The highlight of the museum, the **Danish Prehistory** galleries do an excellent job of bringing to life the 14,000 years of history of the country's earliest occupants – their homes, rituals, beliefs, deaths and burial customs – and charting the gradual move from hunter-gathering to farming to Viking expansion and the arrival of Christianity in Denmark. It's studded with real treasures by any museum's standards – the remarkable number of intact finds on display is due to the preservative quality of the country's peat bogs, which have yielded precious objects ranging from jewellery to whole chariots, thrown in to curry favour with the marsh gods.

Rooms 1–6 document the earliest moments of Stone Age life with various human skulls (many bearing evidence of gruesome deaths), carefully crafted flint tools, axes made from elk bone, stunning amber amulets and necklaces, and a full-sized skeleton of an auroch – a huge (and extinct) indigenous buffalo – replete with hunting wounds. In the excellent **Bronze Age** section a unique collection of 3500-year-old oak coffins – basically hollowed out tree trunks – contain, along with the grisly, desiccated remains of their human occupants, numerous personal items buried with them. The best preserved belongs to the **Egtved Girl (room 9)**, who died in 1370 BC – her clothes, comb, bracelets and blonde hair have all survived eerily intact. Other Bronze Age highlights to look out for include the exquisite **Trundholm Sun Chariot** (1400 BC) in room 12 – an enchanting model made by sun-worshippers that depicts a magical horse-drawn chariot pulling a gold-leaf sun disc across the heavens – and a fine array of *lurs*, sacred horn-like musical instruments used in ritual ceremonies.

The **Iron Age** section boasts a handful of the finest Celtic treasures in Europe. The Celts never managed to conquer Scandinavia but made their influence felt in Denmark through trade and culture – the Danes acquired from them the skills to extract and forge iron from "bog-ore" so ushering out the Bronze Age. In room 16 are the reconstructed remains of the **Dejbjærg Wagon**, a Celtic bronze-clad chariot that was dismantled and laid as a sacrifice in a Jutland bog, while next door is the stunning solid silver **Gundestrup Cauldron**, with its perfectly preserved reliefs of Celtic mythical figures and gods. Room 22 dazzles with a horde of gold artefacts. The original fifth-century AD **Golden Horns, w**ith their delicate decoration of figures and animals and runic inscriptions, are considered to be the most important find from Danish antiquity. What you see here aren't the originals (those were stolen from Christiansborg Slot in 1802 by a goldsmith who melted them down to make jewellery and belt buckles), but reconstructions commissioned by Frederik VII from drawings held in the Royal Treasure Chamber.

The exhibition ends with the **Viking collections**. There had been a sophisticated seafaring culture in the region for centuries, with well-established, extensive trade routes, but it wasn't until 780 AD that the Viking era officially began when a small tribe from Viken used this knowledge of foreign countries – their resources, weaknesses and geography – and combined it with military prowess and state-of-the-art ships to set forth and plunder. The years following 793 AD saw the establishment of colonies in France, Britain and Ireland but though the more familiar story is one of bloodthirsty conquests, the **exhibition** is keen to emphasize the constructive and enduring linguistic, cultural and commercial influences the Vikings had on the countries they settled in. There's a room devoted to the dawn of Christianity in Denmark, as evidenced in the famous Viking monument at Jelling, burial place of Gorm the Old (see p.206), with some exquisite pieces from the site, including a fine silver cup found in a burial chamber. You'll also find the more familiar tools and artefacts on display – clothes, helmets and weapons – as well as shimmering filigree silver jewellery, coins and ingots, many of them from private stashes buried either as sacrificial gifts or as insurance in times of unrest.

Also in this part of the museum is the **Rune Room**, with its section on the ancient Germanic alphabet, used, especially in Scandinavia, from the third century AD to the end of the Middle Ages. There are a number of original, boulder-sized rune stones from Jutland and Lolland – erected by the wealthy in memory of the dead – with translations of the symbols.

The Middle Ages to the present day

Upstairs on the first floor, the story continues with an extensive collection of religious and royal paraphernalia, weapons, furniture and household objects spanning the Middle Ages and the Renaissance. The collection is particularly strong on the relics of **Danish Christianity** – stern-looking late-Viking crucifixes give way to more naturalistic representations, while the Latin alphabet arrives to replace the Germanic runes. There are rooms full of the intricate crafts used to glorify Christ (and the Church), with elaborate **gold altars**, wonderful ceremonial robes and grails. Look out, too, for the practical fifteenth-century **portable altar** (room 104) – *the* must-have travel accessory for the wealthy – in the form of a hinged box that opened up to reveal a diptych of biblical scenes intricately carved in ivory. Other highlights include a fantastic collection of jewel-encrusted rings, made to be worn outside the gloves of the wearer, and an armoury of alarming implements. The displays of royal regalia aren't really in the same league, and many of the more interesting pieces are in Rosenborg Slot (see p.66), but a cabinet in room 114 contains a trio of gold treasures: a tankard given to Christian IV as a christening present; his incredibly ornate display dagger; and Frederik II's ring with the name of his wife, Sofie, touchingly engraved on the inside. After this wonderful array of historical artefacts the collection jumps to the nineteenth century with a disappointing run of portraits of Danish worthies and a series of elaborate seventeenth-century Rococo interiors – the preserved section of the royal palace that served as the home of various crown princes and was left untouched by the museum when it took over the palace in the late 1800s.

On the second floor, the exhaustive "**Stories of Denmark**" picks up the account from 1660 to the present day with an enormous array of objects ranging from royal garments to pop posters to plastic bowls spotlighting key historical and cultural events in the country's history. Weaving together big themes such as "Denmark at War", "The State and the Church" and "Absolute Monarchy", with popular movements including the advent of trade unions, women's rights and current issues such as immigration, it's somewhat overambitious, and is best skimmed through lest the sheer level of detail leaves you rather more dazed than informed.

The ethnographic, classical antiquities and numismatic collections

The bulk of the rest of the museum is taken up by the huge and exceptionally diverse **ethnographic collection**, "Peoples of the Earth". Beautifully displayed in manageable, well-labelled sections, it's a captivating journey through non-European art and culture with Africa, China, India and Japan particularly well represented. Exhibits range from a feathered Peruvian mummy to African jewellery to Native American totem poles to exquisite tea paraphernalia from China. Given the scope, it's wise to focus on particular areas of geographical interest, though the section on **Inuit culture**, spread over the first and second floors and featuring exhibits from northern Canada, Alaska and Greenland, shouldn't be missed – on the first floor, look out for the wonderful coat dating from 1923 and belonging to Tertaq (the Amulet Boy), at six years old the most powerful person in his tribe. It has no less than eighty protective amulets affixed to it, including a grisly array of dead animals, skins and unidentifiable desiccated items, and was acquired in Canada by the Inuit/Danish arctic explorer **Knud Rasmussen** on his fifth Thule expedition. There are more details of Rasmussen's expeditions upstairs where the collection continues with case after case of whalebone carvings, harpoons, sealskin kayaks, furry boots and clothing, and spooky-looking sealskin whaling costumes – the beautiful multicoloured beading and lacework on the festive costumes provides welcome evidence of a lighter side to Inuit life.

Should you have the energy left to climb all the way to the top of the museum, you'll be rewarded with a small selection of **Egyptian** and **classical antiquities**, featuring a few mummies and, more impressively, a good collection of glazed decorative pottery from the city states of Greece; coin and medal enthusiasts might want to feast their eyes on the museum's **numismatic collections** spanning Ancient Greece and Rome, the history of Danish coinage and plentiful exhibits from around the world.

6

Vesterbro and Frederiksberg

The two districts immediately west of the city centre, Vesterbro and Frederiksberg, couldn't be more different. **Vesterbro** has always been determinedly working class, and also has the city's highest multicultural mix; despite encroaching gentrification, it's still Copenhagen's red-light district and one of the most colourful areas of the city, with the broadest selection of affordable ethnic restaurants and shops. In stark contrast to Vesterbro's vibrant and vivid street life, **Frederiksberg**'s wealthy residents tend to stay behind the doors of their grand villas, and the district's spacious and leafy roads are relatively lifeless. Situated on the land leading up to Frederiksberg Slot, the monarch's former summer residence, the area was originally used to grow crops and keep livestock for the royal household, and was ruled directly by the king. Even now it retains a regal aura, and is still administered by its own independent council. Conservative to the core, Frederiksberg is renowned for its low taxes and expensive housing.

Both areas have their share of tourist pulls, though they're fairly spread out. Vesterbro's main daytime attractions are limited to the famous **Carlsberg Brewery**, on the western edge of the district, and the informative **Københavns Bymuseum**. It's at night, however, that the area really comes into its own with its wealth of good, cheap restaurants, trendy bars, clubs and music venues. Most visitors who make it out to Frederiksberg are there either for **Copenhagen Zoo** or the area's real highlight, the sprawling green oasis of **Frederiksberg Have**. With more time to spare, you might want to take in one or two of the area's clutch of small, offbeat museums.

Vesterbro

After the old city ramparts fell in 1851 and construction on areas outside the former defences took off on a massive scale, **Vesterbro** was quickly bought up by entrepreneurs, who crammed in as many housing blocks with minuscule flats as possible. Overcrowded and mismanaged for decades, it was not until the mid-1960s that the area's deplorable state was recognized by the city council. Eventually, in the 1980s, and wise from their experiences at Nørrebro a few years earlier – when locals clashed with police after historic buildings were torn down to make way for concrete housing blocks – it was decided to renovate rather than rebuild. Large sections of Vesterbro have since been restored – flashy streetside cafés have popped up on the corners of Halmtorvet, the preserve, just a few years ago, of drug dealers

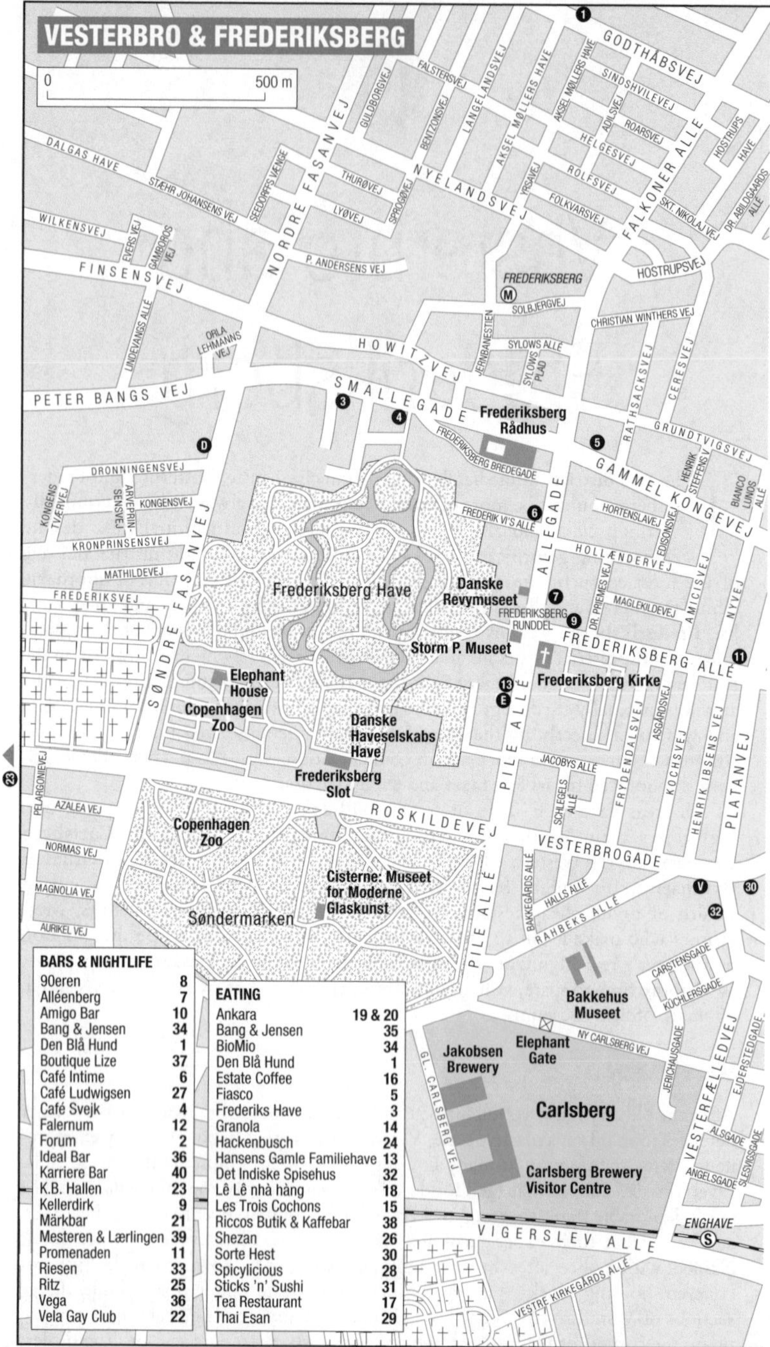
VESTERBRO & FREDERIKSBERG
0
500 m
BARS & NIGHTLIFE
90eren 8
Alléenberg 7
Amigo Bar 10
Bang & Jensen 34
Den Blå Hund 1
Boutique Lize 37
Café Intime 6
Café Ludwigsen 27
Café Svejk 4
Falernum 12
Forum 2
Ideal Bar 36
Karriere Bar 40
K.B. Hallen 23
Kellerdirk 9
Märkbar 21
Mesteren & Lærlingen 39
Promenaden 11
Riesen 33
Ritz 25
Vega 36
Vela Gay Club 22
EATING
Ankara 19 & 20
Bang & Jensen 35
BioMio 34
Den Blå Hund 1
Estate Coffee 16
Fiasco 5
Frederiks Have 3
Granola 14
Hackenbusch 24
Hansens Gamle Familiehave 13
Det Indiske Spisehus 32
Lê Lê nhà hàng 18
Les Trois Cochons 15
Riccos Butik & Kaffebar 38
Shezan 26
Sorte Hest 30
Spicylicious 28
Sticks 'n' Sushi 31
Tea Restaurant 17
Thai Esan 29
Frederiksberg Have
Frederiksberg Rådhus
Danske Revymuseet
Storm P. Museet
Frederiksberg Kirke
Elephant House
Copenhagen Zoo
Danske Haveselskabs Have
Frederiksberg Slot
Cisterne: Museet for Moderne Glaskunst
Søndermarken
Bakkehus Museet
Elephant Gate
Jakobsen Brewery
Carlsberg
Carlsberg Brewery Visitor Centre
FREDERIKSBERG
ENGHAVE
GODTHÅBSVEJ
FALKONER ALLÉ
NYELANDSVEJ
NORDRE FASANVEJ
SØNDRE FASANVEJ
FINSENSVEJ
HOWITZVEJ
SMALLEGADE
PETER BANGS VEJ
GAMMEL KONGEVEJ
ALLÉGADE
FREDERIKSBERG ALLÉ
ROSKILDEVEJ
VESTERBROGADE
PILE ALLÉ
RAHBEKS ALLÉ
NY CARLSBERG VEJ
GL. CARLSBERG VEJ
VESTERFÆLLEDVEJ
VIGERSLEV ALLÉ
VESTRE KIRKEGÅRDS ALLÉ
FREDERIKSBERG BREDEGADE
FREDERIKSBERG RUNDDEL
DALGAS HAVE
WILKENSVEJ
DRONNINGENSVEJ
KRONPRINSENSVEJ
MATHILDEVEJ
FREDERIKSVEJ
PLATANVEJ
HENRIK IBSENS VEJ
KOCHSVEJ
FRYDENDALSVEJ
JACOBYS ALLÉ
HOSTRUPSVEJ
CHRISTIAN WINTHERS VEJ
GRUNDTVIGSVEJ
HOLLÆNDERVEJ
AMICISVEJ
NYVEJ

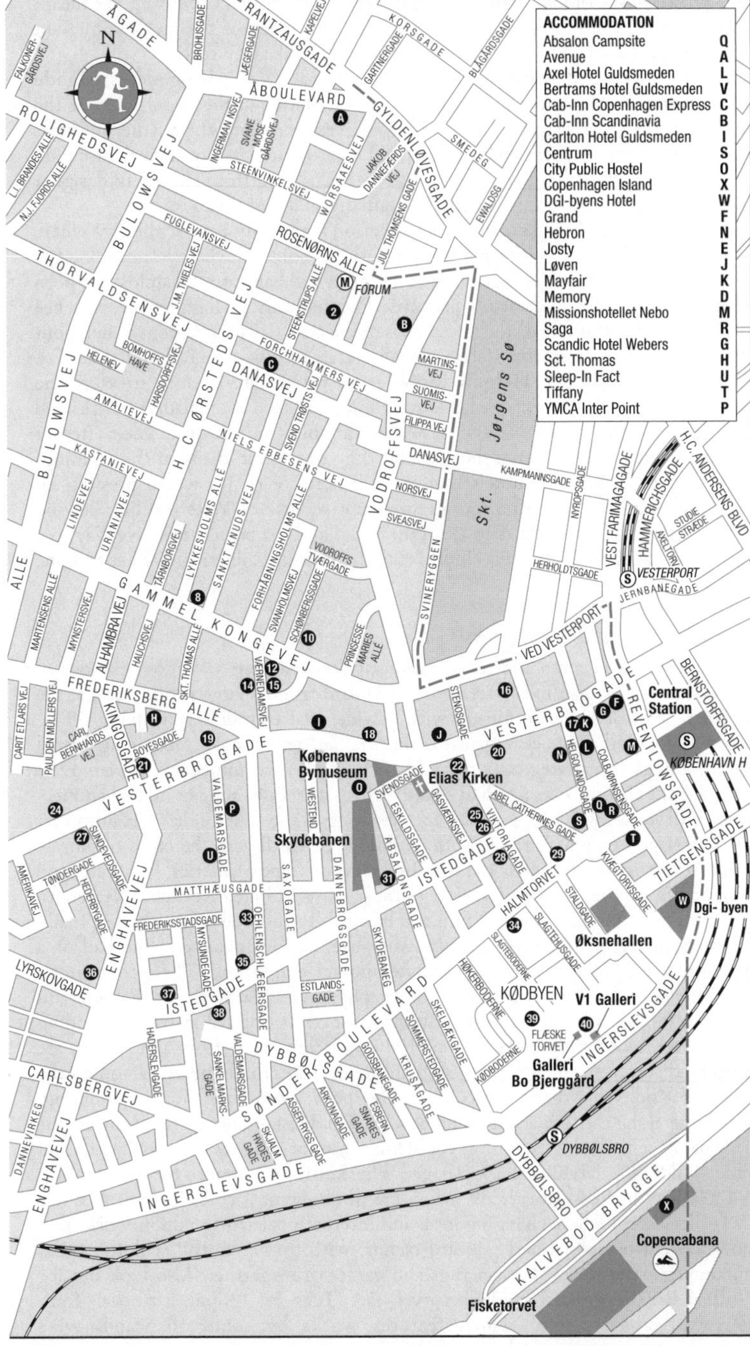

www.roughguides.com

and prostitutes – though sadly the rapid gentrification that's followed has meant that many of Vesterbro's original inhabitants, and much of the area's immigrant community, have had to leave, unable to afford the hiked-up rents.

Vesterbro is crossed by the roughly parallel streets of **Vesterbrogade**, **Istedgade** and **Sønder Boulevard**, running from Central Station at the eastern end of the district to the Carlsberg Brewery in the west. Vesterbrogade, the northernmost of the three, is the district's main artery and one of the city's principal shopping streets. More affordable than Strøget, it sells everything from clothes to designer kitchenware, and also has some good restaurants and nightlife.

The area around Istedgade by Central Station is the only part of the city where you might feel a little vulnerable at night – this is home to what's left of the city's red-light district, and drunks, dealers and junkies still hang around amidst the porn shops, dodgy clubs and tattoo parlours. Paradoxically, a high police presence probably makes this one of the safest areas in the city. Crossing Istedgade here, but decidedly less seedy in themselves, are the city's two so-called "hotel streets" – **Colbjørnsensgade** and **Helgolandsgade**. In a desperate attempt to avoid the district becoming a working-class stronghold, the city council decreed that all houses in the two streets were to have a minimum of four rooms. Their attempt had an unexpected outcome: shortly after they were built, many of the buildings were converted into the hotels that are still here today. It's worth pressing on further along Istedgade for a more representative taste of Vesterbro life; beyond Gasværksvej, the street starts to clean up its act and the porn shops give way to a more workaday mix of cafés, clothes shops, Turkish, Chinese and Thai grocers, and *halal* butchers.

Halmtorvet and Kødbyen

Nowhere is the cleanup and rejuvenation of the Vesterbro area more obvious to the casual visitor than in the area around **Halmtorvet**, a large roundabout at the southern end of Helgolandsgade with a wide dual carriageway running off it. Covered in a rather lifeless expanse of immaculate cream-coloured paving dotted with saplings and strategically placed benches, the area immediately around the roundabout encompasses a trio of bland, bistro-style cafés and has no real connection with Vesterbro's seedy past. More exciting is the south side of Halmtorvet dual carriageway, where the historic buildings of **Kødbyen**, the city's old meat-packing district, have been taken over by a slew of trendy galleries, bars, cafés and restaurants making it one of the city's most edgy and creative hubs. Nearest to Halmtorvet roundabout you'll find the beautifully restored **Øksnehallen** (daily 11am–6pm; admission varies; Ⓦwww.dgi-byen.dk/oeksnehallen), the hall of a 1901-built cattle market now used for temporary exhibitions. These concentrate on contemporary culture, design, photography, art and fashion, but the light and spacious interior is worth a look in itself; most of its original features, including the arched, wood-beamed ceiling typical of market places from the period, are preserved. From Øksnehallen a left turn down Slagterboderne takes you to the heart of Kødbyen, where you could easily spend a couple of hours wandering, refuelling along the way at the many new cafés and restaurants. In here, among the old character-packed warehouses, you'll find a host of galleries in the old white and blue building encircling the U-shaped **Flæsketorvet square**. Most notable is **V1 Gallery** at Flæsketorvet 69 (Mon–Fri noon–6pm, Sat noon–4pm; Ⓦwww.V1gallery.com) where changing local and international artists exhibit works that question current social and political trends, with fun, colourful sculptures that encompass Teletubbies, Persian rugs and gay porn magazines. Also look out for **Galleri Bo Bjerggaard** at Flæsketorvet 85A (Tues–Fri 1–6pm, Sat noon–4pm; Ⓦwww.bjerggaard.com) which features works by some of Scandinavia's best-known contemporary artists. Don't miss **Karriere Bar** at Flæsketorvet 57 (see p.166), which doubles as a café/bar and has every nook and cranny beautifully sculpted and endowed with funky artwork.

Nestling behind the Øksnehallen and signalled by a distinctive concrete climbing tower on the corner of Tietgensgade, the **DGI-byen** centre (Mon–Thurs 6.30am–10pm, Fri 6.30am–8pm, Sat 6.30am –7pm, Sun 9am–6pm; Ⓦwww.dgi-byen.dk) offers superb sports facilities, including the fantastic Vandkulturhuset (Swim Centre; see p.194), a top-of-the-range restaurant, and a pricey hotel designed in classic Scandinavian minimalist style (see p.140).

Københavns Bymuseum and around

On the northern edge of Gasværksvej you will come to Vesterbrogade and the small, triangular **Vesterbros Torv**. Popular in the summer with its outdoor bars and cafés, the square's main feature is the **Elias Kirken**, designed by Martin Nyrop, creator of the Rådhus, in 1908, and exhibiting the same Italian-inspired architecture. At Vesterbrogade 59, the **Københavns Bymuseum** (City Museum; Mon, Tues & Thurs–Sun 10am–4pm, Wed 10am–9pm; 20kr, free on Fri; Ⓦwww.bymuseum.dk) sits behind a detailed model of the city in 1530. A slightly confusing but interesting introduction to the capital's chaotic history, the museum brings the fifteenth- and sixteenth-century city to life through reconstructions of ramshackle house exteriors and tradesmen's signs. Looking at these, the subsequent impact of Christian IV's expansive building programmes (see box, p.50) becomes resoundingly apparent, and there's a large room recording the form and cohesion that this monarch and amateur architect gave the city. The rest of the city's thousand-year history is told with an array of paintings, photos, miniature

Søren Kierkegaard

The name of **Søren Kierkegaard** is inextricably linked with Copenhagen, yet his championing of individual will over social conventions and his rejection of materialism did little to endear him to his fellow Danes. Born in 1813, Kierkegaard believed himself set on an "evil destiny" – partly the fault of his father, who is best remembered for having cursed God on a Jutland heath. Weighed down by his father's endless lectures on the suffering of Christ and the inevitable misery of the world, the young Kierkegaard developed a morbid, depressive and, at the age of 25, deeply religious personality. This combination of periodic depressions and religious devotion led him in 1841 to end his engagement to the love of his life, Regine Olsen, for fear of drawing her into his melancholy and himself away from God. The resulting emotional trauma saw him flee to Berlin where he turned feverishly to writing, with the publication in 1843 of his first book *Either/Or* – a philosophical examination of the conflicting emotions of his doomed love affair – and a concerted writing spell that lasted ten years. Few people understood *Either/Or* with its discussion of the two worlds – the "aesthetic" (man's love of the bodily, sensory, material world and all its sins) and the "ethical" (man's relationship with the spiritual and eternal) – and the individual's resulting "dread" or angst at trying to reconcile the two. Kierkegaard, however, came to revel in the enigma he had created, becoming a "walking mystery in the streets of Copenhagen" (he lived in a house on Nytorv). He was a prolific author, sometimes publishing two books on the same day, and often writing under pseudonyms. His greatest philosophical works, *Either/Or*, *The Concept of Dread* and *Fear and Trembling*, were written by 1846 and are often claimed to have laid the foundations of **existentialism**. Kierkegaard died in 1855, emotionally exhausted by his various quarrels with rival philosophers, writers and the Church itself; it was to be another sixty years before his work gained international recognition.

models and domestic items, all put into context by the excellent audio guides that you pick up at the entrance. Don't miss the small room devoted to **Søren Kierkegaard** (see box, p.92) – filled with caricatures of the man himself, furniture from his home, paintings of his girlfriend Regine Olsen, jewellery, books and manuscripts – which forms a fascinating footnote to the life of this nineteenth-century Danish writer and philosopher.

The collection is housed in a distinguished building of 1787 originally home to the Royal Shooting Brotherhood. They were a pompous group of wealthy citizens that gathered regularly to practise their shooting skills, supposedly to be able to protect the city were it to be attacked, but in reality it was more a snooty sports/social club that had elaborate parties in the sumptuous Banqueting Hall on the first floor with its riot of stuccowork angels which date to an 1896 renovation. Outside, it backs onto the brotherhood's old firing range, Skydebanen, now a children's playground and unremarkable apart from its curious **Skydebanemuren**, a twelve-metre-high red-brick wall adorned with the brotherhood's logo. It was erected in 1887, allegedly to protect passers-by from stray bullets, though rumours suggest that its real purpose was to protect the snobbish brotherhood from the distracting sight of Vesterbro poverty.

Værnedamsvej, north and west of the museum, is a haven for foodies, lined with speciality shops including an impressive selection of traditional butchers, a French bakery (boasting the best croissants in Scandinavia), an ice cream parlour, fishmongers, cheesemakers and ethnic fruit-and-veg shops. It's the ideal place to put together a picnic before heading up to Frederiksberg Have (see p.94).

Carlsberg Brewery

Sadly the world-famous lager (probably the best in the world) is no longer brewed at the site of the massive Carlsberg Brewery complex – production was moved in 2009 to Fredericia where the water quality was deemed better for large-scale production – only a small amount of Jacobsen gourmet lager is now brewed

▲ Elephant Gate, Carlsberg Brewery

within the historic brewery walls. Enthusiasts might nonetheless want to take a look at the multimedia **Visitor Centre** at Gamle Carlsberg Vej 11 (Mon–Wed & Fri–Sun 10am–5pm, Thurs 10am–7.30pm; 60kr; Ⓦwww.visitcarlsberg.dk), in an old brewhouse dating to 1906. The exhibition kicks off with the world's largest collection of beer bottles before offering a detailed tour through the history of brewing in Denmark from the Bronze Age – Egtved Girl (see p.85) had a small pot at her feet containing the first known Danish beer – and the role of beer in Danish social history, with juicy tales including Christian IV's legendary benders. It moves on to the story of the founder, brewer Jacobsen, and Carlsberg itself, complete with models of old workers' quarters, tableaux demonstrating the brewing process, and old brewing machinery, all accompanied by a plethora of videos, photos and diagrams. The assortment of old advertising campaigns makes for lighter entertainment, and there's a section on various countries' per capita Carlsberg consumption – Germany has the highest. It's not nearly as exciting as a noisy brewery in full action, though Carlsberg have at least retained the tradition of handing out beer in the bar at the end of your visit, overlooking the Jacobsen Microbrewery – always the busiest part of the centre.

While you're in the vicinity, have a look at the beautifully carved **Elephant Gate** behind the visitor centre on Ny Carlsberg Vej.

Frederiksberg

"A city within the city" is how the residents of **FREDERIKSBERG** like to describe their independent district. Positioned between the districts of Vesterbro and Nørrebro, it covers a large area – almost twice the size of Indre By – and, with its own industry, shopping mall, city hall and a number of metro stations, tries to be completely self-contained. Away from the main roads you'll find street after street of the district's distinctively grand **villas**, quite unlike the apartment blocks characteristic of residential areas in other parts of the city. The first one was erected in 1846, and between them they represent the work of some of Denmark's most distinguished architects, from Functionalists to Neoclassicists.

Frederiksberg Allé and Runddel

Just beyond Københavns Bymuseum (see p.91), **Frederiksberg Allé** branches off Vesterbrogade to the right. Sloping gently and lined with rows of trees, this long, wide boulevard was originally built by Frederik IV as a private road to his summer residence, Frederiksberg Slot, and even today along its grand length you'll find an impressive array of old apartment buildings and a number of theatres. At **Frederiksberg Runddel** (Circus) the road joins Pile Allé and Allégade and becomes the main entrance to Frederiksberg Have. Look out on the left for the **Frederiksberg Kirke** – a delightful, ivy-clad, 1734 octagonal church built by Dutch farmers coerced here by Christian II to grow vegetables and care for the royal livestock.

As well as being transformed into an open-air ice-skating rink in winter, the *runddel* is home to two eclectic collections. First up, immediately on the left, housed in the former police station, is the entertaining **Storm P. Museet** (May–Oct Tues–Sun 10am–4pm; Nov–April Wed, Sat & Sun 10am–4pm; 30kr; Ⓦwww.stormp-museet.dk), packed with the satirical cartoons that made "Storm P" (Robert Storm Petersen) one of the most popular by-lines in Danish newspapers during the 1920s, as well as his enormous collection of pipes, and other personal effects. A video in English gives some background on the man's work.

A short walk along Allégade, at no. 5, is the **Danske Revymuseet** (Danish Revue Museum; Tues–Sun 11am–4pm; 35kr; Ⓦwww.revymuseet.dk). With hardly any English labelling, you'll have to be a bit of a devotee of revue theatre to get much out of the collection of pictures, theatrical props, costumes, posters, programmes and other artefacts associated with the entertainers who used to amuse – and ridicule – rich city folks on their weekend outings to the Frederiksberg countryside.

Pile Allé

Pile Allé, the road heading south of Frederiksberg Runddel, is famous for the many small, ornate gardens that line its western side, collectively known as **Danske Haveselskabs Have** (10am–sunset; free) and base of the Danish Horticultural Society (the second oldest horticultural society in the world, after the English); the entrance is through the white gate on the left-hand side of the *runddel*. The formally laid out gardens are stuffed with a mishmash of amazing plant environments, the odd peacock strutting about to complete the picture, and make a pretty setting for the jazz concerts hosted here during summer. Further along Pile Allé, amidst a few so-called "family gardens" – popular restaurants formerly catering for palace staff, these days renowned for their sublime traditional Danish lunches accompanied by the obligatory snaps (see "Eating", p.158, for recommendations) – is the **maze**, shaped in the form of a Tuborg beer label. There are great views of Frederiksberg Slot from hereabouts.

Allégade

The road heading north from the *runddel* is **Allégade**, the original main street of the now vanished village of Ny Amager, which housed Dutch immigrant farmers in the seventeenth century. It leads to Gammel Kongevej – Christian IV's main road to Frederiksberg Slot, replaced by Frederiksberg Allé a hundred years later – and Frederiksberg Rådhus, on the corner of Smallegade. One of the city's biggest and most colourful **flea markets** takes place in the car park behind the Rådhus on Saturdays from May to October.

Frederiksberg Have

From the main entrance on Frederiksberg Runddel, the expansive English-style gardens of **Frederiksberg Have** (daily 6am–sunset; free) stretch north towards Smallegade and south towards Frederiksberg Slot amidst a network of pathways, lakes and canals that criss-cross the beautiful lime-tree groves. Throughout the eighteenth century, the city's top nobs came here to mess about in boats, though nowadays you'll have to settle for one of the tours in the large, manned rowing boats that depart regularly from in front of Frederiksberg Slot. The grassy slopes, ponds and fountains attract hordes of picnicking locals in summer, especially when the park becomes a regular venue for live music and theatre. Romantic follies, temples and grottoes abound; look out for the colourful **Chinese Folly** (June–Aug Sun 2–4pm) on one of the park's picturesque islands – it was built in 1799 and used for Frederik VI's tea parties – and the Neoclassical **Temple of Apis**, west of the palace near the zoo, dating from 1804 – and despite the twentieth-century graffiti, a real architectural gem. You can also see the zoo's (see opposite) stunning **elephant house**, which borders the park.

Frederiksberg Slot

At their southern end, the gardens of Frederiksberg Have take on a distinctly more ordered, French-inspired look as they slope up to the pale yellow **Frederiksberg Slot**; the castle and its immediate environs are all that remain of the original Baroque style of the park, the rest having been transformed, according to

▲ Frederiksberg Have

the latest fashions, into English romantic style in the late 1700s. The *slot* (guided tours Jan–May & Aug–Nov on the last Sat of the month at 11am & 1pm; 25kr) was built by Frederik IV in the early eighteenth century on top of Valby Bakke hill, from where it would originally have commanded an uninterrupted view of the city ramparts and the Swedish coastline. Extended many times since, it acquired its present shape under Christian VI in 1735, and was the royal family's summer residence until the mid-1800s, when it was taken over by the Danish Officers' Academy. It's worth joining a guided tour to see the evocative interior, with its imposing stuccowork and ceiling paintings, along with the secret passageway leading down to an enormous marble bathtub (supposedly a secret meeting place of Queen Caroline Mathilde and her lover Count Struensee) and the black-and-white chequered kitchen, where she used to make pancakes. Have a look, too, at the exquisitely fashioned Baroque decorations in the adjacent palace chapel.

Søndermarken

To the south of the *slot*, across Roskildevej, **Søndermarken** is a further sprawling expanse of greenery, equal in size to Frederiksberg Have, though much less rigorously landscaped. It's another of the city's regular summer venues for concerts. The strange glass pyramid structure unceremoniously plonked on the left of the lawn directly in front of the castle is the opening to the rather atmospheric if bizarre **Cisternerne: Museet for Moderne Glaskunst** (Cisternerne: Museum of Modern Glass Art; Feb–Nov Thurs & Fri 2–6pm, Sat & Sun 11am–5pm; 50kr; Ⓦ www.cisternerne.dk) – an underground exhibition of stained-glass works set in the damp environs of the grand former water cisterns.

Copenhagen Zoo

Bordering the southwest corner of Frederiksberg Have, next to Frederiskberg Slot, is **Copenhagen Zoo** (March Mon–Fri 9am–4pm, Sat & Sun 9am–5pm; April, May & Sept Mon–Fri 9am–5pm, Sat & Sun 9am–6pm; early to mid-June

& mid- to end Aug daily 9am–6pm; mid-June to mid-Aug daily 9am–9pm; Oct daily 9am–5pm; Nov–Feb daily 9am–4pm; 130kr; Ⓦwww.zoo.dk), one of the oldest and largest in Europe, with over 2500 animals. Though the zoo is constantly updating the enclosures in line with latest research in order to reproduce the animals' natural environments as closely as possible – their reputable breeding results testify to their success – it's still rather depressing watching the huge bears and big cats pacing around their compounds. The African savannah area in the section south of Roskildevej is a more uplifting, open-plan affair with giraffes, impala and okapi looking a little more at home. The zoo's other star attractions include two Tasmanian devils, a gift from the Australian government to Crown Prince Frederik and his Tasmanian-born wife Mary, and the magnificent new glass-covered elephant house, designed by Norman Foster, with its heated flooring – to keep the elephants' sensitive feet dry and healthy – and the option for the elephants to sleep together as they would in the wild. Should you wish to bypass the rest of the zoo and only see the elephant house, the vista is almost as good from Frederiksberg Have (see p.94) which has the added bonus of being free. The zoo also has a special **children's section** where kids can touch domestic animals such as goats, sheep, cows and horses (see p.199).

Bakkehus Museet

Southeast of Frederiksberg Have, just north of the Carlsberg Visitor Centre, at Rahbeks Allé 28, the **Bakkehus Museet** (Bakkehus Museum; Tues–Sun 11am–4pm; 30kr; Ⓦwww.bakkehusmuseet.dk) is located in what is claimed to be the oldest house in Frederiksberg, dating from the seventeenth century. The museum provides a charming insight into the literary milieu of Denmark's Golden Age; the Rahbæk family – Knud Lyhne Rahbæk, critic, writer and manager of the Royal Theatre and his wife Kamma – lived here from 1802 to 1830, hosting a popular salon for Danish literary personalities such as Hans Christian Andersen and Adam Oehlenschläger (author of the Danish national anthem), who were frequent guests. The peaceful museum preserves the house more or less as the Rahbæks left it, with period furniture, various portraits, personal effects and publications dating to the time. Look out for Rahbæk's study, with his diary open on the desk and, in Kamma's delightfully cosy corner room, papier-mâché replicas of the cakes served at the famous salon. Unfortunately, there's no labelling in English, but the very helpful curator is always willing to answer questions. The kitchen leads through to a succession of rooms given over to almost two hundred tiny portraits of the Danish high and mighty who flocked to Paris from the 1790s onwards to have their profiles immortalized by French portrait artist Gilles Louis Chrétien. In a continuation of the literary traditions of the house, the upstairs apartment is let to a struggling poet of the moment, who gets to live here rent-free for four years.

7

Nørrebro and Østerbro

To the north and east of the city centre are the districts of **Nørrebro** and **Østerbro** (North Bridge and East Bridge), built up in the mid-nineteenth century after the devastation of the British bombardments in 1801 and 1807, when the city's old defences – by now deemed pretty useless – were abolished and the land outside the old ramparts opened up to house the ever-increasing population. Their similar age apart, the two districts have deeply contrasting histories: Nørrebro's is one of deprivation and social struggle followed by more recent immigration, gentrification and today's almost Parisian feel; Østerbro's is one of traditional wealth and privilege – hence the rather smug feel of the district today, though its leafy ambience makes it a pleasant enough place.

Nørrebro

Working-class **Nørrebro** is synonymous with Copenhagen at its most rebellious. As the city expanded beyond the old ramparts, huge slum tenements began to spring up to house Copenhagen's newly industrialized working class, and by the end of the nineteenth century, Nørrebro had established itself as one of the country's most politicized areas – local residents were later instrumental in forming both the Danish trade union movement and the Social Democratic Party, Denmark's biggest political party.

Nørrebro's resilience was expressed in more dangerous circumstances when local residents led the fight against the Nazis during World War II. The immediate postwar period was rather quiet, but by the 1960s residents were again challenging authority, protesting issues from the Vietnam War to local housing concerns. By the 1980s, Nørrebro had given birth to one of Europe's most radical squatting movements, the BZ (see p.100).

In the 1980s, an influx of immigrants to Nørrebro brought much-needed cultural diversity to the city; large numbers of Danish yuppies also moved in, taking advantage of the then low property prices. Their joint presence has been accompanied by a wonderful mix of markets, ethnic food stores and restaurants, and a vast selection of sometimes pretentiously groovy cafés, bars and clubs.

Skt Hans Torv and Politihistorisk Museum

At the heart of the trendy part of Nørrebro is the small **Skt Hans Torv**, formerly working class, now transformed into a hub of gentrified Parisian-style cafés and bars. Home of Copenhagen's young and gifted – or at least rich – this was a favourite hangout of Denmark's "dynamic" forty-something crown prince, Frederik, before he married and started a family.

Just down Fælledvej from Skt Hans Torv is Nørrebro's only – and curiously appropriate – museum, the **Politihistorisk Museum** (Police History Museum;

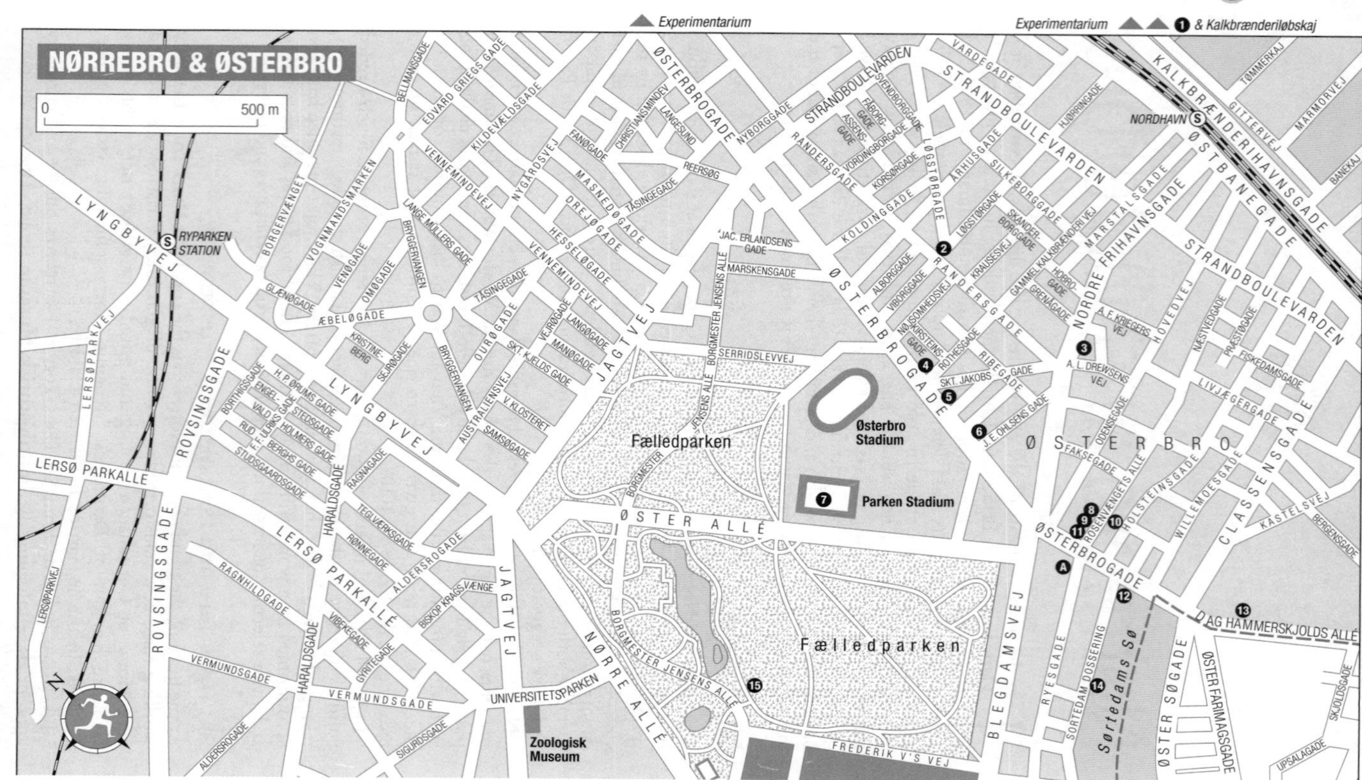
NØRREBRO & ØSTERBRO
0
500 m
Experimentarium
Experimentarium
1 & Kalkbrænderiløbskaj
Ferry to Oslo
Langelinie
NORDHAVN
RYPARKEN STATION
Fælledparken
Fælledparken
Østerbro Stadium
Parken Stadium
Zoologisk Museum
Sortedams Sø
ØSTERBRO
KALKBRÆNDERIHAVNSGADE
ØSTBANEGADE
STRANDBOULEVARDEN
NORDRE FRIHAVNSGADE
RANDERSGADE
ØSTERBROGADE
ØSTER ALLÉ
NØRRE ALLÉ
JAGTVEJ
LYNGBYVEJ
ROVSINGSGADE
LERSØ PARKALLE
LERSØ PARKALLÉ
BLEGDAMSVEJ
CLASSENSGADE
DAG HAMMERSKJOLDS ALLÉ
ØSTER SØGADE
ØSTER FARIMAGSGADE
FREDERIK V'S VEJ
UNIVERSITETSPARKEN
VERMUNDSGADE
HARALDSGADE
BORGMESTER JENSENS ALLÉ
SERRIDSLEVVEJ
MARSKENSGADE
JAC. ERLANDSENS GADE
LØGSTØRGADE
KOLDINGGADE
NYBORGGADE
VENNEMINDEVEJ
HESSELØGADE
DREJØGADE
MASNEDØGADE
NYGÅRDSVEJ
KILDEVÆLDSGADE
EDVARD GRIEGS GADE
BELLMANSGADE
VOGNMANDSMARKEN
BORGERVÆNGET
ÆBELØGADE
BRYGGERVANGEN
OURØGADE
AUSTRALIENSVEJ
SKT. KJELDS GADE
LANGØGADE
MANØGADE
VEJRØGADE
TÅSINGEGADE
LANGE MÜLLERS GADE
VENØGADE
OMØGADE
GLÆNØGADE
KRISTINEBERG
SEJRØGADE
V. KLOSTERET
SAMSØGADE
RAGNAGADE
TEGLVÆRKSGADE
RØNNEGADE
ALDERSROGADE
BISKOP KRAGS VÆNGE
VIBEKEGADE
GYRITEGADE
RAGNHILDGADE
SIGURDSGADE
ALDERSROGADE
LERSØPARKVEJ
BORTHIGSGADE
H.P. ØRUMS GADE
ENGEL-STEDSGADE
VALD. HOLMERS GADE
F.F. ULRIKS GADE
RUD. BERGHS GADE
STUDSGAARDSGADE
FANØGADE
CHRISTIANSMINDEV.
LANGESUND
REERSØG
TÅSINGEGADE
ØSTERBROGADE
SVENDBORGGADE
FÅBORGGADE
ASSENSGADE
VORDINGBORGGADE
KORSØRGADE
ÅRHUSGADE
SILKEBORGGADE
SKANDERBORGGADE
KRAUSESVEJ
GAMMEL KALKBRÆNDERIVEJ
HOBROGADE
GRENÅGADE
ALBORGGADE
VIBORGGADE
NØJSOMHEDSVEJ
KIRSTEINSGADE
ROTHESGADE
RIBEGADE
SKT. JAKOBS GADE
J.E. OHLSENS GADE
A.F. KRIEGERS VEJ
A. L. DREWSENS VEJ
HOVEDVEJ
MARSTALSGADE
HJØRRINGGADE
VARDEGADE
GITTERVEJ
TØMMERKAJ
MARMORVEJ
BANEKAJ
NÆSTVEDGADE
PRÆSTØGADE
FISKEDAMSGADE
LIVJÆGERGADE
ODENSEGADE
FAKSEGADE
ROSENVÆNGETS ALLÉ
HOLSTEINSGADE
WILLEMOESGADE
KASTELSVEJ
BERGENSGADE
RYESGADE
SORTEDAM DOSSERING
SKJOLDSGADE
UPSALAGADE
N

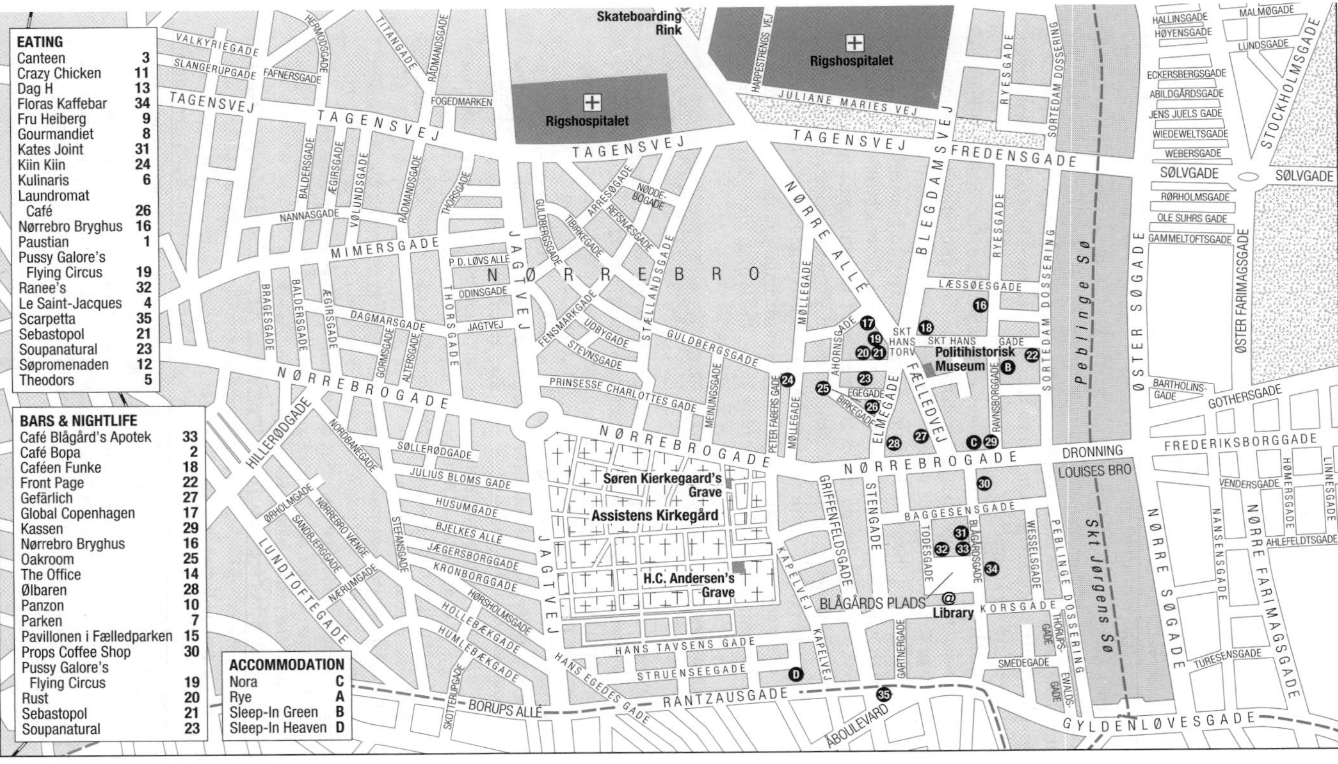
EATING
Canteen 3
Crazy Chicken 11
Dag H 13
Floras Kaffebar 34
Fru Heiberg 9
Gourmandiet 8
Kates Joint 31
Kiin Kiin 24
Kulinaris 6
Laundromat Café 26
Nørrebro Bryghus 16
Paustian 1
Pussy Galore's Flying Circus 19
Ranee's 32
Le Saint-Jacques 4
Scarpetta 35
Sebastopol 21
Soupanatural 23
Søpromenaden 12
Theodors 5
BARS & NIGHTLIFE
Café Blågård's Apotek 33
Café Bopa 2
Caféen Funke 18
Front Page 22
Gefärlich 27
Global Copenhagen 17
Kassen 29
Nørrebro Bryghus 16
Oakroom 25
The Office 14
Ølbaren 28
Panzon 10
Parken 7
Pavillonen i Fælledparken 15
Props Coffee Shop 30
Pussy Galore's Flying Circus 19
Rust 20
Sebastopol 21
Soupanatural 23
ACCOMMODATION
Nora C
Rye A
Sleep-In Green B
Sleep-In Heaven D
NØRREBRO
Skateboarding Rink
Rigshospitalet
Rigshospitalet
Søren Kierkegaard's Grave
Assistens Kirkegård
H.C. Andersen's Grave
Politihistorisk Museum
Library
BLÅGÅRDS PLADS
SKT HANS TORV
Peblinge Sø
Skt Jørgens Sø
DRONNING LOUISES BRO
NØRREBROGADE
JAGTVEJ
TAGENSVEJ
NØRRE ALLÉ
BLEGDAMSVEJ
FREDENSGADE
FÆLLEDVEJ
SORTEDAM DOSSERING
PEBLINGE DOSSERING
ØSTER SØGADE
NØRRE SØGADE
ØSTER FARIMAGSGADE
NØRRE FARIMAGSGADE
GOTHERSGADE
FREDERIKSBORGGADE
GYLDENLØVESGADE
RANTZAUSGADE
BORUPS ALLÉ
ÅBOULEVARD
HILLERØDGADE
LUNDTOFTEGADE
STOCKHOLMSGADE
SØLVGADE
GULDBERGSGADE
STÆLLANDSGADE
PRINSESSE CHARLOTTES GADE
MIMERSGADE
HANS TAVSENS GADE
STRUENSEEGADE
HANS EGEDES GADE
KAPELVEJ
STENGADE
GRIFFENFELDSGADE
BAGGESENSGADE
BLÅGÅRDSGADE
KORSGADE
MØLLEGADE
RYESGADE
LÆSSØESGADE
ELMEGADE
ÆGIRSGADE
BALDERSGADE
BRAGESGADE
THORSGADE
DAGMARSGADE
STEFANSGADE
HUSUMGADE
BJELKES ALLÉ
JÆGERSBORGGADE
KRONBORGGADE
HØRSHOLMSGADE
HOLLEBÆKGADE
HUMLEBÆKGADE
JULIUS BLOMS GADE
SØLLERØDGADE
NORDBANEGADE
VALKYRIEGADE
SLANGERUPGADE
TITANGADE
RÅDMANDSGADE
FOGEDMARKEN
JULIANE MARIES VEJ
HARPESTRENGS VEJ
NANSENSGADE
WESSELSGADE
TODESGADE
GARTNERGADE
SMEDEGADE

Tues, Thurs & Sun 11am–4pm; 30kr), a fascinating, if somewhat macabre, document of crime, detection and incarceration, housed in one of the city's first purpose-built police stations – the infamous Station 6. On the ground floor, the exhibits initially focus on the gruesome methods of social control employed in medieval times, as well as the uniforms and brutal cudgels of the city's early night-watchmen. Look out for the grim, old holding cells (in which you can temporarily lock yourself up) and a pair of impressive antique Nimbus police motorbikes.

The second floor is dedicated almost solely to crime and criminals. One room delves into the history of the various facets of the city's once-illegal sex industry – there's a large collection of porn discreetly held in drawers under the display cases – while another concentrates on forgery and smuggling, and a third on murder. Each exhibit is cross-referençed to drawers holding disturbing photographs of the crime scene from which they were taken – best not to look unless you have a strong stomach.

Back outside, the well-preserved streets around Skt Hans Torv make it difficult to imagine what the area was like pre-gentrification. To capture more of a flavour of the old working-class district with narrow streets of dark, brick tenements, head south from the Politihistorisk Museum along Fælledvej, to Nørrebrogade and the intersection with **Blågårdsgade** on the opposite side. Now a buzzing pedestrianized street, the Blågårdsgade area is at the heart of Copenhagen's immigrant and alternative communities, and also scene of the city's recent bout of gang-related gun crime (see below). South Asian and Middle Eastern immigrants rub shoulders with ex-squatters and protestors, and there's an intriguing multicultural blend of inexpensive restaurants and bars. Further along, the typical inner-city tree-fringed

An arena for protest

The Danes are generally known for their political and social tolerance, but in the 1980s the activities of a radical squatting movement, the **BZ** (a shortening of the Danish word *besæt*, meaning "to occupy"), led to massive and violent street confrontations with the authorities. Based mainly in Nørrebro – then a very run-down area – the BZ's initial aim, apart from alleviating a chronic housing shortage, was to establish an autonomous youth centre outside the control of the city council. After gaining widespread public support, they were given Ungdomshuset (literally "The Youth House"). Even so, increasing confrontation followed, particularly during the eviction of a large squat in Ryesgade in 1985, when thousands of police – the country's biggest ever peacetime deployment – faced down a large group of squatters armed with petrol bombs and sticks.

The **violence** reached a peak in 1993 when, following Denmark's decision to sign the Maastricht Treaty, the police lost control of an anti-EU protest organized by the BZ on Nørrebrogade. In the ensuing chaos, several officers fired into the crowd and eleven demonstrators were shot – some in the back – in the worst incident of civil violence in Denmark's history. Fortunately, nobody was killed.

Today, BZ lacks the popular support it once had, and Nørrebro faces new problems with escalating drug-related gang shootings between Hells Angels and second- and third-generation Danes. In early 2009, after an innocent bystander was shot dead, more than 3000 local residents joined the tearful burial procession down Nørrebrogade to Dronning Louises Bro, sending a clear message to the gang leaders that enough was enough. In the wake of this, and a series of frank and open public meetings attended by local residents, politicians and the police, the streets of Nørrebro quitened a little; however, you can remain certain that if anything happens in the political arena that invokes a mass public response Nørrebro is first port of call for the demonstrators.

▲ Skt Hans Torv

square, **Blågårds Plads**, is converted to an ice-skating rink during winter (see p.192) and surrounded by alfresco dining spots in the summer. Two other streets, both parallel to Fælledvej, are worth looking out for. **Ravnsborggade** to the southeast has an unusual blend of secondhand – some call it antique – furniture and knick-knack shops, interspersed with Danish designer-clothes shops; a perfect Saturday-morning shopping destination. To the northwest, **Elmegade** stands out with its mass of quirky deli-bars – the place to come for eastern European snacks, Japanese sushi and plain old organic sandwiches, and, of course, coffee of every type imaginable. If you want a view while you lunch, then a bench in the sun by the **Sortedams Sø** rampart lake further to the east makes an ideal spot. The semicircle of man-made rampart lakes is a favourite with joggers and Sunday-morning strollers, while numerous lakeside cafés strive to satisfy the never-ending brunch demands.

Assistens Kirkegård

Unmistakable, graffiti-covered yellow walls herald Copenhagen's most famous cemetery, **Assistens Kirkegård** (May–Aug 8am–8pm; March, April, Sept & Oct 8am–6pm, Nov–Feb 8am–4pm; free). Originally positioned in open countryside outside the city's northern gate, the cemetery was founded in 1760 – in an area previously designated for tobacco growing – as a place in which the city's poor could enjoy a decent Christian burial. It wasn't until 1785 that it started to become the eternal resting place of choice for Copenhagen's gentlefolk.

The Kapelvej entrance, where you'll find an information office with maps, is the best place to start. Close by (and well signposted) are the cemetery's two most internationally famous graves, those of **Hans Christian Andersen** and **Søren Kierkegaard**, but don't expect anything grand: both graves, though well maintained, are pretty nondescript. Rather more imposing is the owl-topped tomb of the Bohr family, where Nobel Prize-winning Danish physicist Niels Bohr is interred. Also keep an eye out for the grave of Martin Andersen Nexø, the famous Danish communist and author of *Pelle the Conqueror* (subsequently turned into an Oscar-winning film), and for the "Jazz Corner", where the American Ben Webster is buried alongside several lesser-known Danish jazz musicians.

Assistens' open green spaces offer a welcome respite from the confined streets of Nørrebro, and in summer many locals can be seen picnicking and sunning themselves among the gravestones – if you want to join them, avoid the garden of remembrance, where the ashes of the departed are scattered over inviting grassy lawns.

The city's new Cityringen Metro line (see p.23), due to open in 2018, will have a stop at Assistens Kirkegård's northernmost corner. To make way for the construction it is going to be necessary to move some of the graves in the area. How many graves is still uncertain – estimated numbers range from the Metro Company's 72 to Nørrebro trading association's 2374. Unsurpisingly, local residents are hugely displeased about this. Whether they will muster enough support to stop the construction remains to be seen.

Østerbro

Stretching from the fringes of Fælledparken in the west through to the commercial docks, warehouses and wealthy residences along the Øresund coast to the east, the salubrious district of **Østerbro** stands in marked contrast to the narrow streets and tenements of Nørrebro. Originally a watering hole full of taverns en route to the hunting grounds of Dyrehaven and the amusements at Bakken (see p.106), Østerbro is nowadays predominantly home to Copenhagen's moneyed classes, who luxuriate in the expensive houses along its coastal fringes. Nearer to the city centre, the district's broad avenues are home to ornate apartment blocks and most of the city's embassies, including that of the US, focal point of many a demonstration. More affordable apartment blocks are tucked away in the residential backstreets connecting main thoroughfare Østerbrogade with Strandboulevarden. This is also where many of the area's quainter cafés are found. Behind Strandboulevarden, across the railway tracks, the Nordhavn harbour area has undergone rapid changes in recent years, from industrial harbour to gentrified office zone with a few exclusive restaurants and lifestyle shops. Along Langelinie – a narrow strip of reclaimed land jutting up from the Katellet defences – a new cruise lines' pier has popped up, opposite a row of trendy factory outlet shops. A stone's throw further north is the funky, glass-covered Oslo ferry DFDS terminal that looks almost science-fiction-like at dawn and dusk. Continue north, and you'll come across buildings designed by Denmark's most internationally known architect, Jørn Utzon – famous for the Sydney Opera House – including the Paustian Building now housing a fashionable furniture and indoor design boutique and an exclusive restaurant.

Fælledparken and Parken Stadium

At the western edge of Østerbro lie the enormously popular wide-open spaces and tree-lined avenues of **Fælledparken** (Community Park). Originally pastureland for Copenhagen's livestock, and then shooting range for the Danish military, it reached its present incarnation in 1906 as a recreational space for the city's workers. With children's playgrounds, a skateboarding rink and plenty of grassy space to kick a ball around, the park also features a Scent Garden – in the southeastern corner near the main entrance at Trianglen, the square where Østerbrogade, Nordre Frihavnsgade and Blegdamsvej meet – developed specifically for visually impaired visitors. The park is also the city's main destination for International Labour Day marches on May 1 when speeches are followed by music and people get ridiculously drunk. In addition it hosts free summer concerts and the Lent carnival celebrations (see p.195).

On the eastern fringe of Fælledparken is the huge, 41,000 all-seater **Parken Stadium** (Ⓦwww.parken.dk). There has been a football stadium on this site for almost a hundred years – five of Copenhagen's football clubs played here at one time – and it's now the home of the Danish national team and FC Copenhagen (usually known as FCK), while big-name acts such as Bruce Springsteen, Fleetwood Mac and Madonna also perform here from time to time. In July, there are one-hour tours of the stadium (Tues & Thurs 11am & 1pm; 60kr) in English and Danish, where you're regaled with anecdotes, shown around the grounds, and told about all the technicalities involved in building and maintaining a stadium this large. Next door is the much smaller **Østerbro Stadium**, home to athletics meetings and football team B93 – look out for the splendid entrance on Østerbrogade, topped with bronze figurines engaging in miscellaneous sporting activities. See p.190 for more details about football matches at Parken and Østerbro.

Zoologisk Museum

The area immediately to the west of Fælledparken is occupied by Copenhagen's main hospital, Rigshospitalet, and by various departments of the university, among which is the **Zoologisk Museum** (Zoological Museum; Tues–Sun 11am–5pm; 75kr; Ⓦwww.zmuc.dk), in the modern building at Universitetsparken 15 – look out for the magnificent metallic cockroach, made by Danish sculptor Kim Olesen, on the roof of the entrance. Walk inside, past the stuffed polar bear, and catch the lift up to the fifth floor. First founded in 1622, this is the oldest museum in Denmark and one of the oldest in Europe. Vast collections of old skeletons and stuffed animals are kept in storage – what you actually get to see are two floors of wonderful dioramic exhibitions completed to the minutest detail. On the fifth floor, the theme is Danish fauna over the past 20,000 years, beginning with the Steppe of the Mammoth – with a terrifyingly huge life-size woolly mammoth on display – moving on to more recent inhabitants such as the wild boar and red deer. The sixth floor exhibit moves from the Arctic to the Antarctic via ice floes, rainforests, savannahs and deserts: the close-up views of long-deceased animals such as armadillos, anteaters and various apes are educational, if a bit creepy. Particularly impressive are the stuffed elephant seals, musk oxen and walruses, which are immense – as are the skeletons of Sperm and Greenland Right whales. The museum also has a very popular **children's section** (see p.201).

Experimentarium

The **Experimentarium**, sited in the old Tuborg Brewery bottling hall on the northeastern edge of Østerbro (Mon & Wed–Fri 9.30am–5pm, Tues 9.30am–9pm, Sat & Sun 11am–5pm; 145kr; Ⓦwww.experimentarium.dk), makes for an educational and entertaining few hours, particularly if you've got children (if not, try to visit during a weekday afternoon, as the place tends to get overrun with kids in the mornings). Every six months or so a section of the exhibition changes – check their website for details.

Not strictly a museum, Experimentarium describes itself as a "science centre" where everybody can get a hands-on experience of the physics, biology and chemistry that shape our lives. Most of the exhibits – such as the Emotion Tester, which judges your reaction to pictures of fluffy kittens, naked men/women and sweaty feet – are great fun. There are also lectures giving simple explanations of scientific topics illustrated by down-to-earth experiments using things like bubbles and prisms. Further scientific demonstrations are conducted throughout the museum by guides (called "pilots"), who introduce you to processes ranging from cheese-making to dissection – you can even have a go at cutting up a cow's heart or lung yourself.

The suburbs

Copenhagen's suburbs are, unsurprisingly, relatively quiet and staid places, though there are a few attractions, along with a number of decent sandy beaches, parks and woodland areas, within easy reach of the city centre. To the north, the well-to-do seaside suburb of Charlottenlund has a strip of beach and is home to the **Danmarks Akvarium**, while Klampenborg's beach, Bellevue, is a favourite with trendy city folk, and the suburb is also home to **Bakken** amusement park and the excellent **Ordrupgaard** art museum. A short way inland is the idyllic **Frilandsmuseet** and the curious **Grundtvigs Kirke**, commemorating one of the nation's most celebrated priests and scholars. Southwest of the city you'll find the intriguing **Arken** museum of modern art, while to the southeast is the large island of **Amager**, with its boom town developments in the new suburb of **Ørestaden** and its pleasing mixture of beaches, parkland and nature reserve.

Charlottenlund

North of the centre, a twenty-minute S-Tog ride on line C or a forty-minute #14 bus ride past some of the country's most expensive real estate brings you to the snooty suburb of **Charlottenlund**. From the train station – walk up the station concourse and turn right – it's a ten-minute walk through woods to the immaculate lawns and tree-lined avenues of **Charlottenlund Palace**. (The bus drops you off on the coast road in front of the Akvarium, which means you'll miss the palace grounds.) Built for, and named after, Christian VI's sister Charlotte Amalie in 1731, the palace continued to house numerous royals until 1936, when it was donated to the Danish Ministry of Agriculture. You can't enter the palace but you're free to wander round the gorgeous, leafy gardens.

Charlottenlund's small sandy **beach** is heralded by a stretch of lawn with a small kiosk serving refreshments. To the right are the grass-covered remains of **Charlottenlund Fort**, Copenhagen's most northerly fortification from 1888, closed down in 1932, and now, with its few abandoned cannons and magnificent views, part of the excellent *Charlottenlund Fort* campsite (see p.144).

Back at the kiosk, a hundred metres or so to the north and across the road is the *Jorden Rundt Café* (see p.161), an excellent lunch stop.

Danmarks Akvarium

At the eastern edge of the palace gardens and just off the main coast road, Strandvejen, the **Danmarks Akvarium** (Danish Aquarium; daily: Feb–May, Sept & Oct 10am–5pm, Wed 10am–8pm; June–Aug 10am–6pm, Wed 10am–8pm; Nov–Jan 10am–4pm; 100kr; Ⓦwww.akvarium.dk), at Kavalergården 1, is home to

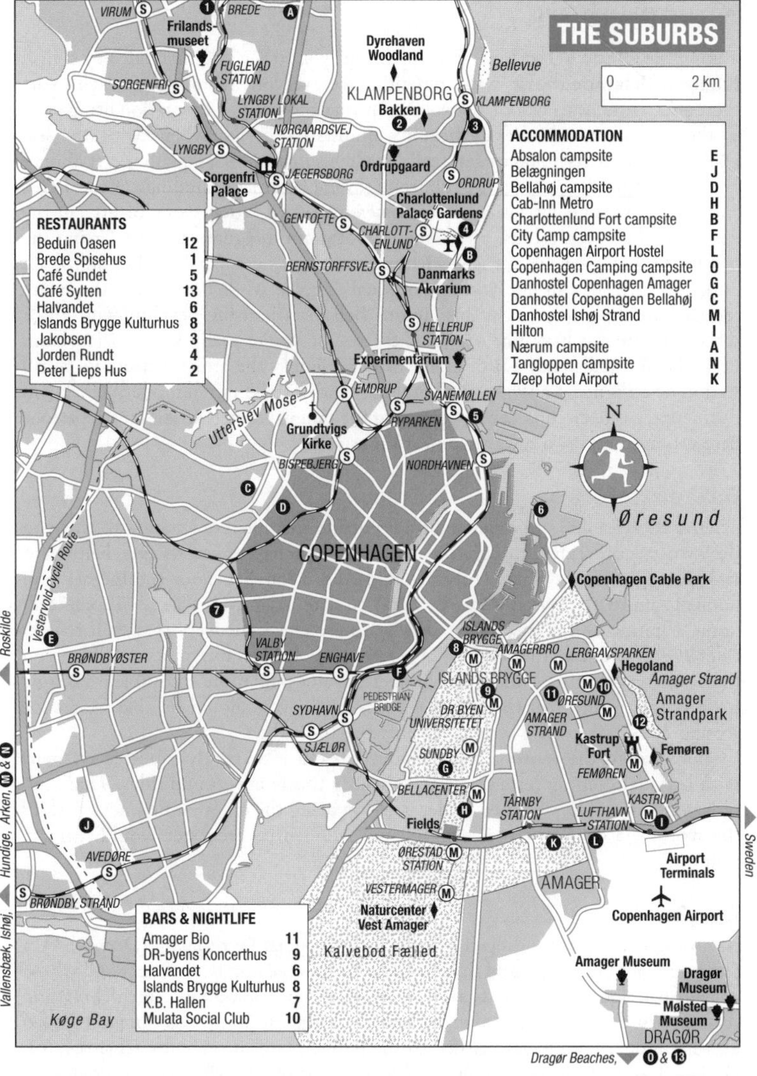

hundreds of species of fish, plus the usual supporting cast of crocodiles, turtles, frogs, octopus, squid and crustaceans. The highlight is the large tropical tank with its exotic collection of colourful creatures and rare corals, along with some sharks, eels and a vicious-looking shoal of piranhas; you can watch them and other inhabitants being fed at various times in the day (check at the desk as you come in). In the basement there are three **touch pools** where you get to handle native marine animals such as hermit crabs, plaice, shrimp and sea anemones. The aquarium is due to move to a spectacular, purpose-built building on the seafront in Amager (see p.109) in 2013; a model of the new building is on display in the foyer.

Klampenborg

Taking the C-line S-Tog to its last stop brings you to the wealthy and very stylish suburb of **Klampenborg**, with something for everyone from sandy beach to art museum to funfair to woodland walks. Turning right out of the station brings you to the very popular **Bellevue beach** – nudists to the left when facing the sea. Danish architect **Arne Jacobsen** really made his mark in Klampenborg, stamping his vision of modernism on the suburb in several landmark buildings of the 1930s and seeing through his vision of *Gesamtkunstwerk* or "total work of art" in the design of the beach cabins, refreshment booths and lifeguard towers. Facing the beach, the Bellevue Teatret and adjacent restaurant, also Jacobsen buildings, are both still furnished in line with his original designs, while beyond are the white terraced apartment blocks of his famous Bellavista housing development, all of whose apartments have fine views of the sea. If you're really keen on Jacobsen, head the short distance south along Strandvejen to the still-functioning petrol station he designed – a white-tiled building with a striking red modern clock and distinctive white circular canopy covering the pumps; there's an ice-cream parlour here too in summer to reward you for the trip.

Bakken

There's always a line of ponies and traps outside Klampenborg station to trot you the two-minute ride through the beautiful Dyrehaven woods (see below) to **Bakken** amusement park (July to mid-Aug Mon–Sat noon–midnight, Sun noon–11pm; late March–June & mid- to late Aug Mon–Sat 2–10pm, Sun noon–10pm; closing times vary in low season so check the website; pass for all 35 rides 199kr, end June to mid-Aug 219kr; Ⓦwww.bakken.dk) for a cool 80kr; you can easily walk it in five minutes so it's better value (and more enjoyable) to haggle for a longer round-trip through the park, which you should be able to get for around 150kr. Traps also wait at the entrance to Bakken.

Compared to the more genteel Tivoli, Bakken is a strictly blue-collar affair, with beer halls, cheap restaurants and cheerily trashy fairground rides. That said, it has a historic side – Bakken prides itself on being the oldest amusement park in the world – a claim the park's antiquated wooden rollercoaster would seem to bear out.

Dyrehaven

Almost entirely surrounding Bakken is the enormous **Dyrehaven** (Deer Park), a former royal hunting ground that is still home to large numbers of deer and whose ancient oak and beech woods are a wonderful spot for walking, picnicking and relaxing. In the middle of the park, and at its highest point, is a unique Rococo hunting lodge, Eremitagen (closed to the public), built in 1736 by Christian VI. Designed by Laurids de Thurah – also known for his contributions to Frederiksberg Slot (see p.121) and the first Christiansborg (see p.33) – this is considered his masterpiece and worth taking a few minutes to appreciate. Strolling back towards Klampenborg along Christianholmsvej, a left turn at the *Peter Lieps Hus* restaurant (see p.161) gives superb views over the Øresund.

Ordrupgaard

A two-kilometre walk west from Klampenborg station, or a short hop on bus #388 towards Lyngby (left out of the station and across the road), takes you to **Ordrupgaard** (Vilvordevej 10; Tues, Thurs & Fri 1–5pm, Wed 10am–6pm, Sat & Sun 11am–5pm; 70kr; Ⓦwww.ordrupgaard.dk), a delightful art museum occupying a 1918 country manor house on the southern edge of Dyrehaven. The curvy concrete extension, added in 2005, was designed by Zaha Hadid and does a pretty good job of blending in discreetly while surrendering none of its modernity. The museum holds the finest collection of **French Impressionist** art in northern Europe with works by Manet, Degas, Monet, Renoir, Pissarro and Sisley among others, all beautifully displayed in the purpose-built main gallery, and there's also a good cache of works by the **Barbizon School**, precursors of the Impressionists, with pieces by Corot and Daubigny. In the adjacent library, Gauguin (who had a Danish wife) is also well represented. Much of the original furniture remains in the house, which provides a fine backdrop to the collections of nineteenth-century **Danish art**, the walls hung with works by the greats of the Golden Age (see p.211) – rural scenes by Skovgaard and Lundbye, Italian scenes by Marstrand, and landscapes, including one of Dyrehaven, by Eckersberg. However, it's the still, monochrome canvases of Hammershøi, with their subtly lit, almost Vermeer-like interiors occupied by solitary dark figures, that most catch the eye. In 2005 the house (open weekends only) of founding father of Danish design, **Finn Juhl**, was added to the grounds; a great chance to see the simplicity and style of classic Danish design in situ. The beautiful grounds provide a suitably tranquil setting and there's an excellent café in the extension.

Frilandsmuseet and Brede Værk

Half an hour north of the city on bus #184 from Nørreport, or by B or B+ S-Tog lines to Sorgenfri station and then a ten-minute walk (turn right out of the station, then left onto Kongevej), is the rural idyll of the **Frilandsmuseet** (Open-air Museum; Easter to mid-Oct Tues–Sun 10am–5pm; free; Ⓦwww.natmus.dk), a wonderful mixture of heritage park and city farm spread across 86 acres of rolling countryside. Established on its present site in 1901 as part of the Nationalmuseet (it had previously been in Kongens Have next to Rosenborg), it displays around eighty beautifully preserved buildings dating back to the seventeenth century from across Denmark and its former territories in southern Sweden, northern Germany and the Faroe Islands. The ticket office provides a map of the lopsided cottages and farmsteads, which are grouped together according to region, and furnished according to various trades – bakers, potters, millers, blacksmiths and so on – offering a vivid picture of how rural communities lived in northern Europe in times past. The museum is also involved in an initiative to conserve Danish breeds of farm animals, and runs a number of events, with staff in period costume engaging in arts and crafts such as weaving and folk dancing.

At the far northern end of the museum, on I.C. Modewegs Vej, is the equally rewarding **Brede Værk** (Industrial Works of Brede; same hours; free; Ⓦwww.natmus.dk) – a large textile mill and factory that operated here from 1832 to 1956, powered by the adjacent Mølleåen river. It's now home to a fine museum, devoted partly to the history of the mill and factory and the local community it supported, and partly to the wider story of the industrialization of Denmark. All of the buildings, from the huge brick bulk of the factory itself to the dye works, workers' cottages, children's nursery (many of the workers in the mill were women) and craftsmen's houses are well preserved, and the museum works hard to bring history to life – the "Active Ticket" enables you to take part in games and activities as well as choosing a "virtual guide" from the past (a mill worker, manager or weaver) to show you around and take you through their day. Next to the factory, **Brede Manor**, the mill owner's grand Neoclassical residence (tours only; June–Aug Sun noon & 1.30pm; 50kr), reveals just how much wealth was made (for some) by the industry. Just beyond the works, the lovely *Brede Spisehus* (see p.161), with its veranda overlooking the small lake, is a beautiful spot for lunch. Brede train station is just opposite; you can catch a small, local train to Jægersborg from here (roughly every 20min), from where B and B+ S-Tog trains continue on to the city centre.

Grundtvigs Kirke and Utterslev Mose

Five kilometres north of the city centre in the suburb of Bispebjerg, and fifteen minutes by bus #6A or a ten-minute walk southwest from Emdrup S-Tog (A line), is the magnificent yellow-brick **Grundtvigs Kirke** (Pa Bjerget 14B; summer Mon–Sat 9am–4pm, Sun noon–4pm; winter until 1pm; Ⓦwww.grundtvigskirke.dk), overlooking the city from the top of Bispebjerg hill. It was designed in 1913 by Peder Vilhelm Jensen-Klint – father of Kaare Klint – as a monument to the Danish theologian and pedagogue N.F.S. Grundtvig (see box below). Resembling a kind of enormous church organ, with parallel yellow-brick buttresses running upwards, the church dwarfs the neighbouring housing, also designed by Klint father and son and built using similar motifs. Inside the church, the cavernous, unadorned space and large, high windows provide a suitably reverential atmosphere, with wonderful acoustics and beautiful natural lighting.

About 1km west of the church – head along På Berget and then Mosesvinget – is the large lake and park of **Utterslev Mose**, an excellent place for biking, walking, sunbathing and picnics. The park stretches about 3km west to the old outer defences at Husum.

Arken

Situated 20km southwest of the city centre on a beautiful windswept beach near the suburb of Ishøj is the stunning **Arken** museum of modern art (Tues & Thurs–Sun 10am–5pm, Wed 10am–9pm; 85kr; Ⓦwww.arken.dk). The obscure location

N.F.S. Grundtvig and the Folkehøjskole

Although less well known internationally than his contemporaries Søren Kierkegaard and Hans Christian Andersen, **N.F.S. Grundtvig** (1783–1872) left the most indelible mark on Danish history and culture. As a man given to manic bouts of frenzied activity – he is still the most prolific Danish author ever, penning tomes on world history, Norse mythology and theology, as well as poetry – Grundtvig forged a career as a Lutheran pastor and scholar, developing the grand humanist vision that would go on to shape almost every aspect of Danish cultural and social life. To many, his lasting legacy was the establishment of the uniquely Danish **Folkehøjskole** (People's High School) system, with residential colleges for adults offering courses in arts, crafts and, more recently, computers and the media. In these schools, Grundtvig's philosophy of equality, democracy, participation and the pursuit of knowledge was put into practice. The first school opened in 1844, and they soon spread throughout the country and abroad. One of the main principles of the Folkehøjskole is to provide an education that eschews the usual authoritarian teacher–pupil relationship in favour of shared experience and knowledge. Schools also avoid competitiveness (there are no exams) and vocational training – the aim is to produce rounded human beings rather than good little workers. If you're interested in attending one, contact the International People's College in Helsingør (Montebello Allé 1, 3000 Helsingør Ⓣ49 21 33 61, Ⓦwww.ipc.dk), one of the few places in Denmark where courses are taught in English. They run a variety of courses varying in length from eight to twenty-two weeks.

– take S-Tog line A or E to Ishøj station, and then bus #128 c... museum – seems almost wilfully perverse for a museum that aspires to be... nationally recognized showcase for contemporary art, but it's worth the trip.

The museum opened in 1996, its design the result of an open competition wo... by young Danish architecture student Søren Robert Lund. His deconstructivist creation – much criticized at the time for detracting from the art itself – pays homage to the maritime location, its intersecting white planes, angles and curves resembling some strange shipwrecked liner – a striking sight when seen from across the dunes. The focus is on art from the 1940s onwards though the bulk of the works are post 1990 and by Nordic artists. Naturally, the big Danish names are here – a series of Asger Jorn's large, colourful canvases adorn the foyer and there are also works by Per Kirkeby among others – though seminal figures such as Jean Arp, co-founder of the Dada group, also get a look in. Contemporary giants of the art world are also represented, including Jeff Koons and **Damien Hirst**, who gets a room to himself with ten works on his favourite existential themes. The museum also holds excellent temporary exhibitions. On the first floor, the restaurant has stunning views over the bay.

While in the area, take the time to explore the beachfront of **Strandparken** running for roughly 7km between the two harbours of Brøndby and Hundige. The ecology of this fabulous man-made stretch of predominantly reclaimed coastline ranges from windblown salt meadow and heather-covered dunes popular with migratory seabirds to artificial islands and fine sandy beaches. This is also the site of the stunningly located *Tangloppen* campsite (see p.145), halfway along the beach and a few hundred metres from Arken. At the park's eastern end, just behind Brøndby harbour, the Vestervoldkanal runs out into the sea. The canal is all that remains of the city's outer rampart ring from 1888 and continues inland – a cycle path runs along its length – in a semicircle for 14km all the way to Utterslev Mose (see opposite).

Amager

Just southeast of the city centre, and connected to it by a series of lifting bridges, is the large island of **Amager** (pronounced "Ama"). Although within walking distance of the city, the area feels quite separate, and the locals – the so-called "Ama'rkaner" (a play on the word "American") – have a reputation for being rougher and tougher than their "mainland" counterparts. Ever-increasing transport links, however, are closing the gap (psychological and physical) between the city and the island; in particular, the **Øresunds Bridge** (see p.126), connecting Copenhagen – via Kastrup and Copenhagen airport on Amager – to Malmö in Sweden, has had a dramatic effect, along with the new metro network that has made a large chunk of Amager accessible by fast public transport.

Islands Brygge

Crossing Langebro from HC Andersens Boulevard and Rådhuspladsen (metro stop Islands Brygge) brings you to the harbour strip of **Islands Brygge**, just south of Christianshavn. Named after the first passenger ferries from Iceland that docked here in the early twentieth century, Islands Brygge was, until the mid-1980s, a working industrial harbour, and off limits to the public; nowadays, however, it is one of the most popular places to hang out on hot summer days. Just next to the bridge, the popular Islands Brygge Harbour Pool (see p.194) marks the start of **Havneparken** – a grassy strip following the coastline for approximately 400m and a pleasant spot to laze in the sun. It also features **Islands Brygges Kulturhus** (see p.161), the local cultural centre, which hosts bands and entertainment year-round.

…centre's laid-back waterfront café/restaurant you can look …evelopments on Kalvebod Brygge on the opposite bank of … along the promenade lining the harbour's edge, the upside-…d wooden ferry on two poles provides cover for Havneparken's … the park's landmark.

…eparken, still on the waterfront, are some of Copenhagen's most …dential developments. A sleek new pedestrian and cycling bridge …aven over to the Havneholmen, and provides a quick route to V… …ypassing the city centre.

Ørestad

Continuing south from Islands Brygge metro station – and pretty much following the route of the metro line – you will come to the largest of Copenhagen's recent developments, the **Ørestad**. Running through the area, the new metro line was initially funded by money raised by selling off the military land that the area sits on. Since then, huge modern residential and commercial developments have cropped up along its route, all exquisitely executed, none of them cheap – and many still empty. One good way to get an impression of the area is to take the metro from Islands Brygge to its terminus at Vestamager. Watch out for the snazzy new **DR-Byen national television centre**, which houses all Denmark's national radio and television activities under one roof and is divided into four segments connected by an internal walkway. One segment in particular stands out, the extraordinary 26,000-square-metre amphitheatre-style concert hall, covered in a cobalt-blue light-penetrating metal screen that shows images from within whenever concerts (see p.171) are playing. Further south, just before crossing the motorway to the airport, is northern Europe's biggest shopping mall, **Fields** (see p.187), built in anticipation of the seventy thousand or so residents that the developers hope will one day call this area home. Next door is one of the city's newest hotels, *Cab-Inn Metro* (see p.142), with its sleek facade designed by Daniel Libeskind (of Ground Zero in New York).

Kalvebod Fælled

Amager's other big draw is the enormous **Kalvebod Fælled** nature reserve. At 2000 hectares, it is not only remarkable for its proximity to the city but it is also an excellent venue for hiking, cycling, horse riding and birdwatching. Reclaimed from the sea during World War II in an effort to create work for unemployed Danes who might otherwise have been deported to Germany, it's now home to an amazing number of predatory birds, including kestrels, blue hawks and buzzards. Until recently, the reserve was a military firing range, and as large areas are still being cleared for potentially explosive debris, it's strongly recommended that you stick to the marked paths.

The **Naturcenter Vestamager**, at the fringe of the reserve, offers **free bike rental** between May and October (call ⓣ35 52 04 03 to book in advance – a good idea during school holidays) and free camping for two nights in designated shelter sites. You can also ride Icelandic ponies with Frederiksens-Isheste (ⓣ60 14 08 44; 150kr per hr). The centre is signed, a short ten minutes' walk from the Vestamager metro station.

Amager Strandpark

Along its eastern coastline, the **beach** area known as Amager Strandpark (ⓦwww.amager-strand.dk) is another big attraction, endowed with three metro stops – Øresund, Amager Strand and Femøren – from north to south. Encompassing a two-kilometre-long artificial island of beautiful, soft sandy beaches connected to the mainland by three short bridges, it's heaving in summer – on a par with the beaches to the north of the city (see p.106) – and has become a regular beach party venue. Facing Sweden across the Øresund and with the Øresunds Bridge to the south, the island's bunker-like, concrete structures, housing free toilets and showers, also give excellent views. Between the island and Amager "mainland" there's a shallow lagoon, ideal for kids, and offering kite surfing, wind surfing, kayaking and other watersports (see p.193), and on the southern end of the island there's a covered market area with a couple of good cafés (see p.160) and popular beach clubs (see p.171). At the northern end of the mainland beach, where Øresundsvej meets Amager Strandvej, the beautifully restored traditional wooden public bathing pier – **Helgoland Søbadeanstalt** – offers free changing facilities and showers (June–Aug 10am–6pm). The pier has three sections: a communal section, where swimwear is obligatory, and two separate male and female nudist sections. At the southern end of the beach, **Kastrup Søbad** (same hours; free) has a five-metre-high trampoline that provides a fabulous launch pad into the water.

Behind the section of the coast called **Femøren** – where during summer weekends music-lovers come in their thousands to inexpensive open-air rock concerts – you'll find **Kastrup Fort**, a remnant of the city's fortification from 1886 that never came into use. During World War II the occupying German army moved in and incarcerated deserters here – the bullet holes in the concrete walls bear witness to the executions that took place.

Dragør

South of Amager Strandpark, on the other side of Copenhagen airport in the southeastern corner of Amager, lies the atmospheric cobblestoned fishing village of **Dragør** (bus #30 from Rådhuspladsen, #350S from Nørreport Station),

▲ Dragør harbour

which, until the opening of the Øresunds Bridge (see p.126), was the departure point for ferries to Sweden. It now mainly survives on tourism and the high incomes of its city-commuting inhabitants – properties in Dragør do not come cheap. Apart from meandering around the quaint streets and lazing on the peaceful south coast beaches, you could check out the couple of good local history museums. The summer-only **Dragør Museum** (May–Sept Tues–Sun noon–4pm; 20kr), by Dragør harbour, is devoted to the maritime history of the village from the thirteenth-century herring trade to the arrival of the Dutch in the early sixteenth century. Docked outside is the *Elisabeth K571* fishing boat, which was used to transport Danish Jews across to Sweden during World War II (see box, p.42); a display gives a full account of the event. Also on the harbour, the *Dragør Røgeri* smokehouse (Easter – Christmas Fri–Sun 10am–3pm) is a great place to stock up on seafood delicacies – not least the fresh fishballs on rye bread which can be munched on benches outside. In the centre of the old village on Dr Dichs Plads, **Mølsteds Museum** (May–Aug Sat & Sun noon–4pm; free) displays paintings by local celebrity Christian Mølsted (1862–1930), known for his atmospheric and colourful land- and seascapes.

The **Amager Museum** (May–Sept Tues–Sun noon–4pm; Oct–April Sun noon–4pm; 30kr), at Store Magleby village on the road leading back to Copenhagen, is housed in two of Amager's old four-winged farmhouses. In the early sixteenth century, Christian II invited a group of farmers from Holland – at the time, a more agriculturally advanced nation than Denmark – to settle here to produce food for the royal household. Twenty-four families arrived, and their descendants stayed for three centuries, continuing to live in the Store Magleby and Dragør area and leaving only for their weekly trips to the Amagertorv market in Indre By. Among their many achievements they were responsible for introducing the carrot to Denmark. The museum comprises two working farms, their interiors kept as they would have been at the time.

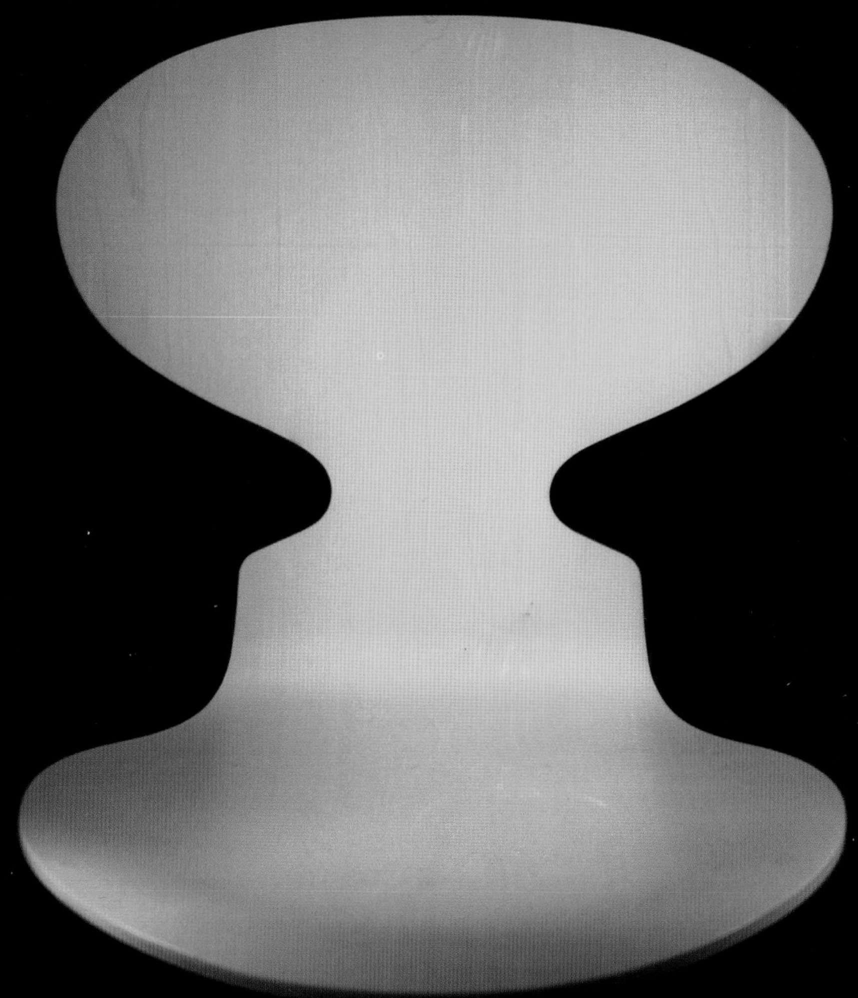

Danish design

The Danes' love affair with design has been going on for a century, its guiding principle – the successful merging of form and function – seen in the capital today in everything from chairs through Bang & Olufsen electronics to the new metro system. Core to the Danish attitude to design is the relationship between the user and the product – the ultimate aim to produce an object that both fulfils its function and is at the same time aesthetically appealing.

Georg Jensen pitcher ▲

Designer Zoo ▼

Gift shop at Dansk Design Center ▲

Designer chairs ▼

Interiors and furniture

Danish designers have always been driven by a democratic, social ideal that good design is a right, as essential in the home as in public arenas. Pioneers of the 1920s such as **Poul Henningsen** and **Kaare Klint** got the ball rolling with their classic designs; the former, depressed by the dreary lighting in most homes, set about designing lamps that transformed rooms with their effective, subtle distribution of light, while the latter reworked furniture design classics for modern needs. But it wasn't until the 1940s and 1950s that Danish design became an international phenomenon with the work of creative visionaries such as **Hans J. Wegner**, who took chair design to new heights with such classics as the Round Chair (1949); interiors and furniture designer **Finn Juhl**, who furnished parts of the UN building in New York; the prolific **Arne Jacobsen**; and **Børge Mogensen**, who went so far as to calculate the average dimensions of household objects and find out how many of each the average person owned in a quest to design the perfect storage system. Danish design soon became synonymous with outstanding craftsmanship, innovative style, pared-down simplicity and purity of line – a combination that has driven design principles ever since. The torch was carried from there on by the likes of **Verner Panton**, with his more futuristic moulded plastic chairs in bright, bold colours, and **Poul Kjærholm**, whose steel-framed chairs have also become timeless classics. The work of these design icons can still be bought in shops throughout the city, either original pieces or new versions made under licence – unsurprisingly neither comes cheap – while cutting-edge shops like Normann and Hay (see opposite) showcase exciting new work.

Arne Jacobsen

For many, the Copenhagen-born architect/designer **Arne Jacobsen** (1902–71) epitomizes the best in Danish design. Still revered, copied, exhibited and coveted, classic "AJ" designs pervade the city's shops, cafés, restaurants and hotels, and the skyline itself. Espousing the modernist idea of **Gesamtkunstwerk** or "total work of art", he turned his hand to everything from furniture to cutlery to buildings, a vision at its most ideologically complete in the swish **Radisson Blu Royal Hotel** (see p.139), for which he designed everything from the door handles to the high-rise building itself. However, it's probably for his iconic **chairs** that he is best remembered: the "Number 7", the "Ant" (a groundbreaking plastic, armless chair with an insect-like nipped-in waist), the "Swan" and the "Egg" – the last two designed specifically for the hotel and famous for their natural, curvy shapes that suggest the presence of the human form even in its absence.

▲ Shopping at Hay

▼ Radisson Blu Royal Hotel

Top design spots

▸▸ **Dansk Arkitektur Center** Temporary exhibitions and an excellent bookshop. See p.56.

▸▸ **Dansk Design Center** The country's showcase for cutting-edge design exhibitions. See p.82.

▸▸ **Illums Bolighus**, **Hay**, **Normann** and **Paustian** Hit the shops for a taste of the latest in Danish design. For more on shopping for design, see p.184.

▸▸ **Klampenborg** Some of the best of Jacobsen's architecture lives in this nearby suburb. See p.106.

▸▸ **Kunstindustrimuseet** Excellent exhibition on twentieth-century design. See p.73.

▼ Exhibition at the Dansk Design Center

Skuespilhus ▲

Den Sorte Diamant ▼

Operaen ▼

Architecture

The most famous Danish-designed structure – Jørn Utzon's Sydney Opera House – may be on the other side of the world, but the current generation of home-grown architects are building on the country's rich architectural tradition to create inspiring waterfront landmarks in Copenhagen itself. The combination of natural materials and forms with cutting-edge techniques remains foreground: the exteriors of two modern masterpieces – **Den Sorte Diamant** (Schmidt, Hammer & Lassen; 1996) and **Operaen** (Henning Larsen; 2005) – may be forbidding glass-and-steel visions of functional simplicity, but their interiors are organic, human spaces, with tiers of wave-like, wood-floored balconies in the former and a curved maplewood-enclosed auditorium in the latter. This philosophy extends to industrial design; the driver-less **metro** system is a model of functional simplicity – skylights in stations shed natural light onto platforms while the trains have wide, spacious carriages with wall-mounted seats to allow for easy cleaning of the floors. Danish designers are also pioneering the ecological dimensions of design – the stunning **Skuespilhus** (Boje Lundgaard & Lene Tranberg, 2008), housing the Royal Theatre, uses energy-saving heating and cooling systems, ingeniously converting the body heat from the previous night's audience into liquid form and reusing it as underfloor heating, and recycling the water from the adjacent harbour to cool the building. The **DR-Byen** national TV and radio centre was also designed, in part, by Danish architects (Vilhelm Lauritzen Arkiteckter, 2009), though its stunning concert hall, clad in a screen that shows images from within, is the work of the French Jean Nouvel.

Out of the city

The area around Copenhagen is steeped in history, with a plethora of castles, museums and sites of natural beauty offering a huge range of opportunities for day-trips or longer stays, and all easily accessible on fast public transport links from Copenhagen's Central Station. Heading **north** up the coast, you can stop off at the **Karen Blixen Museum** or the excellent collection of modern art at **Louisiana**, before continuing on to **Helsingør**, with its magnificent castle of *Hamlet* fame, from where it's just a short side-trip to a string of villages and fantastic beaches along the north coast. Nearby, inland, is the grand **Frederiksborg Slot** in the town of Hillerød, while, to the west of the city, is the unmissable ancient Danish capital of **Roskilde**, with its fascinating Viking ship museum and impressive Domkirke – burial place of Danish royalty since the Reformation.

You needn't confine yourself to Denmark on your day-trips: the southern Swedish medieval town of **Malmö** is within easy reach across the Øresunds Bridge; once Denmark's most important city after Copenhagen, this historic regional capital has the museum-packed **Malmöhus castle** as its main attraction, and a pleasant, strollable centre bustling with Copenhageners looking for bargains.

North Zealand

The **coast north of Copenhagen**, as far as Helsingør, rejoices under the tag of the "Danish Riviera", a label that neatly describes its line of tiny one-time fishing hamlets, now inhabited almost exclusively by the wealthy. It's best seen on the hour-long bus journey (#388) north to Helsingør from Klampenborg, itself the last stop on line C of the S-Tog system. There's also a frequent fifty-minute train service between Copenhagen and Helsingør; it's quicker than the bus, but you won't see much, since views are obscured by trees almost the entire way. Heading inland from the north coast takes you past Hillerød, home of the stunning Frederiksborg Slot and Museum of National History, precariously positioned across three small islands on an artificial lake. Transport to Hillerød from Helsingør and the north coast is limited to slow regional trains, one line heading south from Gilleleje and one southwest from Helsingør.

Karen Blixen Museum

A visit to the **Karen Blixen Museum** (May–Sept Tues–Sun 10am–5pm; Oct–April Wed–Fri 1–4pm, Sat & Sun 11am–4pm; 50kr; Ⓦwww.karen-blixen.dk), 25km north of Copenhagen at Rungsted Strandvej 111, is easily combined with a

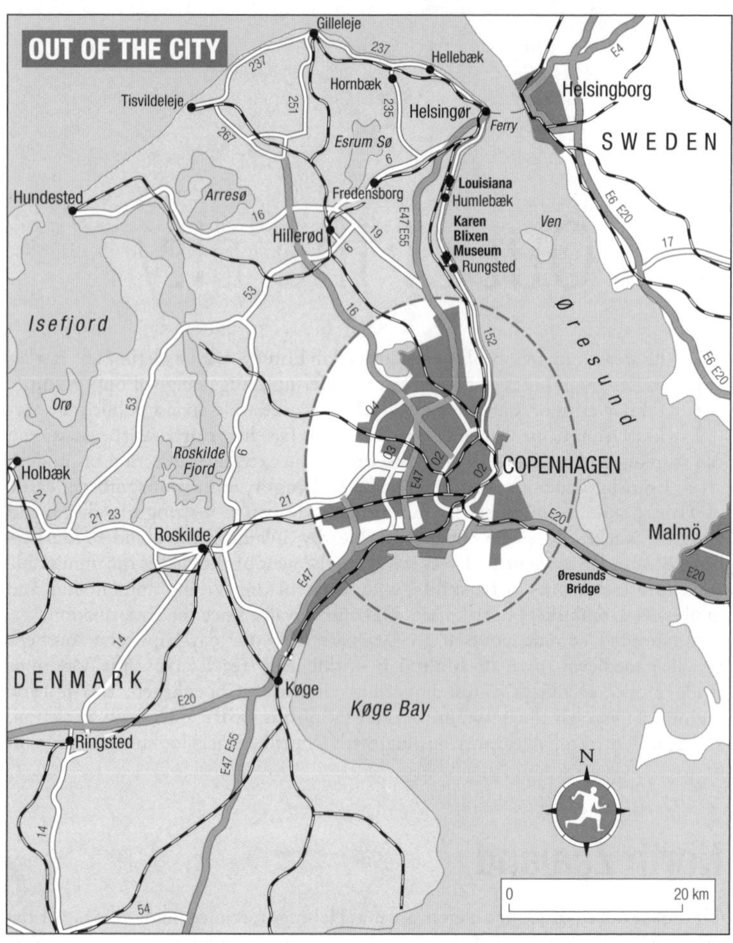

trip further up the coast to Louisiana and Helsingør. The museum is housed in the family home of the writer who, while long a household name in Denmark for her short stories (often written under the pen name of Isak Dinesen) and outspoken opinions, enjoyed a resurgence of international popularity in the mid-1980s when the film *Out of Africa* – based on her 1937 autobiographical account of running a coffee plantation in Kenya and her love affair with the dashing English hunter Denys Finch-Hatton – won seven Oscars. Often nominated for the Nobel Prize for Literature, she never actually won it; Ernest Hemingway, on winning the award in 1954, said it should have gone to her.

Blixen lived in the house after her return from Africa in 1931 until her death in 1962, and much of it is maintained as it was during her final years. Upstairs, a small exhibition describes her eventful life – her father committed suicide and she married the twin brother of the man she loved, among other things – amply illustrated with glamorous photos of her with various celebrities, while exhibits include a collection of first editions and the tiny typewriter she used in Africa. The

living quarters (timed admission) feature a short film of her life and work, a gallery showing a collection of her paintings and drawings (she was an accomplished artist but dropped out of art school in her late teens) and several rooms with furniture, personal effects and photographs, including many of Denys Finch-Hatton, left as they were when she died. The light-filled study at the end is where she wrote most of her books, surrounded by mementos of her time in Kenya and with lovely views out to sea. The museum is backed by delightful woodlands, established as a **bird sanctuary** by Blixen, and also her final resting place – a simple **grave** beneath a huge beech tree. The ticket office can provide a map of the grounds and you can follow the path back on to Rungstedvej, from where it's five minutes' walk back to the station.

The closest station is Rungsted Kyst, on the *regionaltog* line, from where it's a fifteen-minute walk to the house – turn left out of the station, right onto Rungstedvej, then right at the harbour, from where the house is signposted – or a short ride on bus #388. Bus #388 also makes the longer ten-kilometre journey from Klampenborg S-Tog station.

Louisiana Museum of Modern Art

Situated in Humlebæk, a coastal village three train stops before Helsingør, **Louisiana Museum of Modern Art** (Tues–Fri 11am–10pm, Sat & Sun 11am–6pm; 90kr; ⓦwww.louisiana.dk) is a compelling mixture of unusual architecture and outstanding modern art in a wonderful setting on the Øresund coast. The superbly displayed and wide-ranging **permanent collection** – divided between the museum buildings and the sculpture garden outside – reflects most of the important art movements of the second half of the twentieth century.

The entrance is through a nineteenth-century villa, beyond which a modern extension opens into a twisting (and sometimes confusing) sequence of glass corridors that trace a roughly circular shape through various airy yet intimate gallery spaces. All the way round, the galleries offer stunning views out over the gardens and interact with sculptures outside. Start walking clockwise around the gallery, through a section usually given over to temporary exhibits, to reach a tall, purpose-built gallery that houses one of the museum's highlights – a striking collection of **Giacometti's** gaunt bronze figures together with many of his original sketches. A little further on is the museum's outstanding collection of works by the **CoBrA** movement (named after the cities of Copenhagen, Brussels and Amsterdam), a left-wing collective of artists formed in 1948 and characterized by their distinctive and colourful abstracts – there are works by Appel, Corneille and Heerup and a whole room devoted to the characteristically tortured abstracts of Asger Jorn, one of Denmark's most renowned artists. You'll also find small rooms dedicated to the bright, Constructivist works of Rodchenko and Delaunay, with their straight lines and simple colours, and large spaces filled with German artist Anselm Kiefer's energetic canvases. There's also a good representation of **Pop Art**, with works by Warhol, Rauschenberg, Robert Ryman and Lichtenstein providing the backdrop to Claes Oldenburg's models of oversized cigarette butts and a lunchbox, and Jim Dine's stark *White Bathroom*. **Contemporary art** is also well represented, boosted by the recent acquisition of *A Closer Grand Canyon* by David Hockney, a *Maman* spider by Louise Bourgeois and works by Sam Taylor-Wood, Jonathan Meese, Doug Aitken and video artists Gary Hill and Bill Viola, among others.

The grounds **outside overlook** an old harbour, the small copses and lawns scattered with around sixty pieces of world-class sculpture, some of it specifically designed for this site. Here you'll find the flat, abstract sculptures of Alexander Calder rubbing shoulders with Max Ernst's surreal creations, and Henry Moore's dramatic *Bronze Woman* perched on a small hill, with the Øresund and distant Sweden providing a stunning backdrop. Louisiana also has an imaginative **children's wing** (see p.201), and regular **concerts** of chamber music and solo recitals are held in the Concert Hall, often featuring internationally renowned performers (see the website for details). The excellent **café** offers lovely food and sea views.

Louisiana is on the northern edge of Humlebæk, at Gammel Strandvej 13; it's a short signposted walk from the train station, or bus #388 stops right outside.

Helsingør

Some 45km north of Copenhagen and just 45 minutes on the *regionaltog* from Copenhagen, **HELSINGØR** is strategically positioned on the four-kilometre strip of water linking the North Sea and the Baltic, facing the Swedish town of Helsingborg on the opposite coast. The town's wealth was founded on the Sound Toll of 1429, which was levied on passing ships right up until the nineteenth century, when shipbuilding restored some of Helsingør's fortunes after the toll was abolished. Today, it's the ferries crossing to and from Sweden that account for most of the town's livelihood, with boatloads of Swedes taking advantage of the easily accessible (and relatively cheap) booze, though the local economy is also significantly bolstered by the many visitors who come each year to see the mighty Kronborg Slot.

Kronborg Slot

Tactically placed on a sandy curl of land extending seawards into the Øresund, the **Kronborg Slot** (April & Oct–Dec Tues–Sun 11am–4pm; May–Sept daily

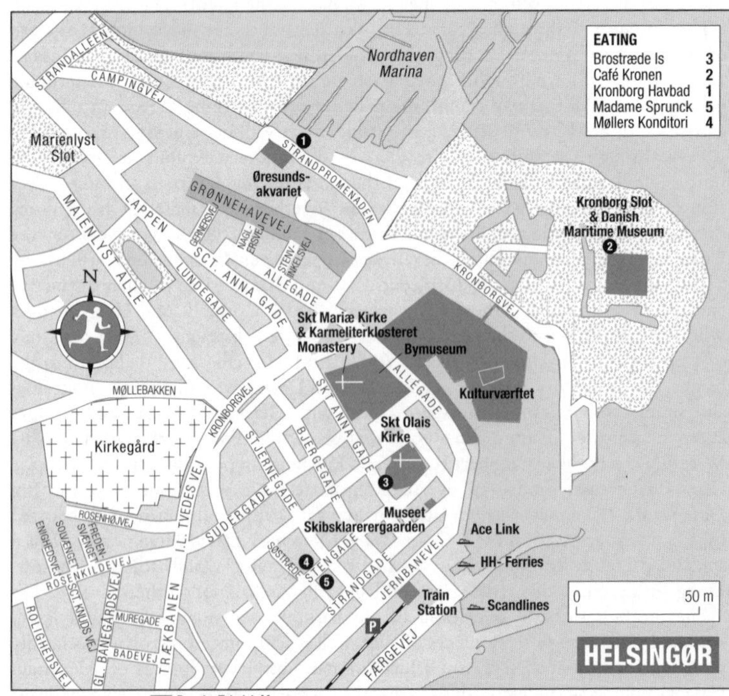

10.30am–5pm; Jan–March Tues–Sun 11am–3pm; 65kr, joint ticket with Handels og Søfartsmuseet 90kr; Ⓦwww.kronborg.dk), a fifteen-minute walk from the train station, dominates Helsingør. Famous principally as the setting – under the name of Elsinore Castle – for Shakespeare's *Hamlet*, it's still uncertain whether the playwright actually ever visited Helsingør (see box, p.118), but the association endures in Kronborg's thriving trade in *Hamlet* souvenirs and the annual staging of the play in the castle grounds – a tradition started in 1816. In 2000, the castle was awarded UNESCO World Heritage Site status and a ten-year project was initiated to restore the building to the height of its glory; be prepared for a little disruption in some rooms due to ongoing work. **Guided tours** of the royal chambers take place in English daily at 11.30am and 1.30pm, and well-informed attendants also hover in every room ready to answer questions.

Constructed in the fifteenth century by **Erik of Pomerania**, the fortress of Krogen was for hundreds of years the key to control of the Øresund (Helsingborg on the other side of the strait was also under Danish rule), enabling the Danish monarchs to extract a toll from every ship that passed through it. During the sixteenth century, **Frederik II** rebuilt (and renamed) the castle as a splendid Renaissance palace with sumptuous interiors, commissioning Dutch architect Antonius Van Opbergen, who took his ideas from the Dutch Renaissance buildings of Antwerp. Upon completion in 1585 it stood in all its grandeur as the largest castle in northern Europe and its international reputation soon caught Shakespeare's ear. However, in 1629, during the reign of Frederik's son, **Christian IV**, the castle was largely destroyed by a massive fire – only the royal chapel survived – and the cost of rebuilding it would have bankrupted the struggling Danish state had Christian IV not doubled the Sound Toll. Christian's castle had lavish Baroque interiors – liberally sprinkled with his distinctive monogram – though he opted to rebuild the exterior to the same Renaissance style. His enjoyment of the castle (supposedly his favourite) was short-lived; just twenty years after the fire, the hapless fortress was bombarded and overrun by the Swedes, who carted off most of its treasures. Over the next three centuries, the castle was largely given over to military use, being deemed too uncomfortable for the royals – in 1924, the military moved out and a major restoration programme began.

Even now, as you enter the castle via a series of gates, bridges, moats, earthen ramparts and brick defences, you get a sense of its former power, with antique cannons pointing menacingly out across the narrow sound. Crossing over the final bridge, you go through the forbidding Dark Gate, to the small forecourt and castle courtyard. The main keep is rather ornate, with plenty of Renaissance features, two spindly towers roofed with green copper jutting out into the usually blustery sky, and another tower providing a fully functioning lighthouse. The **interior** isn't as grand as you might expect: white walls and wood floors long ago replaced the more lavish gilt-leather wall cladding and black-and-white floor tiles, and the furniture, though beautiful, is rather sparse. That said, the rooms are still impressive: the second floor houses the **private apartments**, with the King's Chamber and Queen's Chamber adorned with magnificent fireplaces and fine, circular ceiling paintings. On the third floor, the **ballroom**, at 62m, is the longest hall in northern Europe and a stunning space, though sadly lacking most of its original features. The paintings hanging along its length are from a series commissioned by Christian IV for Rosenborg Slot (see p.66); fourteen splendid tapestries woven in 1590 and part of a series depicting Danish kings once decorated the ballroom during festivities, seven of them are now on display in the **Little Hall**. In the **Corner Room** – part of the guest suite of James VI of Scotland (later James I of England) and his wife, who was Christian IV's sister – you can see the original flooring that was once laid throughout the castle. From here on, it's a lighter,

Kronborg and Hamlet

The origins of the story of a tragic Danish prince stretch back far beyond Shakespearean times. The earliest mention of a character called **Amled** can be found in a story, derived from Icelandic and Celtic sagas, written around 1200 by one of Bishop Absalon's scribes, a certain Saxo Grammaticus. An Elizabethan version of the Hamlet story, thought to have been written by **Thomas Kyd**, had already appeared on the London stage twenty years before Shakespeare's *Hamlet* was produced in 1602. Quite how the semi-mythical Danish prince and the very real Danish castle became connected isn't entirely clear, though it's probable that Elizabethan England got wind of Kronborg from sailors who had passed through the Øresund, returning with stories of the mist-shrouded fortress that subsequently metamorphosed into Shakespeare's Elsinore. Another vague theory has it that Shakespeare spent part of his so-called lost years, between 1585 and 1592, in Kronborg rather than in Spain as was previously believed.

brighter affair in the series of panelled and stuccoed eighteenth-century chambers of Frederik V.

Be sure to see the beautiful **Chapel**, directly across the courtyard from the ticket office: the only part of the castle to survive the fire of 1629, its elaborate and colourful carving, at its zenith in the royal pew opposite the pulpit, gives an idea of the richness of the castle's original Renaissance interiors. An altogether gloomier atmosphere pervades the dark, labyrinthine **casemates** (cellars; guided tours daily 11am & 1pm) where the body of Holger Danske, a mythical hero from the legends of Charlemagne, is said to lie, ready to wake again when Denmark needs him – although the Viking-style statue depicting the legend detracts somewhat from the cellars' authentic aura of decay. For the time being the castle also houses the **Handels og Søfartsmuseet** (Danish Maritime Museum; same hours as the castle; 50kr; joint ticket with Kronborg Slot 90kr; Ⓦwww.maritime-museum.dk), a well-displayed jaunt through the history of Danish seafaring up to the modern-day domination by the Maersk shipping dynasty, featuring what is reputedly the world's oldest ship's biscuit, ship figureheads of busty Viking maidens, and the usual nautical trinkets and paintings. There are interesting sections on the Sound Toll, the Danish East India Company and the valuable work of the ice-breaking ship *SS Storebjørn* from 1922, whose lovely wood-panelled officers' saloon, complete with table laid for dinner, is a sight to behold. A huge (and pricey) new development in the former boatyard area, entitled Kulturværftet (culture yard), is due to be completed in 2012. The area will house a multitude of cultural institutions including a theatre and library; as part of this development, the Søfartsmuseum is going to move into the former dry docks. Until then, a large section of the harbour area will be cordoned off, but you will still be able to take a stroll along the **coastal batteries** for views over the Sound, open from sunrise to sunset.

The Town

Helsingør itself is a lively town with a well-preserved **medieval quarter**. At its heart is the bustling pedestrianized main street, **Stengade**, linked by a number of narrow alleyways lined with rickety half-timbered houses, to **Axeltorv**, the town's small market square (markets are held April–Nov on Wed, Fri & Sat mornings) and a good spot to linger over a beer. Near the corner of Stengade and Skt Anna Gade is the town's cathedral, the red-brick, copper-spired **Skt Olai's Kirke** (daily: May–Aug 10am–4pm; Sept–April 10am–2pm), extensively remodelled and expanded over the centuries from its humble origins as a Romanesque church founded in 1200. Inside, the white walls set off the run of dark portraits of past rectors, en route to the fussily ornate white and gold altar. Just beyond is the fifteenth-century **Skt Mariæ Kirke** (daily: mid-June to mid-Sept 10am–3pm; mid-Sept to mid-June 10am–2pm) with its pretty red-brick cloister, and the adjacent **Karmeliterklosteret** (guided tour only, summer daily 2pm; 20kr), the best-preserved medieval monastery in Scandinavia. Erik of Pomerania gave the site to Carmelite monks in 1430; following the Reformation, in 1541, the monastery was turned into a hospital for the old and poor, during which time it prided itself on its brain operations. The unnerving tools of this profession are still on show next door, at Skt Anna Gade 36, in the **Bymuseum** (Town Museum; Tues–Fri & Sun noon–4pm, Sat 10am–4pm; 20kr), an otherwise rather dry trawl (no English labelling) through Helsingør's history. You'll get a better sense of what the town was all about at the **Museet Skibsklarerergaarden** (Shipping Agent's House; Tues–Fri noon–4pm, Sat 10am–2pm; 30kr), on Strandgade 91, a gorgeous eighteenth-century building once occupied by agents responsible for collecting the Sound Toll. The rooms have been reconstructed much as they were during the last days of the toll (it was abolished in 1857) and there's also a shop done out in period style – now selling a motley selection of treats and trinkets.

There's not much else to keep you in town; those with kids might want to walk ten minutes north of the centre to the harbour at Strandpromenaden 5, where the **Øresundsakvariet** (Øresund Aquarium; June–Aug daily 10am–5pm; Sept–May Mon–Fri 10am–4pm, Sat & Sun 10am–5pm; 55kr; Ⓦwww.oresundsakvariet.ku.dk) is home to a collection of local sea critters, some of which can be approached close up in the "touch basin". A further fifteen minutes' walk northwest out of town (continue to the end of Skt Anna Gade and follow the signs straight ahead), the stately Neoclassical pile of **Marienlyst Slot** (daily noon–4pm; 30kr) was built in the eighteenth century as a royal summer residence – ideally situated to make the most of the cooling sea breezes and stunning views. There's not much to see in the Louis XVI-style interior; the rooms are largely devoid of furniture with just the odd gilt mirror and chandelier to set the tone, but the collection of paintings, most of local seascapes and the brooding Kronborg over the centuries, are wonderfully atmospheric and include a few by Golden Age painter C.W. Eckersberg. You can walk up behind the palace into the hilly gardens (the ticket desk will give you a map) where you'll find a shady glade and a statue marking the supposed site of "Hamlet's Grave". The *slot* was closed for renovations at the time of writing but should – all being well – open again in late 2010. In the other direction out of town, southwest along Kongevejen (bus #805 from the train station, towards Espergærde), is the **Danske Teknisk Museum**, Fabriksvej 25 (Danish Science and Technology Museum; Tues–Sun 10am–5pm; 65kr; Ⓦwww.tekniskmuseum.dk), a huge hangar filled with planes, trams, fire engines, cars, steam locomotives and the like.

Eating and drinking

Stengade offers the full range of fast food, cafés and **restaurants**. For light lunches or snacks, *Møllers Konditori*, at no. 39, is a lovely old-fashioned bakery and café that's been here since 1855. For something more substantial, there's also *Madam Sprunck* at no. 48, a characterful, old timbered building in a tiny courtyard; the cosy café serves up good pasta, burgers and salads. Not to be missed is the award-winning *Brostræde Is* **ice cream** on Brostræde: immense, home-made, and delicious.

Away from the centre, *Café Kronen*, in the castle approaches, is an excellent spot for traditional Danish smørrebrød (try the herring platter for 115kr) or an atmospheric dinner, with a three-course gourmet menu at 350kr (book on

☎49 20 00 35). In a similarly impressive location, with lovely views across the harbour, *Kronborg Havbad*, Strandpromenaden 6 (☎49 20 20 45), is a bright, modern restaurant specializing in fish.

Onwards from Helsingør: the North Zealand coast

A long day-trip from Copenhagen would allow you to see a little of the beautiful (and very popular in summer) North Zealand coast, which boasts some of the best beaches in Zealand and a clutch of attractive fishing towns. The glorious sandy swathes at **Hellebæk** and **Hornbæk** (the best option for an overnight stay) are within easy reach of Helsingør, either by bike, local bus or a network of private trains, while the fishing town of **Gilleleje** – just forty minutes by train from Helsingør – is a lovely spot for a fish lunch or dinner.

Hellebæk and Hornbæk

A string of fine beaches can be found by following Nordre Strandvej from Helsingør towards the sleepy village of **HELLEBÆK**, some 5km north. At Hellebæk itself, part of the beach is a well-known, if unofficial, venue for nude bathing. Trains from Helsingør stop at Hellebæk and then continue for 7km to **HORNBÆK**, blessed with excellent beaches, dunes and fabulous views over the sea towards Kullen, the rocky promontory jutting out from the Swedish coast. Harbour and beaches aside, there's little to see in the town itself, but there's a lovely pine forest – **Hornbæk Plantage** – bordering the beaches to the east of town. The excellent **tourist office** (mid-June to Aug Mon 10am–7pm, Tues–Fri 10am–5pm, Sat 10am–2pm; rest of the year closed Tues; ☎49 70 47 47, Ⓦwww.hornbaek.dk), in the library (with free internet) just off the main street, has maps of the forest with trails marked and can advise on cycle hire.

For **food**, nothing beats the delicious fresh fish and seafood sold from a hatch on the side of the fish shop *Fiskehuset* (hatch: summer daily 11am–8pm; shop: Mon–Fri 9am–5.30pm, Sat & Sun 9am–2pm) on the harbour; there are tables outside, but their takeaway menu means you can eat delicious fresh fish anywhere along the beach. If you'd prefer something more formal, head for *Restaurant Hansen's Café* (Ⓦwww.hansenscafe.dk) on Havnevej 9, which has bags of olde-worlde charm, great Danish-French cooking and alfresco seating in summer.

Gilleleje

From Hornbæk, trains continue along the coast to **GILLELEJE** (15min) another appealing fishing town that does a roaring tourist trade. The town's beaches aren't the best along the coast, but there's a pretty working **harbour** bristling with boats and lined with restaurants serving the local catch – *Restaurant Gilleleje Havn* does excellent traditional lunches; further along the harbour, *Adamsen's Fisk*, next to the smokehouse and shop of the same name, is a small kiosk selling a variety of fish-filled rolls and sushi starting from 35kr.

It's worth walking at least some of the footpath that runs along the top of the dunes, where, in 1835, **Søren Kierkegaard** took lengthy contemplative strolls, later recalling: "I often stood there and reflected over my past life. The force of the sea and the struggle of the elements made me realize how unimportant I was." Ironically, so important has Kierkegaard become that a monument to him now stands on the path bearing his maxim: "Truth in life is to live for an idea."

Hillerød and around

The inland town of **HILLERØD** is forty minutes by S-Tog from Helsingør, and a similar distance from Copenhagen (last stop on S-Tog line E). Hillerød itself is unremarkable, but it basks in the glow of the glorious **Frederiksborg Slot**, a castle that, for sheer splendour and romance beats the more famous Kronborg hands down, lying decorously across three small islands within an artificial lake and set within magnificent Baroque gardens. Bus #703 runs from the train station to the castle, or it's a twenty-minute walk, following the signs (*Slottet*) through the centre.

Frederiksborg Slot (daily: April–Oct 10am–5pm; Nov–March 11am–3pm; 60kr; Ⓦwww.frederiksborgmuseet.dk) was originally the home of Frederik II and birthplace of his son Christian IV, who, at the turn of the seventeenth century, began rebuilding the castle in an unorthodox Dutch Renaissance style. It's the unusual aspects of the design – a prolific use of towers and spires, Gothic arches and flowery window ornamentation – that still stand out, despite the changes wrought by a serious fire in 1859 and subsequent restoration.

Since 1882, the interior has functioned as a **Museum of National History**, largely funded by the Carlsberg Brewery magnate Carl Jacobsen and intended to heighten the nation's sense of history and cultural development. It's a good idea to get an audioguide (20kr) to get the most out of the sixty-odd rooms charting Danish history since 1500. Many are surprisingly free of furniture and household objects, and attention is drawn to the ranks of portraits along the walls – a motley crew of flat-faced kings and thin consorts who between them ruled and misruled Denmark for centuries. **The Rose** has been reconstructed to look as it did in the time of Christian IV, when it served as a dining room, its low vaulted ceiling and imitation gilt-leather creating a lavish yet intimate space. On the first floor, the **chapel**, where Denmark's monarchs were crowned between 1671 and 1840, is exquisite, its vaults, pillars and arches gilded and embellished, and the contrasting black marble of the gallery riddled with gold lettering. The shields, in tiered rows around the chapel, are those of the knights of the Order of the Elephant – an honour begun by the king in the late seventeenth century that continues to the

▲ Frederiksborg Slot

present day (Churchill and Montgomery were recipients but it's now limited to Danish royalty and foreign heads of state). From the chapel, head through room 23 along the Privy Passage to Christian V's **Audience Chamber** (room 24) – the only living quarters from the seventeenth century to have been preserved and a Baroque triumph of stucco and marble flourishes. The **Great Hall**, above the chapel, is a reconstruction, but this doesn't detract from its beauty. It's bare but for the staggering wall and ceiling decorations: tapestries, wall reliefs, portraits and a glistening black marble fireplace. In Christian IV's day the hall was a ballroom, and the polished floor still tempts you to some fancy footwork.

Set aside some time for the **Modern Collection** on the third floor – effectively Denmark's national portrait gallery with paintings, busts and photos of more recent royals, politicians, scientists, writers and artists, including Karen Blixen, the explorer Knud Rasmussen, Niels Bohr, and a rather camp and gory self-portrait by Lars Von Trier. Room 82 is devoted to the current royal family – look out for Andy Warhol's portrait of Margrethe II.

Away from the often crowded interior, the **Baroque gardens**, on the far side of the lake, are astonishingly intricate, with a cascade of canals and fountains (summer only) and some excellent views of the castle from their stepped terraces. The quickest way to them is through the narrow **Mint Gate** to the left of the main castle building, which adjoins a roofed-in bridge leading to the King's Wing. From the castle you can take the **footpath** that skirts the lake into town – it's a pretty ten-minute walk to Torvet, Hillerød's main square. In summer, you can also do a thirty-minute trip on the lake aboard the *M/F Frederiksborg* **ferry**, which leaves every half-hour from outside the castle (mid-May to mid-Sept Mon–Sat 11am–5pm, Sun 1–5pm; 20kr).

Practicalities

The **tourist office** is in the library (free internet access) at Christiansgade 1 (Mon–Wed 10.30am–6pm, Thurs & Fri 10.30am–4.30pm, Sat 10am–2pm; ⓣ48 24 26 26, ⓦwww.hillerodturist.dk), off Frederiksgade. For good **food**, you needn't even leave the castle confines: *Spisestedet Leonora* (daily: April–Oct 10am–5pm; Nov–March 11am–4pm), set in one of the gatehouses, serves fantastic smørrebrød starting at 59kr a piece – one should suffice unless you're really hungry. In the town itself, don't miss possibly the county's best coffee, served at the rustic *Café Kaffemøllen* not far from the castle at Møllestræde 6. They also do salads and sandwiches, as well as delicious cakes.

Fredensborg Slot

While in Hillerød, it's worth making a detour to a current royal residence – the picturesque **Fredensborg Slot** (July daily 1–4.30pm; guided tours 50kr; joint ticket with the Reserved Garden 75kr) in the small town of Fredensborg (10min on the train back towards Helsingør). Built by Frederik IV to commemorate the 1720 Peace Treaty with Sweden, the palace is only open in July, when the queen is away staying at her summer home, Marselisborg, in Århus. During this period there are also guided tours of the so-called **Reserved Garden** next to the palace where you'll find the queen's veggie patch and herb garden, and a grand orangery stuffed with citrus trees, olive trees and the like. The rest of the extensive **Baroque gardens** – grand, seemingly endless, tree-lined avenues radiating out from the palace down to the waters of the beautiful Esrum Sø – are open year round (daily dawn–dusk; free). In the gardens, be sure to see **Normandsalen**, seventy life-size sandstone statues of eighteenth-century Norwegian and Faroese peasant folk arranged in a grassy amphitheatre; replicas of originals, carved in

1773, that were intended as an ethnographical record of the folk costumes of the region. For **food**, head down to the lakeside *Skipperhuset* (May–Oct Tues–Sun noon–5pm; book ahead on ⓣ48 48 17 17) for a beautifully presented traditional Danish lunch.

Roskilde

West of Copenhagen, the ancient town of **ROSKILDE** was seat of the country's ecclesiastical and royal power from the eleventh to the fifteenth centuries. There's been a community here since prehistoric times, and Roskilde Fjord later provided a route to the open sea that was used by the Vikings. But it was the arrival of Bishop Absalon in the twelfth century (see p.35) that made the place the seat of the Bishops of Zealand and the base of the Danish church – and, as a consequence, the national capital for a while. However, as Copenhagen's star rose, helped by the new wealth brought by herring fishing on the Øresund and the establishment in 1479 of Copenhagen's university, Roskilde's waned, and, after the Reformation, the bishops moved to the new capital as many of the town's convents, monasteries and

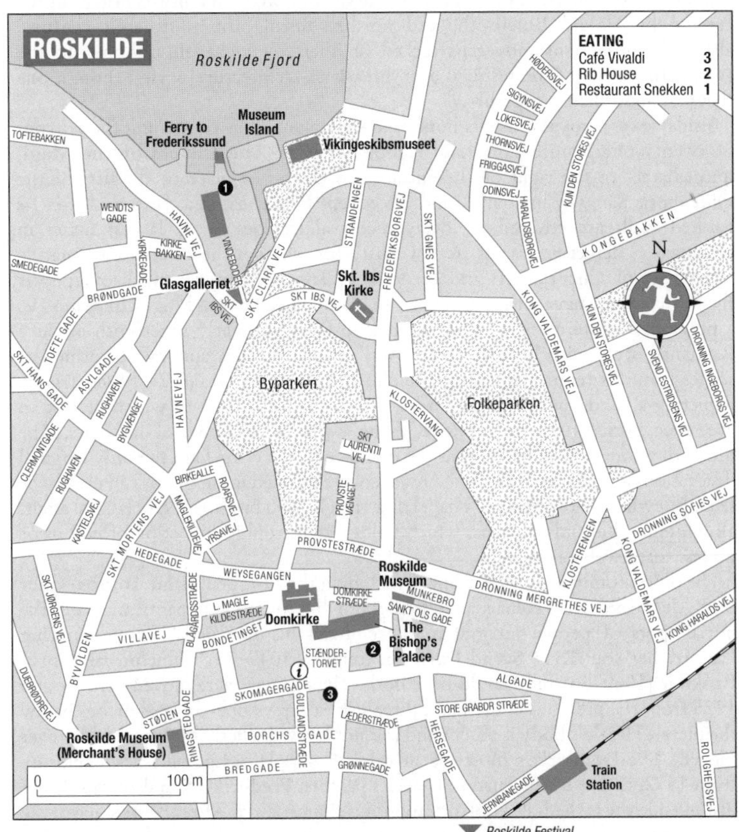

churches were destroyed. Roskilde came to function mainly as a market for local rural communities.

All this history is conveniently packed into a relatively small area, easily explored on foot. From the train station, it's a short walk down the hill to the small, largely pedestrianized **town centre** with its main shopping streets of Algade and Skomagergade and tangle of quiet, narrow streets around the **Domkirke**. Just to the north of the Domkirke, the green hilly stretch of Byparken, once the stronghold of Viking power, leads down to the harbour, home of Roskilde's other big draw, the **Viking Ship Museum**. It's a relaxing day out – except during the first week of July when the town undergoes a complete transformation and is packed with revellers attending the famous **Roskilde Festival** (see p.196).

The Domkirke

The major pointer to the town's former status is the enormous Gothic **Domkirke** (April–Sept Mon–Sat 9am–5pm, Sun 12.30–5pm; Oct–March Tues–Sat 10am–4pm, Sun 12.30–4pm; 25kr; guided tours in English summer only Mon–Fri 11am & 2pm, Sat 11am, Sun 2pm; 20kr; Ⓦ www.roskildedomkirke.dk), one of Scandinavia's most important religious buildings, and a UNESCO Heritage Site. The brick-built cathedral, high on the hill overlooking the fjord, was founded by Bishop Absalon in 1170 on the site of a wooden tenth-century church erected by Harald Bluetooth, and finished during the fourteenth century, although subsequent monarchs tacked on their own chapels right up to the twentieth century. The result is a mishmash of architectural styles, though one that just about hangs together.

Inside, several **royal chapels** house the elaborate coffins containing the remains of twenty-one Danish kings and eighteen queens. **The Chapel of the Magi**, immediately to the right of the entrance, is the burial place of the first of the Oldenburg Kings, Christian I, and his queen, Dorothea, and dates to 1462. Its vaulted walls are covered in lovely medieval frescoes – the largest intact in Denmark – depicting scenes from Christ's life, though the ostentatious marble sarcophagi of Christian III and Frederik II, also here, pretty much overpower them. Across the nave is the chapel of Denmark's most famous king, **Christian IV**, a previously austere resting place jazzed up in typical early nineteenth-century Romantic style with bronze statues, wall-length frescoes and vast paintings of scenes from his reign, including Wilhelm Marstrand's *Christian IV on the Trinity*, depicting a bandaged Christian on his ship during the battle in which he lost an eye. Also buried here are his wife, Anne Cathrine, and two of his heirs. The intricate wrought iron gratings at the entrance to the chapel are the only original decorations and date to 1620 – the royal couple's gilded monograms can clearly be seen. Elsewhere, **Frederik V**'s chapel dates to 1778 – a brighter, Neoclassical affair, all white marble and columns, which holds a claustrophic collection of coffins of no less than twelve monarchs.

The oldest tombs are in the chancel, including the so-called **Pillar Tombs** – four piers, decorated with Renaissance frescoes of the tombs' occupants, marking the burial spots of people integral to the church's history: Estrid, sister of King Canute, her son, King Svend Estridson (reigned 1047–76), Vilhelm, Bishop of Roskilde (1060–73) and Harald Bluetooth. Their graves were moved here around 1225 from the previous church and three still occupy stone-covered niches below the piers – Harald's body is absent and it is not known whether it was actually ever moved. The Domkirke's most recent tomb, a simple octagonal brick enclosure from 1972, is that of the current Queen's parents, **Frederik IX** and Ingrid. It lies just outside the cathedral. Look out too for the animated medieval **clock** above the main entrance: just before the hour a model of Skt Jørgen (Saint George) gallops forward on his horse to wallop the dragon and the hour is marked by the creature's squeal of death.

Upstairs in the Great Hall, the small **Cathedral Museum** (April to mid-June Mon–Fri 11am, 1pm & 2pm, Sat 10am, Sun 1pm & 2pm; mid-June to Aug Mon–Fri every 30min between 11.05am and 2.35pm, Sat every 30min between 9.05am and 11.35am, Sun every 30min between 1.05pm and 3.35pm; Sept Mon–Fri noon & 1pm, Sat noon, Sun 1pm & 2pm; Oct–March Tues–Fri noon & 1pm, Sat noon, Sun 1pm & 2pm) provides an engrossing introduction to the cathedral's colourful history.

At the western, chancel, end of the cathedral, the thirteenth-century **Arch of Absalon** (a roofed passageway only accessible to the Danish clergy) feeds into the yellow Baroque **Bishop's Palace**, built in 1733. The incumbent bishop nowadays confines himself to one wing, while the others have been turned into showplaces for (predominantly) Danish art. The main building (entrance at Stændertorvet 3) houses the **Museet for Samtidskunst** (Museum of Contemporary Art; Tues–Fri 11am–5pm, Sat & Sun noon–4pm; 40kr, free on Wed; Ⓦwww.samtidskunst.dk), which hosts temporary exhibitions, while the west wing is home to the **Palæfløjen** gallery (Tues–Sun noon–4pm; free), run by Roskilde Art Society, which, in summer, extends outdoors with a collection of striking sculptures beneath the fruit trees of the bishop's garden.

Vikingeskibs Museet

North of the town centre, a fifteen-minute stroll though Byparken takes you to the **Vikingeskibs Museet** (Viking Ship Museum; daily 10am–5pm; May–Sept 95kr; Oct–April 60kr; free guided tours in English daily July & Aug, Sat & Sun only May, June & Sept; Ⓦwww.vikingeskibsmuseet.dk), one of the country's finest museums. Its huge glass hall overlooks Roskilde Fjord, a stunning backdrop to the remains of five Viking vessels: a deep-sea trader, a merchant ship, a man-of-war, a ferry and a longship. The ships were discovered at the bottom of the fjord in 1958 where they had been sunk to block invading forces from Norway. Together, they give an impressive indication of the Vikings' nautical versatility, their skills in boat-building and their far-ranging travels, while the accompanying text does a good job of portraying a balanced view of Viking history – they sailed abroad not only to rape and pillage, as much historiography would suggest, but also to find places where they could settle down and farm. Try to catch the film downstairs first (shown in English on request), which goes into fascinating detail about the project to restore the ships, helping to bring the main exhibits alive. Check out also the new exhibition on the **Sea Stallion** – a fully functioning reconstruction of the museum's great longship or man-of-war – that in 2007/08 sailed to Dublin and back.

On the adjacent **Museum Island** there are demonstrations on all aspects of Viking craftsmanship from boatbuilding to jewellery-making, while berthed in the small **museum harbour** is the amazing collection of reconstructions of Viking ships. During the summer, you can experience their seaworthiness first-hand – you'll be given an oar when you board and be expected to pull your weight as a crew member (50min; 75kr).

The rest of town

The **Roskilde Museum**, close to the cathedral at Skt Ols Gade 18 (daily 11am–4pm; 25kr; Ⓦwww.roskildemuseum.dk), is a fine local history museum, with Viking gold and Bronze Age grave finds and strong sections on medieval pottery and antique toys. Look out for the strange photos that satirist Gustav Wied (who lived in Roskilde for many years and whose rooms are reconstructed here) took of his family. The museum also has an old **merchant's house** at Ringstedgade 6–8 (Mon–Fri 11am–5pm, Sat 10am–2pm; free), with a grocer's shop kitted out in 1920s style, where you can buy traditional salted herring and sugar loaves, and a small **craft museum** with various workshops and tools of carpenters, coachbuilders and the like.

There are also a couple of diversions close to the harbour. At Skt Ibs Vej 12, the **Glasgalleriet** (April–Sept, Nov & Dec Mon–Fri 10am–5.30pm, Sat & Sun 11am–4pm, Jan–March & Oct Mon–Fri 10am–5.30pm, Sat 11am–4pm; free; Ⓦwww.glasgalleriet.dk) is a good little glasswork gallery in the old Roskilde Gasworks between the harbour and Byparken where you can watch the glass being blown and buy any pieces you like. A little way to the east along Skt Ibs Vej you come to the well-preserved ruin of **Skt Ibs Kirke** (St James's Church), built in 1100 at the height of the town's ecclesiastical glory when there were no less than fourteen churches here. Just to the west of the church, in a quiet cobbled seating area, is **Skt Ibs Kilde**, one of over twenty ancient springs and wells (*kilde* is Danish for spring) dotted around the town in various states of ruin. Roskilde was famous for its curative water – some of its springs were considered holy – and over the centuries "Roskilde Water" was transported to Copenhagen to alleviate the digestive complaints of its overfed kings and courtiers. The town's most effusive, still-functioning spring is on Maglekildevej, where water gushes out of Neptune's head.

Practicalities

Roskilde is just thirty minutes from Copenhagen Central Station. The **tourist office** is at Stændertorvet 1 (April–June Mon–Fri 10am–5pm, Sat 10am–1pm; July & Aug Mon–Fri 10am–5pm, Sat 10am–2pm; Sept–March Mon–Thurs 10am–5pm, Fri 10am–4pm, Sat 10am–1pm; Ⓣ46 31 65 65, Ⓦwww.visitroskilde.com). Good **eating** options include *Café Vivaldi*, centrally located at Stændertorvet 8, a modern, brasserie-style place serving brunch, sandwiches, salads and burgers and a post-5pm menu of pasta and meat or fish mains. Or try *Rib House*, Djalma Lunds Gaard 8, whose hearty lunch menu of ribs, steaks and burgers is among the city's best deals. Down at the harbour there's *Restaurant Snekken* at Vindeboder 16, a good all-rounder, which does traditional Danish food as well as omelettes, burgers and sandwiches. You could also rustle up a picnic from the Irma supermarket at 21 Skomagergade, and head for Byparken.

Across to Sweden

Historically and culturally, Denmark and southern Sweden are closely linked. For centuries, Danish rule extended across the Øresund, and the connections continue today, most visibly in the splendid **Øresunds Bridge** that links the two countries. Historic **Malmö** – the main city of the area – is an easy day-trip from Copenhagen, and the journey across the bridge makes a spectacular start to the day: from Copenhagen airport, a four-kilometre tunnel brings you out onto the equally long artificial island of Peberholm, from where the eight-kilometre suspension bridge runs to the town of Lernacken, just south of Malmö. The bridge has two levels – the upper for a four-lane highway and the lower for two sets of train tracks – and comprises three sections: a one-kilometre-long central high bridge and approach

▲ Øresunds Bridge

bridges to either side, each over 3km long. All the way along the views of the Øresund are stunning.

Getting to Malmö is easy; though, at a prohibitive 550kr for a return ticket across the bridge by car, it's worth taking the **train**: Malmö is on the same line as Copenhagen airport, so services from Central Station are frequent (three per hour during the day), and the journey to Malmö Central, bang in the middle of town, takes just 35min.

Malmö

Founded in the late thirteenth century, **MALMÖ** rose to become Denmark's most important city after Copenhagen. Their interconnected histories mean that in many ways Malmö has more in common with Copenhagen than with the rest of Sweden, although most Swedes would profusely deny this. The Malmö dialect of Swedish is very similar to Danish, and Danish kroner are accepted everywhere. With groceries and clothes comparatively cheap in Sweden, Malmö is also a popular shopping destination for Copenhageners.

The high density of herring in the sea off the Malmö coast brought ambitious German merchants flocking to the city, an influence that can still be seen in the striking fourteenth-century St Petri kyrka. Erik of Pomerania gave Malmö its most significant medieval boost when, in the fifteenth century, he built the **castle** and mint, and gave the city its own flag – the gold-and-red griffin of his family crest. It wasn't until the Swedish King Karl X marched his armies across the frozen belt of water to within striking distance of Copenhagen in 1658 that the Danes were forced into handing back the southwestern counties to the Swedes. For Malmö, this meant a period of stagnation, cut off from nearby Copenhagen and too far from its own uninterested capital. Not until the full

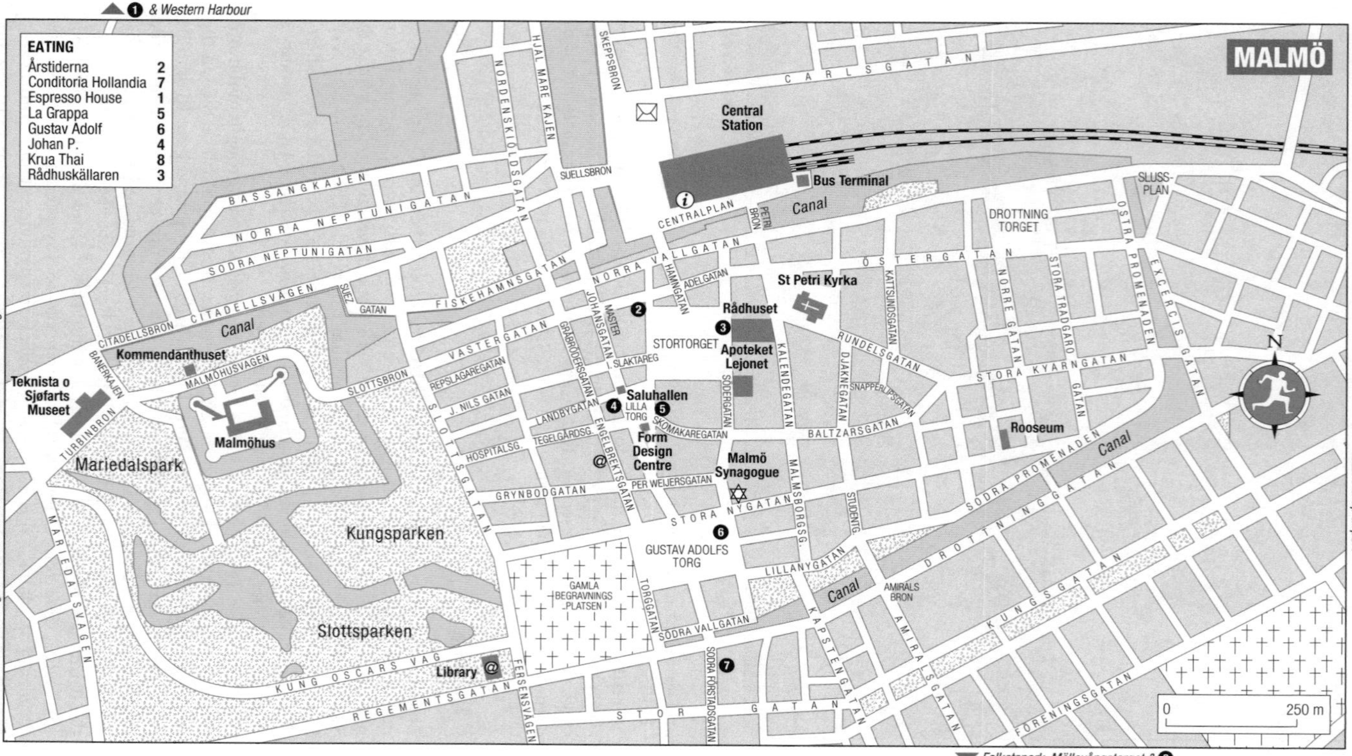
MALMÖ
EATING
Årstiderna 2
Conditoria Hollandia 7
Espresso House 1
La Grappa 5
Gustav Adolf 6
Johan P. 4
Krua Thai 8
Rådhuskällaren 3
1 & Western Harbour
Öresund bridge
Ribersborg Park & Kallbadhuset
Sturup airport
Folketspark, Möllevångstorget & 8
Central Station
Bus Terminal
Canal
St Petri Kyrka
Rådhuset
Apoteket Lejonet
Stortorget
Saluhallen
Lilla Torg
Form Design Centre
Malmö Synagogue
Rooseum
Gustav Adolfs Torg
Gamla Begravnings Platsen
Kommendanthuset
Malmöhus
Teknista o Sjøfarts Museet
Mariedalspark
Kungsparken
Slottsparken
Library
Drottning Torget
Sluss-Plan
Carlsgatan
Skeppsbron
Suellsbron
Hjalmare Kajen
Nordenskiöldsgatan
Bassangkajen
Norra Neptunigatan
Sodra Neptunigatan
Citadellsvägen
Suez Gatan
Citadellsbron
Banerkajen
Turbinbron
Malmöhusvägen
Slottsbron
Fiskehamnsgatan
Vastergatan
Repslagaregatan
J. Nils Gatan
Hospitalsg.
Slottsgatan
Grynbodgatan
Centralplan
Petri Bron
Norra Vallgatan
Hamngatan
Adelgatan
Master Johansgatan
Gråbrödersgatan
I. Slaktareg
Landbygatan
Tegelgårdsg.
Engelbrektsgatan
Skomakaregatan
Per Weijersgatan
Södergatan
Kalendegatan
Östergatan
Kattsundsgatan
Rundelsgatan
Djaknegatan
Snapperupsgatan
Baltzarsgatan
Norre Gatan
Stora Tradgaro Gatan
Stora Kyarngatan
Ostra Promenaden
Excercis Gatan
Sodra Promenaden
Drottninggatan
Stora Nygatan
Malmsborgsg.
Studentg.
Lillanygatan
Amiralsbron
Amiralsgatan
Kungsgatan
Kapstengatan
Föreningsgatan
Torggatan
Sodra Vallgatan
Sodra Förstadsgatan
Stor Gatan
Fersensvägen
Kung Oscars Väg
Regementsgatan
Mariedalsvägen
0 250 m

thrust of industrialization, triggered by the tobacco merchant Frans Suell's enlargement of the harbour in 1775, did Malmö begin its dramatic commercial recovery, and the city's fortunes remained buoyant over the following two centuries.

In the last decade the new university and the opening of the Øresunds Bridge have attracted an influx of investment and development that has helped to create an upbeat, energetic and likeable atmosphere. The attractive medieval centre, delightful parks and the sweeping beach are all major draws; the plentiful restaurants are another inducement to visit.

City transport and tours

The city centre is easy to walk around; should you need a **bus**, tickets cost 16SEK and are valid for an hour; a 200SEK magnetic card is also available and can be used by several people at the same time. In summer, you can **rent bikes** from Fridhems Cykelaffär (Ⓣ040 26 03 35; 120SEK per day) on Tessins väg 13, near Malmöhus.

Leaving from the quay outside Central Station, the "Rundan" tourist **boat** (daily every hour on the hour: May to mid-June noon–5pm; mid-June to end Aug 11am–7pm; end Aug to mid-Sept noon–3pm; mid- to end Sept 1–3pm; 100SEK; Ⓦwww.rundan.se) winds its leisurely way along the lovely canals that encircle the old city and out into the harbour, taking in most of the main sights. The trip takes about fifty minutes, with English commentary if requested.

The City

As you stand outside the nineteenth-century train station, with its ornate red-brick arches and curly-topped pillars, the **canal** in front of you forms a rough rectangle encompassing the **Old Town** directly to the south and the moated castle, the **Malmöhus**, with its cluster of museums, to the west, surrounded by a series of attractive interconnecting parks. South down Hamngatan is the main square, **Stortorget**, heart of the old town; and further south the hub of multiethnic Malmö; to the west lies the appealing **beach** area; while to the north the rapidly redeveloping Western Harbour, with its love-it or loathe-it landmark, the **Turning Torso Skyscraper**.

The Old Town

Stortorget, the city's main square, is home to a series of handsome, mostly nineteenth-century, buildings, amongst which the **Rådhuset** of 1546 draws most attention. A pageant of architectural fiddling and statuary, the building's original design was destroyed during remodelling in the nineteenth century, which left the present, finicky Dutch Renaissance exterior. The cellars, home to the *Rådhuskällaren* restaurant (see p.132), have been used as a tavern for more than four hundred years. The crumbling, step-gabled red-brick building on the opposite side of the square was once the home of sixteenth-century mayor and Master of the Danish Mint, Jørgen Kock; Danish coins were struck in Malmö on the site of the present Malmöhus, until irate local Swedes stormed the building and destroyed it in 1534. In the cellars here you'll find the *Årstiderna* (also known as *Kockska Krogan*, see p.132) restaurant, the only part of the building accessible to visitors.

Head a block east, behind the Rådhuset, to reach the Gothic **St Petri kyrka** on Göran Olsgatan (daily 10am–6pm), dark and forbidding on the outside, but light and airy within. The church has its roots in the fourteenth century and, although Baltic in inspiration, the final style owes much to German influences, for it was beneath its unusually lofty and elegantly vaulted roof that the German community came to pray. The ecclesiastical vandalism of whitewashing over medieval roof murals started early at St Petri – almost the whole interior turned white in 1553 – and consequently your eyes are drawn to the pulpit and four-tiered altarpiece, both of striking workmanship and elaborate embellishment. The only part of the church left with its original murals is a side chapel, the **Krämare Chapel** (Merchant's Chapel). Added to the church in the late fifteenth century as a Lady Chapel, it was considered redundant at the Reformation and sealed off, thus protecting the paintings from the zealous brushes of the reformers.

Södergatan, Malmö's main pedestrianized shopping street, leads south of Stortorget down towards the southern canal via the pleasant Gustav Adolfs Torg; at the start of Södergatan, take a peek inside **Apoteket Lejonet** from the 1890s. Gargoyled and balconied on the outside, the pharmacy interior is a busy mix of inlaid wood, carvings and etched glass.

Despite the size of Stortorget, it still proved too small to suffice as the sole city square, so in the sixteenth century **Lilla Torg**, formerly marshland, was sewn on to the southwest corner. Looking like a film set, this little square with its creaky old half-timbered houses, flowerpots and cobbles is everyone's favourite part of the city. During the day, people congregate for a drink in one of the many cafés and to wander around the summer jewellery stalls. At night, Lilla Torg explodes in a frenzy of bar activity. From the beginning of the twentieth century until the 1960s, the whole of Lilla Torg was a covered market; the sole vestige of those days is **Saluhallen**, to the right as you enter the square from Stortorget. A bustling collection of enticing food stalls – Greek, Italian, Japanese, Thai and seafood among others – it's a cool retreat on a hot afternoon and a great place to pick up lunch.

At the square's southeastern corner, walk through the gateway into the tiny, cobbled courtyard where, in addition to a handful of boutiques and craft shops, you'll find the stylish **Form/Design Center** (Tues, Wed & Fri 11am–5pm, Thurs 11am–6pm, Sat & Sun 11am–4pm; free; Ⓦ www.formdesigncenter.com), housed in a seventeenth-century grain store and celebrating Swedish design. It carries mostly temporary exhibitions, but the shop is a cornucopia of funky designer kitchenware, toys and textiles, and there's a nice café, too.

Malmöhus and around

Take any of the streets running west from Stortorget or Lilla Torg and you soon come up against the edge of **Kungsparken**, within striking distance of the fifteenth-century castle, **Malmöhus** (daily: June–Aug 10am–4pm; Sept–May noon–4pm; 40SEK, includes entry to Kommendanthuset), the most intact Renaissance castle in Scandinavia. For a more dramatic approach, walk west (away from the station) up Citadellsvägen; from here the low castle with its grassy ramparts and two striking red circular keeps is straight ahead over the wide moat.

Originally Denmark's mint, Malmöhus was destroyed by the Swedes in 1534. Two years later, a new fortress was built on the site by the Danish king Christian III, only to be of unforeseen benefit to his enemies who, once back in control of Skåne, used it to repel an attacking Danish army in 1677. Serving as a prison for a time (the Earl of Bothwell, Mary Queen of Scots' third husband, was its most notable inmate), the castle's importance waned once back in Swedish hands, and it was used for grain storage until opening as a museum in 1937. It's now more of a **museum complex**, its diverse collections spread throughout the castle itself and a modern extension.

Arguably, the pick of the museums is the **Malmö Konstmuseum** (Art Museum), upstairs to the left, whose fine collection of paintings, furniture, ceramics and glassware is exhibited chronologically in a series of beautiful period interiors from the mid-sixteenth-century Renaissance through Baroque, Rococo, pastel-pale Gustavian and Neoclassical. A stylish *jugendstil* (Art Nouveau) interior is equally impressive, while other rooms feature Functionalist and post-Functionalist interiors. The collection is particularly strong on twentieth-century and contemporary Nordic art. Look out for the fine landscapes of Swedish painter **Carl Fredrik Hill**, his *Villa by the Seine* showing the influence of the Barbizon School and French realism following a sojourn in Paris in 1873. There are also wonderful examples of modern **Scandinavian silverware** with luminaries such as Georg Jensen and Swedish designer Vivianna Toron Bülow-Hübe well represented.

On the ground floor, the **Naturmuseet** (Natural History Museum) features the usual taxidermal parade, but the live section – the small aquarium, vivarium and nocturnal room brimming with bats and other night-time furry critters – is a real draw for the kids. The lack of English labels, plus old-fashioned displays of flints, bones, pots and chunks of medieval masonry, make the **Stadsmuseet** (Town Museum) a rather indigestible trawl through the area's history since the Stone Age. It's best skimmed through in favour of the more exciting **Power Over People** exhibition, which traces the history of the castle through reconstructions (complete with mannequins, sound effects and so on) of what went on over time in the rooms you pass through; one, for instance, was where the Earl of Bothwell was held prisoner. Having fled Scotland after being accused of Mary Queen of Scots' second husband's murder, a storm brought his ship to Bergen in Norway, where he was recognized and taken to the castle.

One more museum (same hours and ticket as Malmöhus) lies across the road on Malmöhusvagen; the pinky-red building is the **Kommendanthuset** (Governor's House), with a funky café and changing photographic exhibitions upstairs. A little further west is a tiny road, **Banerkajen**, lined with higgledy-piggledy fishing shacks selling fresh and smoked fish in the morning.

The beach and Western Harbour

Formerly home to the Kockum shipyard, the high-tech **Western Harbour** district, a ten-minute walk north of the Malmöhus, or bus #2 from Central Station, is a popular spot for sunbathing and swimming, and for gazing across to the Øresunds Bridge from its marina-side cafés and restaurants. Towering over it all, and visible for miles around, is the quirky 190-metre-high **Turning Torso Skyscraper**, designed by Spaniard Santiago Calatrava. This revolutionary residential tower, the highest building in Scandinavia, consists of nine stacked cubes that revolve through a ninety-degree twist from base to top.

From the Western Harbour, Malmö's sandy **beach** stretches several kilometres southwest of the city, fringed by Ribersborgs Park (bus #32 runs along the park). At the town end of the beach is the **Ribersborgs kallbadhuset**, a cold-water bathhouse with a sauna and café.

Eating

Most of Malmö's **restaurants** are in and around its central squares, with Lilla Torg attracting the biggest crowds. If you want a change of scene, head south of the centre to Möllevångstorget, the heart of Malmö's immigrant community, for cheaper eats and a very un-Swedish atmosphere. Alternatively, stock up at the specialist food stalls within Saluhallen on Lilla Torg.

Årstiderna **Suellsgatan 2, corner of Stortorget ⓣ040/23 09 10**. This is a very fine – but rather pricey – old cellar-restaurant in the former home of Malmö's sixteenth-century mayor Jörgen Kock. Daily lunch specials of traditional Swedish food from 98SEK. Closed Sun.

Conditoria Hollandia **Södra Förstadsgatan 8.** Traditional, pricey *konditori* south of the canal, with a window full of delicious chocolate fondants.

Espresso House **Sundspromenaden, Western Harbour.** An outlet of the coffeehouse chain serving excellent chocolate cake, muffins, ciabattas and Indian chai – milky tea with cardamom. All best enjoyed (weather permitting) on the lovely terrace sporting bridge views.

La Grappa **Lilla Torg 4 ⓣ040/12 50 65.** Designer restaurant with a pleasant terrace, serving beautifully presented Italian dishes from 129SEK.

Gustav Adolf **Gustav Adolfs Torg 43.** Long-established, slightly staid but popular café-restaurant in a grand, white-stuccoed building with outside seating. Open late at weekends.

Johan P. **Saluhallen, Lilla Torg ⓣ040/97 18 18.** Great fish and seafood restaurant, centrally located, pricey, but perfect for a treat – lighter food such as gravadlax, caviar or shrimp salad goes for 105SEK or so while mains will set you back around 200SEK. Closed Sun.

Krua Thai **Möllevångtorget 12 ⓣ040/12 22 87.** In the big square south of the city centre, this place serves the best Thai food in town, with an informal ambience that's more domestic than haute cuisine.

Rådhuskällaren **Stortorget**. Gloriously atmospheric setting beneath the town hall, with dishes at around 200SEK and a delicious daily economy meal for 85SEK. Outside seating in summer.

Listings

Listings

10

Accommodation

Accommodation in Copenhagen is varied but relatively expensive, with prices easily on a par with other Western European capitals. Most of the hotels in the city centre are aimed either at tour groups or business travellers – they generally have good service and amenities but can be a bit characterless. With the looming recession a number of new so-called discount hotels – simple and clean but with minimal service – have also sprung up to cater for the budget-conscious business traveller. A wave of modern **designer and boutique hotels** offers trendy and surprisingly good-value alternatives. Hotels in Copenhagen are awarded up to five stars by HORESTA, the Danish hotel association. The number of stars is an indication of the hotel's amenities – TV, minibar, restaurant, and so on – rather than an indication of comfort or cleanliness, and determines the price they can charge. **Room rates** are generally most expensive in summer, though in the majority of big hotels prices rise and fall on a daily basis according to demand. Rates at business-oriented hotels tend to fall at weekends; in touristy hotels they fall in winter (the Christmas period aside). Always check **hotel websites** for **special rates** – particularly at weekends, and if you can book well in advance – and packages.

Rooms fill up quickly during the summer high season (July & Aug) and around Christmas. If you have a hotel in mind you should book ahead during these times, but if you're willing to take a chance, you can make great savings by using the **hotel-booking service** at the Copenhagen Right Now tourist office (see p.30). Queues can be lengthy, however, and they charge 100kr. The tourist office at the airport (see p.22) offers a similar service for just 70kr, and is less busy. **The tourist office** also has a website (Ⓦ www.bookcopenhagen.dk) and phone line (Ⓣ 70 22 24 42) via which you can book a room in advance without a fee. In low season, or when things are quiet, you may be able to get a really good deal like this. Copenhagen Right Now also offers free internet terminals where you can book a room yourself via their website.

Guesthouses, and **private rooms** in local homes, are an affordable option. Check Ⓦ www.bedandbreakfast.dk – but be aware that some smaller hotels also market themselves as guesthouses through this site. Note also that the price of a "bed and breakfast" (from 325kr per night) doesn't actually include breakfast, and in some cases breakfast isn't even on offer. If you're on a budget, you can choose from a number of variable **hostels** and **sleep-ins** scattered around the city centre and suburbs, or a handful of campsites further out. For stays longer than a couple of weeks, an **apartment** will be most cost-effective. The efficient and friendly agency HAY4YOU, Vimmelskaftet 49 (Ⓣ 33 33 08 05, Ⓦ www.hay4you.dk) has a range of central options for short- or long-term stays.

The rates quoted here are for the cost per night of a **standard double room** mid-week in high season. Unless stated, **breakfast** is included in the price. Note that these are **rack rates** and that big discounts are often to be had if you book online or in advance. Unless the city is packed due to a big event it is seldom that you will actually be quoted the rack rate.

Hotels

Copenhagen has experienced a hotel boom in recent years. In the past, most of Copenhagen's classier hotels were concentrated in the desirable canalside area around **Kongens Nytorv** and **Nyhavn**, on the eastern side of Indre By, with a smattering around the Peblinge and Sortedams rampart lakes west of the city centre. These are now facing strong competition from a number of international chains that have rooted themselves firmly at the airport, around **Sydhavnen** and right in the city centre, as well as several new exciting **designer hotels** in great, central locations. Most of the **budget hotels** are just west of Central Station, in **Vesterbro**, with the majority clustered along the ever-so-slightly seedy (though rarely dangerous) streets of Helgolandsgade, Colbjørnsensgade and Istedgade. The area is also home to a number of mid-range hotels, and there are further mid-price options around Nyhavn canal, on the other side of Indre By, and out towards the suburbs of Nørrebro, Frederiksberg and Ørestaden.

Indre By

Staying in Indre By has the benefit of being close to all the action: some of the city's more unusual hotels are squeezed in among the many historical buildings here, and you'll find good restaurants and bars on almost every corner. The following hotels are on the map on p.44.

71 Nyhavn Nyhavn 71 ⓣ33 43 62 00, ⓦwww.71nyhavnhotel.dk. Bus #29; Kongens Nytorv metro. In an excellent location, right on the harbour at the quiet end of Nyhavn and around the corner from the new playhouse, this is a charming hotel full of character from its former days as two grocery warehouses. There's a warm, comfy feel to the place, helped by the beautifully restored interior – all white-washed walls, beamed ceilings and hefty timber pillars. Standard rooms are small but cosy – many have beams – and tastefully furnished. For more space and harbour views, go for a superior or suite. The hotel has its own bar and restaurant, free internet access and wi-fi. Breakfast not included. 2050kr.

Copenhagen Strand Havnegade 37 ⓣ33 48 99 00, ⓦwww.copenhagenstrand.dk. Bus #29. Located on the waterfront in a converted warehouse from 1862, this is a friendly and comfortable option in a quiet spot with fine views over to Christianshavn. There's a nod to the building's past in the lobby's rustic brick walls hung with maritime pictures. Standard rooms are a bit small but comfortably furnished. Larger options are also available – only suites have harbour views. Breakfast included. Rates reduced substantially at weekends. 1635kr.

D'Angleterre Kongens Nytorv 34 ⓣ33 12 00 95, ⓦwww.remmen.dk. Bus #1A, #15, #26, #350S; Kongens Nytorv metro. Copenhagen's answer to the Ritz, this prestigious five-star dates back to 1755 and has been first choice for pretty much every politician, celebrity and pop star who has visited the city ever since. The ultra-stylish classically furnished rooms contain every conceivable amenity, and there's also a luxurious spa, indoor pool, fitness centre and two gourmet restaurants, though breakfast isn't included in the price, and parking costs extra, too. 3125kr.

First Hotel Skt Petri Krystalgade 22 ⓣ33 45 91 00, ⓦwww.hotelsktpetri.com. Bus #6A; Nørreport S-Tog/metro. Located in a former discount department store in a quiet street in the heart of the trendy Latin Quarter, there is nothing cut price about the five-star *Skt Petri*, the only Danish member of Design Hotels (ⓦwww.designhotel.com). It's slick, classy and glamorous throughout from the black-liveried porters to the ultra-trendy lobby and café with wi-fi and international newspapers. Rooms, from small to suite, feature large beds, stylish furnishings, wooden floors and bright prints on the walls – some have balconies, so ask when booking. All have wi-fi, internet and cable TV. There's a brasserie serving French classics, and if you're lucky you might get in to the cocktail lounge *Bar Rouge* (it tends to host mostly private parties). 1995kr.

Jørgensen Rømersgade 11 ⓣ33 13 81 86, ⓦwww.hoteljoergensen.dk. Bus #5A, #14, #40, #42, #43 or #350S; Nørreport S-Tog/metro. One of the few inexpensive options in the centre and within ten minutes, walk of Strøget, the friendly and relaxed *Jørgensen* offers good-value rooms with or without en suite facilities. They're all comfortable and well furnished, and there's a good buffet breakfast included. The family rooms and dorm-style accommodation (see p.142) ensures a congenial mix of young travellers, families and tourists. 800kr; 675kr shared bathroom.

Kong Arthur Nørre Søgade 11 ⓣ33 11 12 12, ⓦwww.kongarthur.dk. Bus #5A or #350S. Located in a largely residential area by Peblinge Sø, this lovely hotel has a comfortable lobby that doubles as a bar (open 24/7) and is beautifully furnished with a stylish mix of modern and period furniture (the odd suit of amour and shield providing a link to the hotel's name). Rooms (all with internet and cable TV) are tastefully decorated in muted tones, though some are quite small and views are limited. There's a courtyard where you can relax with a drink, and the spa is free to guests. Breakfast buffet is organic and costs extra (135kr). The hotel is carbon neutral, and electric cars can be rented from reception. Free parking. 1550kr.

Sømandshjemmet "Bethel" Nyhavn 22 ⓣ33 13 03 70, ⓦwww.hotel-bethel.dk. Bus #29; Kongens Nytorv metro. This former seamen's hostel right in the heart of Nyhavn is an excellent budget option in this often expensive area. The decor is a little dated, but rooms are clean and comfortable and the atmosphere is welcoming. Corner rooms have great views and are worth paying a bit more for. A small breakfast café serves cakes and coffee. 845kr.

Hotel Twentyseven Løngangstræde 27, ⓣ70 27 56 27, ⓦwww.hotel27.dk. Bus #6A. A recent addition to the city's designer hotels, this is an edgy and exciting place to stay. There's an informal ambience, from the risqué artwork to the glamorous Honey Ryder Cocktail Lounge to the dildo-vending machine in the ladies' toilets. At *Ice Bar CPH* next door (see p.163) you can knock back shots at tables made of ice. The rooms are pure Scandinavian style with light oak floors, fluffy rugs, red-lacquer wardrobes and black slate bathrooms. There's free tea, coffee and fruit, and you can also pay for half-board and have the evening buffet. Rates are surprisingly reasonable, along with their range of gimmicky but good-value "lifestyle packages" (check website for details). Free wi-fi. 1000kr.

Christianshavn

The following hotel is on the map on p.55.

CPH Living Langebrogade 1C ⓣ61 60 85 46, ⓦwww.cphliving.com. Bus #5A or #12. If you fancy being lulled to sleep by the gentle rolling of waves, this new hotel boat might be just the place. With just twelve beautifully decorated rooms, this sleek, fully automated option (there's no reception; you check in using your credit card), floating in Inner-havnen, has a floating restaurant moored right next to it, and a private sundeck from where you can look across at the Black Diamond glinting in the water. Breakfast not included. 1000kr.

Frederikstad

Hotels in Frederikstad cater mainly to a business clientele, but the area is quieter than others, near lots of museums, the harbour and green spaces, and with plenty of good restaurants. The following hotels are on the map on p.64.

Christian IV Dronningens Tværgade 45 ⓣ33 32 10 44, ⓦwww.hotelchristianiv.dk. Bus #26. In a quiet spot on a pleasant street halfway between Rosenborg and Amalienborg castles, this is a good-value, friendly and cosy hotel, though it lacks the modern pizzazz of other similarly priced options. The rooms are comfortable, well presented and a good size, and there's free access to a nearby fitness centre. All rooms have internet and wi-fi. Free tea, coffee, fruit and cake. Good deals available, especially at weekends. 1525kr.

Comfort Hotel Esplanaden **Bredgade 78 ⓣ33 48 10 00, ⓦwww.choicehotels.dk. Bus #1A or #15.** Set in a lovely, quiet location near Kastellet and the Little Mermaid, this pleasant and relatively small, no-frills hotel – one of the Choice Hotels chain – has decent, plain en-suite rooms, with the choice of bath or shower and all with wi-fi. Breakfast (95kr) is not included. Great offers during weekends and winter. 1349kr.

Copenhagen Admiral **Toldbodgade 24–28 ⓣ33 74 14 14, ⓦwww.admiralhotel.dk. Bus #29.** Housed in an impressive two-hundred-year-old granary in a great location on the waterfront and only two minutes from Nyhavn, this large, handsome hotel exudes comfort, style and professionalism. The six-storey building has kept its rustic maritime interior with impressive vaulted brick ceilings and huge wooden beams throughout. Rooms are comfortable and classy with oak beams and furniture by top Danish designers Trip Trap; half have great views of Inderhavnen and cost around 250kr more. Doubles come in variable sizes. The breakfast buffet (115kr) is not included. There's a classy Conran-designed restaurant, *Salt*, and *Salt Bar* on the ground floor. 1580kr.

Rådhuspladsen and around

Staying here will put you at the centre of things – close to Central Station, Tivoli, the shopping streets of Indre By and several major museums. As a result, hotels tend to be pricey, though there are a couple of affordable options. Most of the options below are on busy main roads; if you're a light sleeper, ask for a room away from the noise. The following hotels are on the map on p.78.

Hotel Alexandra **HC Andersens Bld 8 ⓣ33 74 44 44, ⓦwww.hotel-alexandra.dk. Bus #2A or #250S; Central Station or Vesterport S-Tog.** This homely and charming hotel offers something different with its unique retro theme of Danish design from the 1930s, 1940s and 1950s. The beautifully furnished rooms all boast real Danish furniture classics – a few (for which you'll pay around 500kr extra per night) have even been done out completely in the style of designers such as Arne Jacobsen, Hans Wegner and Finn Juhl. 1745kr.

Cab-Inn City **Mitchellsgade 14 ⓣ33 46 16 16, ⓦwww.cabinn.com. Bus #5A, #30, #66 or #250S; Central Station.** The only budget option in the area, offering a reasonably comfortable place to bed down in a central location near Tivoli and Central Station. Small, functional ferry-cabin-style rooms (for 1–3 people) with bath, TV, phone, internet and kettle (and free tea and coffee). Breakfast 60kr. 675kr (based on 2-person occupancy).

Copenhagen Plaza **Bernstoffsgade 4 ⓣ33 14 92 62, ⓦwww.profilhotels.dk. Central Station.** The *Plaza*'s slightly worn exterior and position next to Central Station might put some off, but inside it's a very friendly, welcoming hotel. There's an intriguing mixture of gentlemen's club ambience – dark wood panelling, heavy furniture and subdued elegance in the lobby and fabulously old-fashioned Library Bar – and, on the accommodation floors, light, modern murals based on Hans Christian Andersen's tales. Rooms are a good size and well furnished, but some overlook the train tracks, so request the Tivoli side if possible. Breakfast not included. 1345kr.

Hotel Fox **Jarmers Plads 3 ⓣ33 13 30 00, ⓦwww.hotelfox.dk. Bus #5A; Central Station.** Great-value, funky, friendly little hotel – the 61 rooms have been individually decorated and furnished by a team of young European designers, and though some (1960s psychedelic movies, Manga) may be too garish to live with for long, they all use their space creatively and with flair. Doubles come in medium, large and extra large; some have showers, some baths, so state your preferences when booking. Breakfast – great coffee and pastries – is served on aeroplane-style compartmentalized trays in the bright and cosy lobby, while drinks can be taken up to the roof terrace. Part of the same chain as Kong Arthur so there's free entrance to their spa. Bikes and rollerblades for hire. 1100kr.

Marriott **Kalvebod Brygge 5 ⓣ88 33 99 00, ⓦwww.marriott.com/cphdk. Bus #30 or #66; Central Station.** In a great harbourfront spot at the end of Bernstorffsgade, the high-rise *Marriott* offers all the American-style amenities you could want – large, plush, well-equipped rooms (many with harbour or city views), restaurant, terrace café (summer only), bar, gym, sauna and solarium, and expensive shops. Prices vary considerably according to demand and drop at weekends, so check their website for special deals. Breakfast not included. 1799kr.

Radisson Blu Royal Hotel Hammerichsgade 1 ⓣ33 42 60 00, ⓦwww.radissonblu.com. Bus #6A or #26; Central Station or Vesterport S-Tog. Built in 1960, this five-star place bills itself as the first designer hotel in the world – the work of Danish architect/designer Arne Jacobsen, from the high-rise building down to the door handles. Several renovations later, it remains faithful to its original style and decor, a time capsule back to the jet-set glamour of the 1960s – the huge lobby has a glamorous sweeping staircase, and a classy bar that's perfect for a pre-dinner drink. The rooms aren't that big, but they are a model of tasteful Danish design, with AJ furniture, pastel fabrics, maple-wood panelling and stylish lighting. The gourmet *Alberto K* restaurant on the twentieth floor adds to the luxurious ambience with its fine views over the city. Rates reduced at weekends. Breakfast not included (195kr). 1995kr.

The Square Rådhuspladsen 14 ⓣ33 38 12 00, ⓦwww.thesquare.dk. Bus #2A, #5A, #6A or #350S; Central Station or Vesterport S-Tog. Great hotel, slap-bang in the centre (hence no parking) and offering significant discounts (around twenty percent) at the weekends. The spacious, stylish lobby is scattered with gorgeous, red Arne Jacobsen swan chairs; the modern design is carried through into the smartly decorated, comfortable rooms. Those overlooking the square get some traffic noise, so if you like quiet, request a room further back. Breakfast (there's no restaurant) is served on the sixth floor with views over the city. 2050kr.

▲ The Square

Vesterbro

The multicultural district of Vesterbro is packed with some of the city's most affordable hotels – with a couple of more pricey options – and a number of cheap ethnic restaurants. The following hotels are on the map on p.88.

Absalon Helgolandsgade 15 ⓣ33 24 22 11, ⓦwww.absalon-hotel.dk. Bus #10; Central Station. On the corner of Istedgade, this large but friendly three-star family hotel, with a one-star annexe, offers a wide choice of rooms (some en suite), plus a number of deluxe doubles and suites. It's nothing special but it's reasonably priced, convenient and clean, and soundproofing keeps things nice and quiet. Free Internet access in the lobby and chargeable wi-fi throughout. 750kr–990kr.

Axel Hotel Guldsmeden Helgolandsgade 7–11 ⓣ33 31 32 66, ⓦwww.ibishotel.com. Bus #6A; Central Station. The newest member of the Danish Guldsmeden hotel chain, Axel is a four-star boutique hotel at the nice end of Colbjørnsensgade. Beautifully decorated rooms feature traditional Balinese wooden furniture and modern accents – including free wi-fi. The light and cheery public areas house an organic courtyard bar and restaurant, and there's a spa to die for. 1305kr.

Bertrams Hotel Guldsmeden Vesterbrogade 107 ⓣ33 25 04 05, ⓦwww.hotelguldsmeden.dk. Bus #6A. Another member of the Danish Guldsmeden hotel chain, *Bertrams* is exquisitely done up in French colonial style with dark wooden interiors and fake furs lying around. Rooms are fairly large, bright and breezy, and come with shower or bath. Breakfast is from *Emmery's* next door – in itself, reason enough to stay here. There's parking (95kr) just down the road at the Vesterbrogade 66 branch, free wi-fi throughout, plus bike hire for 120kr per day. 1745kr.

Carlton Hotel Guldsmeden Vesterbrogade 66 ⓣ33 22 15 00, ⓦwww.hotelguldsmeden.dk.

Bus #6A or #26. Almost opposite the Københavns Bymuseum, this small, charming hotel occupies a nineteenth-century building. All rooms are done out in French colonial style, with a laudable attention to detail, and some have small balconies, though the view isn't that enticing. There is free wi-fi in the café and lobby area and beautiful breakfast from *Emmery's*. Parking 95kr. 1745kr.

Centrum Helgolandsgade 14 ⓣ33 31 31 11, ⓦwww.dgi-byen.dk. Bus #10; Central Station. One of the trendier options in this area, the recently revamped *Centrum* has cool, modern decor – black leather sofas and cosy lighting in the lobby, tasteful whites, creams and pale wooden furniture in the modestly sized rooms (all en suite). Guests get free access to the DGI-byens swim centre. 1395kr.

Copenhagen Island Kalvebod Brygge 53 ⓣ33 38 96 00, ⓦwww.copenhagenisland.com. Dybbelsbro Station. With stupendous views across Innerhavnen, this sparkling new large hotel next to Fisketorvet shopping mall and the Copencabana harbour pool, designed by the famous Utzon team of architects, is difficult to fault. Rooms are stylishly furnished with Scandinavian design, there's free wi-fi throughout and a free fitness centre on the top floor. 1725kr.

DGI-byens Hotel Tietgensgade 65 ⓣ33 29 80 50, ⓦwww.dgi-byen.dk. Bus #1A; Central Station. Excellently located for sporty types or families travelling with kids, the *DGI-byens Hotel* is part of the leisure centre of the same name; guests get free access to the swim and fitness centre. Its a beautiful example of minimalist Scandinavian design, with large, immaculate rooms with light, pine floors. 1695kr.

Grand Vesterbrogade 9 ⓣ33 27 69 00, ⓦwww.grandhotel.dk. Central Station. Popular with British travellers, trainspotters and businessmen, the en suite rooms at the old-fashioned *Grand*, at the Tivoli end of Vesterbrogade, come in different shapes and sizes and are all tastefully decorated with classic British furniture. The convenient location near Central Station makes it a superb choice if you're planning to travel around a lot. 1155kr.

Hebron Helgolandsgade 4 ⓣ33 31 69 06, ⓦwww.hebron.dk. Bus #6A; Central Station. This three-star Best Western hotel at the quiet end of Helgolandsgade, near Vesterbrogade, is popular with Danish business travellers who don't mind the bland decor. Rooms (all en suite) vary in size; some on the Helgolandsgade side have small balconies. Free tea, coffee and internet in the lobby area. Massively reduced rates at weekends (845kr). 1350kr.

Løven Vesterbrogade 30 ⓣ33 79 67 20, ⓦwww.loeven.dk. Bus #6A or #26. One of central Copenhagen's real bargains, offering affordable, no-frills accommodation in plain but pleasantly decorated rooms sleeping up to six (mostly en suite). Breakfast isn't included, but there's a large and well-equipped kitchen and a good breakfast café downstairs. The major drawback is the noise – rooms facing the courtyard are quieter. En suite 690kr, shared 490kr.

Mayfair Helgolandsgade 3 ⓣ70 12 17 00, ⓦwww.choicehotels.dk. Bus #6A; Central Station. Part of the Choice hotel chain but one of the most characterful hotels in this street, with olde-English-style rooms complete with flat screen TV, minibar, and tea- and coffee-making facilities – plus carved wooden beds, leather armchairs and tasteful fabrics. There's also a cosy lobby and bar area. Breakfast buffet and a light dinner included in the price. 1295kr.

Missionshotellet Nebo Istedgade 6 ⓣ33 21 12 17, ⓦwww.nebo.dk. Central Station. Next door to Central Station – take the back exit – this well-run Danish Mission hotel (profits go to a homeless shelter on Vesterbro) is one of the best deals this close to the centre. Rooms – some en suite – are simple but adequate and clean, and staff are friendly. There's also free internet access, chargeable wi-fi in the rooms, and bike hire for 100kr a day. 699–899kr.

Saga Colbjørnsensgade 18–20 ⓣ33 24 49 44, ⓦwww.sagahotel.dk. Bus #10; Central Station. This friendly, laid-back family hotel at the grotty, but cheap, end of Colbjørnsensgade is a good budget option. Simple, pleasant rooms – mostly en suite – with some triples and quadruples popular with families and backpackers. Free internet in the lobby. Bike hire 125kr per day. 750–950kr.

Scandic Hotel Webers Vesterbrogade 11B ⓣ33 31 14 32, ⓦwww.scandic-hotels.dk. Bus #6A, #26; Central Station. Occupying a busy corner on Vesterbrogade, this child-friendly place offers modern comforts and nicely furnished, smallish rooms ranging from singles to suites. Ask for rooms facing the courtyard (open for drinks in summer) if you want to avoid street noise, though the soundproofing is good. Much cheaper at weekends and during the summer, but you'll need to book early. 1850kr.

Tiffany Colbjørnsensgade 28 ⓣ33 21 80 50, ⓦwww.hoteltiffany.dk. Bus #10; Central Station. Small, charming and welcoming hotel, a cut above most in the area – the large, well-furnished double or family rooms come with free wi-fi and mini-kitchens comprising a microwave, fridge and toaster. Continental breakfast is left in the fridge, with freshly baked rolls left at your door each morning. Non-smoking. 1345kr.

Frederiksberg

Frederiksberg's tree-lined residential streets provide a calm setting, though restaurants are thin on the ground. The following hotels are on the map on p.88.

Avenue Åboulevard 29 ⓣ35 37 31 11, ⓦwww.avenuehotel.dk. Bus #67, #68, #250S; Forum metro. Comfortable and welcoming place on the border between Frederiksberg and Nørrebro, with spacious rooms tastefully decorated in classic Scandinavian style. There's a breakfast buffet (served outdoors in the summer), free wi-fi throughout and free parking. Rates often fall at weekends. 1195kr.

Cab-Inn Scandinavia Vodroffsvej 55 ⓣ35 36 11 11, ⓦwww.cabinn.com. Bus #29; Forum metro. The Cab-Inn concept was inspired by passenger cabins on the Oslo ferry, and the small rooms, flip-up tables and tiny showers certainly make you feel like a passenger on an overnight boat. But they're clean, functional (with free wi-fi) and safe, and the unbeatably low price makes this one of the top budget hotels in town. The **Cab-Inn Copenhagen Express** (**Danasvej 32–34 ⓣ33 21 04 00**) is only open March – Oct. Both are wheelchair accessible. Breakfast buffet (60kr) not included. Parking 80kr per day. 775kr.

Josty Pile Allé 14A ⓣ38 86 90 90, ⓦwww.josty.dk. Bus #18 or #26. Picturesque hotel with just seven rooms (1 single, 4 doubles and 2 suites, so book well in advance) in a lovely position on the edge of Frederiksberg Have. Primarily used for weddings and functions (which can make it a bit noisy at weekends), *Josty* was built as a restaurant in 1813 by sculptor Agostino Taddei, and still preserves its original romantic Italian style. The en-suite rooms are a bit worn but the beautiful location by the park still makes it an ideal spot for a romantic break. 900kr.

Sct. Thomas Frederiksberg Allé 7 ⓣ33 21 64 64, ⓦwww.hotelsctthomas.dk. Bus #26. In a great location just beyond the junction with lively Vesterbrogade, near the delis and foodshops on Værnedamsvej and a 10-minute walk from Frederiksberg Have. The friendly owners, pleasant rooms (some with shared facilities) and easy-going atmosphere have made it popular, so be sure to book ahead (a couple of months in high season). Tea and coffee and buffet breakfast are included in the price. Wi-fi in the room costs 50kr per day and they rent out bikes for 100kr per day. Parking 75kr per day. 995kr.

Nørrebro and Østerbro

There's not much available in these residential districts, which makes them appealing if you want to live side-by-side with locals. The following hotels are on the map on p.98.

Nora Nørrebrogade 18B, Nørrebro ⓣ35 37 20 21, ⓦwww.hotelnora.dk. Bus #5A or #350S. This excellent hotel spans four floors of a residential apartment block. Spacious, comfortably decorated rooms come with fridge, tea- and coffee-making facilities and free wi-fi. Popular with business travellers. Free parking in the back yard. 1300kr.

Rye Ryesgade 115, Østerbro ⓣ35 26 52 10, ⓦwww.hotelrye.dk. Bus #1A, #14 or #15. Near Fælledparken, Parken Stadium and busy Østerbrogade with its array of good places to eat and drink, *Rye* is a home away from home. On the second and third floor of an old apartment block, the sixteen comfortable rooms (one shower for every two rooms) come with slippers and housecoat, and free wi-fi. There is also a large breakfast buffet with home-made bread. One of the best budget hotels in Europe. 800kr.

The suburbs

The development of the Ørestad area on Amager has led to a crop of new hotels. There are also a couple of options convenient for the airport. The following hotels are on the map on p.105.

Cab-Inn Metro Arne Jakobsens Allé 2, Ørestad ⓣ32 46 57 00, ⓦwww.cabinn.com. Ørestad metro. Just a short train ride away from Central Station and the airport, and a short metro ride from the city centre, this new Cab-Inn hotel is by far the best of the chain, with a stunning exterior designed by Daniel Libeskind and comfortable rooms. The huge Fields shopping mall is next door. Breakfast buffet 60kr; free wi-fi throughout. 615kr.

Hilton Copenhagen Airport, Ellehammervej 20, Kastrup ⓣ32 50 15 01, ⓦwww.hilton.com. Copenhagen Airport Station. One of Copenhagen's top hotels, the *Hilton* attracts celebrities and security-conscious politicians to its twelve floors of absolute luxury. As with Hiltons elsewhere, it houses superb restaurants and a range of fitness facilities – at a price. It's connected to the airport via internal walkways. 2595kr.

Zleep Hotel Airport Englandsvej 333, Kastrup ⓣ32 46 46 10, ⓦwww.zleep.dk. Tårnby Station. Housed in a former red-brick nursing home, with a large free car park in front, this hotel is largely self-serviceable: you slide your credit card through a slot by the front door and a key card pops out. Rooms are on the small side but beds are comfortable and there's a popular restaurant next door. Wi-fi is chargeable and the airport is just a short train ride away. Rates vary hugely – you can make massive savings by booking in advance online. 1099kr.

Hostels and sleep-ins

Copenhagen has a great selection of **hostels** and **sleep-ins** (often run by volunteer staff and geared towards backpackers, and some have age restrictions). They're mostly aimed at school groups and the hordes of young Swedes who descend on the city during the summer looking for cheap alcohol and thrills, but some are quieter, with private rooms, which can work out good value if you're in a small group. **Prices** are roughly the same everywhere (105–145kr for a dorm bed); sheets (you're generally not allowed to use sleeping bags) and breakfast cost around an extra 40kr each. **Availability** is only likely to be an issue in high summer (June–Aug), when you should call ahead or turn up early on the day you want to stay. At hostels run by Danhostel (the Danish branch of Hostelling International; ⓦwww.danhostel.dk), you'll also have to pay for guest HI membership if you're not already a member.

Unless otherwise stated, none of the places listed below has a curfew, and all are open all year.

Indre By

The following places are on the map on p.44.

Danhostel Copenhagen Downtown Vandkunsten 5 ⓣ70 23 21 10, ⓦwww.copenhagendown town.dk. Bus #6A. Great, new, central hostel with a fun, cultural vibe – they host live music and art exhibitions. The café serves great coffee, breakfast (65kr), reasonably priced snacks and evening meals, and there's also a kitchen and TV room. With a range of two-to-four person rooms (some en suite) and dorms – all light, bright and newly renovated – it's very popular, especially with students and families. Bike rental, safety boxes, internet access and bed sheets/towels for hire (60kr). Book ahead, especially at weekends. En-suite double 549kr. Dorm 75kr per person.

Jørgensen Rømersgade 11 ⓣ33 13 81 86, ⓦwww.hoteljoergensen.dk. Bus #5A, #14, #40, or #350S; Nørreport S-Tog/metro. Great hostel-cum-hotel (see p.137) offering three dorms with six to twelve beds, with a TV in each room and breakfast included. You can rent sheets for 50kr. Very central, and popular with gay travellers. 150kr per person.

Rådhuspladsen and around

The following hostel is on the map on p.78.

Danhostel Copenhagen City HC Andersens Bld 50 ⓣ33 11 85 85, ⓦwww.danhostel.dk. Bus

#5A or #250S; Central Station. Trendy and bright HI "design" hostel in a multistorey building overlooking the harbour and the green copper spires of the city. With over one thousand beds in 4- to 6-person rooms (all en suite) and dorms (single sex and mixed), it's the largest city-hostel in Europe. Linen/towel hire 60kr. Breakfast 69kr. Rooms with 1–4 beds 740kr. Dorm 185kr per person.

Vesterbro

The following places are on the map on p.88.

City Public Hostel Absalonsgade 8 ⓣ33 55 00 81, ⓦwww.citypublichostel.dk. Bus #6A or #26. Easy-going and handily placed hostel, ten minutes' walk from Central Station next to the Københavns Bymuseum. There's a noisy 68-bed boy-only dorm on the lower floor, and less crowded 6- to 32-bed mixed rooms on other levels – girls only in a 24-bed dorm – plus a kitchen and a barbecue. Open May–Aug. 24hr check-in. Bedding 40kr extra, breakfast 30kr. 125kr–165kr per person depending on dorm size. Cash only.

Sleep-In Fact Valdemarsgade 14 ⓣ33 79 67 79, ⓦwww.sleep-in-fact.dk. Bus #6A or #26. In the heart of Vesterbro, this is a sports centre out of season and has sports facilities for hire when serving as a sleep-in. The eighty beds are divided between two large hall-type rooms, which can get very noisy. Open July & Aug only; reception 7.30am–noon & 3pm–3am. Small breakfast included in the price. 120kr per person.

YMCA Inter Point Valdemarsgade 15 ⓣ33 31 15 74, ⓦwww.ymca-interpoint.dk. Bus #6A or #26. Run by the Danish YMCA/YWCA, with 28 dorm beds in 4-, 6- and 10-bed rooms. Open July to mid-Aug. Curfew 12.30–7am (check-in 8–11.30am & 3.30pm–12.30am). Sheets (15kr) and blankets (25kr) can be rented. No breakfast. 105kr per person.

Nørrebro and Østerbro

The following places are on the map on p.98.

Sleep-In Green Ravnsborggade 18, Nørrebro ⓣ35 37 77 77, ⓦwww.sleep-in-green.dk. Bus #5A or #350S. In the centre of hip Nørrebro, this eco-conscious hostel is run by students and staff of the training school for organic production that the building houses for the rest of the year. It has bright rooms with 8, 20 and 38 beds, free wi-fi, and organic breakfast and snacks sold at the reception/chill-out room. Extra charge for bedding (30kr). Max age 35. Open June–Oct. 125kr per person. Lockout noon–4pm.

Sleep-In Heaven Struenseegade 7, Nørrebro ⓣ35 35 46 48, ⓦwww.sleepinheaven.com. Bus #250S. Among the city's smallest Sleep-Ins, next to Assistens Kirkegård, with two large dorms with triple bunks, plus two tiny "bridal suites" (which still share a bathroom). Quite crammed, so potentially noisy. Also has lockers, free wi-fi and takes credit cards. Sheets 30kr, breakfast 40kr. Max age 35. 135kr per person.

The suburbs

The following places are on the map on p.105.

Belægningen Avedørelejren, Vester Kvartergade 22, Hvidovre ⓣ36 77 90 84, ⓦwww.belaegningen.dk. Bus #1A to Avedøre school; S-Tog to Avedøre Station, then bus #133. Located in the old army barracks of Avedøre, next door to the Zentropa film production company (home to Von Trier and the Dogme concept), this hostel has quiet 2-, 3-, 4- and 7-bed rooms, a small kitchen, and a restaurant, *Avedørelejren*, nearby. The only drawback is the distance from town. Free internet access and sheets included in the price. No age restriction. Open all year. Check-in Mon–Fri 8am–7.30pm, Sat & Sun 9am–5.30pm. 460kr for a double, 110kr for a dorm bed.

Copenhagen Airport Hostel Amager Landevej 181, Kastrup ⓣ32 11 46 40, ⓦwww.copenhagenairporthostel.dk. Bus #30 from Central Station and Tårnby Station or a ten-minute walk from Terminal 1 at Copenhagen airport – take the free airport bus from Terminal 3. A great new option if you want to be near the airport or beaches at Amager Strandpark. Located in a large villa with four dorms of various sizes packed with bunk beds, a well-stocked bar with pool table, and a nice garden. Bedding 50kr. 112kr per person.

Danhostel Copenhagen Amager Vejlandsallé 200, Amager ⓣ32 52 27 08, ⓦwww.copenhagenyouthhostel.com. Bus #30 or Bellacenter metro and a 500m walk. A large 155-room three-star HI hostel on Amager, with simple but adequate two- to five-bed rooms, about half with en-suite bathroom, plus laundry, kitchen and net café (20kr/hour). Despite its size *Amager* tends to be fully booked during summer so it's essential to book in advance. There's free parking, and reception is open 24hr. Breakfast 55kr, sheets 40kr. Closed Dec. En-suite doubles for HI members 510kr, non-members 580kr, dorm beds for HI members 145kr, non-members 180kr.

Danhostel Copenhagen Bellahøj Herbergvejen 8, Brønshøj ⓣ38 28 97 15, ⓦwww.youth-hostel.dk. Bus #2A. More homely than its rivals, and situated in a residential part of the city – a 15min bus ride from the centre – *Bellahøj* has 4-, 6- and 14-bed rooms (sheets 50kr). There's a fully equipped kitchen and cheap laundry facilities, too. Reception is open 7am–8pm, check-in between 2pm and 5pm; and there's a dorm lockout from 10am to 1pm. Breakfast buffet 55kr. Closed Jan. HI members 140kr, non-members 175kr.

Danhostel Ishøj Strand Ishøj Strandvej 13, Ishøj ⓣ43 53 50 15, ⓦwww.ishojhostelt.dk. Ishøj Station then bus #300S. Out near Arken and some beautiful beaches, this well-run and comfortable five-star HI hostel has spacious en-suite rooms sleeping up to six, plus a restaurant. Check-in daily 2–6pm. Members 175kr, non-members 210kr.

Campsites

The Danes love camping, and have some brilliant **campsites**. Some of those near Copenhagen are in peerless locations by beaches or in woods, and all are easily accessible by public transport. There's little difference in price among them (60–80kr per person per night, plus up to 40kr per tent). Most also have full hook-ups for trailers and camper vans, and many also have **cabins** – usually small huts without bedding (this can generally be hired) with kitchenettes. They're a great self-catering option if you don't want to live in the city, but are often booked a year in advance. There's generally a basic rate for renting cabins by the day or by the week, on top of which you need to add things like electricity and a cleaning bill. Most of the campsites also have facilities such as laundries, kitchen areas with cookers, TV rooms, bike hire, internet access (either wi-fi or an internet café), playgrounds and the like.

Some campsites may ask for a **Camping Card Scandinavia** (90kr), which is available at most sites and valid for a year. Alternatively, a transit pass costs 20kr per night. Prices quoted below are per person per night and not for the pitch. For locations of the following sites, see the map on p.105.

Absalon Korsdalsvej 132, Rødovre ⓣ36 41 06 00, ⓦwww.camping-absalon.dk. Bus #1A to Avedøre Havnevej, then a 10-minute walk. A friendly campsite about 9km west of the city (exit 24 on E47), *Absalon* has good facilities for campers or those with caravans, and pleasant new cabins sleeping up to six (from 650kr per day). Open all year. 73kr.

Bellahøj Hvidkildevej 66, Bellahøj ⓣ38 10 11 50, ⓦwww.bellahoj-camping.dk. Bus #2A. One of the cheapest of Copenhagen's campsites, and near the city centre, *Bellahøj* is rather grim, with temporary facilities and little cover from the elements, but one plus point is its proximity to the excellent open-air Bellahøj public baths and the amazing view of the city from its hilltop location. There are also some simple cabins sleeping 2 (325kr) and 4 (475kr). Open June–Aug. 65kr.

Charlottenlund Fort Strandvejen 144, Charlottenlund ⓣ39 62 36 88, ⓦwww.campingcopenhagen.dk. Bus #14. Situated in the old fort at beautiful Charlottenlund beach, this excellent campsite is the best within easy striking distance of the city centre (the bus stops right outside). There are also sites for camper vans and trailers. If you're camping, try to get a pitch around the back, where there's greater protection from the elements. Open May to mid-Sept. 95kr.

City Camp Vasbygade ⓣ21 42 53 84, ⓦwww.citycamp.dk. Located close to the harbour, right behind the Fisketorvet shopping centre, *City Camp* offers safe parking for up to a hundred camper vans, and facilities such as

Food and drink

Sampling Copenhagen's traditional cuisine is a delight: the emphasis is on locally grown seasonal food, simple and flavour-packed. An ideal eating day would start with a crispy, flaky morning pastry, followed at lunchtime with a heavily laden smørrebrød (open sandwich) piled with a variety of toppings and washed down with a glass of ice-cold beer, plus – if you're feeling festive – a shot of snaps.

Typical Danish bread ▲

Eating alfresco ▼

Danish pastries ▼

Baked goods

Local bakers get up before dawn to have freshly made bread ready for the breakfast table. Try the **rundstykke** (literally "round piece"), a crispy roll baked with seeds and grain, and eaten with butter and jam or cheese. Follow this with a freshly made pastry and a cup of coffee and you have the traditional Danish breakfast.

Don't expect Danish pastries to resemble those you'll find at home, however: they're less sweet and sticky, and much more flaky and crispy (in Denmark, Danish pastry is actually called *wienerbrød*, "Viennese bread", because the art of flaking pastry was learnt from bakers in Vienna). Try the pristine **hanekam** ("rooster's comb"), a simple comb-shaped flaky pastry decorated with sugar and sliced almonds, or the aptly, if horribly, named **bagerens dårlige øje** – "baker's infected eye" – flaky pastry adorned with a gooey splodge of sweet custard or jam in the middle.

Best bakeries

▸▸ **Lagkagehuset** Torvegade 45, Christianshavn. Amazing bread, baked in traditional stone ovens, plus great pastries and cakes. Sit-down available. See p.152.

▸▸ **Rhein van Hauen** Ostergade 22 (and other outlets). Thirty years of organic baking to its credit, serving mouth watering *rundstykker* and *wienerbrød*.

▸▸ **Emmery's** Various citywide branches. Innovative bread – including spelt and moist sourdough.

If you'd rather **sit down** and enjoy your pastry in comfort, try *Café Europa* (p.148), *Royal Café* (p.150), *Konditori & Café HC Andersen* (see p.155) and *La Glace* (p.149).

Smørrebrød

A quintessentially Danish delicacy – different in style and flavour, even, from the Swedish smörgåsbord – the **smørrebrød**, or open sandwich, is eaten at lunch. The concept is simple and the end result scrumptious: a thin slice of rye bread (good for the digestion) is spread with butter (Danish, of course) or pork fat, layered with a selection of fish or sliced meats, and topped with a combination of thick dressings and raw or pickled vegetables, or, in a few cases, raw egg or caviar. Herring is key to a good smørrebrød spread, whether raw in herbal and spicy marinades, fried and pickled with onion, or smoked in various infusions of wood smoke and spices.

You can order your toppings from a list of ingredients; construct your own sandwiches from a buffet; or have your smørrebrød served ready-made. To the uninitiated, it can be a bit of a mystery as to which spreads, slices and toppings go well together, but café and restaurant staff are only too happy to help – smørrebrød combinations are ingrained in the Danish psyche. Some combos have names: **dyrelægens natmad** ("vet's midnight snack") is liver pâté topped with a square of broth jelly, cress and a slice of salted beef; **sol over gudhjem** ("sunset over Gudhjem") consists of smoked herring (preferably from Bornholm) covered with chives, radish slices and a raw egg yolk; **stjerneskud** (starburst) is a piece of fried plaice topped with remoulade and prawns, decorated with caviar and a slice of lemon. Usually two or three pieces of traditional, heavily laden smørrebrød will fill you up; the finger-food sized "smushi" served at the *Royal Café* (see p.150) allows you to try a few more, and non-traditional, combinations.

▲ Smoked fish

▼ "Smushi" at the Royal Café

Microbrews ▲

Sunset drinks ▼

Beer sign ▲

Carlsberg delivery ▼

Beer

In recent years, the ubiquitous Carlsberg has had its monopoly somewhat threatened by **microbreweries** from home and abroad. Among the smaller Danish breweries, companies such as **Thisted Bryghus**, in West Jutland, and **Bryggeriet Svaneke**, on Bornholm, are making major impressions on the Copenhagen beer scene, attracting fiercely loyal followers.

In the warm summer months, a cold **høker** beer – the generic name for any beer bought in a shop and drunk outside – can't be beaten. In Denmark, drinking alfresco – on beaches, parks or simply on a city bench – is seen as an appreciation of life and the great outdoors, so do what the locals do: stock up at a corner shop and find a spot you like.

Best beer spots

▸▸ **90eren** A veritable Carlsberg temple serving the uncarbonated version of the Danish brew virtually straight from the barrel. See p.166.

▸▸ **Bryggeriet Apollo** Brewers' pub next to Tivoli, which produces a different beer – always organic, always delicious – every month. See p.165.

▸▸ **Charlie's Bar** Small, British-run place in the city centre whose outstanding selection of fresh, unpasteurized ales and ciders are pulled from eighteen taps. See p.163.

▸▸ **Nørrebro Bryghus** Microbrewery in Nørrebro, with a gourmet restaurant upstairs and a bar downstairs, serving award-winning home-brews such as Stuykman Witt wheat beer, Czech pilsner, New York lager and the local Ravnsborg Rød. See p.159.

▸▸ **Ølbaren** Intimate place packed with bottles from all over the world, and with in-the-know bartenders. See p.167.

showers and washing machines. You can also have breakfast delivered to your door. Open June–Aug. Check-in 8am–10pm. 75kr per camper and 75kr per person per day.

Copenhagen Camping Bachersmindevej 13, Dragør ⓣ32 94 20 07, ⓦwww.copenhagen camping.dk. Train to Tårnby Station then take bus #350S and get off at Store Magleby Strandvej, from where it's an easy five-minute walk (a 30min journey in total). Brand new campsite just outside Dragør and 12km outside the city centre, with beaches on one side and a bird reserve on the other. The site includes luxurious self-contained cabins sleeping up to six (from 575kr per day) plus a few excellent value cabins sleeping two (375kr). Open all year. 70kr.

Nærum Ravnebakken, Nærum ⓣ45 80 19 57, ⓦwww.camping-naerum.dk. Jægersborg station, then private train to Nærum. Fifteen kilometres north of the city centre, in a pleasant setting beside some woods, this site is very family-oriented, with great play areas for the kids. Basic cabins are also available (400kr for up to 4 people). Open April to mid-Sept. 69kr.

Tangloppen Ishøj Havn, Ishøj ⓣ43 54 07 67, ⓦwww.fdmcamping.dk. Ishøj Station, then bus #128. Right next door to Arken (see p.108), and facing onto a picturesque lagoon, *Tangloppen* is a wonderful place if you want a beach, modern art and not much else – shelter is minimal, and tents take a battering here in bad weather. There's also a cheap café selling grilled food, and a number of stunningly positioned cabins sleeping up to eight (460kr for up to 4 people; 670kr for up to 8). Open April to mid-Oct. 77kr.

11

Eating

Copenhagen's **restaurant** scene has seen a dramatic increase in the quantity and variety of establishments in the last decade or so, punching above its weight in the Michelin star category – the city now has a total of thirteen starred restaurants, more than Rome and Madrid – and establishing itself on the international culinary scene with highly original places like *Noma* (see p.152), focusing on the best of Nordic produce. This renewed vigour and excitement at the top has filtered down, with the result that trendy new places offering fancy fusion food or modern takes on traditional Danish cooking open up on an almost monthly basis, though there's still plenty of old-fashioned restaurants offering excellent, traditional Danish food. Despite the cost, Danes love to dine out and, as soon as summer arrives, the city is transformed as cafés and restaurants spill out onto the pavements – for those less than balmy nights, most will turn on gas heaters or provide you with blankets to help along that *hygge* ("cosy") feeling.

For the vistor, the **food** is all part of the Copenhagen experience, be it tucking into a plate of herring by the harbour, starting your day with one of the city's popular and very filling brunch deals, or paying through the nose for beautifully presented **seafood** in a gourmet restaurant. Don't miss the delicious and quintessentially Danish lunch phenomenon of **smørrebrød**, or open sandwich – a slice of delicious bread topped off with anything from herring to beef tartar to prawns, and always beautifully garnished. It's one of the highlights of a visit to the city, better still when washed down with another Danish delight – an invigorating shot of **snaps** (many restaurants have a snaps menu; failing that, just ask the waiter what goes best with what). Smørrebrød is best sampled in one of the many traditional smørrebrød restaurants, cosy and often packed cellar places open at lunchtime only and for which you're advised to book ahead – we've highlighted a few of the best on p.148. For a less expensive option head for one of the many smørrebrød shops that, around lunchtime, sell ready-made takeout smørrebrød to the city's workforce. Another speciality not to be missed is the famous **Danish pastry** – available in most cafés but best bought straight from the excellent and plentiful **konditorier** (patisseries) and eaten on the move or in the *konditori*'s coffee bar.

Eating out in Copenhagen can be **expensive**. Just a cup of coffee and a Danish might cost around 60kr, while, in the evening, dining out at any of the more formal **restaurants** will generally set you back at least 150kr for a main course, with a decent bottle of wine costing upwards of 200kr. That said, daytime set menus can prove an affordable way to sample the city's finer, more adventurous cuisine, while combining breakfast and lunch in one of the city's many **brunch** options (see p.151), or lunching on a couple of classic Danish smørrebrød at around 49kr a piece is a good way to enjoy local food relatively cheaply. In addition, among the usual fast-food options the ubiquitous **pølser stands** offer various surprisingly tasty hot dogs and burgers. For a list of the best places to eat on a budget, see the box on p.160.

Though Copenhagen is a long way behind London or New York in terms of quality and diversity of **ethnic restaurants**, Vesterbro and Nørrebro have a large array of **Turkish** and **Indian** places – probably the city's cheapest eating-out options – along with Asian noodle joints and (slightly pricier) **Thai** restaurants and Japanese **sushi** places. Such places tend to offer the best range for **vegetarians**, too, though most restaurants offer at least a couple of meat-free dishes (see p.155 for a list of the best).

Note that the **opening hours** given for each listing are for the venue's actual closing time; the **kitchen often closes** one or, in the case of café/bars, two hours earlier. Note also that many restaurants are closed Sunday or Monday – be sure to double-check before you set out. Most places have English-language menus; failing that the waiting staff usually speak at least enough English to translate. Note that some cafés and restaurants levy a surcharge of up to five percent for paying with a **foreign credit card** – check the menu's small print or ask first.

For more on Danish food see the **Food and drink** colour section and, for a glossary of food terms, see pp.225–227.

Indre By

Indre By has cafés and restaurants on virtually every street corner. The area's many offices and businesses also mean that most restaurants have an excellent lunch menu; indeed, for some, lunch is the busiest time of the day. The following places are on the map on p.44.

Den Anden Fortunstraede 7 ⓣ33 14 64 00, ⓦwww.madklubben.info. Tues–Sat 5.30pm – midnight. More central, sister restaurant (Den Anden means "the other one") of the very successful *Madklubben* (see p.153) offering a Mediterranean-influenced menu of beautifully presented, classic, delicious mains like confit of duck, fillet of beef or rack of lamb. Choose from the three-, four- or five-course menus at 200kr, 250kr and 300kr respectively (side orders are extra). Great value. Booking advisable.

Atlas Bar Larsbjørnsstræde 18 ⓣ33 15 03 52, ⓦwww.atlasbar.dk. Mon–Sat noon–midnight. On trendy Larsbjørnsstræde in the basement underneath *Flyvefisken* restaurant, the popular *Atlas Bar* features a globetrotting menu (lunch 95kr plus, dinner 120kr plus) that leans towards the exotic (and often spicy) with dishes like Manila chicken, Pakistani lamb and ostrich on skewers – though more sedate options like fishcakes and lasagne also feature – on a blackboard menu that changes daily. Portions are large and delicious. Also excellent, freshly pressed vegetable and fruit juices. Best to book at lunchtime.

Barbarellah Nørre Farimagsgade 41 ⓦwww.barbarellah.dk. Tues–Thurs 2pm–2am, Fri & Sat 2pm–4am. *Barbarellah*, with its easygoing, loungey vibe, funky bar and DJ (from 9pm, 8pm on weekends), is the creation of three siblings from Chile, who make mean cocktails and cook up good South American food. Choose from the "lounge menu", with its tasty snacks like churrasco sandwich (a Chilean sandwich with fine cut beef, avocado, aioli and salad), nachos, burgers and tapas (from around 85kr), or the "restaurant menu", with starters like Chilean lentil soup and Bolivian potato salad followed by mains (from 165kr) like fillet of Argentinian beef. The chocolate chilli mousse is a great way to finish.

Bibendum Vincafe & Butik Nansensgade ⓣ33 33 07 74, ⓦwww.vincafeen.dk. Mon–Sat 4pm–midnight. This small, rustic wine bar with mismatched tables and chairs is a bit of a treasure, serving up a short list of delicious tapas combos with a Spanish/Middle Eastern influence and small taster plates of charcuterie, cheese and olives from 55kr. In addition to the wide range of excellent imported wines (also sold in the shop), there's a good range of aperitifs, digestifs, pale ales and some Belgian beers, too. Round things off with the fantastic coffee imported from northern Italy. Booking essential.

Café & Ølhalle "1892" Rømersgade 22 ⓣ33 33 00 18, ⓦwww.arbejdermuseet.dk. Daily 11am–5pm. It doesn't come much more atmospheric and old-fashioned than this. Situated in the basement of the Arbejdermuseet (see p.51), cosy *Ølhalle* has been restored to its 1892 appearance and specializes in food from that era – traditional Danish lunch food, such as *bidesild* (strongly flavoured pickled herring) washed down with snaps. There are plenty of small dishes for around 59–99kr – herring, roast beef with home-made remoulade, *fiskefrikadeller* and the like – while the lunch platter gives you a taste of a few dishes for 148kr. Booking advisable.

Café Fiat Kongens Nytorv 18 ⓣ33 14 22 77, ⓦwww.f-i-a-t.dk. Mon–Thurs & Sun noon–4pm & 5.30pm–midnight, Fri & Sat 5.30pm–1am. On the north side of Kongens Nytorv, *Fiat* offers authentic Italian food with a delicious lunch menu of antipasti, pasta (from 125kr) and wood-fired, thin-crust Neapolitan style pizzas (from 115kr); in the evening you can also get secondi piatti like braised rabbit leg with polenta, osso bucco, or grilled steak fiorentina, from around 195kr. Three-course menu available for 375kr. Takeaway available.

Café Hovedtelegrafen Købmagergade 37 ⓦwww.cafehovedtelegrafen.dk. Tues & Thurs–Sat 10am–5pm, Wed 10am–8pm, Sun noon–4pm. Most people bypass the exhibitions in the Post & Tele Museum and take the lift straight to this rooftop café. Cool, modern and light, with fine views over the rooftops, it's a relaxing spot. Try posh open sandwiches from 89kr, salads, fish and steaks from around 125kr – or just coffee and a piece of gorgeous cake.

Cap Horn Nyhavn 21 ⓣ33 12 85 04, ⓦwww.caphorn.dk. Daily 9am–1am. One of the more reliable, friendly and good-value options along this touristy stretch. Sit by the canal and tuck into a lunch of herrings or gravadlax for around 54kr or, if you're after something more substantial, the tasty organic burgers with salad and potatoes for 129kr. The evening menu features solid, no-fuss pasta dishes and meat or fish mains like leg of lamb, steak or lobster from 129kr. There's always a vegetarian option. For dessert, you can't beat the home-made chocolate truffles.

Custom House Havnegade 44 ⓣ33 31 01 30, ⓦwww.customhouse.dk. Daily 9am–1am. Terence Conran's Danish venture is a typically stylish gastrodome, with three restaurants, two bars and a deli housed in the renovated former customs house on the harbourfront. Of the three restaurants, the clubby Danish/European *Bar and Grill* steakhouse (daily lunch and dinner; mains from 150kr) is the most informal, with decent steaks, burgers and fish and lots of regional Danish produce. The Italian *Bacino* (Mon–Fri lunch & dinner, Sat lunch only; mains from 155kr) at the other end of the building has lighter decor and a classier vibe. You could also head upstairs for great sushi, teriyaki and charcoal-grilled meat and fish in *Ebisu*, the elegant Japanese alternative (Tues–Sat dinner only; mains from 160kr). Outside seating on the quayside in summer. Booking advisable.

L'Education Nationale Larsbjørnsstræde 12 ⓣ33 91 53 60, ⓦwww.leducationnationale.dk. Mon–Sat 11.30am–midnight, Sun 4.30–10pm. Everything in this cosy, rustic café comes from France – even the butter on the table. All the classics are here – lunchtime favourites such as croque monsieur, baguettes, omelette and moules frites give way in the evening to large portions of hearty French country cooking like rabbit ragout or lamb casserole. Expect to pay upwards of 49kr for lunch and, in the evening, 89kr for a starter, 199kr for a main course.

Europa Amagertorv 1 ⓦwww.europa1989.dk. Mon–Thurs & Sat 7.45am–midnight, Fri 7.45am–1am, Sun 9am–11pm. In a great spot, overlooking bustling Amagertorv and with ample outdoor seating, the stylish, large, glass-fronted *Europa* is a welcome stop along Strøget. Excellent coffee, great Danish pastries, breakfasts and brunch (from 159kr), delicious salads and sandwiches for lunch (from 125kr) and classic fish and meat mains in the evening (from 159kr).

Flyvefisken Larsbjørnsstræde 18 ⓣ33 14 95 15, ⓦwww.atlasbar.dk. Mon–Sat 5.30–10pm.

Simply delicious smørrebrød

The following are a few of the best spots in the city to sample **smørrebrød**. For more on smørrebrød see the Food and drink colour section.

Aamanns p.153
Hansens Gamle Familiehaven p.158
Ida Davidsen p.153
Kanal Cafeen p.155
Slotskælderen Hos Gitte Kik p.150
Søpromenaden p.160
Told & Snaps p.151

Upstairs from, and affiliated to, the equally popular *Atlas Bar* and with a good view of goings-on in trendy Larsbjørnsstræde, *Flyvefisken* is a great place to start the evening in one of the city's liveliest quarters. Its Thai menu features all the favourites – soups, curries, fishcakes, noodles and satays – served amid a stylish blend of modern Danish decor with tasteful Thai touches. Main courses from 130kr.

La Galette Larsbjørnsstræde 9 ⓦwww.lagalette.dk. Mon–Sat noon–4pm & 5.30–10pm, Sun 4–10pm. Tucked away in a back yard with outdoor seating in summer, this cosy, excellent-value and authentically Breton (the flour for the galettes is imported from Brittany) pancake joint offers the savoury and sweet buckwheat kind with a range of fillings; you can wash it down with a jug of equally authentic cider. From 35kr for a plain galette to 110kr for a galette with caviar and smoked salmon filling.

La Glace Skoubogade 20. Mon–Thurs 8.30am–5.30pm, Fri 8.30am–6pm, Sat 9am–5pm, Sun 11am–5pm. Time seems to have stood still in the city's oldest patisserie, the scrumptious *La Glace*, with primly dressed waitresses ministering to a genteel clientele who come for the beautifully sculpted, cream-heavy cakes and pots of real hot chocolate. If all that sounds too much, you could settle for a coffee and a Danish.

Den Grønne Kælder Pilestræde 48 ⓣ33 93 01 40. Mon–Sat 11am–10pm. "The Green Kitchen" is a busy but relaxed vegetarian cellar restaurant, offering scrumptious seasonal hot dishes like vegetable stews and mushroom and spinach lasagne and a tempting array of unusual main-course salads. Dinner is relatively cheap, compared to other city-centre restaurants, starting at 95kr for very generous portions. Also organic wines, beer and home-made bread. Note that it doesn't accept foreign credit cards.

Kong Hans Kælder Vingårdsstræde 6 ⓣ33 11 68 68, ⓦwww.konghans.dk. Mon–Sat 6pm–midnight. With a Michelin star since 1983 and a romantic setting in the vaulted cellar of a medieval building on the site of what was once King Hans' vineyard, this is one of Denmark's best restaurants. Choose from two simple and elegant French-influenced menus: "Signature", an à la carte selection (820kr plus for three courses) of the restaurant's classic cuisine with starters like oysters, langoustines or foie gras, and mains such as black lobster and tenderloin of Danish beef; and "Innovation", a seven-course taster menu with, as the name suggests, more experimental dishes like king crab with chanterelle mushrooms preserved in elderflower vinegar, for a set price of 1100kr. Pricey stuff, but for sheer quality, atmosphere and a sense of occasion, it's hard to beat. Booking essential.

Krogs Fiskerestaurant Gammel Strand 38 ⓣ33 15 89 15, ⓦwww.krogs.dk. Mon–Sat 6pm–midnight. One of the city's oldest, best and most expensive fish restaurants, located on the canalside where fisherwomen used to sell their catch. The high-ceilinged interior has been faithfully restored to its original 1910 appearance, right down to the colour of the paint, and oozes elegance with its gilt-framed mirrors and nineteenth-century paintings. If you can justify paying the high prices, you'll be rewarded with beautifully presented, locally sourced dishes like fried scallops with oyster mayo and clamfoam, Limfjord oysters, butter-fried Baltic salmon and the house speciality – bouillabaisse à la Krogs. À la carte starters begin at around 175kr; mains from 300kr; the three-course set menu, at 575kr, is a great way to sample the exquisite food. Booking essential.

Marius Nørre Farimagsgade 55 ⓣ33 11 83 83, ⓦwww.cafe-marius.dk. Tues & Wed noon–11pm, Thurs noon–1am, Fri noon–2am, Sat 11am–2am, Sun 11am–4pm. This Chicagoan corner café prides itself on serving the "best brunch in town", and they're not far wrong. On weekends (11am–3pm) they offer two American brunches – one including chorizo and potato pancakes (105kr), the other bacon, hash browns and buttermilk pancakes (99kr) – and an array of side orders. At other times choose from a wider menu of freshly made wraps, burgers, salads and great home-made pasta for lunch; more pasta, stir fries and steaks for dinner (from 119kr). Booking recommended for brunch.

Nyhavns Færgekro Nyhavn 5 ⓣ33 15 15 88. Daily 9am–1pm. The "Ferry Inn" is a good lunchtime option along this restaurant-heavy stretch and, for the uninitiated, offers a great way of getting to grips with Danish herring – a lunchtime herring buffet with ten types for 119kr. There's also the "Nyhavn Selection" with five pieces of smørrebrød for 179kr, and smørrebrød from 54kr a piece.

Paludan Bogcafé Fiolstræde 10. Mon–Fri 9am–7pm, Sat 10am–5pm. In the heart of the Latin Quarter and with a textbook-toting student clientele, this pleasant bookshop-café is a good spot to enjoy inexpensive coffee, croissants and cakes or a lunchtime salad or sandwich in between browsing the bookshops on Fiolstræde.

Pasta Basta Valkendorfsgade 22 ⓦwww.pastabasta.dk. Mon–Thurs & Sun 11.30pm–2am, Fri & Sat 11.30am–2am. Big, central and a good late night option, *Pasta Basta* is a favourite final stop for partygoers (the kitchen stays open till 1.30am), and extremely popular with young locals at all times. The all-day buffet of pasta and salads for 89kr is great value and there are plenty of other pasta dishes and fish and meat mains from around 159kr.

Peder Oxe Gråbrødretorv 11 ⓣ33 11 00 77, ⓦwww.pederoxe.dk. Daily 11.30am–1am. Situated in a charming, old ochre-coloured building on a picturesque square (outdoor seating in fine weather), this popular French-inspired café/bistro is an old favourite with locals. Busy for both lunch and dinner, it offers a small menu of brasserie staples like moules frites and steak, with a few Danish-inspired fish and shellfish options. The main attraction, though, is the juicy organic "oxe-burger" made with finest beef (129kr) – for an extra 45kr you can help yourself to the salad buffet. The lunchtime smørrebrød option is good value at 138kr for three pieces.

Quote Kongens Nytorv 8 ⓣ33 32 51 51, ⓦwww.cafequote.dk. Mon–Wed 8am–midnight, Thurs 8am–1am, Fri 8am–2am, Sat 10am–2am, Sun 11am–midnight. A large, modern, café/restaurant with outside seating right on Kongens Nytorv. Watch the comings and goings on the square while enjoying morning coffee and breakfast or choose from the wide-ranging, if somewhat pricey, lunch menu of international sandwiches – croque monsieur, club sandwich and smørrebrød – as well as omelettes, soups, salads and great burgers with fat, hand-cut chips. The evening menu, Modern European with a strong French bias, features favourites like foie gras and moules frites in addition to mains like seared yellow fin tuna or entrecôte béarnaise from 145kr. Evening booking advisable.

Riccos Kaffebar Studiestraede 24. Daily 8am–10pm. This cosy, friendly little basement coffee house on funky Studiestraede has a strong local following who come for its delicious home-baked filled rolls, smoothies, milkshakes and some of the best coffee in town. Healthy, homely breakfasts like boiled eggs, muesli or bread and cheese set you up for the day; there's also internet access and seating at the rear where you can plug in your laptop. This is the sister branch of the original, *Riccos*, on Istedgade (see p.157). Takeaway available.

Rice Market Hausergade 38 ⓣ35 35 75 30, ⓦwww.ricemarket.dk. Mon–Thurs 5pm–midnight, Fri & Sat 5–11pm, Sun 5–9pm. This modern Asian bistro (owned by the same people as *Kiin Kiin*, see p.158) dishes up an excellent, largely Thai menu, though Chinese and Japanese dishes do get a look in. It's reasonably priced – from around 200kr you can tuck into starters like dim sum, Thai fishcakes or tempura followed by mains such as Thai green curry, noodle soup or wok-fried scallops with chilli.

Riz Raz Kompagnistræde 20 ⓦwww.rizraz.dk. Daily 11.30am–midnight. *Riz Raz*'s hot and cold Mediterranean veggie buffet is one of the city's best (and healthiest) budget options – all the fresh salads, pasta, falafel, rice and feta cheese you can eat for 79kr (89kr in the evening). There's also a meatier menu including kebabs and steaks. As you'd expect, it's usually packed, but turnover is high and there's outdoor seating. There's another branch at Store Kannikestræde 19.

Royal Café Amagertorv 6 ⓦwww.theroyalcafe.dk. Mon–Fri 10am–7pm, Sat 10am–6pm, Sun 11am–5pm. In a small courtyard next to Royal Copenhagen, the high-ceilinged, quirkily decorated *Royal Café* is a chic place to stop for coffee or a pot of tea (lots of varieties on offer) with a delicious cake or biscuit. Alternatively, try the café's innovative "smushi" concept – mini-smørrebrød at 45kr each or 165kr for four, including a shot of snaps. While you wait you can read the glossy magazines or browse the eclectic and pricey stuff for sale, from candles to kids' clothes to accessories. Some outdoor seating.

Slotskælderen Hos Gitte Kik Fortunstræde 4. Tues–Sat 11am–5pm. It may not look much from the outside but this cosy, old-fashioned basement restaurant is one of the best places in town to sample smørrebrød. There's no menu – just walk up to the table, presided over by Gitte herself, pick your toppings from the heaped plates of delicacies, and the made-up smørrebrød will be brought over to you. 46–95kr per piece.

Sommersko Kronprinsensgade 6 ⓦwww.sommersko.dk. Mon–Wed 8am–midnight, Thurs 8am–1am, Fri 8am–4am, Sat 9am–4am, Sun 10am–midnight. Friendly, laid-back, Parisian-style café/brasserie on a boutique street attracting a young and trendy clientele. Great for morning coffee and croissant or a delectable brunch (80–115kr); lunch options include French classics like onion soup and steak frites, along with staple sandwiches, burgers, omelettes and salads. In the evening, innovative pasta dishes, fish and meat mains are served till 11pm.

Sporvejen Gråbrødretorv 17 ⓦwww.sporvejen.dk. Daily 11am–midnight. One of the city's more unusual restaurants and a hit with kids, *Sporvejen* is housed in the last of Copenhagen's old trams with old tram-stop signs and tram paraphernalia covering the walls. The food is cheap, cheerful and great value, with burgers, generous omelettes and home-made chips from around 50kr. Outdoor seating in summer.

Stella Kompagnistraede 18 ⓦwww.cafestella.dk. Mon–Wed & Sun 9am–1am, Thurs–Sat 9am–5am. Cosy, low-lit, late-opening, corner café/bar (some outdoor seating) on pedestrianized Kompagnistraede, serving up generous portions of filling food at reasonable prices to a largely young crowd. Brunch, wraps, burgers, salads and sandwiches at lunchtime (from 74kr), as well as nachos and noodles. In the evening, mains start at 99kr for pasta, steak and fish; start the evening off with a cocktail (40kr on Thurs; 65kr at other times). Kitchen closes at midnight.

Told & Snaps Toldbodgade 2 ⓣ33 93 83 85, ⓦwww.toldogsnaps.dk. Mon–Sat 11.30am–4pm. Situated just off Nyhavn and a cut above most of the restaurants along here, this traditional, family-run lunchtime smørrebrød place focuses on quality food rather than fashion with a long list of toppings from which you tick off your choices. The curried herring and home-made meatballs are delicious, but it's all good, especially when accompanied by one of the home-made aquavits or a beer from the Nørrebro brewery.

Vandkunsten Rådhusstræde 17. Mon–Fri 8am–5pm. A great place to pick up a delicious sandwich to go and sit and eat by the canal, this small Italian shop sells home-made focaccia and ciabatta filled to bursting with pastrami, mozzarella, sun-dried tomato, avocado and the like (from 33kr). They also do takeaway pastas and salads.

Brunch

Most cafés offer a range of **brunch** options, from a restrained yoghurt, muesli and fruit combo to American-style blowouts with pancakes, eggs and bacon. They're usually very good value, at around 60–120kr, and available until at least 2pm (sometimes all day), either plated up or as all-you-can-eat buffets. The following are some of the best brunch spots in the city:

Bang & Jensen	p.156
Café Wilder	p.152
Canteen	p.159
Marius	p.149
O's American Breakfast & Dinner	p.154
Sommersko	p.151
Stella	p.151
Sult	p.154

Victor Ny Ostergade 8 ⓣ33 13 36 13, ⓦwww.cafevictor.dk. Mon–Wed 8am–1am, Thurs–Sat 8am–2am, Sun 11am–11pm. An old-timer on the Copenhagen food scene, this large, bustling, French-style brasserie with smart, efficient waiters is still going strong and offers something for everyone from its French/Danish menu, be it morning coffee and croissant, lunchtime herring, coq au vin or croque monsieur in the brasserie (from 95kr) or oysters, fish and foie gras from around 165kr in the adjacent, posher restaurant (Mon–Thurs noon–3pm & 6–10.30pm, Fri noon–3pm & 6–11pm, Sat noon–4pm & 6–11pm, Sun 6–10pm). Restaurant booking advisable.

Wok Shop Ny Adelgade 6 ⓦwww.wokshop.dk. Mon–Fri noon–2pm & 5.30–10pm, Sat 6–10pm. Excellent Thai restaurant with plenty of seating and a huge menu of fresh, fragrant, spicy soups, satays, noodle dishes and curries, most of which are available for takeaway.

Zirup Laederstraede 32 ⓦwww.zirup.dk. Mon–Thurs & Sun 10am–midnight, Fri & Sat

10am–2am. One of several cafés along this pedestrianized stretch, and probably the most popular, trendy Zirup is always packed at lunchtime with locals tucking into the huge brunch plates (from 99kr), sandwiches (from 89kr), quesadillas and burgers. The evening menu offers good-quality, filling standards – burgers, pasta, stroganoff, grilled chicken breast and the like – for a reasonable 129kr.

Christianshavn

Laid-back Christianshavn is a great spot to linger over a meal, which you can follow with a walk along the pretty Wilders Kanal; it also offers the unique experience of eating out in the hippie haven of Christiania. The following places are on the map on p.55.

Bastionen og Løven Voldgade 50 ⓣ32 95 09 40, ⓦwww.bastionen-loven.dk. Mon–Fri noon–midnight, Sat 10am–midnight, Sun 10am–5pm. Set in the old miller's house next to Lille Mølle, up on the ramparts and with outside seating, this is a charming, relaxed spot for traditional Danish food. The lunchtime menu offers delicious salads or smørrebrød from 65kr – try the delectable *kalveleverpostej* (calves' liver paté) and soups in winter; in the evening, main courses start at 185kr. The overpriced weekend brunch is best avoided.

Café Wilder Wildersgade 56 ⓦwww.cafewilder.dk. Mon 9am–midnight, Tues & Wed 9am–1am, Thurs & Fri 9am–2am, Sat 9.30am–2am, Sun 9.30am–midnight. Popular and relaxed locals' café, great for coffee and croissants, sandwiches or salads, and usually packed on Sundays with brunch junkies tucking into the "Wilder's brunch" (10am–2pm; 95kr) – a generous helping of egg, bacon, sausage, yoghurt, cheese and fruit.

Christianshavns Bådudlejning & Café Overgaden neden Vandet 29 ⓣ32 96 53 53, ⓦwww.baadudlejningen.dk. Mid-April to mid-Sept 9am–midnight. Floating in Christianshavns Kanal on a large pontoon, this place has a café serving light breakfasts (25kr), famous fish balls, and sandwiches and salad lunches (from 55kr), and a slightly finer table-clothed restaurant devoted to Danish/French cuisine.

DACafé Strandgade 27B ⓦwww.dac.dk. Mon–Fri 11am–4pm. On the first floor of the beautifully restored Dansk Architektur-center warehouse, this café has possibly Copenhagen's best views from its glass-encased bird-box balcony that hovers over the waters of Innerhavnen. The menu is limited to well-prepared sandwiches, soup of the season, cake of the day and a delightful lunchtime buffet (noon–1.30pm). Arrive early if you want a table in the bird-box.

Era Ora Overgaden Neden Vandet 33 ⓣ32 54 06 93, ⓦwww.eraora.dk. Mon–Sat noon–3pm (kitchen closes 2pm) & 7pm–midnight (kitchen closes 10.30pm). In a lovely location by the Wilders Kanal and with a romantic courtyard for summer dining, *Era Ora* serves top-flight Italian cuisine – all ingredients are seasonal and most are sourced from Italy. You'll pay for the quality, with lunchtime menus starting at 325kr and evening four- to seven-course menus from 650kr, but for Italophiles looking for a special meal, it's hard to beat. Book well in advance.

Kanalen Wilders Plads 2 ⓣ32 95 13 30, ⓦwww.restaurant-kanalen.dk. Mon–Sat 11.30am–midnight. Intimate, romantic and elegant canalside restaurant in a pink eighteenth-century building with indoor and canalside seating. The traditional Danish lunchtime menu includes a herring platter (115kr) and fried plaice with remoulade (135kr); the evening set menu also focuses on local ingredients (360kr for three courses; 300kr for the equally delightful veggie version).

Lagkagehuset Torvegade 45. Mon–Fri 6am–7pm, Sat & Sun 6am–6pm. At the absolute epicentre of Christianshavn – both geographically and socially – this fantastic bakery/café buzzes with life throughout the day. Laden with a mouthwatering array of home-made Danish pastries, fruity muffins and cakes, this is also a great place to pick up a coffee and a bite to eat by the canal. A notice board advertises everything from lift-shares to Jylland to rooms for rent and, with free wi-fi, the counter seating by the large windows is always packed.

Morgenstedet Langgaden, Christiania ⓦwww.morgenstedet.dk. Tues–Sun noon–9pm. Cosy Christiania favourite serving great-value vegetarian and vegan food from an organic kitchen. There are usually five dishes – salads, stews, curry, ratatouille and the like – on offer, costing between 75kr and 95kr. BYOB.

Noma Strandgade 93 ⓣ32 96 32 97, ⓦwww.noma.dk. *Noma*, with two Michelin stars and right up there on the world's best restaurant lists, is *the* place for modern, inventive and unusual Scandinavian cuisine. The quirky, ever-changing menu relies totally on seasonal ingredients from the North Atlantic countries cooked by traditional methods, so there's a good deal of pickling, salting and drying, and lots of musk ox, lumpfish, Danish blood sausage, fungi and berries. Housed in a former warehouse, *Noma*'s decor is as modern and stylish as you'd expect – exposed bricks, white paint, animal skins draped over expensive chairs – and its location, overlooking the harbour, completes the whole experience. With three-course set dinner menus costing upwards of 845kr, the lighter three-course lunch menu at 395kr might be the way to go if you're counting your pennies. Book three months in advance for dinner.

Spicey Kitchen Café Torvegade 56. Daily 5–10pm. Like stepping into a busy Middle Eastern truck stop. The curries, around 65kr, are excellent – most of them made with chicken or lamb. Also fantastic kebabs (from 50kr) and a range of good veggie dishes. You may have to wait for a table in the rather cramped interior. Takeaway available; credit cards not accepted.

Spiseloppen The Loppe Building, Bådsmandsstræde 43, Christiania ⓣ32 57 95 58, ⓦwww.spiseloppen.dk. Tues–Sun 5–11pm. Upstairs from the music venue *Musikloppen*, this excellent restaurant has a reputation far beyond Christiania's borders for serving superb food from a changing but always imaginative small menu of international dishes. Meat and fish mains start at 165kr, and there's always a good vegetarian option. Very popular, so book ahead.

Rosenborg and Frederikstad

Cafés and restaurants in upmarket Rosenborg and Frederikstad are clustered along the busy streets of Gothersgade and Store Kongensgade. Hours can be erratic: some do a brisk lunch trade with local office workers and are open weekdays only. The following places are on the map on p.64.

Aamanns Øster Farimagsgade 12. Mon–Sat noon–3pm & 6–9.30pm. Excellent restaurant next to a deli of the same name run by a popular Danish TV chef called Adam Aamann who is especially famous for his smørrebrød. The range (lunch only) is extensive – try the three pieces with herring (115kr) or selected meats (165kr). For dinner the menu stays traditional, and simple, with offerings such as skate with crushed new potatoes or fried foie gras with cherries and glazed beetroot (two courses 255kr).

Coffee Factory Gothersgade 21. Mon–Fri 7.30am–7pm, Sat 9am–6pm. Small, friendly coffee bar serving the finest coffees from around the world for the *feinschmecker* (someone who can taste which estate a coffee comes from). Also cakes, pastries and sandwiches.

Ida Davidsen Store Kongensgade 70 ⓣ33 91 36 55, ⓦwww.idadavidsen.dk. Mon–Fri 10.30am–4pm. The Davidsen family has been serving up smørrebrød since 1888; Ida and her husband opened this basement place in 1974 and the menu now runs to more than 200 options. It's an institution, known by everyone, and still as popular for lunch as ever. The interior is cosy and old-fashioned and the waiters will help you choose.

Kafferiet Esplanaden 44. Mon–Fri 8am–6pm, Sat & Sun 10am–6pm. On a cold winter's day, after having seen Kastellet and the Little Mermaid, get warm again at *Kafferiet*. Choose from a wide choice of excellent coffees and croissants, cakes and sandwiches. In summer, freshly squeezed fruit juices and smoothies may suffice.

Den Lille Fede Store Kongensgade 15 ⓣ33 33 70 02, ⓦwww.denlillefede.dk. Mon–Sat 5.30–10pm. Literally "the little fat one", this cosy restaurant serves excellent Mediterranean-inspired food with mouth-watering dishes like creamy onion soup, baked cod with olives and tomato, and fillet of pork with herb risotto. The only decision is whether to go for five or seven courses (325kr/448kr). For an extra 225kr/350kr you'll get a different and perfectly chosen glass of wine to accompany each dish. It's not a cheap evening out, but good value: the food is really good, imaginatively but not fussily cooked and presented, and the service is excellent. Booking advisable.

Madklubben Store Kongensgade 66 ⓣ33 32 32 34. Mon–Sat 5.30pm–midnight. A trendy yet relaxed atmosphere, rustic Danish cooking with a modern twist, and good portions at reasonable prices have helped make this relative newcomer madly popular. The frequently changing menu typically features delicious starters like lumpfish roe or pork with smoked crackling, followed by unpretentious mains like leg of chicken with home-made sausage or braised beef with beetroot. Choose from one- to four-course menus from 100–250kr. Side dishes are 25kr but big enough to share. Booking advisable.

Mormors Bredgade 45 ⓦwww.mormors.dk. Mon–Fri 9.30am–4pm, Sat 11.30am–3pm. Gorgeously nostalgic and homely, with retro 1940s furnishings, *Mormors* is a great spot to enjoy a sandwich or home-made cake – the choc chip scones are heavenly – washed down with coffee from the huge 150-year-old grinder. Old-fashioned sweets and trinkets are also on sale, and there's a small gift shop.

O's American Breakfast & Dinner Gothersgade 15. Mon–Fri 9.30am–10pm, Sat & Sun 4am–10pm; another branch at Øster Farimagsgade 27 (Mon–Fri 9.30am–3pm, Sat & Sun 9.30am–4pm). Full-on American diner with a vast assortment of fry-ups that could satisfy your calorie count for an entire week. Especially recommended are the filling breakfast/brunches (from 79kr) that come with pancakes, hash browns, sausages and eggs, and – at the Gothersgade branch – can be enjoyed as early as 4am at weekends. Dinner (only at Gothersgade) includes soul food from "N'awlins"; chicken gumbo (129kr) is among the favourites.

Raasmus Oubaek Store Kongensgade 52 ⓣ33 32 32 09, ⓦwww.rasmusoubaek.dk. Mon–Fri 6pm–midnight. Cosy, intimate restaurant run by ex-Michelin chef Rasmus Oubaek, who cooks excellent French cuisine. All dishes (85–185kr) come in one (generous starter) size and the idea is that you pick three – though, given the rich flavours, two should suffice. It's mostly perfectly cooked classics – boeuf béarnaise, snails in garlic, foie gras – with a few modern dishes like turbot with mussels and a couple of divine pasta options. Excellent desserts, too (70kr). Booking essential.

Sult Vognmagergade 8B ⓣ33 74 34 17, ⓦwww.cinemateket.dk. Tues–Sun noon–10pm. Occupying part of Cinemateket (see p.67), this large, bright, modern bistro dishes up a wide-ranging menu of global cuisine. Well-prepared dishes leave the open kitchen all day, from herring, burgers, Caesar salads and club sandwiches (from 85kr) at lunch to scrumptious evening meals such as braised shank of lamb or baked Norwegian king crab (mains from around 145kr). There's a great all-you-can-eat brunch buffet at the weekends (10am–3pm; 195kr including coffee/tea and juice).

Sushitarian Gothersgade 3 ⓣ33 93 30 54, ⓦwww.sushitarian.dk. Mon–Wed noon–11pm, Thurs–Sat noon–midnight, Sun 5.30–11pm. Among the city's best sushi places, with good Californian-style sushi, sashimi, tempura, teriyaki grills, noodle dishes and veggie options. There's a small upstairs section where you can sit on cushions on the floor; they also have tables, chairs and counter seating if you prefer. À la carte dishes from 75–165kr; sushi from 175kr for eight pieces. Also takeaway.

Taste Store Kongensgade 80–82 ⓦwww.tastedeli.dk. Mon–Thurs 11am–4pm, Fri 11am–5.30pm. Great for lunch, this small, exquisite café/bakery/deli/chocolate shop near the Marmorkirken has a French owner whose dedication shines through in the largely organic sandwiches, tarts, salads, soups and home-made cakes, muffins and cookies that cannot be bettered. The daily hot special (95kr, 65kr to go) is a bargain. Takeaway available (and much cheaper) so, weather permitting, take your food and head for a bench in Amalieparken.

Traktørstet på Rosenborg Øster Voldgade 4A ⓣ33 15 76 20, ⓦwww.traktoerstedetrosenborg.dk. Daily 11am–4pm; closed Mon Nov–May. By the gatehouse of Rosenborg Slot, charming *Traktørstet* gives traditional Danish food a modern twist. Prices are fairly reasonable, considering the location, starting at 89kr for three types of herring smørrebrød and from 115kr upwards for the likes of plaice, steak or lamb. It's often crowded and it can be hard to find a seat, so book a table or, on a warm day, sit outside. Booking essential.

Umami Store Kongensgade 59 ⓣ33 38 75 00, ⓦwww.restaurantumami.dk. Mon–Thurs & Sun 6–10pm, Fri & Sat 6–11pm. One of the trendiest restaurants in town, with sleek, ultra-modern decor and a fabulous menu of French-accented Japanese food – grilled veal tenderloin with wasabi and truffle sauce, for example. With food ranging from the relatively inexpensive soup and noodle dishes (from 125kr) to sushi and sashimi (120kr for 6 pieces) to prime Japanese wagyu beef at 200kr per 50g, *Umami* caters for most budgets. You'll find no other place in town like it. Takeaway available Mon–Sat 5–9.30pm. Booking advisable.

Vespa Store Kongensgade 90 ⓣ33 11 37 00, ⓦwww.cofoco.dk. Closed Sun. One in the excellent "cofoco" (Copenhagen Food Company) chain, whose increasingly successful format offers classic cooking at affordable prices. This one specializes in Italian food served in a stylish and relaxed setting – plain furniture and white walls covered with Dolce Vita-era black-and-white photos of Italians enjoying themselves. The set five-course menu (275kr) follows the traditional antipasti, primi, secondi, dolci format, with Italian liqueurs to finish it all off perfectly. There's a five percent surcharge for foreign credit cards. Booking advisable.

Rådhuspladsen and around

The noisy, amusement-packed area around the Rådhus isn't that great for restaurants, tending more towards fast-food outlets, though there are a few good spots. For recommendations in Tivoli itself, see the box on p.80. The following places are on the map on p.78.

Café Bjørg's Vestervoldgade 19 ⓣ33 14 53 20. Mon–Thurs & Sun 10am–midnight, Fri & Sat 10am–2am. This busy, trendy café-bar on the edge of Indre By serves decent sandwiches, salads, burgers and brunch (9am–1pm, till 2pm on weekends; 99kr) by day and a more expensive menu (main courses from 112kr) featuring regulars like pasta and steak by night.

Glyptoteket Dantes Plads. Tues–Sun 10am–4pm. The Ny Carlsberg Glyptotek's café, set in the gallery's beautiful glass-domed, palm-filled Winter Gardens, makes for one of the best lunchtime settings in town. The food is excellent, too, with open sandwiches (89kr), great home-made cakes and wonderful coffee; or you could fill up on the delicious 169kr brunch. Come on a Sunday and you won't have to pay the museum entrance fee.

Kanal Cafeen Frederiksholm Kanal 18 ⓣ33 11 57 70. Mon–Fri 11.30am–4pm. This rather cramped but wonderfully atmospheric smørrebrød place dates back to 1852. The politicians' stable boys used to lunch here; now it's a haunt of the politicians themselves, munching their way through a selection of the 36 toppings on offer (from 44kr; English list available). All the standards are here – a variety of herring, beef tartar with egg yolk and smoked eel with scrambled eggs to name a few. Booking essential.

Konditori & Café HC Andersen Rådhusarkaden, Vesterbrogade 1B. Mon–Thurs & Sat 8am–6pm, Fri 8am–7pm, Sun noon–6pm. The location may not be the most appealing – in the shopping centre next to Tivoli – but this welcoming, relaxed café is very convenient if you're exploring the Tivoli area, and is usually packed with shoppers and sightseers tucking into sandwiches, rolls and salads, cakes and great Danish pastries, all made fresh on the premises. Takeaway available.

Lagkagehuset Vesterbrogade 4A ⓦwww.lagkagehuset.dk. Daily 7.30am–6.30pm, till 8pm July & Aug. Almost opposite the entrance to Tivoli, this central branch of the excellent bakery chain has some seating (in and out) and serves its trademark quality sandwiches from 45kr, plus pastries, cakes and coffee. Or go for a takeout and people-watch from a bench in Rådhuspladsen.

Restaurant Nimb Bernstorffsgade 5 ⓣ88 70 00 00, ⓦwww.nimb.dk. Daily 11.30am–10pm. Part of the Nimb complex in Tivoli (see box, p.80) but with a street entrance for diners who don't want to go to the fair. This laid-back brasserie has an open kitchen so you can see the food cooked in front of you. Lunch (11.30am–2pm) is classic, delicious Danish – herring, roastbeef on rye, fish fillet or beef from 79–170kr. In the evening starters such as oysters or smoked salmon are followed by fish and meat mains; expect to pay around 450kr for three courses. Sunday brunch buffet (10.30am–2pm) is great value at 195kr, with goodies from the on-site Logismose dairy and deli including

Vegetarian Copenhagen

Most restaurants have at least a couple of vegetarian options on the menu. The following have the greatest range of veggie dishes:

Atlas Bar	p.147
Den Grønne Kælder	p.149
Hackenbusch	p.156
Det Indiske Spisehus	p.158
Morgenstedet	p.152
Paustian	p.160
Riz Raz	p.150

home-made butter and marmalade, as well as all the sausages, pancakes, eggs and fruit you can eat. Booking advisable in high season.

Wagamama Tietgensgade 20. Mon–Thurs & Sun noon–11pm, Fri & Sat noon–midnight. Large, bright branch of the ubiquitous chain, dishing up unfailingly delicious steaming bowls of Asian soup, curries or noodles at very reasonable prices. Dishes, all in the 80–110kr price bracket, range from chilli chicken ramen to mandarin and sesame beef salad, with several good veggie options on offer, too.

Vesterbro

With its significant multicultural population, Vesterbro is your best bet if you fancy an ethnic meal, and is also home to the city's largest range of more affordable restaurants. The following places are on the map on p.88.

Ankara Vesterbrogade 96 ⓦwww.restaurant-ankara.dk. Mon–Sat 11am–midnight, Sun 1pm–midnight. Whether you're on a budget or not, *Ankara*'s all-you-can-eat Turkish buffet for 49kr until 4pm (79kr 4–11pm) is a great filler – delicious meaty stews, rice and vegetables, accompanied by a variety of fresh salads. If you're not venturing this far up the street, there's another, bigger branch at Vesterbrogade 35.

Bang & Jensen Istedgade 130 ⓦwww.bangogjensen.dk. Mon–Fri 8am–2am, Sat 10am–2am, Sun 10am–midnight (kitchen closes 10pm, 7.30pm on Sat). At the quieter end of Istedgade – no sex shops here – this popular café has a weekday breakfast buffet (8–10.30am; 60kr) and thereafter brunch until 4pm (85kr), featuring a wide range of unusual foods that you can combine as you wish – try the *ymer* (a mild, creamy yoghurt) with maple syrup. Sandwiches, pasta, tapas, tortillas and quiches are offered from lunch onwards. The place transforms into a popular cocktail bar on Saturday evenings (see p.165).

BioMio Halmtorvet 19 ⓦwww.biomio.dk. Mon–Thurs & Sun 11.30am–10pm, Fri & Sat 11.30am–midnight. New, totally organic restaurant on the outskirts of Kødbyen. It's a bit concepty – you're given a card when you arrive to place your order at the bar and to check out with once you're done. It's all self-service (they call you when your food is ready) and the limited menu very seasonal. The spicy beef noodles for 125kr are a good bet, washed down with a draught Jakobsen beer.

Estate Coffee Gammel Kongevej 1 ⓦwww.estatecoffee.dk. Mon–Fri 8am–10pm, Sat & Sun 10am–10pm. Small coffee house at the southern edge of the lakes. A wide range of single estate coffees are served in the usual, and more unusual, ways – great for a satisfying caffeine hit. Alternatively, there are many varieties of tea and crème Valrhona hot chocolate, with Valrhona brownies and delicious banana and chocolate muffins too.

Granola Værnedamsvej 5. Mon–Thurs 7am–6pm, Fri 7am–7pm, Sat 9am–5pm, Sun 9am–4pm. Superb 1930s-style coffee bar/ice cream parlour done out in pretty pastels with authentic old coffee grinders and the like, serving excellent early bird breakfasts (60kr for a breakfast platter without coffee) and delightful sandwiches from 65kr. Also excellent fresh fruit smoothies.

Hackenbusch Vesterbrogade 124 ⓦwww.hackenbusch.dk, ⓣ33 21 74 74. Mon & Tues 11am–9pm, Wed–Sat 11am–10pm, Sun 11am–6pm. Laid-back place serving three types of brunch (one veggie) until 2pm (from 85kr), and burgers and sandwiches, heaped with salad, in the café-bar at the front. The excellent Mediterranean-style restaurant at the back has steak and fish mains, with a daily special for 98kr and always one veggie option. Try the spicy and delicious "frog burger" (75kr) – its ingredients are a well-kept secret (don't worry: it's actually made of beef) – on offer on Tuesdays (65kr including a beer) in the restaurant.

Lê Lê nhà hàng Vesterbrogade 40 ⓦwww.lele-nhahang.dk. Mon–Thurs & Sun 11.30am–11pm, Fri & Sat 11.30am–2am. Hugely popular Vietnamese restaurant on bustling Vesterbrogade across from Det Ny Theater with simple French colonial-style decor. Food is also simple but elegant and tasty. Lunch starts at 70kr for six wonton with turkey and crab, or choose dishes such as rice-noodle soup, cold rice-noodle salad, and beef, pork or chicken baguettes with pickled vegetables dowsed in fresh herbs. At dinner, the choices are more varied and prices max out at 165kr. Arrive early for dinner (they don't take bookings) or prepare for a long wait at the Tiger Bar (which serves Vietnamese beer, of course). There's a takeaway further up the road at Vesterbrogade 56 where you can get the same salads plus some sushi-style Vietnamese fast food.

Les Trois Cochons Værnedamsvej 10 ⓣ33 31 70 55, ⓦwww.cofoco.dk. Mon–Sat noon–2.30pm & 5.30pm–midnight, Sun 5.30pm–midnight. Part of the popular Cofoco (Copenhagen Food Company) chain, this French-style brasserie offers excellent-value three-course evening meals for 275kr. Starters and desserts are pre-set, and for mains you get to choose between beef, fish and veal – no veggie option – all freshly made and rustically presented. If there are two of you, you both have to pick the same mains. For lunch, there's a choice between six Danish and French classics such as the open potato sandwich (85kr) and moules marinière (95kr). Booking essential.

Riccos Butik & Kaffebar Istedgade 119. Mon–Fri 9am–11pm, Sat & Sun 10am–11pm. One of the best coffee joints in town with a small seating area in the back room. The owner describes himself as a coffee nerd, and if he's not working behind the counter, he's travelling the globe in search of the finest beans. Apart from coffee in various forms – cold as well as hot – there are also cakes and Italian ice cream.

Shezan Viktoriagade 22. Daily 11.30am–11.30pm. Denmark's first Pakistani restaurant, established in 1978, may be a bit shabby round the edges but it's still going strong. The fiery curries (from 60kr) come in mild, medium and strong – be warned, even medium burns your tongue off.

Sorte Hest Vesterbrogade 135 ⓣ33 25 22 23. ⓦwww.sortehestspisested.dk. Wed–Fri noon–3pm & 5.30pm–midnight. Small, atmospheric and informal place run by a Michelin-starred chef who decided to downsize so he could have more direct contact with his customers – it will probably be him that welcomes you when you arrive. The largely Mediterranean menu is limited to only two starters (from 100kr) and two main courses (from 170kr), plus a few extras such as cheese platter and dessert, all beautifully prepared with great attention to detail.

Spicylicious Istedgade 27 ⓣ33 22 85 33. ⓦwww.restaurantspicylicoius.dk. Mon–Thurs 5–11pm, Fri & Sat 5pm–midnight, Sun 5–10pm. Great Thai/Vietnamese restaurant overlooking the livelier end of Istedgade. The name says it all: the food is spicy and it's delicious. Mains from 115kr for beef noodle soup to 120kr for Bahn Xeo – crispy prawn and chicken pancakes.

Sticks 'n' Sushi Istedgade 62 ⓣ33 23 73 04, ⓦwww.sushi.dk. Mon–Thurs & Sun 10am–11pm, Fri & Sat 10am–midnight. Fifth branch of this ubiquitous Japanese chain that has taken Vesterbro by storm. The menu changes seasonally, and apart from the usual range of sushi and maki rolls there's also a selection of bento boxes (Japanese lunch boxes) with different morsels in separate compartments (from 169kr). This large branch also has a bar (opens at 10pm) with a good selection of Japanese beer.

Tea Restaurant Helgolandsgade 2. Daily noon–11pm. Excellent-value Chinese restaurant serving well-prepared, authentic food primarily from Hebei province. Among the many delicacies are mouthwatering Hai Xian dumplings (179kr) and Peking duck with a twist. Also a wide variety of Chinese green teas.

Thai Esan Lille Istedgade 7 ⓣ33 24 98 54. Mon–Thurs & Sun noon–11pm, Fri & Sat noon–midnight. Using fresh ingredients from the numerous Thai food shops in the area, the very popular and often crammed *Thai Esan* serves a wide range of cheap, hot food in a fairly authentic Thai atmosphere. Good choices are the chicken in oyster sauce for 85kr, or the Tom Yom shrimp soup for just 80kr.

Frederiksberg

Posh, residential Frederiksberg is hardly a fruitful hunting ground for restaurants, though there are several places worth taking dinner in after wandering the area's great parks and gardens. The following places are on the map on p.88.

Den Blå Hund Godthåbsvej 28 ⓣ38 87 46 88, ⓦwww.cafedenblaahund.dk. Mon–Wed 9.30am–11pm, Thurs & Fri 9.30am–1am, Sat 10am–2am, Sun 10am–10pm. Mediterranean-style café-restaurant featuring enormous sandwich platters and tapas, plus a fabulous brunch until 2pm (classic, vegetarian and deluxe; 89–99kr). Speciality main courses include grilled goats' cheese with crab tails (95kr) and chicken salad with bacon and cold curry sauce (85kr). In summer, tables are moved across the road to Axel Møllers Have.

Fiasco Gammel Kongevej 176 ⓣ33 31 74 87, ⓦwww.fiasco.dk. Tues–Sat 5.30–10pm. Stylish, upmarket Italian restaurant a stone's throw from Frederiksberg Rådhus offering outstanding food from Florence. The antipasti platter is a work of art, and there's a choice of classic pastas and salads or more full-on primi and secondi dishes in refined but relaxed surroundings. The three-course set menus are good value at 285kr.

Frederiks Have Smallegade 41 ⓣ38 88 33 85, ⓦwww.frederikshave.dk. Mon–Sat noon–2.30pm & 5–9.30pm. Right next to Frederiksberg Have – take the northern exit and the entrance is around the corner on Virginiavej – this popular restaurant is in a picturesque villa with outdoor seating in summer. Try the fabulous fish platter (98kr) or the poached and smoked poulard in vinaigrette (also 98kr) for lunch, or the three-course evening menu (365kr, or 618kr including wine) featuring things like poussin in chestnut sauce.

Hansens Gamle Familiehave Pile Allé 10–12 ⓣ36 30 92 57, ⓦwww.hansenshave.dk. Daily 11am–midnight. This historic outdoor restaurant (under a sliding roof during winter) offers some of the city's most stunning open sandwiches, with a fantastic spread of herring, cold meats and cheeses, all lavishly decorated with fresh salad, pickles, fried onions and other smørrebrød essentials. Beautifully prepared traditional hot meals, such as *biksemad* (109kr) and *flæskesteg* (168kr) are also on offer.

Det Indiske Spisehus Vesterfælledvej 8 ⓣ33 21 90 80. Daily except Tues 5–10pm. Small, no-frills place near the Carlsberg Brewery, serving up some of the city's best and cheapest Indian food. Plenty of filling veggie options; try the thali – dhal, pickles, vegetables, yoghurt, potatoes, chapati and rice for 95kr. Booking advisable at weekends.

Nørrebro

Possibly the hippest part of town, with a variety of venues tucked around Skt Hans Torv and Blågårdsgade; this is also a good area to grab brunch. The following places are on the map on p.98.

Floras Kaffebar Blågårdsgade 27 ⓦwww.floraskaffebar.dk. Mon–Thurs 10am–10pm, Fri & Sat 10am–11pm, Sun 10am–8pm. Friendly café on the occasionaly tense Blågårds Plads (see p.101). Known predominantly as a coffee place with many exotic brands on offer, *Floras* also serves an array of daily specials, plus soups, sandwiches and home-made cakes, in an easy-going atmosphere. Brunch daily until 3pm (98kr). Come back at night for cheap beer.

Kates Joint Blågårdsgade 12 ⓣ35 37 44 96. Daily 5.30–10.30pm. Small, intimate and somewhat grungy place, where you can find dishes from most corners of the world (the blackboard menu changes daily). Jamaican jerk chicken is a perennial favourite; cheapest is tandoori chicken and rice for 90kr. There's always a huge stack of English-language magazines in the corner.

Kiin Kiin Guldbergsgade 21 ⓣ35 35 75 55, ⓦwww.kiin.dk. Mon–Sat 5.30pm–midnight. Awarded a Michelin star in 2008, after which prices immediately shot up, this wonderful Thai restaurant serves extraordinarily delicious food. Choose between the early-bird four-course theatre menu (5.30–7.30pm; 450kr), or the full-on six-course menu from 6pm (750kr), which features dishes such as Thai caviar and lime, chanterelles with coconut, quails' eggs served with orchid salad and smoked mackerel dipped in cane sugar. Booking essential.

Laundromat Café **Elmegade 15 ⓦwww.thelaundromatcafe.com. Mon–Thurs 8am–midnight, Fri 8am–2am, Sat 10am–2am, Sun 10am–midnight.** Icelandic café-cum-laundry where you can wash down your brunch or light meal with mugfuls of coffee or beer while your clothes are being washed in the back room (34kr for a large load plus detergent, 1kr/min for tumble driyer). A basic brunch starts at 85kr (125kr for a larger portion at weekends) and salads and sandwiches/burgers cost between 72kr and 110kr. There's a second, equally popular branch on Århusgade 38 in Østerbro.

Nørrebro Bryghus **Ryesgade 2 ⓣ35 30 05 30, ⓦwww.noerebrobryghus.dk. Mon–Wed 11am–midnight, Thurs–Sat 11am–2am, Sun 10am–5pm.** Super-hip brewery restaurant in a former factory building with restaurant upstairs and the brewery and bar downstairs (see p.167). Food is either made with beer, or to go well with beer, with monthly changing three-, four- and five-course set menus (325kr/355kr/398kr). The curry sorbet with beer and white chocolate is quite unique. Their Sunday brunch (10am–3pm) which comes in two versions (Brewer's brunch and the lighter Brewer's Wife's brunch) is also very popular – although it doesn't come with beer.

Pussy Galore's Flying Circus **Skt Hans Torv 30 ⓣ35 24 53 00, ⓦwww.pussy-galore.dk. Mon–Fri 8am–2am, Sat & Sun 9am–2pm.** Modern café-bar on trendy Skt Hans Torv. With its minimalist decor *Pussy*'s – as it's known locally – is less pompous than its French neighbour *Sebastopol*, and the food is great. The infamous brunch pulls in a large crowd, but earlier still the breakfast plate proves good value at 25kr. Café-style sandwiches (from 70kr) and full-on meals (from 79kr for a burger) also come recommended, as does the extensive alcohol selection (see p.167).

Ranee's **Blågårds Plads 10 ⓣ35 36 85 05, ⓦwww.ranees.dk. Tues–Sun 5–11pm.** Rustic Thai restaurant serving authentic dishes from the Mekong delta area, with most main courses costing 145kr. Try Kanon chin nam jaa (Thai fish balls with banana flowers). In summer there's outdoor seating on the square.

Scarpetta **Rantzausgade 7 ⓣ35 35 08 08, ⓦwww.cofoco.dk. Daily 5.30pm–midnight.** Newest member of the popular cofoco (Copenhagen Food Company) chain – this time an Italian version – serving excellent starter-sized dishes of gnocchi, pasta, risotto, pizza, carpaccio and the like, a bit like Italian tapas. The five-dish combo goes for 275kr. Hugely popular, so booking is recommended.

Sebastopol **Skt Hans Torv 32 ⓣ35 36 30 02, ⓦwww.sebastopol.dk. Mon–Wed 8am–midnight, Thurs & Fri 8am–2am, Sat 9am–2am, Sun 9am–midnight.** French-style café on hip Skt Hans Torv serving petit déjeuner (croissant or pain au chocolat) for 30kr and plat déjeuner (brunch) for 120kr from 8am onwards. The outdoor seating in summer can hardly be bettered, with the gentle trickling of the fountain in the background. In the evening, when it's a popular spot for a drink, the menu includes things like steak frites (190kr) and coq au vin (160kr).

Soupanatural **Guldbergsgade 7, ⓦwww.soupanatural.dk. Mon & Tues 8am–10pm, Wed & Thurs 8am–midnight, Fri 8am–2am, Sat noon–2am, Sun noon–10pm.** Funky, tiny place across the street from *Rust* (p.171), specializing in hot organic breakfast porridge using a different mix of grains every day (25kr) plus fabulous home-made smoothies, and from 11am, a wide range of outstanding soup (from 35kr) – everything totally organic. In the evening the place turns into a cocktail bar.

Østerbro

Lacking the trendy appeal of neighbouring Nørrebro, Østerbro's restaurants are more glitzy. The following places are on the map on p.98.

Canteen **Nordre Frihavnsgade 52 ⓦwww.canteen-cph.dk. Tues–Sat 10am–4pm.** Consistently voted the city's best brunch spot, this friendly corner café serves light and delicious meals prepared with the utmost attention to detail. Arrive early if you want to try their popular brunch (until 3.30pm; 60–115kr) or come later for delicious sandwiches such as chicken, bacon and apple chutney (72kr).

Crazy Chicken **Rosenvængets Allé 1 ⓣ35 26 41 42. Mon–Fri 10am–9pm, Sat & Sun noon–9pm.** On the corner of Østerbrogade, this small chicken joint is a great place to buy supplies for a picnic in Fælledparken. The chicken sandwich combos (from 45kr) are excellent, as are the half (40kr) and whole (70kr) roasted chickens fresh from the spit; the serve-yourself salads (44kr) are tasty, too. A few tables next to the counter allow you to eat in if you'd rather.

Dag H **Dag Hammarskjolds Allé 36–40 ⓣ35 25 35 35, ⓦwww.dagh.dk. Mon–Wed 8am–11pm, Thurs & Fri 8am–midnight, Sat 10am–midnight, Sun 10am–10pm.** Parisian-style café with outdoor seating, near the American Embassy and a stone's throw from the lakes. Busy throughout the day, especially with young families, *Dag H* offers quality coffee and wonderful cakes, plus an eclectic mix of Danish and international salads, sandwiches and burgers (from 109kr), and dinners (from 169kr).

Fru Heiberg **Rosenvængets Allé 3 ⓦwww.fruheiberg.dk. Mon–Thurs & Sun 5–10pm, Fri & Sat 5–11pm.** Small, relaxed French/Danish restaurant with a tiny, well-thought-out menu – try the fabulous bouillabaisse (165kr) or traditional Danish *stægt flæsk* (105kr). They also do some unusual cocktails such as the Vladimir Cosmo – Clementine-infused vodka, orange brandy, cranberry juice, ginger and lime.

Gourmandiet **Rosenvængets Allé 7 ⓣ39 27 10 00, ⓦwww.gourmandiet.dk. Thurs–Sat 5.30pm–midnight.** Butcher's shop that opens up a small corner section to serve probably the best steak you've ever had. Totally organic and locally reared, it's not surprising that it comes at a price. The 600g T-bone steak, for instance, goes for 400kr. Booking essential.

Kulinaris **Østerbrogade 98 ⓦwww.kulinaris.dk. Daily 10am–8pm.** Excellent little sandwich joint, convenient for Fælledparken and Parken Stadium, that specializes in organic Thai sandwiches – chicken or beef – topped with peanut sauce, chilli and cheese (small 45kr, large 65kr). There are many other delicious options and "sandwich meals" – sandwich, chips and soft drink.

Paustian **Kalkbrænderiløbskaj 2 ⓣ39 18 55 01, ⓦwww.bobech.net. Mon–Sat noon–3pm & 6pm–midnight.** *Paustian* is one of Copenhagen's most adventurous Michelin-starred gourmet restaurants, scenically located overlooking the Kalkbrænderi harbour. Housed in the same building as the exclusive Paustian designer furniture shop (see p.186), this is undoubtedly among the restaurants of choice for the style-conscious and rich. The chef is famous for his unusual combinations (such as cod with pineapple vanilla) and the fixed menus – the surprise-laden "Alchemist" (750kr), and the vegan or vegetarian (depending on the diner) "Chlorophyll" (600kr) – come highly recommended.

Le Saint-Jacques **Skt Jakobs Plads 1 ⓣ35 42 77 07, ⓦwww.letzonline.dk. Daily 11am–midnight.** Exquisite French restaurant serving rustic country cooking at a price. There's both indoor and outdoor seating in summer, and apart from the recommended home-smoked salmon (lunch or evening starter; 98kr) and fish of the day mains (lunch 165kr, dinner 195kr), *Saint-Jacques* also does a popular weekend brunch (11am–1pm; 155kr).

Søpromenaden **Sortedam Dossering 103. Daily 11am–5pm.** Lovely lunch spot specializing in Danish smørrebrød (from 49kr). Tick off your choices of bread and toppings from a long, long list (or go for the platter for 139kr) and enjoy the tranquil lakeside setting.

Theodors **Østerbrogade 106 ⓣ35 26 66 66, ⓦwww.theodors.dk. Mon–Thurs 11am–midnight, Fri & Sat 11am–2am, Sun 11am–8pm.** Part café with outdoor seating, part posh French restaurant, all stylishly decorated with wooden panelling and Art Deco chandeliers. The restaurant serves delectable items such as pork tournedos served with Danish asparagus and crisp ham (215kr), while the café excels in well-prepared smørrebrød, sandwiches and salads (58–105kr). Also a good weekend brunch spot (until 2pm; 135kr).

Budget eating

The following offer generous portions of good food at very reasonable prices.

La Galette	p.149
Den Grønne Kælder	p.149
Pasta Basta	p.150
Riz Raz	p.150
Spicey Kitchen Café	p.153
Spicylicious	p.157
Sporvejen	p.151
Stella	p.151

The suburbs

Beduin Oasen **Amager Strandpark ⓦwww.beduinoasen.dk. April–Sept daily noon–10pm. Femøren Station.** At the southern end of the beach near the canal leading into the lagoon, *Beduin Oasen* is a chilled-out spot run by a Palestinian who has set up a couple of large tents should you need protection from the wind. From the falafel, hummus, and aubergine salads to the kebabs and the burgers, it's all well-prepared and cheap (mains from 50kr), and the charming proprietor keeps everybody smiling.

Brede Spisehus I.C. Mødewegs Vej, Brede ☎45 85 57 67, ⓦwww.bredespisehus.dk. Tues–Sat 11.30am–11pm, Sun 11.30am–3pm. Follow up a visit to the Frilandsmuseet and Brede Værks (see p.107) with a classic Danish lunch at this charming, old-fashioned restaurant in Brede village. There's a lovely veranda and gardens overlooking the pretty lake, and the food is great – plenty of herring, fish and beef (lunch dishes from around 89kr; three-course menu for 265kr). See p.107 for travel details.

Café Sundet Sejlklubben Sundet, Strandvænget 45 ☎39 29 30 35, ⓦwww.sundet.dk. May to mid-Oct Mon–Fri & Sun 11am–3pm & 5–11pm. S-Tog to Svanemøllen station; turn right onto Strandvænget and head for the harbour. A ten-minute train journey north from the city centre, *Café Sundet*, in the Sundet sailing club in Svanemøllen Harbour, is one of the city's best inexpensive places to eat. With its beautiful harbourside setting, outdoor seating and fine home cooking for less than 100kr, this can hardly be bettered. There's an outdoor grill n summer.

Café Sylten Søndre Strandvej 50, Dragør ☎32 94 01 49, ⓦwww.sylten.dk. Mon–Sat 11am–10pm, Sun 10am–9pm. Bus #350 towards Dragør; get off at Vierdiget and walk for five minutes towards the beach. Wonderful "destination" café tucked away on a beautiful protected salt marsh on the edge of Dragør beach. People travel for miles to enjoy the lovely view from the terrace while munching on well-prepared café dishes such as grilled goats' cheese salad or the fabulous carpaccio (both 109kr). Extremely busy at weekends for the extensive brunch buffet (149kr including coffee and juice).

Halvandet Refshalevej 325, Refshaleøen ⓦwww.halvandet.dk. April–Sept 10am–sunset/midnight. Large, über-cool beach venue in an old industrial complex on the western coast of Refshaleøen facing the Little Mermaid on the opposite bank. Access is easiest with the DFDS canal boat (the green hop-on-hop-off route) or by water taxi (Flyvefisken ☎32 96 49 64). Served On a couple of huge terraces covered with beach chairs and large white mattresses which you can book for the day, food here is simple and tasty, with three breakfast options (10am–noon; 35kr), brunch until 2pm (145kr), sandwiches and salads. At 5pm, they light the barbecue and the spare ribs (155kr) and the best sausages (105kr) come out. Also lots of beach activities and a lively evening venue (see p.168).

Islands Brygges Kulturhus Islands Brygge 18. Mon–Wed & Sun 10am–11pm, Thurs–Sat 10am–midnight. Bus #12. Next to the harbour pool on the banks of Inderhavnen, *Islands Brygges Kulturhus* is a popular cultural centre with live gigs and a waterfront café offering excellent food at reasonable prices. Try the herring platters (65kr) for lunch or the lamb chops with grilled artichoke for dinner (149kr). On hot summer days after 4pm you can also grill yourself a steak on the barbecue out front while enjoying great views across the harbour

Jacobsen Strandvejen 449, Klampenborg ☎39 63 43 22, ⓦwww.restaurantjacobsen.dk. Tues–Sat noon–3pm & 6–10pm, Sun 10.30am–4pm. Klampenborg Station. Named after its designer, Arne Jacobsen, this fabulous restaurant is the epitome of Danish cool, situated in the most stylish of suburbs and with beautiful views out over the Øresund. Furnished throughout with Jacobsen's designs, the place is often packed with trendy folk checking out the decor while sampling the delightful Danish/Modern European menu which offers plenty of delicious fish, seafood and meat dishes. It's all reasonably priced; the three-course lunch menu is 245kr; evening three-course menu 290kr.

Jorden Rundt Standvejen 152, Charlottenlund ⓦwww.cafejordenrundt.dk. Mon–Fri & Sun 10am–10pm, Sat 10am–8pm. Charlottenlund S-Tog Station (line C) and bus #14 and #166. Near the Danmarks Akvarium and the Charlottenlund beach and campsite, this popular roadside rotunda café is housed in an old tram waiting room. It offers coffee and cakes, delicious filled rolls, sandwiches and salads (from 68kr) as well as savoury pancakes, pasta and chilli con carne (112kr). Plenty of outside seating.

Peter Lieps Hus Dyrehaven 8 ☎39 64 07 86, ⓦwww.peterliep.dk. Tues–Sun 10am–6pm, summer till 8pm. Klampenborg Station. Originally a hunter's lodge, this cosy old thatched restaurant, opposite the entrance to Bakken, is the perfect spot for a hot chocolate and Danish pastry after a stroll in Dyrehaven. It also does smørrebrød and a range of heartier lunchtime food (from 116kr) like *fiskefileter* with fried potatoes and delicious remoulade, with an evening menu of meat and fish. The outside seating in the park is lovely.

12

Drinking

Drinking is a favourite pastime for many Danes, with liberal licensing laws, a relaxed attitude to alcohol and the lowest prices in Scandinavia (a combination that has proved irresistible to the hundreds of thirsty Swedes who cross the Øresund each weekend and drink themselves senseless in Copenhagen's bars). The distinction between eating and drinking establishments is often blurred, and places that are worthy lunchtime stops can be equally good for a few cold beers the same evening.

Lager-style **beer** is still without doubt Denmark's staple drink although the most common brands – Tuborg and the ubiquitous Carlsberg – are being overtaken by a growing number of both domestic and international small and microbreweries. Beer is usually sold by the bottle, less frequently in 250ml or 500ml draught measures – bottled beer can be cheaper than draught (25–40kr per bottle; draught beer can cost up to 90kr for 500ml). Most Danish breweries also tend to brew special "Christmas" and "Easter" beers – a bit stronger than normal to enhance the festive feel. The days when they are released – "J-Day" and "P-Day" ("J" for *Jul* and "P" for *Påske* – Christmas and Easter respectively) see beer enthusiasts all around the country venturing out to taste the latest offerings. Guinness and draught British and Irish ales can generally only be found in British- and Irish-themed pubs, and are quite pricey. **Wine** is usually available in most bars, though it is still predominantly drunk with meals and, apart from in a few select wine bars, you won't usually have the same choice as in restaurants. **Cocktail bars** are also a colourful feature of Danish nightlife, with interesting and eclectic drink lists.

Opening hours vary according to police licensing and the bar owner's inclination, though you'll be able to find somewhere to drink at any time; most locals know of at least one so-called "Death Route" – an extensive pub-crawl – to ensure 24-hour drinking. As the evening moves on, people head to more lively dancing venues, often ending before breakfast in a traditional *værtshus* with billiards and a jukebox.

Smoking is not permitted in bars and cafés if they're above a certain size or serve food. We've noted which ones still allow smoking below.

For a **glossary** of Danish drinks, see "Language", p.227.

Indre By

Indre By has plenty of atmospheric joints with charm, along with a few new glitzy cocktail bars that rival their equivalents in trendy Nørrebro. The following places are on the map on p.44.

1105 Kristen Bernikows Gade 4. Wed 5pm–1am, Thurs & Sat 5pm–2am, Fri 4pm–2am. Award-winning cocktail bar near Kongens Nytorv with large comfy sofas that could easily swallow you up for the night – especially once the drinks start kicking in. Cocktails here are a delight, and the famous bartender Hardeep Rehal – winner of two Danish cocktail-mixing championships – has a huge following.

Bankeråt Ahlefeldtsgade 29. Mon–Fri 9.30am–midnight, Sat & Sun 10.30am–midnight. On the corner of Nansensgade, this laid-back, lively café, usually packed with locals, is renowned for its quirky decor (an assortment of macabre mannequins sporting stuffed animal heads). Also does inexpensive light meals.

Bibendum Nansensgade 45. Mon–Sat 4pm–midnight. Small, crowded wine bar in a Nansensgade cellar, with a huge selection of wine, most of which is served by the glass (from 45kr). Also great tapas (see p.147) to soak up the alcohol.

Bloomsday Bar Niels Hemmingsensgade 32. Daily noon–2am. Irish bar named after the day in James Joyce's *Ulysses* when his "stream of consciousness" takes place. It's not a theme pub, though, and it has a good selection of ales and ciders – both of which make it especially popular with Copenhagen's large Irish population. Other attractions are a large-screen TV showing football, and pool tables and darts in a big room at the back. Irish music sessions on Sunday afternoons.

Bo-Bi Bar Klareboderne 14. Daily 10am–2am. Home to Copenhagen's oldest bar counter – an idea first introduced to the city by a New York-returned sailor in 1917 – this small, atmospheric drinking hole is now patronized by inner-city professional types, artists and journalists.

Café Floss Larsbjørnsstræde 10. Mon 2pm–2am, Tues–Sat 1pm–2am. Grungy low-life bar, where artists and creative souls gather for full-on drinking sessions. To facilitate this, there's a Guldøl (Tuborg's strong gold beer) and tequila happy hour between 10pm and 11pm. There's a pool table in the basement.

Café Globen Turesensgade 2B. Mon & Thurs 5–11pm, Tues & Wed 5–10pm, Fri 3pm–1am. The Danish version of the National Geographic society's club, run by members of De Berejstes Klub (the "well-travelled club") and featuring talks every Thursday about globe-trotting experiences. The café is well stocked with exotic drinks and there's a library with guides to most corners of the world – including lots of Rough Guides! Free wi-fi.

Charlie's Bar Pilestræde 33. Mon–Wed 2pm–2am, Thurs–Sat noon–2am, Sun 2–11pm. *Charlie's* is the only bar in Denmark that has been awarded the prestigious Cask Marque for its vast selection of high-quality real ales, the vast majority from the UK and Ireland. A small, crowded place so arrive early if you want a seat. Smoking permitted.

The Globe Nørregade 45. Mon & Tues 2pm–midnight, Wed & Thurs 2pm–2am, Fri 2pm–3am, Sat noon–3am, Sun 2–10pm. Loud and spacious Irish pub, with lots of televised European and American sport. Your fellow drinkers are more likely to be tourists or Danish theatre folk than expats from the Emerald Isle. A good range of ales from around the globe, and fish and chips for 80kr. Smoking as well as non-smoking sections.

Heidi's Bier Bar Vestergade 18A. Mon & Sun 4pm–2am, Tues & Wed 4pm–3am, Thurs & Sat 4pm–5am, Fri 2pm–5am. Kitschy Austrian beer-hall-type place where braid-wearing waitresses in Tyrolean dresses handle half a dozen jugs of beer at once. Drinks include ice-cold shots of Jägermeister and Paulaner Weissbier, and a plate of sausages and potato salad goes for 55kr. Especially popular with younger groups.

Hviids Vinstue Kongens Nytorv 19. Mon–Thurs & Sun 10am–1am, Fri & Sat 10am–2am. Proper old-fashioned *vinstue* dating back to 1723 – Hans Christian Andersen, who lived just around the corner, was a regular – whose many tiny crowded rooms are patrolled by uniformed and respectful waiters. There's a good selection of Danish beers (27 at last count) and a great lunch deal – three pieces of smørrebrød and a Tuborg for 55kr. Outdoor seating on Kongens Nytorv square in summer, and justifiably famous *gløgg* in winter.

Ice Bar Løngangstræde 27. Mon–Thurs 11am–midnight, Fri & Sat 11am–1am, Sun 11am–10pm. Next door to the trendy *Hotel Twenty seven*, of which it is a part, *Ice Bar* is the city's most unusual spot for a drink. Don your designer cape and gloves and enter the sub-zero room completely made out of huge blocks of Swedish ice. Everything here is made of ice – the walls, the bar, tables, chairs, stools, even the glasses. Entrance is in 45-minute timed slots; the fee of 150kr includes the gloves and cloak, plus one free cocktail.

Nord Bar Klosterstræde 23. Fri & Sat 8pm–4am. Offshoot of the hugely popular *Nord* nightclub, which is the only place in town exclusively for people over 30; this is a quieter bar for those over 30 who just want to hang out and hear themselves think.

Nyhavn 17 Nyhavn 17. Mon–Thurs & Sun 10am–2am, Fri & Sat 10am–3am. Located on fashionable Nyhavn, this is a cross between a British pub and a maritime museum, with old iron diving helmets, ships' figureheads, anchors and rudders scattered around the dimly lit interior – the gleaming brass bar fittings are the only bright feature. Popular among tourists and Danes alike, with moderately priced draught beers and an excellent selection of Scottish single malt whisky.

Palæ Bar Ny Adelgade 5. Mon–Wed 11am–1am, Thurs–Sat 11am–2am, Sun 4pm–1am. Around the corner from Kongens Nytorv, *Palæ* is a classy neighbourhood bar with the usual range of beer and live jazz every third Sunday. Smoking permitted.

Ruby Nybrogade 10. Mon–Wed 4pm–1am, Thurs–Sat 4pm–2am. Glitzy yet chilled out cocktail bar around the corner from *Danhostel Downtown* (see p.142) serving beautifully presented and delicious cocktails that are guaranteed to impress. Which is what this place is about – cocktail appreciation – so bring an open mind and a heavy wallet. Very popular, so you may have to wait in line to get in. Over-25s only.

Tryk Bar Møntergade 24. Mon–Wed noon–2am, Thurs noon–3am, Fri noon–5am, Sat 2pm–5am, Sun 2pm–2am. A really nice, fairly traditional bar just across from the Kongens Have, with well-priced beer and shots, particularly during its early evening happy hour, and a good selection of different ales.

Christianshavn

Nightlife on Christianshavn is dominated by Christiania, but there are also a few traditional drinking dens. The following places are on the map on p.55.

Eiffel Bar Wildersgade 58. Mon–Wed & Sun 9am–2am, Thurs–Sat 9am–3am. Next door to the smart *Café Wilder* (see p.152), this traditional drinking den couldn't be more different. Rumours of its shady past – featuring assorted sailors and can-can girls – add to the atmosphere, while the old carved mirrors and the tricolour hanging outside take you back to Paris in the 1930s. This is one of the few places in the city where smoking is still permitted.

Nemoland Christiania. Mon–Thurs & Sun 10am–2am, Fri & Sat 10am–3.30am. One of Christiania's two main watering holes, and among Copenhagen's most popular open-air bars, with occasional live gigs during summer, when it's packed with tourists and shoppers enjoying their purchases from nearby Pusherstreet. It's quieter during the winter, with regulars playing backgammon or billiards.

Woodstock Pusherstreet, Christiania. Daily 9am–5am. Housed in a former military

Alfresco drinking

In addition to all the bars we've listed on Amager, the following places have nice outdoor seating.

Alléenberg Alfresco drinking in a tranquil garden in smart Frederiksberg. See p.166.

Den Blå Hund Sit outside on Axel Møllers Have – you may catch one of the jazz concerts that are sometimes held here. See p.158.

Front Page Enjoy a view of the waters of the rampart lakes with the city seemingly miles away. See p.167.

Hviids Vinstue Traditional old *vinstue* whose tables spill out onto busy Kongens Nytorv in good weather. See p.163.

Nemoland At the heart of the "Free City" of Christiania, and a good place to people-watch. See p.164.

The Office Cocktail bar where you can chill out in swings outside, while enjoying the view of the rampart lakes. See p.168.

Pavillonen I Fælledparken A tranquil spot in the centre of Fælledparken. See p.168.

Promenaden Parisian-style café in the most regal-feeling part of Frederiksberg with outdoor seating shaded by the beech trees lining the wide avenue. See p.167.

Props Coffee Shop At the heart of downtown Nørrebro, this small bar spills out onto the pedestrian street in front on sunny days. See p.167.

Pussy Galore's Flying Circus and **Sebastopol** Right on trendy Skt Hans Torv – *the* places to be seen. See p.167.

Zum Biergarten A pretty, secluded beer garden close to the city centre. See p.165.

barracks, chilled-out *Woodstock* is the place to enjoy a laid-back drink (and perhaps a smoke) in a ramshackle bar kitted out with old garden furniture and full of 1960s spirit.

Frederikstad and around

Bars are extremely thin on the ground in Frederikstad, possibly because the royals don't want too much night-time disturbance. The following places are on the map on p.64.

Andy's Bar Gothersgade 33B. Daily 11pm–6am. A so-called morning-pub, where the city's partygoers head when they can dance no more. Always crowded and noisy; you'll soon be chatting to your bar companions like they're long-lost friends.

Gold Prag Gothersgade 39. Mon–Wed 5–10pm, Thurs–Sat 4pm–midnight. Authentic Czech drinking den in a dark, narrow room packed tight with tables and richly decorated with knick-knacks. It is also a decidedly non-vegetarian restaurant, but the main attraction is the cheap Czech beer (35kr for 500ml) – Urquell, Budvar and Kozal – plus some delicious Czech liqueurs.

Kruts Karport Øster Farimagsgade 12. Mon–Thurs noon–midnight, Fri & Sat noon–2am, Sun 2–7pm. Closed Aug. Small Parisian-style neighbourhood café that has Denmark's largest whisky selection (mainly Scotch single malts) and for years was the only bar in Copenhagen selling absinthe. Whisky tastings and cigar evenings in winter – smoking is still allowed here.

Rådhuspladsen and around

The bright lights of Rådhuspladsen set the tone for the area's nightlife. With a few exceptions, places tend to be large, flashy and aimed at tourists. The following places are on the map on p.78.

Bryggeriet Apollo Vesterbrogade 3. Mon–Thurs 11.30am–midnight, Fri & Sat 11.30am–2am, Sun 3pm–midnight. Close to Central Station, this place offers *Bryggeriet*'s home-brewed beer amid gleaming vats, copper kettles and heavy wooden tables; food is available, too, in the bright upstairs section. Each month, with much brouhaha, a new (organic) brew is launched and judged by a beer-loving celebrity. This, plus a pilsner and a strong beer is all that's on offer. If you want more excitement, you can have it served in a Belgian litre *kwak*, similar to a short-yard glass. It's all a tad pricey.

Zum Biergarten Axeltorv 12. Mon–Wed 3pm–midnight, Thurs 3pm–2am, Fri 2pm–5am, Sat 3pm–5am. Lively Bavarian *bierstubbe* housed in the old waterworks building in front of Palads cinema by Vesterport Station, offering Oktoberfest atmosphere with long rickety wooden tables and huge litre-mugs of delicious German micro-brewery beer. When the weather allows, you can sit in the beautiful secluded beer garden, and food is prepared on an open grill.

Vesterbro

Plenty of bars – especially cocktail bars – line Istedgade, from Central Station down to Enghave Plads, as well as along Vesterbrogade. The following places are on the map on p.88.

Bang & Jensen Istedgade 130. Mon–Fri 8am–2am, Sat 10am–2am, Sun 10am–midnight. High stucco ceilings and a mahogany counter left over from its former incarnation as a pharmacy add to the character of this place, which is usually packed before concerts at *Vega* (see p.171) and on Saturday nights when *Ingeborgs Cocktail Saloon* takes over, and the in-house DJ plays electronic jazz grooves. One of the pricier places in Vesterbro.

Boutique Lize Enghave Plads 6. Wed 8pm–midnight, Thurs 8pm–2am, Fri & Sat 8pm–4am. Heaving cocktail bar across the square from *Vega* (see p.171) with a good selection of draught beer as well – both imported and from local microbreweries. Packed with people sipping drinks while deciding what to try next – the Tokyo Iced Tea comes especially recommended. Prices are reasonable, possibly because none of the cocktails is that strong.

Café Ludwigsen Sundesvedsgade 2. Mon–Wed noon–2am, Thurs noon–5am, Fri & Sat noon–6am, Sun 3pm–2am. One of those outrageously popular late-night bars (despite the "café" in the name, there's no food) where the young, free and desperate congregate en masse in the small hours for no good reason. If you want to meet the locals, this is your best bet.

Falernum Værnedamsvej 16. Daily 8am–2am. Cosy tapas bar which doubles as a breakfast café. But it's the wine that makes this place unique – lots of delicious varieties from around the globe, many of them sold by the glass.

Ideal Bar **Enghavevej 40. Wed 9pm–4am, Thurs–Sat 9pm–5am.** Housed in the *Vega* music complex (see p.171), this stylish bar has a laid-back attitude and excellent cocktails. A relaxed post-gig atmosphere, with handy, large leather sofas. Things don't really get started here until after midnight, when the dance tunes start playing.

Karriere Bar **Flæsketorvet 57. Fri & Sat 3pm–4am.** Hugely trendy bar-club-art space in the equally trendy Kødbyen meatpacking district. Packed to the gills most nights with hipsters, beautiful people and their acolytes. Great space for celeb-spotting.

Märkbar **Vesterbrogade 106A. Tues & Wed 4pm–2am, Thurs–Sat 4pm–5am, Sun 4pm–2am.** Behind the decrepit facade alternative rock/punk is played in a dark, underground Berlinesque setting. There's good German *weissbier* on offer – which is attraction enough for some.

Mesteren & Lærlingen **Flæsketorvet 86. Wed & Thurs 6pm–midnight, Fri & Sat 6pm–2am.** Laid-back new place in the middle of the Kødbyen district (see p.90) housed in what used to be the workers' canteen. A stark contrast to the über-stylish *Karriere Bar* nearby, with little fuss and a deck that the DJ owners use to play their classic blues, jazz and soul.

▲ Enjoying Copenhagen's bar scene

Riesen **Oehlenschlægersgade 36. Wed & Thurs 8am–2.30am, Fri & Sat 8pm–3.30am.** Basic, no-frills student hangout with indie music, an affordable selection of imported beer and the obligatory cocktail menu – this is Vesterbro after all.

Ritz **Viktoriagade 22. Thurs–Sat 9pm–5am.** On the corner of Istedgade in the basement beneath *Shezan* restaurant (see p.157), this grungy new Berlinesque place has quickly become Copenhagen's party capital. With DJs every night – mostly rock on Thursday, mainly electronic the rest of the week – there's a refreshingly unpretentious feel, and cocktails are served in plastic cups.

Frederiksberg

Apart from the few places listed below, Frederiksberg isn't much of an area for nightlife. Allégade is the liveliest street, attracting the post-theatre crowd. The following places are on the map on p.88.

90eren **Gammel Kongevej 90. Mon–Wed & Sun 11am–1am, Thurs–Sat 11am–2am.** Famous for its painstakingly pulled draught beer, an operation that takes roughly fifteen minutes, *90eren* is the only bar in Copenhagen that serves uncarbonated Carlsberg beer (from the nearby brewery). The strong hops flavour is reminiscent of English real ale and – supposedly – very similar to the original Carlsberg beer produced in the mid-nineteenth century.

Alléenberg **Allégade 4. Tues–Sat 10pm–5am.** Decorated with Danish theatre memorabilia, this lively bar is the preferred watering hole of the local Frederiksberg theatre wannabes – they'll probably give you a tune on the piano at some point – and the last stop of the night for the neighbourhood's high-school students who, for reasons unknown, fondly refer to it as "The Psychopath".

Den Blå Hund **Godthåbsvej 28. Mon–Wed 9.30am–11pm, Thurs–Fri 9.30am–1am, Sat 10am–2am, Sun 10am–10pm.** By day, people come here to drink coffee, read newspapers and chat. After sunset, the draught beer begins to flow and, on a few nights a week, there's live jazz. In summer, tables spread out across busy Godthåbsvej to Axel Møllers Have, where covered seating is available, serviced by tray-balancing white-aproned waiters. Good food, too (see p.158).

Café Svejk Smallegade 31. Tues–Sat noon–2am, Sun & Mon noon–midnight. Near Frederiksberg Have, in a red wooden townhouse extension, *Svejk* has a good selection of draught beer from the Czech brewery Bohemia Regent and the German brewery Moritz Fiege. There's also occasional live jazz, and a large-screen TV showing important football matches.

Promenaden Frederiksberg Allé 58. Mon–Sat noon–2am, 11am–midnight. Under the beech trees lining regal Frederiksberg Allé, this Parisian-style café has nice outdoor seating and one claim to fame: a visit by Salman Rushdie in 1996. His photo, wearing a Tuborg Christmas hat, is still displayed proudly on the wall above where he sat.

Nørrebro

People head to Nørrebro if they want to be "seen"; the bars are mostly trendy places where the clientele has thought long and hard about what to wear that night. The following places are on the map on p.98.

Café Blågård's Apotek Blågårds Plads 20. Daily 3pm–2am (in summer from noon). Homely bar, still patronized by some of the left-wing activists who used to clash on this square with the police during the 1970s. They're now joined by a less-committed crowd who come to sample the bar's many wines and Urquell draught beer. Gets jam-packed during weekends, when there's also live jazz, blues or rock.

Caféen Funke Blegdamsvej 2. Mon–Wed & Sun 2pm–2am, Thurs–Sat 2pm–5am. Refreshingly laid-back place on hip Skt Hans Torv, this is one of the oldest cafés on the square and still going strong, with cheap beer, a Tuesday-night backgammon tournament, and live music or stand-up comedy a couple of nights a week. Reasonably priced food available, too.

Front Page Sortedam Dosseringen 21. Mon–Wed, Sat & Sun 11am–1am, Thurs & Fri 11am–2am. Attractive lakeside café-bar, especially popular in summer, when tables are moved outdoors and you can enjoy a relaxing drink while contemplating the city from afar. In winter, service moves inside to a cosy cellar.

Gefärlich Fælledvej 7. Tues 5pm–1am, Wed & Thurs 5pm–3am, Fri & Sat 5pm–4.30am. Funky two-storey bar-cum-nightclub-cum-restaurant with DJs playing every night from 10pm and an upstairs bar transforming into a cocktail bar from 11.30pm.

Kassen Nørrebrogade 18. Wed 8pm–1am, Thurs 8pm–3am, Fri 2pm–4am, Sat 8pm–4am. A stone's throw from *Nora* hotel (p.141), this small place is one of the city's top cocktail bars, preparing their own unique array of very tasty drinks for around 60–70kr each. The Friday happy hour(s) (3–10pm) offers two-for-one cocktails and beer. Smoking permitted.

Nørrebro Bryghus Ryesgade 2. Mon–Wed 11am–midnight, Thurs–Sat 11am–2am, Sun 11am–5pm. Immensely popular brewpub in an old factory, with a range of homebrews that sell out quicker than they can be bottled. Pricey restaurant, too (see p.159).

Oakroom Birkegade 10. Tues 7pm–midnight, Wed & Thurs 7pm–2am, Fri & Sat 7pm–3am. Another new, popular cocktail bar, this one with a classy interior designed by award-winning architect Kasper Rønn.

Ølbaren Elmegade 2. Mon 9pm–1am, Tues–Thurs & Sat 4pm–1am, Fri 3pm–1am. A small, crowded place frequented by beer enthusiasts, with a wide range of beer from all over the world, and absolutely no Tuborg or Carlsberg. Tell the bartender what flavours you like, and he'll find a beer to suit. Unfortunately, this personal service can be – endearingly – slow.

Props Coffee Shop Blågårdsgade 5. Mon–Wed 11am–midnight, Thurs–Sat 11am–2am, Sun noon–11pm. Small, laid-back bar-cum-secondhand furniture shop; should you suddenly decide that you can't live without the chair you've sat on all evening, check the price tag. In summer furniture spills out onto the street and at weekends the place is heaving.

Pussy Galore's Flying Circus Skt Hans Torv 30. Mon–Fri 8am–2am, Sat & Sun 9am–2am. Named after Honor Blackman's nubile Bond Girl in *Goldfinger*. You'll be stirred if not shaken by delicious cocktails and outdoor seating on one of Nørrebro's hippest squares – definitely a place to be seen. Also a restaurant; see p.159.

Sebastopol Skt Hans Torv 2. Mon–Wed 8am–midnight, Thurs & Fri 8am–2am, Sat 9am–2am, Sun 9am–midnight. Glitzy Parisian-style café with outdoor seating on the cobbles of lively

Sankt Hans Torv square. Crowded at weekends with well-groomed professionals warming up for the night.

Soupanatural Guldbergsgade 7. Mon & Tues 8am–10pm, Wed & Thurs 8am–midnight, Fri 8am–2am, Sat noon–2am, Sun noon–10pm. Small, super-hip joint (also a restaurant; see p.159) across from *Rust* featuring fabulous and affordable cocktails that, as far as possible, are organic. Seating is organized around two large tables, so it's almost impossible not to get chatting with your neighbour.

Østerbro

Østerbro is mostly residential, with the few places listed below – at all of which you could easily while away a few hours – being the exception to the rule. The following places are on the map on p.98.

The Office Sortedam Dosseringen 83. Wed, Thurs & Sat 7pm–2am, Fri 5pm–2am. Run by a Kiwi and a Brit, this basement bar facing the lakes fills up in the early evening with people waylaid on their way home from work. With both indoor and outdoor seating (outdoors on swings!), there's always room for one more. They specialize in cocktails with unusual names such as Not Broccoli, Extreme Prejudice and Knowledge.

Panzon Rosenvængets Allé 6. Mon–Thurs 4pm–midnight, Fri & Sat 4pm–2am. Fantastic little tapas bar with more than fifty own-import wines, sold by the glass as well as bottle, a good selection of European and North American beer, and lovely tapas to soak it all up. A tad pricey.

Pavillonen i Fælledparken April–Sept Mon–Fri noon–10pm, Sat & Sun 11am–5am. Pretty little pavilion café in the middle of Fælledparken with outside benches ideal for enjoying the tranquil park while sipping a cool draught lager. Free salsa lessons Mon & Wed 7–10pm.

Amager

The best places to go for a drink on the island of Amager are all near the waterfront. The following places are on the map on p.105.

Halvandet Refshalevej 325, Refshaleøen. April–Sept 10am–sunset/midnight. Large beach café-bar in a derelict industrial complex on the western coast of Refshaleøen. Access is easiest with the DFDS canal boat (the green hop-on-hop-off route) or by water taxi (Flyvefisken ⓣ32 96 49 64). Enjoy the view of the Little Mermaid on the opposite bank while lounging on a beach chair or a mattress sipping on something from the vast drinks menu – including a good range of champagne and other bubblies.

Islands Brygge Kulturhus Islands Brygge 18. Mon–Wed 10am–11pm, Thurs–Sat 10am–midnight, Sun 10am–11pm. The café/bar at this culture centre next to the harbour pool on the banks of Inderhavnen has outdoor seating with great views across the harbour. Drinks are not too expensive and there's a good selection of draught lagers from home and abroad.

Mulata Social Club Amager Strandvej 110. April–Sept daily noon–midnight. Lively new beach bar across the road from Amager Strandpark (see p.110) modelled on a Cuban social club with lots of music and fun goings-ons throughout the day. As it's an outdoor place, and Danish summers are reliably unreliable, it's a good idea to check out the weather forecast before heading this way; evening gigs tend to be cancelled if it's raining. There's also a popular barbecue buffet in the evenings.

13

Live music and clubs

Though more subdued during the week, Copenhagen is Scandinavia's party town at the weekend, with a range of nightlife to suit the widest – and wildest – tastes. The city's liberal drinking laws – the most relaxed in Scandinavia – pull in punters from across the region, particularly Swedes, who descend on the city in search of a good time. A wide range of **bars** (see pp.162–168) and **clubs** cater to fun-lovers of all ages, with every sort of music from bebop to bhangra.

There's also a raft of **live music** venues. Traditionally, the **jazz** scene has always been the city's liveliest – a number of respected American jazz musicians such as Dexter Gordon and Ben Webster lived here during the 1960s and 1970s – and the annual jazz festival is world renowned. There's a decent local **rock** scene, while many big-name international acts include Copenhagen on their tours (and many more turn up for the huge **Roskilde Festival** – see p.196). A number of smaller places double as cafés or restaurants during the day and bars in the evening, before becoming live music venues or nightclubs after midnight.

You can buy **tickets online** or by **phone** for gigs at most of the larger venues listed below. Their websites will either link you through to **Billetlugen** (Ⓦwww.billetlugen.dk, Ⓣ70 26 32 67; Mon–Fri 10am–5pm) which gives you the option of printing the ticket or having it posted to you for a fee, or **Billetnet** (Ⓦwww.billetnet.dk, Ⓣ70 15 65 65; Mon–Sat 10am–8pm) which can post it to you for a fee or allow you to pick it up, for 10kr, at their outlets. There's one at Vesterbrogade 3 (beside Tivoli's main entrance) and at all post offices. Tickets are also usually sold at the door a couple of hours before the gig starts.

For English-language **listings** information, pick up the *Copenhagen Post* (Ⓦwww.cphpost.dk) from the Wonderful Copenhagen tourist office on Vesterbrogade, or check Ⓦwww.aok.dk and Ⓦwww.kulturnaut.dk. The tourist office has details of **free outdoor summer concerts** and festivals at Fælledparken (see p.102).

Live music

Indre By

The following places are on the map on p.44.

Copenhagen Jazzhouse Niels Hemmingsensgade 10 Ⓣ33 15 47 00, Ⓦwww.jazzhouse.dk. Mon–Thurs & Sun 6pm–midnight, Fri & Sat 6pm–5am. Copenhagen's premier jazz venue, this large, smart, two-level club is frequented by jazz-lovers of all ages. Gigs start at 8pm weekdays and 9pm Fridays and Saturdays, with music ranging from traditional jazz and funkjazz, fusion and neobop to world music at its best. On Fri & Sat the *Natklub* nightclub (see p.172) takes over at midnight (or whenever the gigs finish) and continues until the early hours of the morning.

Din Nye Ven **Sankt Peders Stræde 34 ⓦwww.myspace.com/dinnyeven. Mon & Tues 1pm–midnight, Wed 4pm–midnight, Thurs 1pm–1am, Fri & Sat 1pm–2am.** Homely, rustic café that transforms into a packed live music venue one or two nights a week, generally with pop-rock and urban-hip-hop. Also a nightclub.

Drop Inn **Kompagnistræde 34 ⓣ33 11 24 04. Mon–Fri 11am–5am, Sat noon–5am, Sun 2pm–5am.** A cosy café-cum-jazz bar that has live jazz, blues or folk music every night starting at 10pm – and often for free. In the summer, there's indoor and outdoor seating, and sandwiches and light meals available all day.

La Fontaine **Kompagnistræde 11 ⓣ33 11 60 98. Daily 7pm–5am.** The city's oldest jazz venue, with live jazz Fri & Sat 11pm–3am and Sun 9pm–1am. Frequented largely by up-and-coming Danish hopefuls, this is the place to come if you're into small smoky rooms and surprise appearances by visiting big names. Later in the evening the stage is thrown open to aspiring performers in the audience.

Huset Magstræde **Rådhusstræde 13 ⓣ33 69 32 00, ⓦwww.husetmagstraede.dk.** With loads of different cultural venues under one roof, *Huset Magstræde* offers jazz at *1.Sal* on the first floor (around 60kr); *Musikcaféen* on the third floor features up-and-coming mostly Scandinavian bands (also around 60kr). Gigs nightly at around 9pm. Advance tickets for *Musikcaféen* through ⓦwww.gaffabillet.dk.

Det Hvide Lam **Kultorvet 5 ⓣ33 32 07 38. Mon 10am–midnight, Tues & Wed 10am–1am, Thurs–Sat 10am–2am, Sun noon–1am.** Traditional jazz in a small, dark basement bar with no stage but loads of atmosphere, and musicians giving it all they've got most nights. During the day you're welcome to eat your packed lunch here as long as you buy drinks.

Mojo **Løngangstræde 21C ⓣ33 11 64 53, ⓦwww.mojo.dk. Daily 8pm–5am.** Live music nightly in this small venue with plenty of down-at-heel ambience, popular with blues aficionados of all ages. Music starts around 9.30pm and is followed at weekends with a DJ until closing. Less-established local acts get things going before the big names come on stage. Either free or around 60kr.

The Rock **Skindergade 45–47 ⓣ33 91 39 13, ⓦwww.the-rock.dk.** The oppressive former law courts provide a perfect setting for the aggressive music played at this dark live-music venue devoted to heavy metal and hardcore rock. Bands start at 9pm and are sometimes follow by a heavy-metal disco. From 70kr.

Studenterhuset **Købmagergade 52 ⓣ35 32 38 60, ⓦwww.studenterhuset.com. Mon noon–6pm, Tues & Thurs noon–1am, Wed noon–2am, Fri & Sat from noon, Sun 3–6pm.** Student union club next door to Rundetårn with lots going on throughout the week. The downstairs café hosts live music from around 9.30pm on Thursdays (primarily jazz), Fridays and Saturdays (a wide range of up-and-coming Danish and international bands). 20–60kr.

Christianshavn

The following places are on the map on p.55.

Loppen **Christiania ⓣ32 57 84 22, ⓦwww.loppen.dk.** Most nights – around 9pm – this cool converted warehouse on the edge of Christiania hosts both established and experimental Danish rock, jazz and performance artists, and quite a few visiting British and American ones, too (some free, others 60–200kr).

Operaen **Christiania ⓣ32 57 29 09, ⓦwww.operaen.net.** Upstairs in one of Christiania's old warehouses on Pusherstreet, *Operaen* is a very laid-back venue with live gigs most nights except Tuesday (film night), ranging from blues to hip-hop. Sunday is blues day from 3–9pm.

Frederikstad

The following is on the map on p.64.

Jazzcup **Gothersgade 107 ⓣ33 15 02 02. Mon–Thurs 11.30am–5.30pm, Fri 11am–7pm, Sat 10am–6pm.** An ingenious arrival on the Copenhagen jazz scene, this original café-cum-CD-shop-cum-music-venue has live jazz every Friday (3.30pm) and Saturday (2.30pm). Some of the best Danish and international musicians play here, including names from the world music circuit. 40–60kr.

Rådhuspladsen and around

The following places are on the map on p.78.

Pumpehuset **Studiestræde 52 ⓣ33 93 19 09, ⓦwww.pumpehuset.dk.** The city's spacious former pumphouse is one of its best concert venues with a capacity of up to six hundred. A broad sweep of up-and-coming or fading international rock acts and big Danish names perform about eight times a month. 60–250kr.

Tivoli ⓣ33 15 10 01, ⓦwww.tivoli.dk. Surprisingly good, sometimes even groundbreaking, live outdoor rock-pop every Friday night at 10pm from April to September – with a good crowd and decent weather it can be great fun. Entry is free with general Tivoli admittance.

Vesterbro and Frederiksberg

The following places are on the map on p.88.

Forum Julius Thomsens Plads ⓣ32 47 20 00, ⓦwww.forumcopenhagen.dk. Large sports, flea market and performance venue around the corner from the *Cab-Inn* hotels in Frederiksberg, hosting the occasional huge international pop or rock act such as Oasis, Green Day and Pink. From 300kr.

Vega Enghavevej 40 ⓣ33 25 70 11, ⓦwww.vega.dk. In a former union hall, this top music venue retains its 1950s and 1960s decor while showcasing plenty of modern alternative rock. *Vega* houses two stages: Store Vega, accommodating 1500, hosts international names; Lille Vega, with room for "only" 500, is used for smaller bands or when the big names want an intimate atmosphere. At the weekends it becomes *Vega Nightclub*. Keep your eye out for local and visiting luminaries: Björk apparently loves the place. Up to 400kr.

Nørrebro and Østerbro

The following places are on the map on p.98.

Café Blågård's Apotek Blågårds Plads 20, Nørrebro ⓣ35 37 24 42, ⓦwww.kroteket.dk. Daily 3pm–2am (in summer from noon). Low-key place catering for a slightly older crowd that come here to listen to live jazz, blues, rock or world music every Monday, Friday and Saturday, when it gets packed. Monday is jazzjam and free; Fri and Sat 20kr.

Global Copenhagen Nørre Allé 7 ⓦwww.globalcph.dk. Fri & Sat 9pm–1am. Excellent world music venue run primarily by volunteers as a not-for-profit organization. Gigs every Friday and Saturday (9pm–1am) include such diverse genres as reggae, Balkan fusion, Afrocuban rumba and Russian folk. Tickets from 60kr; 20kr discount for students.

Parken Øster Allé 50 ⓣ35 43 31 31, ⓦwww.parken.dk. The country's main football stadium and FCK's home ground, hosting concerts with international megastars four to five times a year. A large sliding roof weatherproofs it year round. From 400kr.

Rust Guldbergsgade 8, Nørrebro ⓣ35 24 52 00, ⓦwww.rust.dk. Wed–Sat 9pm–5am. One of the best-known venues in town, this multifaceted place on busy Skt Hans Torv hosts up-and-coming live indie rock, hip-hop and electronic music acts from across the globe on its main stage. Downstairs, the very hip *Rust Natklub* specializes in electro, hip-hop, house and cool, funky grooves. Over-20s only after 11pm. 30–300kr.

The suburbs

The following places are on the map on p.105.

Amager Bio Øresundsvej 6 ⓣ32 86 02 00, ⓦwww.amagerbio.dk. Converted cinema, now one of the city's largest and most popular live-music venues, hosting big names from the local and international music scene such as Macy Gray and Yes. Tickets start at 150kr.

DR-byens Koncerthus Emil Holms Kanal 20, Ørestad ⓣ35 20 62 62, ⓦww.dr.dk/koncerthuset. Stunning state-of-the-art concert venue mainly devoted to classical music but also hosting the occasional rhythmic band such as Thomas Dybdahl from Norway and posh pop acts such as the French Nouvelle Vague. From 150kr.

Femøren Amager Strandpark ⓦwww.amager-strand.dk. June–Aug. Huge, inexpensive open-air rock concerts by top local bands and international acts on a temporary stage a stone's throw from Amager beach.

K.B. Hallen Peter Bangsvej 147 ⓣ38 71 41 50, ⓦwww.kbhallen.dk. The city's oldest sports stadium which has hosted live concerts since it was reconstructed in 1945 (it was bombed during the war) including legends such as Josephine Baker and The Beatles. Still going strong, it features big international acts such as Backstreet Boys and the Pet Shop Boys. From 400kr.

Clubs

Indre By

The following places are on the map on p.44.

Club Mambo **Vester Voldgade 85 ⓣ33 11 97 66, ⓦwww.clubmambo.dk. Thurs 8pm–3am, Fri & Sat 9pm–5am.** Increasingly hip salsa bar, long popular among the city's small South American community. Free salsa and merengue classes (Thurs 9–10pm, Fri & Sat 10pm & 11pm). Thurs free, Fri & Sat 60kr.

Din Nye Ven **Sankt Peders Stræde 34 ⓦwww.myspace.com/dinnyeven. Mon & Tues 1pm–midnight, Wed 4pm–midnight, Thurs 1pm–1am, Fri & Sat 1pm–2am.** When this bar doesn't have a live band playing, it becomes a popular nightclub with DJs spinning chill-out tunes and world music.

Diskotek In **Nørregade 1 ⓣ33 11 74 78, ⓦwww.discotekin.dk. Fri 11pm–8am, Sat 11pm–10am.** Three nightclubs under one roof: *La Hacienda*, a Spanish-inspired club playing soul and R&B, the more electronic *The Dance Floor*, and the *Jukeboksen* where you can make requests from lists on the tables. All three – you can move freely between them – are pretty mainstream, catering for a young audience. *Diskotek In*'s free-bar concept – you pay a fixed fee (women pay about fifty percent less than men) after which you can drink your fill of beer, wine and champagne all night – is wildly popular. 75–150kr.

▲ Clubbing in Copenhagen

Faust **Skindergade 20 ⓦwww.faust.dk. Wed & Thurs 6pm–midnight, Fri & Sat 6pm–5am.** Basement club on Skindergade dedicated to Goth music genres – neo-folk, horror-punk, darkwave. Weekdays free, weekends around 50kr.

Natklub **Niels Hemmingsensgade 10 ⓣ33 15 26 00, ⓦwww.jazzhouse.dk. Fri & Sat midnight–5am.** When the live gigs are finished at *Copenhagen Jazzhouse* (see p.169) *Natklub* takes over with in-house DJs spinning Latin, house, acid jazz, bossa nova and old-school disco tunes. 65kr.

Woodstock **Vestergade 12 ⓣ33 11 20 71, ⓦwww.woodstock.dk. Thurs–Sat 10pm–5am.** Basically a large dance floor and not much else, *Woodstock* pulls in a fun-loving older crowd willing to bop to anything with a beat – predominantly retro music, going all the way back to Elvis. Thursday 100kr with free bar; Friday & Saturday 50kr.

Rosenborg and Frederikstad

The following places are on the map on p.64.

Culture Box **Kronprinsessegade 54 ⓣ33 32 50 50, ⓦwww.culturebox.com. Thurs–Sat 11pm–5am.** Dedicated to electronic music – techno, electro, electronica, drum'n'bass and dubstep – with a constant influx of up-and-coming DJs, this is Copenhagen's most happening nightclub. It has a steady following of regulars, so you may have to wait to get in. Around 60kr.

Nasa/Kulørbar **Boltens Gård ⓣ33 93 74 15, ⓦwww.nasa.dk. Nasa: Fri & Sat midnight–6am; Kulørbar: Thurs 10pm–5am, Sat 11pm–5am.** You don't have to be rich and famous to come here, but it helps, and you'll certainly need to dress up to have any chance of getting in. *Nasa*, on the top floor, is the more exclusive – it's members only, but you might be able to talk your way in if you look the part – and is the haunt of Danish and visiting movie and music stars. *Kulørbar* is marginally more relaxed and easier to get in, though you'll still need to slip on a posh party frock. *Kulørbar* 60kr.

Rådhuspladsen and around

The following places are on the map on p.78.

Nord Natklub Vesterbrogade 2E ⓦwww.nordlounge.dk. Sat 10pm–5am. Fun nightclub across from Tivoli for the over-30s (so, yes, if you're a young-looking 31 you'll need to bring some ID!) that gets heaving after midnight, primarily playing 1980s and 1990s rock and pop. Also an excellent cocktail bar with table service. 90kr.

Rosie McGee's Vesterbrogade 2A ⓣ33 32 19 23, ⓦwww.rosiemcgee.dk. Mon, Tues & Sun 11pm–3am, Wed & Thurs 11pm–4am, Fri 11pm–5am, Sat 11pm–6am. A stone's throw from Rådhuspladsen, *Rosie McGee's* pub-style venue attracts many Anglophone visitors. There's a restaurant and bar downstairs with occasional DJs and live gigs during the week, but it's the upstairs nightclub spanning two floors, and encompassing three dance floors and five bars, that gives life to the place, pumping out mainstream pop until dawn. Friday & Saturday 60kr after 10pm, rest of the week free.

Vesterbro and Frederiksberg

The following places are on the map on p.88.

Kellerdirk Frederiksberg Allé 102, Frederiksberg ⓣ33 25 22 53, ⓦwww.kellerdirk.dk. Fri & Sat 11.30pm–4.30am. A restaurant and theatre café during the week, until it throws open its disco doors, featuring live "copy band" jam sessions until 2am followed by danceable pop/rock disco from the 1980s and 1990s. With very limited seating, the options are either to dance or stand by the bar; most choose to dance. Frequented by an "older" audience (25–40) that has opted to avoid the hassle of inner-city clubs. 80–100kr.

Vega Natklub Enghavevej 40, Vesterbro ⓣ33 25 70 11, ⓦwww.vega.dk. Fri & Sat 11pm–5am. One of the top clubs in the city, part of the immensely popular *Vega* (see p.171) and offering all you could want for a fantastic night out. The actual club is based in Lille Vega and sees resident and internationally renowned guest DJs raising the roof with funky beats and soulful sounds. There's also an upstairs chill-out lounge with soothing tunes and fancy cocktails and, out front, *Ideal Bar* (see p.166) which hosts Zoot Suit every Thursday between 8pm and 5am – a swing club with free lessons until midnight. Gets very busy after 1am. 60kr after 1am.

Nørrebro and Østerbro

The following places are on the map on p.98.

Café Bopa Løgstørgade 8, Østerbro ⓣ35 43 05 66, ⓦwww.cafebopa.dk. Thurs 11.30pm–2am, Fri & Sat 11.30pm–5am. Hugely popular café-bar in a remote corner of Østerbro, offering late-night boogying. Guest DJs play mostly mainstream dance tunes that appeal to the very mixed crowd. Free.

Gefärlich Fælledvej 7, Nørrebro ⓦwww.gefarhlich.dk. Tues 5pm–1am, Wed & Thurs 5pm–3am, Fri & Sat 5pm–4.30am. Funky two-storey bar-cum-nightclub-cum-restaurant with the city's hottest DJs every night from 10pm.

Global Copenhagen Nørre Allé 7, Nørrebro ⓦwww.globalcph.dk. Fri & Sat 9pm–1am. World music venue with DJs – world musicians themselves – taking over after the live bands have finished playing. From 60kr, 20kr discount for students.

Rust Guldbergsgade 8, Nørrebro ⓣ35 24 52 00, ⓦwww.rust.dk. Wed–Sat 11pm–5am. Crowded, multilevel venue named after Mathias Rust, who famously landed his small plane on Moscow's Red Square in 1987. His adventure resulted in the pan-Scandinavian peace initiative, the Next Stop Sovjet, which was based in this building. *Rust* subsequently began to host live bands and still has the occasional gig. Attractions today include the small basement nightclub, which offers serious underground electronic dance music. Upstairs, there's a laid-back, minimalist cocktail bar and a larger main stage and dance floor where guest DJs play hip-hop, house and cool, funky grooves. Only over-21s after 11pm. 60kr.

14

Classical music, theatre and cinema

With three new big-budget, high-profile music and performing arts venues completed since 2005, Copenhagen's cultural scene is going through an unprecedented period of expansion. And though traditionally strong on the "high" arts – **opera**, **ballet**, **classical music** and **theatre**, which receive most of the government's subsidies, an increasing number of more experimental ventures have broken through in the last couple of decades, particularly in the arena of alternative theatre and **film**.

Until recently, the Royal Opera, Royal Ballet and Royal Theatre all jostled for space in the grandiose **Det Kongelige Teater** on Kongens Nytorv; now the Royal Opera has its own building, the fabulous waterfront Opeaen (see p.61) on Holmen, opened in 2005, while the Royal Theatre has its own state-of-the-art venue – the Skuespilhuset – inaugurated in 2008, almost directly across the harbour. The "Old Stage" on Kongens Nytorv is now mainly given over to ballet and some opera. They all still operate under the banner, however, of Det Kongelige Teater, which produces a booklet of the season's repertoire, available from the tourist office and the theatre itself, with details of all of the productions – opera, theatre, concerts and ballet – across its various venues. Alternatively, check out their website at Ⓦwww.kglteater.dk. You can buy tickets online, from their ticket hotline (Ⓣ33 69 69 69; Mon–Sat noon–4pm), from the box office at August Bournonvilles Passage 1, just off Kongens Nytorv (Mon–Sat 2–8pm) or from the other sources mentioned below. If you don't mind leaving it till late, go in person to the box office; they hold back around 25 tickets for that day's evening performance at Det Kongelige Teater and Opeaen, which can be bought in person on the day. You can get some real bargains if you're willing to leave it really late – unsold tickets for that evening's performances are sold off from 4pm onwards at a fifty percent discount.

Grand projects aside, the city has a plethora of smaller venues for music and drama – from churches and minor theatres to more quirky locations like the **Rundetårn** and the **Teatermuseet**. For details on where to find English-language **listings** information, see p.26.

Tickets for all the large (and many of the smaller) venues reviewed below can be bought through **Billetnet** (see p.169).

Classical music and opera

Copenhagen is home to a number of top-class ensembles – including the Zealand Symphony Orchestra, the Academic Orchestra and Choir, and the excellent Danish National Symphony Orchestra/DR and Danish National Choir (Ⓦwww.dr.dk/dnso), which have stunning premises at the **Koncerthuset** at DR-byen in Ørestad. There are also regular classical music concerts in many of Copenhagen's grandest **churches**, including Vor Frue Kirke, Vor Frelsers Kirke, Trinitatis Kirke, Marmorkirken, Skt Petri Kirke and the church in Kastellet – a free quarterly programme listing all these concerts is available from the churches themselves or from the Wonderful Copenhagen tourist office; most are either free or very modestly priced. Look out, too, for concerts in the city's **museums** and in the Queen's Hall of Den Sorte Diamant. Finally, Tivoli has its own concert hall, which puts on world-class classical music concerts.

Opera in the city received a huge boost with the completion of the Opeaen on Holmen, home to the Royal Danish Opera and Royal Danish Orchestra (the world's oldest orchestra, dating back to 1448), under the artistic direction of Kasper Bech Holten. Here, the familiar classics continue to predominate – works by Puccini, Mozart, Wagner, Strauss, Verdi and Rossini – though the extra space now means that more contemporary productions by modern composers are now on the programme. Note that a few operas per season are still performed on the Old Stage in Kongens Nytorv. Most performances are in Danish, Italian or German, with occasional supertitles in English. Thanks to subsidies, **tickets** are reasonably priced, though it depends on the production and, of course, where you want to sit – for the more popular classics, expect to pay 90–833kr. Every summer the Royal Danish Opera goes out and about with its **Open-Air Opera** – two free, open-air performances (usually highlights of the coming season at Det Kongelige Teater; see Ⓦwww.kglteater.dk) staged in one of the city's green spaces. Arrive early to get a spot, and bring a picnic.

Classical music and opera venues

DR-byens Koncerthus Emil Holms Kanal 20, Ørestad Ⓦwww.dr.dk/koncerthuset. DR-Byen Metro. Copenhagen's classical music scene has its own acoustic heaven in the form of the brand new, state-of-the-art National Concert Hall, located out on Amager (see p.110). This is the home of DR's orchestral, choral and ensemble companies, principally the Danish National Symphony Orchestra/DR, the Danish National Chamber Orchestra and the DR Radio Choir. There are four concert halls in all – three smaller ones hosting performances of choral works and chamber music – while the main concert hall is for symphony concerts and guest performances. There's plenty of other non-classical music on offer here too, be it free jazz in the foyer, big band jazz from the DR Big Band, rhythm and blues or large rock and pop concerts. Tickets from DR-butikken, the on-site shop and box office (Ⓣ35 20 62 62; Mon–Wed & Fri noon–5pm, Thurs noon–6pm, Sat 11am–2pm) or from Billetnet and Billetlugen (see p.169)

Det Kongelige Teater Kongens Nytorv, Indre By Ⓣ33 69 69 69 (Mon–Sat noon–4pm), Ⓦwww.kglteater.dk. Despite the arrival of the new opera house, Copenhagen's grandest theatre still stages a few fairly conservative operas and classical concerts. Tickets (100–1200kr) for popular works sell out very fast.

Opeaen Holmen Ⓣ33 69 69 69, Ⓦwww.kglteater.dk or Ⓦwww.operaen.dk. The city's opera house has two stages – the opulent, maple-encased, gilt-ceilinged main stage "Store Scene", with seating for up to 1700, and the much more intimate "Takkelloftet" (Tackle Loft), used for more experimental productions and chamber music.

Rundetårn Købmagergade, Indre By Ⓣ33 73 03 73, Ⓦwww.rundetaarn.dk. This quirky venue offers regular chamber-music recitals, classical soloists and choral works, along with the annual Copenhagen Guitar Festival (July/Aug). Free, or relatively cheap (50–100kr).

Den Sorte Diamant Koncertsal Christians Brygge 9, Slotsholmen Ⓣ33 47 47 47, Ⓦwww.kb.dk. Stunning waterfront venue hosting frequent performances from solo pianists and string ensembles – it even has its own resident string quartet.

Tivolis Koncertsal **Tietgensgade 20, Indre By ⓣ33 15 10 12, ⓦwww.tivoli.dk.** Tivoli's concert hall stages a variety of classical performances and some opera, often featuring the major national orchestras.

Theatre and dance

The Royal Danish Playhouse – Skuespilhuset – opened in 2009, has revitalized the city's **theatre** scene, offering a varied programme from classics to contemporary Danish drama. Most are performed in Danish, though there are frequent guest directors and companies from all over the world with the odd performance in English. In the past decade or so, several youthful and dynamic theatres and companies have appeared, though as many only stage Danish-language productions, they're unlikely to be of interest to most visitors – unless you head for some of the more experimental performances where dialogue is sparse and not too integral to the experience. Alternatively, you could see whether there's anything playing by the **London Toast Theatre** (ⓦwww.londontoast.dk), a well-established English theatre company, based in Copenhagen, which performs English-language plays, comedies and musicals in the mainstream city theatres, including an ever-popular Christmas cabaret in Tivoli's Glassalen. The free English-language city listings magazine *Copenhagen This Week* also has a section "Theatre in English". There are also English-language productions of **Hamlet**, staged in the summer in Kronborg Slot in Helsingør; check with the tourist office for details.

Copenhagen has a small but thriving **dance** scene – although there's only one venue, Dansescenen, specifically devoted to this, other theatres occasionally stage dance performances. For **ballet** lovers, there's the fairly traditional repertoire of the Royal Ballet, staged at Det Kongelige Teater and Opeaen, as well as several performances in Tivoli during the summer and at Christmas. If you're in the city in mid-August, you can catch the free open-air ballets in the atmospheric surroundings of Kastellet (ⓦwww.kglteater.dk for details).

Ticket prices can be steep even for fringe performances: at least 150kr, or less late on the day of performance. A free monthly programme, *Teater Kalenderen* (ⓦwww.teaterkalenderen.dk), covering theatre and dance, is available at the theatres themselves, at the Tivoli ticket centre and at the tourist office; alternatively check out ⓦwww.kulturnaut.dk and www.aok.dk.

Theatre and dance venues

CaféTeatret **Skindergade 3, Indre By ⓣ33 12 58 14 (Tues–Fri 4–6pm), ⓦwww.cafeteatret.dk.** Part theatre, part trendy café (featuring its own programme of events) frequented by actors and arty types, CaféTeatret puts on a range of innovative performances – theatre, dance, cabaret – mostly in Danish.

Dansescenen **Øster Fælled Torv 34, Østerbro ⓣ35 43 20 21 (Mon–Fri 5–7pm), ⓦwww.dansescenen.dk.** The only place in Copenhagen with regular performances of modern dance, showcasing top Scandinavian ensembles on its two stages plus the work of the current choreographer in residence. The Dansescenen programme (available from the Tivoli ticket office) has a section in English.

Det Kongelige Teater **Kongens Nytorv, Indre By ⓣ33 69 69 69 (Mon–Sat noon–4pm), ⓦwww.kglteater.dk.** Copenhagen's oldest theatre provides all the gilt and velvet pomp you could ask for. Since the arrival of the new opera house and playhouse the "old stage", as it is affectionately known, is now largely given over to the Royal Danish Ballet and their repertoire of classic and modern ballet. Note that some ballet is also performed in the new opera house (see p.61).

Folketeatret **Nørregade 39, Indre By ⓣ33 12 18 45 (Mon–Fri 1–6pm, Sat noon–3.30pm),**

Ⓦwww.folketeatret.dk. One of the oldest theatres in town. The main stage (Store Scene) tends to put on musicals and family-oriented stuff; the smaller Hippodromen shows more experimental work, as does the tiny stage, Boxen; Snoreloftet sticks to cabaret. The Christmas shows are always a hit.

Gasværket Nyborggade 17, Østerbro ⓣ39 27 71 77 (Mon–Fri 2–6pm, Sat 2–4pm), Ⓦwww.gasvaerket.dk. Set in an old gasworks, this is one of the hippest theatres in town, with new plays and innovative musical theatre productions – no weighty classics here. Occasional performances in English.

Krudttønden Serridslevvej 2, Østerbro ⓣ35 42 83 62, Ⓦwww.krudttonden.dk. The small "Powder Keg Theatre" is a live music/theatre/comedy venue that puts on a range of plays and monologues – the latter by locally founded "That Theatre Company" – some of which are in English.

Skuespilhuse Skt Annæ Plads 36, Frederikstad ⓣ33 69 69 69, Ⓦwww.kglteater.dk or Ⓦwww.skuespilhus.dk. The city's stunning new playhouse offers a wide-ranging programme of drama across three stages – the main stage seating around 650, the second stage, Portscenen, with seating for 200 and the small Studio stage with capacity for 100.

Film

The Danes' love affair with celluloid stretches back to the 1920s, when the country's thriving studios looked for a time as though they would become Europe's answer to Hollywood. The success was spearheaded by internationally renowned director Carl Theodor Dreyer, with his series of dark, dramatic pieces such as *The Master of the House* (1925) and the French-produced *The Passion of Joan of Arc* (1928); he continued to make films until his death in the 1960s. Nowadays, the **Danish film industry** is booming again with a new set of film-makers achieving international critical acclaim, in particular the group originally associated with Dogme 95 (see box, p.178), including its founder, Lars von Trier, and Thomas Vinterberg. Von Trier's controversial films such as *Breaking the Waves* and *Dancer in the Dark* made his directorial name worldwide, and his star continues to rise as actors like Nicole Kidman, star of *Dogville*, and Willem Dafoe, who starred in the violent *Antichrist*, come on board, lured by the prospect of challenging, non-Hollywood roles.

Danes are keen cinemagoers, and despite the inevitable predominance of mainstream Hollywood flicks in the city's **cinemas**, there's usually at least one Danish production on offer. Foreign-language films get good representation, too; most films are screened in their original language, with Danish subtitles. The city's arthouse cinemas, particularly Cinemateket at the **Filmhuset**, home to the Danish Film Institute and Vester Vov Vov, always have offbeat offerings. Most cinemas offer cheaper **tickets** earlier in the day (before 6pm), with prices being staggered up to the most expensive evening and weekend screenings – from about 60kr–80kr. At weekends, it's definitely worth booking ahead. Cinemas are not part of the Billetnet or Billetlugen systems.

In 2009, the established **Night Film Festival** and **Copenhagen International Film Festival** merged into one – **CPH:PIX** (Ⓦwww.cphpix.dk) – held over ten days every Spring. The focus is on Danish and European film, with a competition for budding directors, an international jury, around 170 special screenings, plus seminars and interviews.

The weekly pamphlet *Film Kalenderen* (available in English on Ⓦwww.aok.dk) includes details of almost all of Copenhagen's movie offerings and is available free in most cinemas; Cinemateket produces its own monthly **listings**, and the free city paper *metroXpress* also has a film calendar.

Dogme 95 and Lars von Trier

Established in 1995, **Dogme 95** was founded in reaction to Hollywood domination with its reliance on special effects and massive budgets. Basically a manifesto drawn up by Lars von Trier and Thomas Vinterberg and dubbed the "Vow of Chastity", it aimed to enhance cinematic realism by a series of rules – the film must be in colour, only hand-held cameras and natural lighting are allowed, shooting must be done on location with no props and sets, and no special costumes, special effects or extraneous soundtracks are permitted. Although the four main exponents of the movement – von Trier, Vinterberg, Søren Kragh Jacobsen and Kristian Levring – are all Danish, anyone can make a Dogme film if it follows the manifesto, and over thirty accredited Dogme films have been made in a variety of countries. That said, the best-known Dogme films are Danish – a selection of the best is reviewed below. Ironically, the Dogme Secretariat closed in 2002 for fear that Dogme was becoming too much of a genre in itself (one of the rules of the "Vow of Chastity" was no genre films), and claiming that it and the original founders had "moved on". Although the movement still exists, films no longer have to receive official accreditation to be called a Dogme film – they simply have to follow the manifesto. Von Trier continues to make films through his highly successful film company Zentropa, started in 1992 with producer Peter Albaek Jensen. Zentropa has made more than seventy films, including the Dogme films, and now also includes a large studio complex, Filmbyen; both are based in the Copenhagen suburb of Hvidovre.

The Idiots (1998), Lars von Trier. One of von Trier's most disturbing (and least politically correct) films, this mockumentary about a group of friends who feign mental disability in public, inciting unrest wherever they go, showed von Trier's characteristic lack of fear of controversial material.

Festen (The Celebration) (1998), Thomas Vinterberg. The film that made Vinterberg's name, Festen tells the story of a family gathering to celebrate the father's 60th birthday; things turn dark when the son accuses the father of sexual abuse. Terrific performances make this engrossing, if uncomfortable, viewing.

Mifune's Last Song (1999), Søren Kragh Jacobsen. A touching romance of a son returning home to take over his parent's farm.

Italian for Beginners (2000), Lone Scherfig. An international hit, this charming, low-key romcom tells the story of the social misfits and outsiders who find varying degrees of love and fulfillment in an Italian language class. Set in Copenhagen.

Cinemas

Cinemateket at Filmhuset Gothersgade 55, Indre By ⓣ33 74 34 12, ⓦwww.cinemateket.dk. Closed Mon. Home of the Danish Film Institute, this three-screen, state-of-the-art complex shows the best of Danish and international arthouse film – the more eagerly anticipated films sell out quickly, so bookings are advisable. The Benjamin theatre shows children's films and free documentaries, and there's also a trendy restaurant, a decent book and DVD shop and fantastic cinematic archives (see p.67).

Cinemaxx Fisketorvet Kalvebod Brygge 57, Vesterbro ⓣ70 10 12 02, ⓦwww.cinemaxx.dk/koebenhavn. Multiscreen complex in a mall showing the latest from Hollywood. Not worth a special trip unless you plan to go shopping beforehand.

Dagmar Teatret Jernbanegade 2, Indre By ⓣ33 14 32 22, ⓦwww.dagmar.dk. Mostly mainstream movies in this popular five-screen cinema in the heart of Copenhagen. There's a bust of Carl Theodor Dreyer, who was the cinema's manager for a short period.

Empire Bio Guldbergsgade 29F, Nørrebro ⓣ35 36 00 36, ⓦwww.empirebio.dk. Very popular cinema with huge, comfy seats and a good selection of Danish and international film.

Gloria Biografen Rådhuspladsen 59 ⓣ33 12 42 92, ⓦwww.gloria.dk. Small cinema right in the centre of the city, with an eclectic programme of mainstream, specially imported and arthouse movies. It also sells arthouse films through its own DVD-distribution arm, some of which can be hard to find elsewhere. A cinebuff's delight.

Grand Teatret Mikkel Bryggers Gade 8, Indre By ⓣ33 15 16 11, ⓦwww.grandteatret.dk. Very central cinema, in the heart of Indre By, showing the best of mainstream international films.

Husets Biograf Rådhustræde 13, Indre By ⓣ33 32 40 77. On the second floor of the Huset building, this small cinema shows esoteric, arthouse movies.

Imperial Ved Vesterport 4, Vesterbro ⓣ70 13 12 11, ⓦwww.biobooking.dk. Copenhagen's largest cinema, and the usual site for gala openings and premieres. The enormous single screen – the biggest in Scandinavia, with reclining seats and a stunning sound system – shows mainly middle-of-the-road Hollywood blockbusters.

Palads Axeltorv 9, Indre By ⓣ70 13 12 11, ⓦwww.biobooking.dk. One of the world's first multiplexes and probably the most colourful cinema on the planet, this Copenhagen landmark, with its famously gaudy exterior, shows the latest mainstream movies on its seventeen screens.

Park Bio Østerbrogade 79, Østerbro ⓣ35 38 33 62, ⓦwww.parkbio-kbh.dk. One of the oldest in town, this atmospheric single-screen cinema tends to show a mixture of the better Hollywood offerings and the more commercial arthouse films coming towards the end of their runs. It also has a decent café-bar.

Tycho Brahe Planetarium og Omnimaxteater Gammel Kongevej 10, Vesterbro ⓣ33 12 12 24, ⓦwww.tycho.dk. Copenhagen's IMAX screen shows a mixture of non-fiction natural world and cosmic wonder films, although there's the odd 3D offering, too. You'll need to rent headphones for English translation.

Vester Vov Vov Absalonsgade 5, Vesterbro ⓣ33 24 42 00, ⓦwww.vestervovvov.dk. Three-screen arthouse cinema, with a decent bar and café for pre-flick nibbles. Also a large and fairly comprehensive collection of film posters, some of them for sale.

15

Gay Copenhagen

Being the capital of a country where homosexuality has long been legal, and where gay and lesbian couples are allowed to marry and adopt children, has led to Copenhagen becoming one of the world's **premier gay cities**. Heads don't generally turn if a gay or lesbian couple are seen kissing or holding hands, and its main cruising spot, H.C. Ørstedsparken, has been equipped with "birdboxes" containing condoms and lubricating gel. Police here don't chase out cottaging men, but protect them from homophobic violence.

Paradoxically, Copenhagen's liberal traditions mean that there are fewer specifically gay and lesbian venues than in less tolerant cities. The national organization for gays and lesbians, the **Landforeningen for Bøsser og Lesbiske** (LBL), at Nygade 7 (Ⓣ33 13 19 48, Ⓦwww.lbl.dk; Mon 9am–6pm & Thurs 3–6pm) offers **information** on the gay and lesbian scene in Denmark, and a very useful online gay guide (Ⓦwww.gayguide.dk). Also available at all major gay hangouts is the monthly *Out and About* magazine – mostly in Danish – published by Copenhagen Gay Life (Ⓦwww.copenhagen-gay-life.dk), a network of gay and gay-friendly businesses and organizations that also produces a good English-language *Gay City Map of Copenhagen* with listings marked.

The city's hugely popular annual gay-pride march – **Copenhagen Pride** (Ⓦwww.copenhagenpride.dk; see p.197 for more) – is held in August, with an all-night party after the parade. Also on the annual agenda is the Copenhagen Gay and Lesbian Film Festival, which takes place over nine days in October (Ⓦwww.cglff.dk), and the legendary midsummer beach party at Amager Strandpark organized by LBL.

Accommodation

Apart from the places listed below, you can also find rooms (from 400kr) in gay or gay-friendly accommodation by contacting the German-based Enjoy Bed & Breakfast (Ⓣ+49 30 236 236 10, Ⓦwww.ebab.dk). Unless otherwise stated, the following places are on the Indre By map on p.44.

Carsten's Guest House Christians Brygge 28, 5th floor (ring the bell marked "Carsten Appel"), Indre By Ⓣ33 14 91 07, Ⓦwww.carstensguesthouse.dk. Bus #5A or #66; ten minutes' walk from Central Station or Rådhuspladsen. See map, p.78. This guesthouse has a very friendly and international atmosphere, though the rooms are a bit small and the walls thin. There's a great roof garden, a comfortable and attractive lounge, plus a kitchen for guests' use. Dorm beds 175kr. 585kr.

Copenhagen Rainbow Guesthouse Frederiksberggade 25, Indre By Ⓣ33 14 10 20, Ⓦwww.copenhagen-rainbow.dk. Rådhuspladsen bus station. *Rainbow* is a gay-only guesthouse in an excellent position on Strøget, just off Rådhuspladsen, with five rooms, some en suite, and all with TV and tea- and coffee-making facilities. The rate includes a buffet breakfast, and there's free wi-fi. 790kr.

Hotel Windsor Frederiksborggade 30, Indre By ⓣ33 11 08 30, ⓦwww.hotelwindsor.dk. Bus #5A; Nørreport Station. On the second and third floor of a residential apartment block, this long-established and unpretentious gay hotel has some en-suite rooms, some with shared facilities. Continental breakfast buffet included. 625kr.

Restaurants, bars and clubs

Unless otherwise stated, the following places are on the Indre By map on p.44.

Amigo Bar Schønbergsgade 4, Frederiksberg. Daily 10pm–6am. See map, p.88. Fun gay bar popular with gay and straight folk alike, not least for its karaoke.

Café Intime Allégade 25, Frederiksberg. Daily 6pm–2am. See map, p.88. Small, cosy piano bar frequented by a good mix of gay and straight people with a thing about musicals. On Monday & Tuesday the floor is open for wannabe performers.

Can Can Mikkel Bryggers Gade 11, Indre By. Mon–Thurs & Sun 2pm–2am, Fri & Sat 2pm–5am. Small, friendly, inexpensive bar during the day, alive and bustling at night when mostly frequented by gay men.

Centralhjørnet Kattesundet 18, Indre By ⓦwww.centralhjornet.dk. Daily noon–2am. Copenhagen's oldest gay bar, frequented predominantly by older gay men: welcoming, unpretentious and very cheap, with a lively atmosphere and famous jukebox featuring a vast selection of kitsch pop. Live gigs most Thursday nights between November and April, with fantastic drag queen performances.

Chaca Studiestræde 39, Indre By. Wed–Sat 7pm–5am. Predominantly lesbian bar spread over two floors with lots of different events; games nights, speed-dating and karaoke nights are the most renowned. Good cocktails, too.

Code Rådhusstræde 1, Indre By. Wed & Thurs 4pm–midnight, Fri & Sat 4pm–5am. This new addition to the gay scene attracts a good gay and lesbian mix. It's a café during the day and a lounge bar at night with DJ and dance floor.

Cosy Bar Studiestræde 24, Indre By. Mon–Thurs & Sun 10pm–6am, Fri & Sat 10pm–8am. Popular dance and late-night/early-morning cruise venue (mostly gay men but a lot of straight people too) for the partygoer with stamina. DJ Tuesday & Thursday–Saturday.

Jailhouse Studiestræde 12, Indre By. Mon–Thurs & Sun 3pm–2am, Fri & Sat 3pm–5am. Popular basement bar, primarily frequented by gay men, designed as a jail with drinking "cells", handcuffs lying around and waiters dressed as wardens. The first-floor restaurant (Thurs–Sat), also mainly gay, serves good-value daily specials.

Masken Studiestræde 33, Indre By. Mon–Thurs & Sun 2pm–3am, Fri & Sat 2pm–5am. Nearly every segment of the city's gay and lesbian population makes it to this raucous bar at some point during the week, possibly because of the cheap beer. The "girls' night" in the basement on Thursdays seldom attracts the crowds, while Fridays are for young gays and lesbians and can be very cruisey.

Mens Bar Teglgårdsstræde 3, Indre By. Daily 3pm–2am. The city's most macho bar, popular with leather-clad men and those who enjoy a walk on the butch side; you won't find any women or straights here – they're simply not let in. There's a popular free brunch the first Sunday of every month.

Oscars Rådhuspladsen 77, Indre By. Daily noon–2am. A traditional first port of call on a night out, the very popular *Oscars* serves good, classic Danish food as well as every kind of soft and alcoholic drink imaginable. Can get cruisey late on.

Vela Gay Club Viktoriagade 2–4, Vesterbro. Wed & Thurs 9pm–midnight, Fri & Sat 9pm–5am. See map, p.88. Hugely popular oriental-style place that began life as a predominantly lesbian venue – it serves "pussy-tails" as well as cocktails – but now attracts party-goers of all persuasions.

16

Shopping

Shopping is one of the highlights of a visit to Copenhagen, with an abundance of eclectic and original shops offering a refreshing alternative to the predictable selection of chain stores. Denmark's fine tradition of innovative **design** (see *Danish design* colour section), can be found everywhere in stylish shops selling everything from clothing through furniture, glassware and lighting to stereo equipment. Quality is very high – as are prices. Most of the city's top shops – particularly fashion, furniture and interior design – are in **Indre By**, traversed by Strøget, the world's longest (and oldest) pedestrianized shopping street, with the latest in Danish fashion design and interiors clustered in the trendy streets heading west off Købmagergade. With no real traffic to dodge or excessive distances to cover, shopping here is a real pleasure. Another great shopping area is Ravnsborggade and its surrounding streets in **Nørrebro** where a vibrant mix of antique, vintage and secondhand shops, designer clothes stores and one-offs are contained in a relatively small area, while the lively Vesterbrogade and Istedgade in up-and-coming **Vesterbro** offer a great combination of cheap clothing shops and funky boutiques. In summer it's also worth checking out the outdoor **flea markets**.

Opening hours are roughly Monday to Thursday 10am to 6pm, Friday 10am to 7pm, Saturday 10am to 4pm (5pm in summer), though be warned that many close around 2/3pm on Saturday. Hardly any open late or on Sundays, though for food and basic supplies, a few central supermarkets (see p.188) have longer hours. Failing that, the supermarket in Central Station is open daily from 8am to midnight. We've only given opening hours in reviews if they differ greatly from those above. If you're shopping for wine or beer, note that shops aren't allowed to sell alcohol after 8pm.

For information on children's clothing and toy shops see p.202.

Fashion

As far as **clothes** go, you can find pretty much whatever you want without leaving Indre By. The main shopping thoroughfares of **Strøget** and **Købmagergade** are lined with the likes of Benetton, Diesel, Karen Millen, H&M, Zara and French Connection, with a good smattering of quality Danish chains, including Noa Noa, and cheaper discount outlets. The **Østergade** section of Strøget is the place to head for if your budget runs to the likes of Hermes, Prada and Chanel.

Hyper-trendy **Kronprinsensgade**, off Købmagergade, has many of the best and most internationally recognized modern **Danish designer clothes**, though Pilestræde, which cuts across Kronprinsensgade, and the streets stretching further east towards Gothersgade – Gammel Mont, Store Regnegade, Ny Østergade and

Grønnegade – are also rich hunting grounds for Danish design, particularly up-and-coming labels. Larsbjørnsstræde, Studiestræde and Skt Peders Stræde, adjacent to the Latin Quarter, have the best selection of **secondhand and vintage** shops. The area around **Nansensgade**, north of Nørreport Station, is also home to a few small designer clothes shops, as is **Ravnsborggade** in Nørrebro.

Designer clothes

1206 Naboløs 3, Indre By. Stylish menswear from a range of designers and brands, Danish and international, as well as cool casual basics – T-shirts, sweatshirts and the like – by the store's own brand, 1206.

Acne Gammel Mønt 10, Indre By. Flagship store of the Swedish label, whose strength is their trademark jeans and casual wear. Also sells shoes and boots.

Bruuns Bazaar Kronprinsensgade 8–9, Indre By ⓦwww.bruunsbazaar.com. Denmark's first fashion house, Bruuns has established itself as one of Europe's trendiest designer clothes shops, catering for both men and women; it's as expensive and exclusive as you'd expect.

Day: Birger et Mikkelsen Pilestræde 16, Indre By ⓦwww.day.dk. Gorgeous Danish-designer womenswear (there's a menswear outlet in Illum and Magasin) where the focus is on great tailoring, detail and craftsmanship that aims to put glamour into everyday wear.

Dico Ravnsborggade 21, Nørrebro. Housed in one of Ravnsborggade's former antique shops, the Dico label (designed by the son of legendary Stig P, see below) is mainly found on trousers and suits, for both sexes. Classic, stylish and pricey.

Edith & Ella Købmagergade 7, Indre By & Store Kongensgade 19A, Frederikstad. ⓦwww.edith-ella.com. Danish designer Line Markvardsen named her string of boutiques after her two inspirational grandmothers, and theres's definitely a good dose of nostalgia in her fabulous use of florals, knits, satin, chiffon and lace.

Flying A Kronprinsensgade 5, Indre By. Lots of ultra-trendy men's and women's gear from a variety of Danish and international labels, both well-established and up and coming, with everything from funky T-shirts to party frocks and jackets.

Langelinie Pier Langelinie Allé, Østerbro. Daily 11am–6pm. The likes of Diesel, Gucci and Kenzo as well as Danish brands like Noa Noa have factory outlets here with all goods sold at upwards of fifty percent discount.

Munthe plus Simonsen Grønnegade 10, Indre By ⓦwww.muntheplussimonsen.com. Hot fashion to burn a hole in your pocket. The clothes are by Danish designers Naja Munthe and Karen Simonsen who have established an international reputation with garments that blend Far Eastern influences with Scandinavian simplicity.

Nørgaard på Strøget and Mads Nørgaard Amagertorv, Indre By. A family business with two generations of designers, each catering for a different group. Nørgaard på Strøget – the oldest shop – houses women's and teenage wear in all price brackets. Mads Nørgaard is geared towards the trendy man.

Pede & Stoffer Klosterstræde 15 & 19, Indre By. Casual gear for men (no. 15) and women (no. 19) featuring a range of up-and-coming designer labels.

Rützou Store Regnegade 3, Indre By ⓦwww.rutzou.dk. Rising Danish fashion designer Suzanne Rützou makes sensuous, feminine womenswear that's comfortable and versatile; plenty of beautifully designed basics with fine detailing that sets them apart.

Stig P Kronprinsensgade 14, Indre By & Ravnsborggade 18, Nørrebro. The first designer shop to find its way to Kronprinsensgade in the 1970s and still going strong. A broad selection of jeans and smarter wear from well-known designer labels like See by Chloe and Sonia Rykiel as well as Danish designers and Stig P's own designs. The Indre By branch is for women only, whereas Ravnsborggade has a large men's section and also sells its own lingerie collections and kimonos.

Secondhand clothes

Atelier Décor Rømersgade 9, Indre By. Not your regular secondhand shop, this is high-end classy, haute couture stuff with vintage dresses – some antique – and beautiful shoes, gloves and hats to complete the outfit. The stuff of dreams.

Fisk Skt Peders Stræde 1, Indre By. A charity shop with a difference – run for DanChurch Aid, the shop has its own label that takes second-hand clothes and reworks them into funkier, more unique garments. There's a fair-trade coffee shop upstairs too.

København K Studiestræde 32B & Teglegårdsstræde 2, Indre By. This shop pretty much set the trend for those that followed in the area – and is still one of the best places to head for a great range of used and vintage clothing, shoes and accessories.

Retro Skt Peders Stræde 47, Indre By. ⓦwww.retrosales.dk. Lots of carefully chosen retro women's clothing, especially strong on jewellery and accessories.

Sneaky Fox Larsbjørnstræde 15, Indre By. Retro women's clothing, all carefully selected and well displayed, this is a great place to find that special funky dress.

Wasteland Studiestræde 5, Indre By. Trendy retro fashion outlet with a lot of 1970s and 1980s gear – the place to get your original Police or Madonna T-shirt.

Shoes, lingerie and accessories

A Pair Ny Østergade 3 & Nansensgade 39, Indre By ⓦwww.apair.dk. Fantastic range of designer men's and women's shoes – everything from glam stilettos to cool sneakers – as well as a good range of accessories and some casual clothing.

Alli C Læderstræde 1, Indre By ⓦwww.alli-c.dk. Women's shoes and handbags – expensive but unusual one-off designs. Also a stockist of Danish "Sanita" clogs, which come in everything from regular black to pink or furry.

Anne Ammitzbøll Skt Annæ Plads 2, Christianshavn. Lovely jewellery shop selling old and new pieces.

Bruno & Joel Kronprinsensgade 2, Indre By. High quality, classic women's shoes and boots; pricey but stylish and made to last.

Figaros Bryllup Store Regnegade 2, Indre By. Closed Mon. Light, unpolished handmade jewellery using a variety of different metals including 22-carat gold, pink gold and platinum.

Georg Jensen Amagertorv 4, Indre By. Flagship store of the renowned silversmiths, selling a sophisticated mix of classics and more modern designs – beautifully worked brooches, solid rings and elegant watches.

Ilse Jacobsen Kronprinsensgade 11, Indre By. From glam stilettos to her trademark natural rubber lace-up boots with warm cotton fleece lining – now a Scandinavian design icon and the ultimate in practical yet stylish footwear.

Louise Grønlykke Store Standstræde 19, Frederikstad. Beautiful handmade jewellery, mostly gold, inspired by Japanese and North African ornamental styles. Everything is created by Grønlykke herself.

Monique Sko Nygade 6, Indre By ⓦwww.moniquesko.dk. Cool collection of women's footwear by a range of designers – Danish and other – like Ilse Jacobsen, Tommy Hilfiger, Betty Blue and Bumper.

Museums Kopi Smykker Grønnegade 6, Indre By ⓦwww.museum-jewelry.dk. If you've been admiring the amazing Viking jewellery on display at the Nationalmuseet, this excellent, if pricey, shop produces outstanding handmade copies of these and other jewellery finds from the Bronze Age onwards.

Furniture, design and interiors

Denmark's **design** pedigree is second to none and shops abound showcasing the country's continuing contribution to the industry, from classy vintage furniture shops selling original 1940s iconic chairs to funky outlets showcasing the latest in sofa design. Good design and quality is important to the Danes and not seen as the preserve of the rich. In a country where going out to eat is an expensive affair, there's greater focus on entertaining at home, with the important art of table-setting crucial to the creation of a *hygge* ("cosy") atmosphere so integral to Danish social gatherings. This means you'll find a wide range of shops selling imaginative and stylish glassware, crockery, candlesticks, table linen and table decorations.

For an all-under-one-roof crash course in the best of Danish design past and present, you can't do better than the outstanding **Illums Bolighus** (see opposite), though you shouldn't miss the smaller, cutting-edge shops in the streets heading west off Østergade. Admirers of **vintage twentieth-century Scandinavian** furniture and lighting should check out the originals in the high-end vintage shops along exclusive Bredgade in Frederikstad. Finally, if you'd rather rummage through more affordable **bric-a-brac, secondhand and antique shops** you need go no further than Nørrebro and the buzzing streets of Ravnsborggade and Skt Hans Gade.

Bald & Bang Aps **Rømersgade 7, Indre By ⓦwww.bald-bang.com.** Even if your suitcase space is limited, you can take home a piece of Danish designer lighting. Holger Strøm's self-assembly lampshades are formed of identical, interlocking quadrilaterals that can be made up into a range of shapes and sizes – a sort of Lego of the lighting world.

Bang & Olufsen **Kongens Nytorv 26, Indre By ⓦwww.bang-olufsen.com.** The very latest in hi-fi equipment in the city's funky flagship store.

Casa Shop **Store Regnegade 2, Indre By ⓦwww.casashop.dk.** Classic and modern Danish and international design from furniture to watches. Arne Jacobsen is well represented, holding his own against the latest in spindly chairs, stylish sofas and funky lighting.

Designer Zoo **Vesterbrogade 137, Vesterbro ⓦwww.dzoo.dk.** At the western end of Vesterbrogade, this large, bright, two-storey gallery sells the glassware, ceramics, art, jewellery and clothes made by the up-and-coming designers who work in the workshops out the back. They're happy to talk to you about their designs – all contemporary and individual.

▲ Quirky Copenhagen style at Designer Zoo

Georg Jensen **Amagertorv 4, Indre By.** Famous the world over, Georg Jensen silversmiths, which features works by many craftsmen other than the great man himself, has been turning out simple yet stylish silverware – from jewellery and cutlery to candlesticks and tableware – for over a hundred years.

Georg Jensen Damask **Ny Østergade 19, Indre By.** The Danes make an art out of table dressing, and this is as good as it gets – classy tablecloths, napkins, napkin rings and the like.

Hay **Pilestræde 29, Indre By ⓦwww.hay.dk.** Funky, striking furniture – some of the most cutting-edge names in modern Danish furniture design sell here. Also a select range of designer toys, ceramics and trinkets.

Illums Bolighus **Amagertorv 10, Indre By.** Four cool, elegant – and very Scandinavian – floors overflowing with an eye-catching assortment of Danish and international design, from fabulous kitchenware and glassware to Poul Henningsen lamps and Arne Jacobsen furniture classics, though such quality and refinement doesn't come cheap.

Klassik **Bredgade 3, Frederikstad ⓦwww.klassik.dk.** Original Scandinavian modern vintage furniture, lighting, ceramics, art and sculpture – ogle an original Poul Henningsen lamp, and furniture by such luminaries as Hans J. Wegner, Kaare Klint and Arne Jacobsen. At these prices, ogling is about as far as most people get.

Moderna 10 **Ravnsborggade 10A, Nørrebro.** A stand-out on a street where it seems like every other shop is a vintage Danish design or bric-a-brac treasure trove – a good range of Danish classics from furniture to lighting and tableware.

Normann **Østerbrogade 70, Østerbro ⓦwww.normann-copenhagen.dk.** Housed in a former cinema and a worthy rival to Illums Bolighus, this supercool design emporium offers the best and latest in design all under one roof. Plenty of designer fashion from Danish names like Malene Birger and international figures like Marc Jacobs and Ally Capellino, as well as great Scandinavian and Italian furniture, glassware, candlesticks, vases, lamps – the lot.

Paustian Kalkbrænderløbskaj 2, Østerbro ⓦwww.paustian.dk. Stylish furniture shop designed by Danish architect Jørn Utzon (famous for the Sydney Opera House), beautifully situated on the Østerbro harbourfront. Expensive furniture and smaller must-have bits for your home, by local and internationally renowned designers. Also a good in-house café.

Retrograd Gunløgsgade 7, Islands Brygge. A real gem of a place, this small basement shop has an eclectic and irresistible collection of retro design pieces – clocks, coffee pots, toy cars, lamps, tableware, grocery tins. There's bound to be something you can't resist.

Royal Copenhagen Porcelain Amagertorv 6, Indre By. Even if you're not excited by the idea of china, it's worth a peep at one of Denmark's most famous exports, still being produced to centuries-old designs. Each piece is handmade and hand-painted, with the painter's signature on the bottom – hence the extortionate prices.

Something Special Løvstræde 10, Indre By. On a side street by the Rundetårn, this sparkling den of old and new glassware, cocktail shakers, crystal decanters, lighting, jewellery and furniture (designed by the friendly owner) is the place for a special set of snaps glasses.

Bookshops

Central Copenhagen has plenty of **bookshops**, many of which, especially the larger ones, have excellent English-language stock. Most of the big stores are found along Strøget and Købmagergade; the Latin Quarter, particularly **Fiolstræde**, is a rich hunting ground for secondhand gems.

Arnold Busck Købmagergade 49, Indre By ⓦwww.arnoldbusck.dk. Huge, central chain bookstore on three floors selling new titles and with a good English-language fiction section.

Arnold Busck Antikvariat Fiolstræde 24, Indre By. Cramped and slightly stuffy antiquarian and secondhand store with a sprinkling of English-language titles on everything from botany to clocks and a good selection of first editions of twentieth-century fiction classics.

The Booktrader Skindergade 23, Indre By. On a quiet side street off Købmagergade, this rambling secondhand bookstore has a good English-language fiction section (particularly crime) towards the back.

GAD Vimmelskaft 32, Indre By ⓦwww.GAD.dk. In a handy central location halfway down Strøget, this Danish chain has a wealth of new titles and a decent English-language fiction section. There are other branches at Central Station, Fiolstraede 31–33 and Falkoner Alle 21.

Nordisk Korthandel Studiestræde 26–30, Indre By ⓦwww.scanmaps.dk. Great guidebook and map store with friendly staff and an extensive range of travel guides to destinations worldwide, as well as a full range of Denmark maps, for walking, cycling and driving.

Politikens Boghandel Rådhuspladsen 37, Indre By. Large, mainstream bookstore on the town-hall square, with possibly the city's best range of English-language titles.

Tranquebar Borgergade 14, Frederikstad ⓦwww.tranquebar.net. This fantastic bookshop stocks a huge range of travel guides and travel literature – everything from Rough Guides to classic travelogues to glossy coffee-table tomes. They sell ethnic clothing, crafts and trinkets too, and have a comfy café serving fair-trade coffee.

Vangsgaards Fiolstræde 34–36, Indre By ⓦwww.vangsgaards.dk. Three light and spacious floors of antiquarian and second-hand fiction and non-fiction with English-language titles scattered throughout. It also sells old prints.

Department stores and shopping centres

Copenhagen's two department stores are top-class, and also provide a great way of seeing the collections of the country's top designers under one roof, whether you're after clothes, accessories or interior design, while those looking for the big shopping centre experience need look no further than Fields in Amager.

Fields Ørestaden, Amager ⓦ www.fields.dk. Gigantic shopping centre – the largest in Scandinavia – housing, apart from hundreds of international and national chain stores, Denmark's biggest cinema, with 22 screens.

Galleri K Pilestræde 12B, Indre By. A small, exclusive and trendy shopping arcade, housing a rarefied selection of top brands including some flagship stores of classy Danish designers and international names like Agent Provocateur.

Illum Østergade 52, Indre By ⓦ www.illum.dk. The city's most fashionable department store, with almost 500 of the world's best and most luxurious brands on offer, including a good representation of Danish designers – a great place to get a feel for who you like before heading off to their own dedicated stores in the streets nearby. The Illum home department stocks a great range of interior furnishings and tableware, and there are also two coffee shops, two bakeries, a good newsagent with some English-language magazines and an overpriced but convenient supermarket in the basement.

Magasin du Nord Kongens Nytorv 13, Indre By. Dating back to 1871, the grand and very classy Magasin du Nord is Copenhagen's answer to Harrods or Bergdorf Goodman with seven floors of fantastic fashion, homewares and more besides plus a great deli, café, bakery, chocolate counter, newsagent and luxury supermarket Mad & Vin.

Music

If you're after that special bit of vinyl or the latest in jazz, here are a few pointers – all centrally located.

Accord Vestergade 37, Indre By ⓦ www.accord.dk. Plenty of old and new vinyl and lots of cheap CDs and DVDs – a great hunting ground for aficionados. Also a branch at Nørrebrogade 88–90.

Amoeba Recordshop Hyskenstræde 10, Indre By ⓦ www.amoebarecordshop.dk. Specialists in electronic music – the ultra-cool staff will help you find that special import techno, house or hip-hop album.

Beat Pop Gothersgade 58, Indre By. Astounding range of vinyl old and new covering everything from rock to pop to jazz, with an extremely knowledgeable, helpful owner.

Guf Vestergade 17, Indre By ⓦ www.gufmusik.dk. Mainstream pop and jazz are the specialities, with lots of discount CDs.

Jazzcup Gothersgade 107, Indre By. Jazz CD store with a massive selection of both national and international names, as well as an in-house bar and frequent jazz gigs (see p.170).

Jazzkælderen Skindergade 19, Indre By ⓦ www.jazzmusic.dk. Speciality jazz store with a great selection of Danish and international jazz on CD, plus sheet music, videos and flyers for forthcoming gigs. There's a mellow café, too.

Soundstation Gammel Kongevej 94, Frederiksberg ⓦ www.soundstation.dk. Large collection of secondhand CDs, vinyl and DVDs – all genres covered – along with collectibles, memorabilia and posters.

Food and drink

Copenhagen has no shortage of delis and excellent bakeries where you can get the vital ingredients for a picnic or pick up something special to take home – jars of pickled and marinated herrings, cheeses, remoulade, rye bread and snaps or the bitter aperitif Gammel Dansk make good consumable souvenirs. Away from Indre By, the small street of Værnedamsvej, northwest of the Bymuseum in Vesterbro and lined with an array of delicatessens, bakeries and colourful fruit and veg shops, is the place to hunt out **gourmet food**. The city has a good selection of central

supermarkets – usually open Monday to Friday 8/9am to 7pm, Saturday 8/9am to 4pm, with some open on Sundays too. Netto, the cheapest chain, has central branches at Nørre Voldgade 94, Fiolstræde 9 and Landemærket 11. Or there's the more upmarket Irma City (also open 10am–9pm Sundays) in Rådhusarkaden, Vesterbro 1, Vesterbrogade 46, Falkoner Allé 13, Østerbrogade 110, and at Nørrebrogade 3; and Superbrugsen at Nørre Voldgade 15, Christianshavns Torv 2 and Halmtorvet 25 (this branch also open Sun 10am–4pm) in Vesterbro. Note too that both Illum and Magasin (see p.187) have – pricey – supermarkets in their basements.

Bakeries

Det Rene Brød **Elmegade 6, Nørrebro.** Home-made organic bread with a beautiful, flavour-packed texture. Two more outlets in Østerbro on Rosenvængets Allé 17 and Ndr Frihavnsgade 54.

Emmerys **Store Standstræde 21, Indre By** Ⓦ**www.emmerys.dk.** Trendy bakery where the young, rich and health-conscious queue every weekend for their organic non-dyed, non-yeast bread. Plenty of scrumptious cakes on offer, too. Also outlets on Østerbrogade 51, Vesterbrogade 34 & Nørrebrogade 8.

Lagkagehuset **Torvegade 45, Christianshavn.** Right opposite the metro station and easily identifiable by the ever-present queue, this sumptuous bakery produces amazing bread baked in traditional stone ovens, plus great pastries and cakes. There's another branch in the Copenhagen Right Now tourist office on Vesterbrogade (see p.30).

Rhein van Hauen **Østergade 22, Indre By.** The king of Danish bakeries, with nearly thirty years of organic baking to its name. Mouth-watering *rundstykker* (crispy bread rolls) and pastries. Also branches at Store Kongensgade 45 & Gammel Kongevej 177.

Delis and speciality food shops

A.C. Perch's Thehandel **Kronprinsensgade 5, Indre By.** One of Europe's oldest teashops, founded in 1835, Perch's retains much of its delightful original wooden interior, around which waft the wonderful aromas of teas from across the globe.

Elm Street **Elmegade 8, Nørrebro.** Delicious home cooking, including Danish meatballs, and a couple of Thai specialities as well. A few tables but mostly takeaway.

Gammel Strand Ø log Vin **Naboløs 6, Indre By.** Over two hundred different beers – Danish and international.

Granola **Værnedamsvej 5, Frederiksberg.** Chocolates, jams, coffees, teas and ice cream are the specialities in this cute little retro shop/café (see p.156).

Løgismose **Bernstorffsgade 5, Indre By.** Bang opposite Central Station, this fabulous deli is part of the Nimb complex in Tivoli (see p.80) but there's also a street entrance for non-Tivoli-goers. Aside from the inevitable jars of herring, cheeses, cured meats, remoulades, preserves and the like, you'll find more unusual delicacies to try or take home as souvenirs, and there's also the produce made by their own dairy and delicious home-made chocolates.

Peter Beier Chokolade **Skoubougade 1, Indre By.** Delicious, beautifully packaged chocolates sold by weight.

Solhatten **Istedgade 85, Vesterbro.** Great organic health-food store selling fresh produce and a good range of meat alternatives and soya products. Also some healthcare products and herbal remedies.

Sømods Bolcher **Nørregade 24 & 36, Indre By.** Using century-old recipes – no chemical additives – this shop makes a range of tasty boiled sweets; you can also watch the elaborate sweet-making process.

Vinbutikken **Nansensgade 45, Indre By.** Attached to the lovely wine-bar Bibendum (see p.163), this little wine shop offers a great selection from Italy, France, Spain and Australia.

Speciality shops

Christiania Cykler **Christiania, Christianshavn.** Next door to the *Månefiskeren* music café and bar, this is the home of the Pedersen bike – an age-old design created to make cycling on cobbled streets more comfortable – which is produced and sold here.

Games **Jorcks Passage, Indre By.** Traditional board games and toys, ranging from functional pocket chess sets to suave Italian leather backgammon boards.

Johnny **Skindergade 21, Indre By ⓦwww.johnny.dk.** Run by Aids-Fondet, the Danish Aids foundation, Johnny, as you'd expect, sells just about every brand, flavour, texture, shape and size of condom on the market. Also sells femidoms. Mon–Wed noon–5.30pm, Thurs & Fri noon–8pm, Sat 10am–3pm.

Sögreni of Copenhagen **Skt Peders Stræde 30A, Indre By ⓦwww.sogreni.dk.** Beautiful handmade bicycles, including ones made to your own specifications.

Tranhuset **Amager Strandvej 112, Amager ⓦwww.tranhuset.dk.** This unique shop is packed with traditional arts, crafts, clothes and food from Greenland, Iceland, the Faroe Islands and Denmark. All the seal-fur coats, sealskin boots and bags, bone and tooth figurines, and chunky woolly mittens you can handle.

Markets

You'll be able to hunt for a piece of bargain Royal Copenhagen porcelain or Holmegaard glass at one of the city's several summer **flea markets**, most of them centrally located and with nearby cafés. If you're here at Christmas, especially with kids, don't miss the Christmas markets; the best are at Tivoli, in Christiania and along Nyhavn.

Det Blå Pakhus **Holmbladsgade 113, Amager. Sat & Sun 10am–4pm.** A year-round weekend fixture, Copenhagen's largest indoor flea market boasts 4500 square metres of uninhibited clutter, featuring objects of every conceivable size, shape, form and value. Entrance fee.

Frederiksberg Rådhus **Gammel Kongevej, Frederiksberg. April–Oct Sat 9am–3pm.** Popular trading place for locals, and, thanks to this prosperous neighbourhood's wealthier residents, you might turn up a few better-than-usual wares, particularly in the fashion department.

Gammel Strand flea market **Gammel Strand, Indre By. May–Sept Fri 7am–6pm & Sat 8am–6pm.** The most central (thus overpriced) and beautifully located flea market, by the canal on Gammel Strand, sells the usual range of old china, bric-a-brac, paintings and glassware.

Israels Plads **Israels Plads, Indre By. April–Oct Sat 8am–2pm.** On the children's playground behind the fruit and veg market off Frederiksborggade, this Saturday flea market sees a great mix of professional dealers selling serious antiques and ordinary Joes emptying their attics.

Kongens Nytorv Arts & Crafts Market **Kongens Nytorv. April–Aug Sat 10am–5pm, first Sun of the month 11am–4pm.** A chance for the city's creative types to get out of their workshops and studios and show off their work to the general public; everything from handmade jewellery to paintings to ceramics and clothing.

Nørrebro market **Along the wall of Assistens Kirkegåard, Nørrebro. April–Oct Sat 6am–3pm.** This is the city flea market where, if you search patiently, you may unearth some real bargains from Royal Copenhagen porcelain to antique chairs.

Økologiske Torvegade **Blågårds Plads, Nørrebro. May–Sept Sat 11am–4pm.** Organic market in the heart of trendy Nørrebro, offering a wealth of vegetables, meat, bread, milk, fish and some non-food products in a jovial neighbourhood atmosphere.

17

Sport and outdoor activities

In terms of health and fitness, the Danes are a contradictory lot: the country has one of Europe's highest rates of smoking- and drinking-related deaths, yet also, thanks to massive government funding, boasts some of the best public sports facilities in the world. Far and away the country's most popular sport is **football**, an enthusiasm that has been nourished by some excellent performances from the national team during the past two decades. **Golf**, **badminton**, **squash** and **swimming** are also well catered for (**tennis** less so), while **handball** – particularly women's handball – and **ice hockey** (winter only) are popular spectator sports. If you're keen to catch a game of the former, contact Dansk Håndbold Forbund (Ⓣ43 26 24 00, Ⓦwww.dhf.dk). Copenhagen's proximity to the sea means there are also plenty of opportunities for **water-based activities** such as windsurfing, kayaking and fishing, while, if you're here in summer, you shouldn't pass up the chance to swim in one of the open-air **harbour pools**. Back on land, the city's many parks and jogging paths offer the chance for **running**.

DGI-byen (Ⓦwww.dgi-byen.dk), the city's ultra-modern showpiece **sports centre**, is right in the centre, behind Central Station, at Tietgensgade 65. There are usually a few people getting to grips with the climbing wall at the entrance, while inside you'll find a state-of-the-art swimming complex (see p.194), bowling alley and spa (though no gym), as well as a decent café and restaurant.

All the venues listed below are within easy reach of the city centre.

Fitness centres

Scandinavia's leading health-club chain, **SATS** (Ⓦwww.sats.com), has several branches in the city. The most central is at Vesterbrogade 2D (Ⓣ33 32 10 02), in the Scala centre, opposite Tivoli. Other branches include Købmagergade 48, Indre By next to Rundetårn (Ⓣ33 89 89 11), Vesterbrogade 97 (Ⓣ33 25 13 10), Øster Allé 42 in the Parken Stadium, Østerbro (Ⓣ33 55 00 78) and Bragesgade 8, in Nørrebro (Ⓣ35 81 27 81). A number of the hotels also host in-house fitness centres, including *Copenhagen Island* (see p.140), *Hilton* (p.142), *Marriott* (p.138), *Bertrams Hotel Guldsmeden* (p.139) and *The Square* (p.139).

Football

The 2006 World Cup and Euro 2008 aside, when they failed to qualify for the finals, the Danish national team has enjoyed a good degree of success over the last

Roligans

During the 1986 World Cup in Mexico – the first the Danes had ever qualified for – the Danish football team's exemplary performances on the field were matched by the country's football fans off it. These supporters of the national team became known as the **roligans** – a play on the words *rolig* ("relaxed") and "hooligan" – and their good humour, colourful hats and face paintings compared strikingly to the boorish behaviour of many rival fans. The Roligans' finest hour came during Denmark's victory at the 1992 European Championship, leading to the biggest street party ever seen in the country, and they still turn up in reasonable numbers to all Denmark's home games in Parken stadium, though you might find their antics a bit annoying if you've come to watch the football, rather than to Mexican wave. Check out their website at Ⓦwww.roligan.dk, where you can buy Viking hats decked out in the red and white of the national team.

twenty years. This and a number of Danish players, including Peter Schmeichel, the Laudrup brothers and Daniel Agger, have played for Europe's largest clubs. **Football** has become the country's most popular sport, but that said, the domestic game in Denmark is fairly low-key compared to the big European leagues – there were no professional clubs in the country until 1985 – and though there's plenty of football played in the Copenhagen area, don't expect big crowds or high-quality games unless you're seeing the national side or the city's two biggest teams, Brøndby and FC København (usually known as FCK). Matches are usually played on Sundays at 3pm, and the season lasts roughly from late July to early June, with a winter break from December to mid-March. **Tickets** for Brøndby, FCK and international games are available through Billetnet or Billetlugen (see p.169) or at the respective stadiums. Danish fans are noted for their relaxed and good-natured behaviour (see box above).

Founded in 1992, **FCK** (Ⓦwww.fck.dk) is the country's richest club, thanks in part to the fact that they own their home ground (also the venue for international games), the enormous Parken stadium (see p.103), which also rakes in cash from occasional rock concerts. FCK are now firmly established in the top flight of the Superliga, winning the league seven times since they were founded. Games are well attended, with an average gate of about 15,000–20,000, though this still only half fills the 40,000-capacity stadium. If FCK are playing Brøndby, it's well worth going along to see the rivals slug it out against a backdrop of noisy support. Tickets cost around 190kr, and you'll need to book in advance for big matches (see above). If you want a more intimate atmosphere, try next door at Østerbro Stadium, where **B93** – a team in Denmark's semi-professional second division – play; tickets (90kr) are available on the gate.

Brøndby (Ⓦwww.brondby.com), currently coached by Euro 92 champion Kent Nielsen, are from the working-class suburbs south of the city. Founded in 1964, they became the country's first professional football club when they turned pro in 1985. Brøndby have won the league several times since, and have enjoyed successful campaigns in European competitions. Brøndby's smaller stadium has atmosphere, and even though the crowds have dwindled, numbers still rival FCK. Tickets cost from 110kr; take the S-Tog to Glostrup and then bus #135 or #500S.

Golf

The gentle, rolling countryside surrounding the capital is perfect for golf, and the Copenhagen region is home to over thirty courses, with most clubs renting out equipment. The city boasts a wonderful eighteen-hole course at the **Copenhagen Golf Club**, 2 Dyrehaven, Lyngby (Ⓣ39 63 04 83, Ⓦwww.kgkgolf.dk; Mon 8am until 30min before sunset, Thurs 8am–2.45pm, Fri 11am until 30min before sunset, Sat & Sun 1pm until 30min before sunset; green fees 300kr; S-Tog to Lyngby station, then bus #182 and a 15min walk), set in the middle of a deer sanctuary, beautiful woodlands and meadows. The oldest club in Scandinavia, it has a friendly atmosphere, along with a restaurant and bar. **Copenhagen Pay & Play**, Skebjergvej 46, 2765 Smørum (Ⓣ44 97 01 11, Ⓦwww.smorumgolfcenter.dk; daily 8am–10pm), 2.5km from Ballerup, is open year round to everyone – green fees range from 60kr to 375kr depending on day of the week (Fri–Sun are more expensive), number of holes played (6-hole pitch-and-putt, 9-hole or 18-hole course) and your level.

Ice skating and ice hockey

Come winter, temporary **outdoor skating rinks** pop up all over the city between December and February; they are free and offer skate hire for around 45kr per hour. The most central are: Kongens Nytorv; Blågårds Plads, Nørrebro; and Frederiksberg Runddel, at the main entrance to Frederiksberg Have. There's also a temporary winter-only **indoor** ice-skating rink at Ryparkens Idrætsanlæg (Oct–March Mon–Fri noon–2.45pm, Sun 4–6.30pm), at Lyngbyvej 110 (Ⓣ39 20 38 80; 35kr, kids 15kr, skate hire 35kr per hour), next to Ryparking S-Tog station.

Ice hockey is an enormously popular spectator sport in Denmark, played at a national and international level. The two best teams in the Copenhagen area are Rødovre Mighty Bulls and Rungsted Cobras. If you're keen to catch a game, contact the Danish Ice Hockey Union (Ⓣ43 26 26 26, Ⓦwww.ishockey.dk) for details of local matches.

Running

In addition to the city's many parks, the paths bordering Copenhagen's lakes on the western edge of Indre By are great for scenic, relatively uncrowded **running**. Conveniently traversed by bridges at regular half-mile intervals or so, you can choose circuits of varying distances – a complete circuit of Skt Jørgen Sø, Peblinge Sø and Sortedams Sø is around four miles. Other popular, shorter, jogging routes follow the water's edge along the bastions of Christianshavn (see p.57), southwest from Torvegade to Langebro; or along the Frederikstaden coast from Amaliehaven gardens at Amalienborg, north through Kastellet and on to the Little Mermaid. The city council has also demarcated a number of running routes (from 1km to 16km) in the Nørrebro and outer Nørrebro area, starting at the lakeside end of Læssøesgade. Routes are marked with a yellow triangle with a running man inside, the distance run written underneath.

On the third Sunday of May, many of the prettiest areas of Copenhagen are cordoned off to make way for the **Copenhagen Marathon** (Ⓦwww.copenhagenmarathon.dk) during which around ten thousand participants of all ages and abilities, from professional athletes to fun-runners, take over the streets, cheered by more than twice that number of spectators. If you're fit enough and want to give it a try, contact Sparta (Ⓦwww.sparta.dk).

Tennis, squash and badminton

Playing tennis is no longer as prohibitively expensive as it used to be, and courts are getting slightly easier to come by, although it's advisable to book at least a week in advance. Tennis courts – none of them in central Copenhagen – include the indoor and outdoor courts at the B93 tennis club at Svanemølleanlægget 10, Østerbro (Ⓣ82 56 33 00; bus #1A, #14 or Svanemøllen S-Tog); indoor courts at Ryparkens Idrætsanlæg (see opposite) and Syndby Idrætspark Englandsvej 62, Amager (Ⓣ32 58 20 20; bus #5A to Øresundsvej, from where it's a ten-minute walk); and the outdoor court at the *Hotel Norlandia Mercur*, Vester Farimagsgade 17 (Ⓣ33 12 57 11; Vesterport S-Tog). Fees start at around 120kr per hour plus 25kr to hire rackets.

Badminton is a far more widely played – and cheaper – sport than tennis in Denmark, and the country has produced a couple of world champions in recent years. Courts are available at Nørrebrohallen, Bragesgade 5, Nørrebro (Ⓦwww.noerrebrohallen.dk; Nørrebro S-Tog or bus #5 or #16), for around 70kr per hour (racquet hire 25kr). You can't book over the phone, but call ahead (Ⓣ35 31 05 50) for availability. **Squash** courts are also available at Nørrebrohallen for 90kr per hour.

Watersports and fishing

With its strong links with the sea, Copenhagen is an excellent place to indulge in **watersports**. New and unusual ways of goofing around on the water keep on popping up, especially in the Amager Strandpark area (see p.110). The Surf and Snowboard School (June–Oct; Ⓣ26 73 39 38; Mon–Fri 5–7pm, Ⓦwww.surf.dk) at the northern end of Amager Strandpark rents out everything you need for **kite-** and **windsurfing**, both of which are very popular activities in Denmark; prices start at 145kr per hour for equipment hire, and 7hr beginners' lessons are also available for 980kr. You can also hire kite-surfing kit at Kitecph (Ⓣ27 84 80 80, Ⓦwww.kitecph.dk; 750kr per day) at the southern end of Amager Strandpark, next to Kajak Hotellet (Ⓣ40 50 40 06, Ⓦwww.kajakole.dk), where you can hire a range of **kayaks** and kit, starting at 100kr per hour for a sit-on-top kayak. They also organize hugely fun kayak polo tournaments in the nearby lagoon (145kr per hour to hire a suitable kayak). If you fancy kite surfing but don't feel confident enough to handle both board and kite simultaneously, you could start by balancing on a board while being dragged around by a cable at the Copenhagen **Cablepark** nearby at Kraftsværksvej 20 (mid-April to mid-Oct: June–Aug Mon–Fri noon–8pm, Sat & Sun 10am–8pm, rest of year Mon–Fri 2–6pm, Sat & Sun 10am–6pm; Ⓣ32 96 92 90, Ⓦwww.copenhagencablepark.dk; from 250kr per hour). Copenhagen Adventure Tours (Ⓣ40 50 40 06, Ⓦwww.kajakole.dk) runs excellent and affordable guided **kayak** tours around the **city canals** and harbour area on unsinkable, easy-to-use individual kayaks (see p.25). Or you can hire pretty wooden rowboats, seating four, at Christianshavns Bådudlejning (Ⓣ32 96 53 53, Ⓦwww.baadudlejningen.dk; mid-April to mid-Sept 10am–sunset; 80kr per hour) to paddle around the canals. If you really want to get out to sea, Spar Shipping, at Kalkbrænderihavnen, Lautrupskaj, Østerbro (Ⓣ33 33 93 55, Ⓦwww.sparshipping.dk; bus #26 or Nordhavn S-Tog), organizes day-long (8am–3pm) **fishing trips** (225–250kr, tackle 75–700kr) out into the Øresund; you need to buy a permit (Ⓦwww.fisketegn.dk; 35kr per day, 100kr per week) and to book a few days in advance (one week if you want to hire tackle) and remember to bring warm, waterproof clothing, as the weather can be fierce even during summer. Food and drink is available on board at extra cost.

Swimming and beaches

Copenhagen has plentiful and well-maintained public **swimming pools**. Some also have saunas, and others form part of sports centres offering a range of different activities; most rent towels and swimming costumes for a small fee. If you're here in summer, you might prefer a more exciting and refreshing dip in the harbour itself. There are two open-air **harbour pools**: one at Islands Brygge (June–Aug Mon–Fri 7am–7pm, Sat & Sun 11am–7pm; see p.109), which offers an adult pool, two children's pools and a diving pool; and one at Havneholmen, next to Fisketorvet shopping centre (June–Aug daily 11am–7pm; bus #1A, #30, #65E or Dybbølsbro S-Tog), which also has the mocked-up sandy "Copencabana" beach, complete with volleyball and other sports activities. Both have lifeguards and are free.

In addition, there are numerous great **beaches** within striking distance of the capital. The water is generally pretty cold, although it can get as high as 20°C in summer. The most popular beaches are **Bellevue** (p.106) and **Charlottenlund** (p.104) to the north of the city, and **Amager Strandpark** (p.110), on the east coast of the island of Amager.

Two types of **flag systems** operate on Danish beaches. A blue-and-white FEE (Foundation for Environmental Education) flag indicates that a beach is environmentally sound with good water quality and clean toilet facilities available. A green-and-red flag system operates at the busiest beaches with lifeguards on watch. Red means danger and no swimming; green means it's safe to swim. Going topless is commonplace everywhere; if you want to swim in the nude, find a quiet spot or go to a designated nudist bathing spot; there's one at Helgoland bathing pier (p.111), and another at Charlottenlund Søbad (p.104).

Swimming pools

Bellahøj Bellahøjvej 1–3, Bellahøj ⓣ38 60 16 66. Third week of May to third week of Aug Mon–Fri 7.30am–5.30pm, Sat & Sun 10am–6pm; 30kr. Bus #5A, #68 or #250S. Just twenty minutes' bus ride from the city centre, this pleasant outdoor complex has five heated pools, including two for children and one for babies.

DGI-byen Tietgensgade 65, Vesterbro ⓣ33 29 80 00, ⓦwww.dgi-byen.dk. Mon–Thurs 6.30am–10pm, Fri 6.30am–8pm, Sat 9am–7pm, Sun 9am–6pm; 58kr; swimsuit hire 30kr, with a photo ID as deposit. Right in the heart of the city, in a state-of-the-art complex, this place features a gorgeous elliptical pool, children's pool and diving and climbing area. If you really want pampering, visit the spa, where 245kr buys you access to a sauna, steam rooms, plunge pools and the swim centre; a variety of treatments are also available (at extra cost) by prior appointment (ⓣ33 29 81 00).

Fælledbadet Fælledparken, Borgmester Jensens Allé 50, just off Nørre Alle, Østerbro ⓣ35 39 08 04. June–Aug daily 10am–6pm; 30kr. Buses #184, #185 or #150S. Two outdoor 25-metre pools and a paddling pool for kids, set in the huge park.

Øbro-Hallen Gunnar Nu Hansens Plads 3, Østerbro ⓣ35 25 70 60. Mon, Tues, Thurs & Fri 7am–7pm, Wed 10am–7pm, Sat & Sun 9am–2pm; 30kr. Bus #1A or #14. Beautifully renovated swimming baths dating from the 1930s, complete with sauna and steam bath.

Vesterbro Swimming Baths Angelgade 4, Vesterbro ⓣ33 22 05 00. Mon 10am–8pm, Tues–Thurs 7am–6pm, Fri 7am–4.30pm, Sat & Sun 9am–2pm; 30kr. Bus #1A or Enghave S-Tog. Located up near the Carlsberg Brewery, this complex includes a 25-metre indoor pool, diving area, sauna and solarium.

18

Festivals and events

Copenhagen has a good offering of **festivals** and **events**, particularly in summer, though you're only likely to have heard of Roskilde and the Copenhagen Jazz Festival, both of which have an international reputation. As well as the listings below, which represent some of the best-attended and more popular events, there's a host of smaller, more specialized happenings – check Ⓦwww.visitcopenhagen.com or Ⓦwww.kulturnaut.dk or ask at the tourist office. It's also always worth checking what's on along Nyhavn – this vibrant canalside street is a focal point for annual celebrations like Midsummer's Eve and also hosts various small events throughout the year from a "Day of the Herring" to free tastings of the annual Christmas beers from local breweries and a Christmas market; visit Ⓦwww.nyhavn.com for the full calendar.

The free monthly *Copenhagen This Week* – available from the tourist office and many of the bigger hotels – is a good source of what's-on information, as is the booklet *Major Events in Copenhagen* published annually by the tourist office. Dates given below are a rough indication; always consult the websites for exact dates and locations/routes, as they can vary considerably.

February

Copenhagen Fashion Week One week in Feb and the second week in Aug. Ⓣ70 20 30 68, Ⓦwww.copenhagenfashionweek.com. Well-known and up-and-coming Danish (and some international) designers and photo graphers showcase their work in an extravaganza of exhibitions and shows held across the city in cafés, museums and shops.

April

CPH:PIX Ⓦwww.cphpix.dk. The city's answer to Cannes, this ten-day film festival shows a wide range of Danish and international films, including re-runs of old classics and cult films, foreign films in their original language, and previews.

Queen Margrethe II's birthday April 16. Catch a glimpse of Danish royalty as the queen greets the crowds (well, waves from the balcony anyway) at Amalienborg at noon, accompanied by a suitable display of pomp from the Royal Guards.

May

Copenhagen Carnival Whitsun weekend. Ⓦwww.copenhagencarnival.dk. This weekend-long sequin-and-feather extravaganza attracts crowds of around one hundred thousand with its salsa, samba and African rhythms and skimpy, offbeat costumes. The main parade takes place on Saturday with a procession along Strøget, continuing up Øster Alle to Fælledparken (see p.102) with several themed dance and music stages and a Rio-style "Sambadrome" where the samba parades finish up. Plus stalls selling delicious exotic food, clothing and trinkets.

Copenhagen Distortion Five nights, finishing first Sun in June. Ⓦwww.cphdistortion.dk. A vibrant celebration of street culture, music and fashion. Around eighty organized parties, big and small, in a range of locations from bridges to backyards to buses to boats, followed by after-parties in the clubs and bigger venues. The club nights, which host international DJs and acts, are young and hip, while the free street parties, which start around sunset, attract a more mixed crowd.

Copenhagen Marathon Third Sun in May. ⓦwww.copenhagenmarathon.dk. The city's runners and would-be runners take to the streets in the annual marathon. See p.192 for more details.

May Day May 1. Trade unions march through the city to the open spaces of Fælledparken (see p.102), where there's a rock-concert-cum-political-rally. Most Danish political parties are represented, and although the speeches go on for ever, it's all kept fun and lively with stalls selling ethnic delicacies, Danish bands and, naturally, enormous quantities of beer.

June/July

Sankt Hans Aften (St Hans Night) June 23. ⓦwww.visitcopenhagen.com. The Danes at their patriotic best with an overdose of *hygge* ("cosiness") and bonhomie in towns and villages across the country. An ancient tradition celebrating the longest day of summer, it's a beer-fuelled evening of music, dancing, eating, bonfires and the burning of witch effigies, originally instigated to keep bad forces at bay for the summer. The best places in the city to head for are Nyhavn, Fælledparken, the rampart lakes and the Christianshavn fortifications (near the Torvegade bridge to Amager). It usually starts with the communal singing of Danish folksongs (the most famous, honouring Sankt Hans, was written by Carl Nielsen; see p.000), followed by local bands and a few speeches by city dignitaries.

Roskilde Festival Last week of June to first weekend in July. ⓣ46 36 66 13, ⓦwww.roskilde-festival.dk. Held in fields outside the town of Roskilde (see p.123) over four days and nights (with a pre-festival "warm-up" period of another four days), the Glastonbury-style Roskilde Festival is one of Europe's largest rock events, attracting over 75,000 people, mostly from Scandinavia. The diverse line-up – rock, jazz, indie, hip-hop and more – features a mixture of new and established Danish and international bands and DJs but usually offers at least five big-name acts (recent years have seen Arctic Monkeys, Kanye West and Coldplay) plus pop legends like Madness and the Pet Shop Boys. You can camp (free with a festival ticket), and there's the usual horde of stalls selling food, clothes, jewellery and other festival paraphernalia, as well as an internet café, cinema and dance hall. The festival is a massive boost to the local economy and all profits go to humanitarian

Copenhagen Jazz Festival

Whenever you visit Copenhagen you'll usually stumble across some jazz somewhere in the city, but for ten days from the first Friday in July, it seems the city thinks of little else, as its stages, large venues, museums, cafés, clubs, squares and canals are taken over by around eight hundred events, from big band to experimental, that make up the **Copenhagen Jazz Festival** (ⓦwww.jazzfestival.dk), attracting music lovers from all over the world. The festival showcases a handful of jazz legends – Herbie Hancock, Sonny Rollins and Keith Jarrett are regulars – as well as big names like James Taylor and Chick Corea and new kids on the block like Jamie Cullum, but for many shows the term "jazz" is used in the loosest sense possible, as international musicians come to perform everything from classic bebop to experimental electronica and spoken-word poetry, with popular acts such as Gotan Project and Salif Keita complementing dozens of cutting-edge Scandinavian groups. The largest **venues** are the Det Kongelige Teater, the Black Diamond, Tivoli and the Copenhagen Jazzhouse, but the most exciting performances are often the impromptu ones that get going well after midnight: La Fontaine, at Kompagnistræde 11 (see p.170), and the Børneteatret, in Christiania, are the best bets for late-night, ad-hoc jam sessions – intimate, foot-stomping affairs that seat you just inches away from some of Denmark's hottest musical talents. The festival **programme** is usually published in May and is posted on the website in English. Tickets can range anywhere in price from 50kr to 350kr for larger venues (which usually sell out a few days before the concert), though many performances are free. Tickets for all but the largest shows can be bought at the door.

▲ Swedish band bob hund play Roskilde Festival

causes and community projects. Tickets go on sale from December 1 (via Billetnet Ⓦwww.billetnet.dk, Ⓣ70 15 65 65, Mon–Sat 10am–8pm; or check the festival website for ticket venues in your country of origin) and usually sell out around two weeks before the event. If there are any left, they're sold at the entrances. A ticket for all four days (or eight if you want to attend the warm-up events) will set you back around 1400kr; one-day tickets (for the last Sunday only) cost around 600kr, depending on the country you buy the ticket in.

July/August

Copenhagen Pride **One week in July/Aug. Ⓦwww.copenhagenpride.dk.** A week-long festival of gay events from open-air movie screenings to street parties to Copenhagen Pride Square – an area of food stalls and live entertainment along Frederiksholms Kanal. On the final Saturday (always the first Sat in Aug), the city's gay, lesbian, bisexual and transsexual inhabitants strut their colourful stuff in a flamboyant parade of outlandish frocks, spandex, Lycra and whatever else takes their fancy. The parade route follows Nørrebrogade across the bridge to Nørreport and on to Rådhuspladsen.

August

Kulturhavn **First weekend in Aug. Ⓦwww.kulturhavn.dk.** Making the most of the revamped harbourfront, Kulturhavn (Cultural Harbour) is a three-day annual festival of dance, music, theatre and sports, offering a chance to try activities as diverse as sailing, trampolining, kayak polo or flamenco dancing. All free.

Copenhagen Fashion Week **Usually the second week in Aug and one week in Feb (see p.195). Ⓦwww.copenhagenfashionweek.com.**

Copenhagen Cooking **Last week of Aug. Ⓦwww.copenhagencooking.com.** Popular gastronomic festival highlighting Nordic and Danish cuisine. The city's squares and streets are given over to crayfish parties, food tents, ice-cream tastings and novelty events such as a waiter's relay-race on Nyhavn; meanwhile posh chefs in the city's best restaurants cook up feasts for half the usual price.

Copenhagen Design Week **Last week of Aug/early Sept. Ⓦwww.copenhagendesign.dk.** This event showcases the country's excellent pedigree in design and provides a platform for new designers to show their work. Venues across the city host workshops, lectures and award ceremonies, along with exhibitions on modern architecture (Ⓦwww.cphadd), furniture (Ⓦwww.copenhagenfurniturefestival.dk), textiles and lighting. Many events are free; some sell tickets on the door.

September

CO2PENHAGEN **Ⓦwww.co2penhagen.dk.** Do your bit for the planet and attend the world's first CO_2-neutral festival. Three days of live music events, art, food and fashion across the city with all the energy coming from renewable resources.

Golden Days in Copenhagen **Ⓦwww.goldendays.dk.** Festival showcasing Copenhagen's cultural history with a three-week programme of concerts, exhibitions, theatre and lectures exploring a particular period of Danish history (see p.211).

October

Copenhagen Gay & Lesbian Film Festival (CGLFF) **Ⓦwww.cglff.dk.** For some twenty years CGLFF has brought short films, features and documentaries to Copenhagen's cinemas, attracting straight and gay audiences.

Culture Night **Mid-Oct. Ⓦwww.kulturnatten.dk.** Over three hundred venues, including museums, galleries, libraries, churches and cultural institutions, throw open their doors for an evening (6pm–midnight) of culture, giving the public a chance to see behind the scenes and hosting a wide range of musical, artistic and literary events. Ticket prices vary; a total-access "Kulturkit" ticket covering all events (and including free public transport within the city) costs around 85kr and is available from mid-September from S-Tog stations, the tourist office and participating venues.

Halloween at Tivoli **Usually second or third week of Oct. ⓦwww.tivoli.dk.** One for the kids. Tivoli (see p.79) is transformed during autumn half term into a ghoulish wonderland with all manner of scary decorations and festive treats.

October/November

Copenhagen Autumn Jazz **ⓦwww.jazz.dk.** This week-long jazz fest – offspring of the main jazz festival in July (see box, p.196) – is held in thirty or so of the city's top music venues, offering everything from bebop to swing.

November/December

Christmas A great time to be in the city, as the Danes do Christmas with consummate good taste. Tivoli (mid-Nov to Dec 23) steps up a gear, with a market selling seasonal goodies and themed performances on its many stages. Open-air ice-skating rinks (see p.192) get you in the festive spirit, and there's a parade (usually the last Sat in Nov) through town featuring Santa Claus. Christmas fairs and markets spring up across the city (check with the tourist office for details), including a very popular one along Nyhavn; not to be outdone, Christiania also puts on a good bash, with an excellent market, and a party for the homeless.

New Year's Eve Copenhageners celebrate the New Year with an all-night party, kicking off with a massive fireworks fest on Rådhuspladsen at midnight, attended by revellers in their thousands. Bring your own champagne, and watch out for stray fire crackers.

19

Kids' Copenhagen

Copenhagen is a child-friendly city – the low level of traffic, pedestrianized shopping streets, decent quota of child-centred attractions and abundance of waterways, cycle lanes and green spaces make it easy, relaxing and safe to explore with kids. Unlike most European capitals, Copenhagen is close to several **beaches**, both in the suburbs north of the city (see p.106) and on Amager (see p.109), which has a string of sandy stretches and a wonderful nature reserve. Two **amusement parks**, Tivoli (see p.79) and the lesser known, but just as entertaining, Bakken (see p.106), are fun days out, while most of Copenhagen's larger **museums** cater for children in some way, too.

Of Copenhagen's fine **parks**, **Fælledparken** (see p.102) is especially popular with kids. Along with its wide open spaces – where you can relax and watch them let off steam – a scent garden in the southeastern corner gives young visitors the opportunity to smell and touch plants and rocks. **Kongens Have** (see p.67) stages free puppet shows every summer (June–Aug Tues–Sun 2pm & 3pm) on the Kronprinsessegade side of the park; on the other side, by the Hercules Pavilion, there's a children's play area complete with dragons for clambering on. Spacious **Frederiksberg Have** (see p.94) and **Søndermarken** are also two great open spaces. In summer, football and kite-flying are the two main activities here, or you can rent a rowing boat and experience the park from the old hand-dug canals. During winter, **ice skating** is a favourite pastime – there are free temporary outdoor rinks at Kongens Nytorv, Blågårds Plads and Frederiksberg Runddel at the entrance to Frederiksberg Have (which also has some good hills for sledding). **Boat trips** around the harbour and canal (see p.25) are perennial sure-fire hits.

For more detailed information on any of the following attractions, see the main account in the relevant section of the Guide.

Attractions and sights

Changing of the guard at Amalienborg Daily noon; free. A big pull for children, as one set of splendidly costumed guards marches off and another arrives, sometimes to the accompaniment of a band. At other times, kids can have fun trying to outstare the mannequin-like guards as they stand to attention outside the palace.

Copenhagen Zoo Roskildevej 32, Frederiksberg ⓦwww.zoo.dk. See p.95 for opening hours; 130kr, children 3–11 70kr. One of the oldest and largest in Europe, with over 3300 animals ranging from elephants to apes to polar bears, the Copenhagen Zoo has an excellent Children's Zoo, where they can touch several of the more domesticated inhabitants, as well as pony rides, adventure trails and a playground. *Café K*, as you'd expect, has plenty of children's options; alternatively, there are hot-dog stands and numerous picnic areas.

Danmarks Akvarium Kavalergården 1, Charlottenlund ⓦwww.akvarium.dk. See p.104 for opening hours; 100kr, children 3–11 55kr. As well as the aquarium's vast display of colourful and exotic marine animals, there's a designated children's area with touch pools containing hermit crabs, plaice, shrimp and sea anemones. Try to time your visit with feeding times – Mon–Fri 1.30pm, Sat & Sun 11.30am and 2pm.

DGI-byen Tietgensgade 65, Vesterbro ⓦwww.dgi-byen.dk. Mon–Thurs 6.30am–10pm, Fri 6.30am–8pm, Sat 9am–7pm, Sun 9am–6pm; 58kr, children 2–14 38kr; swimsuit hire 30kr, with photo ID as deposit. The city's flashest swimming complex, with pleasantly warm water, geysers, bubble columns, wave machines and diving platforms.

Guinness World Records Østergade 16, Indre By ⓦwww.topattractions.dk. Mid-June to Aug daily 10am–10pm; Sept to mid-June Mon–Thurs & Sun 10am–6pm, Fri & Sat 10am–8pm; 85kr, children 4–10 43kr, children 11–14 68kr. From the towering statue outside of the world's tallest man, to the endless wacky exhibits inside, kids love this museum of extremes.

Hans Christian Andersen Eventryhuset Rådhuspladsen 57, Indre By ⓦwww.topattractions.dk. Mid-June to Aug daily 10am–10pm; Sept to mid-June Mon–Thurs & Sun 10am–6pm, Fri & Sat 10am–8pm; 67kr, children 4–10 34kr, children 11–14 54kr. A very child-friendly romp through the life and works of the famous writer of children's fairy tales with a mock-up of his study, a short video of his life and numerous animated tableaux (with sound effects and recordings of the stories) of some of his better-known tales.

Rosenborg Østervoldgade 4A, Indre By ⓦwww.rosenborg-slot.dk. See p.66 for opening hours; 70kr, children 0–17 free. A fabulous seventeenth-century fairy-tale castle; the Queen's precious crown jewels, in the Treasury, are a sparkling dream-come-true for many would-be princesses. There's a playground and café in the adjacent park.

Rundetårn Kobmagergade, Indre By ⓦwww.rundetaarn.dk. Daily: mid-May to mid-Sept 10am–8pm; mid-Sept to mid-May 10am–5pm; 25kr; children 5–15 5kr. This quirky tower is a real hit with kids – they can climb the spiralling, cobbled ramp to the top for great views over the city and check out the old bell loft for curios relating to the tower's history.

Tycho Brahe Planetarium Gammel Kongevej 10, Vesterbro ⓦwww.tycho.dk. Tues–Sun 10.30am–9pm, Mon 1–9pm; entry price includes one IMAX or 3D film, 130kr, children 0–13 80kr. (Note: children under 3 are not admitted to the films.) Kids will love the push-button displays in "The Active Universe" exhibition, and the shop full of all things space-oriented. The Space Theatre shows thrilling hourly IMAX or 3D films (you'll need to rent headphones with English translations; 20kr) usually about deep-sea exploration, the natural world, history or space travel.

Museums and galleries

Children's Museum at the Nationalmuseet Ny Vestergade 10, Indre By ⓦwww.natmus.dk. Tues–Sun 10am–5pm; free. This place, spread over several large rooms on the ground floor, is aimed specifically at children between 6 and 12, though there's plenty of interest for toddlers upwards. Kids can clamber on the Viking ship; play hide-and-seek and point cannons in the small medieval castle; wander onto the rooftop of a traditional Pakistani house; draw pictures; cook up a pretend feast in a medieval kitchen; play with crowns, coins and assorted trinkets; or dress up in a variety of costumes.

Experimentarium Tuborg Havnevej 7, Østerbro ⓦwww.experimentarium.dk. Mon & Wed–Fri 9.30am–5pm, Tues 9.30am–9pm, Sat & Sun 11am–5pm; 145kr, children 3–11 95kr. This fascinating, hands-on science centre lets children explore the laws of nature by performing their own experiments. Demonstrations occur throughout the day, and there's a special pavilion for 3 to 6 year olds. See p.103 for more.

Frilandsmuseet Kongevejen 100, Lyngby ⓦwww.natmus.dk. Easter to mid-Oct Tues–Sun 10am–5pm; free. A wonderful mixture of heritage park and city farm set in gorgeous rolling countryside, this is eldorado for kids, with horse-carriage rides, sheep shearing and wool dyeing among many other activities.

Geologisk Museum Øster Voldgade 5–7, Rosenborg ⓦwww.geologisk-museum.dk. Tues–Sun 1–4pm; 40kr, children 3–16 25kr. Exhibits on volcanoes, meteors, minerals galore and

Places to eat with kids

Most cafés and restaurants in Copenhagen are very welcoming to kids and are able to provide a highchair. As with anywhere, the all-day cafés are the best bet for kid-friendly food, but – in addition to the cafés and restaurants in most of the attractions and museums listed here – there are a few places that are particularly welcoming to children or have enough novelty value to keep them amused for a while.

Ankara	see p.156
Dag H	see p.160
Islands Brygges Kulturhus	see p.161
Mormors	see p.154
Peder Oxe	see p.150
Peter Lieps Hus	see p.161
Royal Café	see p.150
Sommersko	see p.151
Sporvejen	see p.151
Wagamama	see p.156

dinosaur bones will keep little ones interested for an hour or two.

Louisiana **Humlebæk ⓦwww.louisiana.dk. Tues–Fri 11am–10pm, Sat & Sun 11am–6pm; 90kr, children under 18 free.** Taking as a starting point different pieces of art from the collections, the Children's Wing (Tues–Sun 11am–6pm) of the fantastic modern art museum (see p.115) is full of artistic materials for kids aged 3 upwards to get creative and messy. Outside an adventure playground, designed by renowned Italian nature-artist Alfio Bonnano, features enormous birds' nests and playhouses made of boats.

Post & Tele Museum **Købmagergade 37, Indre By ⓦwww.ptt-museum.dk. Tues & Thurs–Sat 10am–5pm, Wed 10am–8pm, Sun noon–4pm; 50kr, free on Wed, children free.** The Bumblebee Cave (weekends only) gives kids a chance to make and design their own sheet of stamps, play around with old telephones and write with a quill pen, among other activities. For more on the museum see p.49.

Statens Museum for Kunst **Sølvgade 48–50 ⓦwww.smk.dk. Tues & Thurs–Sun 10am–5pm, Wed 10am–8pm; free.** The Children's Art Museum section of the National Gallery (see p.68) spans three floors and has a cinema, workshop and special child-oriented art exhibitions. Aimed mostly at 6–12 year olds, there are family guided tours at the weekends, with the opportunity to get hands-on in the workshop afterwards.

Viking Ship Museum **Vindeboder 12, Roskilde ⓦwww.vikingeskibsmuseet.dk. Daily 10am–5pm; May–Sept 95kr, Oct–April 60kr, children free.** The fantastic Viking ship museum (see p.124) on the banks of Roskilde fjord has a big room where kids can clamber on a couple of reconstructed Viking vessels, dress in Viking costumes and write their name in Runic letters. Plus demonstrations of Viking handicrafts and boatbuilding.

Zoologisk Museum **Universitetsparken 15, Østerbro ⓦwww.zmuc.dk. Tues–Sun 10am–5pm; 75kr, children 3–16 40kr.** One of the city's most popular museums with school kids, featuring traditional displays of stuffed animals in their reconstructed natural habitats – kids will love the mammoth and the immense Greenland whale skeleton. In a special section they can touch some of the exhibits. For more on the museum see p.103.

Amusement parks and playgrounds

Bakken **Klampenborg ⓦwww.bakken.dk. July to mid-Aug Mon–Sat noon–midnight, Sun noon–11pm; late March–June & mid- to late Aug Mon–Sat 2–10pm, Sun noon–10pm; closing times vary in low season so check the website. Pass for all 35 rides 199kr; free entrance.** The world's oldest amusement park, Bakken's attractions include Denmark's longest and highest Big Dipper, assorted merry-go-rounds and many other fun and breathtaking rides, including a ghost train and a waltzer. There's also a free children's play park with see-saws and swings. Bakken is at the edge of Dyrehaven (see p.106), which is fun to explore by horse-drawn carriage and also a great picnic site.

City playgrounds You can pick up the city council map of all the playgrounds in the greater Copenhagen area from the office next to the bus depot in Rådhuspladsen. Central options include: Nikolaj Plads in Indre By, the playground in Kongens Have, Ostre Anlæg,

Gammel Vagt 5 in Frederikstad, Skt Annæ Plads, two in Ørstedsparken, and Christianshavns Voldgade 36 on Christianshavn.

Tivoli **Vesterbrogade 3, Indre By ⓦwww.tivoli.dk.** **See box, p.80 for opening hours and price details.** An absolute must for families with children, this magical amusement park offers everything a child could want: 26 fun rides from tame to stomach-churning; candy floss, ice cream, balloons and all manner of treats; pantomimes and plenty of opportunities to win colourful and completely useless plastic gadgets or furry toys. Transformed into a winter wonderland over the Christmas period and with a Halloween theme during half term in October. There's also a wonderful saltwater aquarium in the basement of the Concert Hall.

▲ Rollercoaster ride at Tivoli

Shops

BR Legetøj **Bremerholm 4; Frederiksberggade 11; Fisketorvet shopping centre; Købmagergade 9; Nørrebrogade 34; Vesterbrogade 73; Østerbrogade 39–41 ⓦwww.br.dk.** Denmark's main toy-store chain selling a wide selection of games and toys, both local and international brands.

Build-a-Bear workshop **Vesterbrogade 3, at Tivoli main entrance ⓦwww.buildabear.dk.** Kids can pick a bear and make it their own, dressing it up to their heart's content.

Englebørn **Amagertorv 1, Indre By ⓦwww.madsnorgaard.dk. Mon–Thurs 10am–6pm, Fri 10am–7pm, Sat 10am–5pm.** The kids' version of the adjacent his and hers shops owned by Danish designer Mads Nørgaard, this is pricey designer stuff – both Danish designers and international brands like Diesel and Levis – but great for that special purchase.

Games **Jorcks Passage, Indre By ⓦwww.gamesweb.dk. Mon–Fri 10am–6pm, Sat 10am–4pm.** Every kind of board game from old fashioned favourites like chess, dominos, backgammon and solitaire to classic family games like ludo and cranium. Also toys, puzzles, 3D-brainteasers and the like.

Hugin & Mugin **Kompagnistræde 12, Indre By ⓦwww.hugin-mugin.com. Mon–Fri 11am–6pm, Sat 10am–4pm.** Two designers selling comfortable, durable, gorgeous clothes in bold, bright colours and prints. The knitwear is particularly lovely.

Krea **Vestergade 4–6, Indre By ⓦwww.krea.dk. Mon–Thurs 10am–5.30pm, Fri 10am–7pm, Sat 10am–3pm.** A treasure trove of beautifully made wooden toys.

Lego Shoppen **Fisketorvet shopping centre, Vesterbro. Mon–Fri 10am–8pm, Sat 10am–5pm.** The latest offerings from the ever-popular brand, with a play area.

Magasin **Kongens Nytorv, Indre By ⓦwww.magasin.dk.** The city's grandest department store has an excellent toy department with all the familiar brands. Also a good kids' clothing department and wonderful chocolate/confectionery counters in the food hall.

Name It **Vimmelskaftet 42, Indre By.** Part of the successful Danish chain that has gone global selling great quality, reasonably priced unfussy clothes for 0–11 years in funky, modern colours, prints and styles. Former Danish supermodel, Helena Christensen designs some of the ranges.

Pif Paf Puf **Strandboulevarden 108, Østerbro.** Huge baby and child store selling all manner of baby equipment – highchairs, pushchairs, cots, toys, books and clothes. There's a second Pif Paf store, selling only toys, at Nordre Frihavnsgade 23.

Sømods Bolscher **Nørregade 24 & 36, Indre By.** Candy-loving kids will enjoy a visit to this famous sweet shop, where you can watch the skilful process of traditional sweet-making before sampling the scrumptious, rainbow-coloured end products.

Contexts

Contexts

History

Denmark's history is entirely disproportionate to its size. Nowadays a small – and often overlooked – nation, Denmark and the long line of monarchs who have lived in its capital city, Copenhagen, have nonetheless played an important role in key periods of European history, firstly as the home of the Vikings, and later as a medieval superpower.

Beginnings

Although a few tools found in what is now Denmark suggest *Homo sapiens* was present around 200,000 years ago, these cannot be precisely dated and the earliest reliable archeological evidence of **human activity** dates to 80,000 years ago with the remains of a meal eaten near a lake in central Jutland – deer bones prised open for marrow. However, it's likely that settlements of this time were only temporary, as much of the land was still covered by ice. From 14,000 BC, the climate started to warm up, ushering in the end of the Ice Age, and by 11,000 BC the ice had completely melted away from Denmark, leaving vast forests and tundra populated by herds of reindeer. Around this time, tribes from the more southerly parts of Europe arrived during the summer to hunt reindeer for their meat and antlers, which provided raw material for axes and other tools. The hunters established the first permanent settlements and, as the climate gradually warmed and the reindeer headed north, a **Stone Age village culture** developed. A further significant shift occurred around 4000 BC with the cultivation of land and keeping of livestock, and before long, agricultural communities covered the country. With this came a more organized approach to society and religion – the farmers buried their dead in dolmens or megalithic graves, and sacrifices, in the form of flint tools, axes, amber beads and pots containing food, were made to the gods responsible for farming. Many of these objects have survived, preserved in the peat bogs where they were offered up to the deities.

The earliest metal and bronze finds are from 1800 BC, the result of trade with southern Europe. During the **Bronze Age**, foreign trade flourished, with bronze objects becoming a particularly popular commodity; the richness of some pieces, such as the bronze sun chariot dating to 1400 BC (on display in the Nationalmuseet), provides evidence that even at this early date there was contact between Denmark and the Mediterranean cultures of Crete and Mycenae. From this period also come the famous Danish *lurs*, curved metal horns that were blown to call villagers to meetings – a statue of two *lurs*-blowers stands outside Copenhagen's Rådhus – and the excavated coffin of Egtved girl.

After 500 BC, iron gradually replaced bronze as the main material for tools, helped by a ready supply of the raw material in the form of bog ore. Around this time, too, it seems that conflicts between various communities were common, as villages formed alliances to obtain more territory or plunder others' land. However, it was the threat of the advancing Roman Empire – which launched an offensive into northern Germany in 5 AD – that galvanized these hitherto ad hoc fighting units into something more along the lines of mini-armies, equipped with horsemen, archers, soldiers and more sophisticated weaponry. The need to fight didn't arise, as the Romans were beaten back to the areas around the Rhine before they could reach Jutland, but military organization among the various Jutland communities had already made important strides – developments that were then utilized for fighting each other.

The Viking era

Battles for control over individual areas in Scandinavia saw the emergence of a ruling warrior class, and, around 500 AD, a tribe from southern Sweden calling themselves **Danes**, part of a group of peoples who collectively became known as the **Vikings**, migrated southwards and took control of what was known as **Danmark**. The Vikings were seamen, warriors and peasants who grew notorious for their opportunistic raids on surrounding countries – at their peak, they travelled as far as North America and the Caspian Sea. In Denmark itself, the majority of people were farmers: the less wealthy paid taxes to the king, and those who owned large tracts of land provided the monarch with military forces. In time, a **noble class** emerged, expecting and receiving privileges from the king in return for their support, while law-making became the responsibility of the *ting*, a type of council consisting of district noblemen. Above the district *ting* there was a provincial *ting*, charged with the election of the king. The successful candidate could be any member of the royal family, which led to a high level of feuding and bloodshed.

The **first Danish state** – established by the Viking Godfred, King of Jutland – emerged some time around 800 AD, encompassing most of the Jutland peninsula. A century later, the Norwegian chieftain Hardegon conquered the peninsula and began to expand eastwards over the rest of Denmark, establishing the foundations of the modern Danish nation, the oldest in Europe – the present Danish monarchy can be traced back to his son, Gorm the Old. Shortly afterwards, **Christianity** became the national religion. Benedictine monks had started arriving in Denmark in 826, but it wasn't until the baptism in 961 of Gorm the Old's son, **Harald** ("**Bluetooth**"), that Christianity became Denmark's state religion – even if his reasons for doing so (to make peace with the Franks to the south) were not entirely spiritual. Harald gave permission to a Frankish monk, **Ansgar**, to build the **first Danish church**, and Ansgar went on to take control of missionary activity throughout Scandinavia. Harald was succeeded by his pagan son **Sweyn I** ("**Forkbeard**"), who tolerated Christianity, despite suspecting the missionaries of bringing a German influence to bear in Danish affairs. From 990, Sweyn relaunched attacks on England (Viking attacks on the English had been intermittent since the late eighth century) for what seems to be primarily economic motives; a severe reduction in the availability of silver from Arabia saw a shift in focus to England as a potential source of income through exaction of tribute. By the time of Sweyn's death in 1014, Ethelred's England was all but under Danish rule, though continued resistance and struggle meant that it took a further two years for Sweyn's son Knud (Canute) to be accepted as English king, marrying Ethelred's widow into the bargain. By 1033, the Danes controlled most of southern Sweden, the whole of England and Normandy, and dominated trade in the Baltic. This was the zenith of Viking power, and it's from this period that we get the first historical record of the small fishing village of **Havn** (literally "Haven" or "Harbour", and later to become København or Copenhagen), when it was mentioned in 1043, after the Norwegian King Magnus sought refuge there following his defeat in a sea battle in the Øresund.

The Middle Ages

A century of violent **internal struggles**, not only between different would-be rulers but also among the Church, nobility and monarchy, weakened Viking power in Denmark, and it wasn't until the accession of Valdemar the Great in 1157 that the country was once again united and free of factional fighting. Valdemar strengthened the crown by ending the elective function of the *ting*, and shifting the power of choosing the monarch to the Church. Technically, the *ting* still influenced the choice of king, but in practice hereditary succession became the rule.

One of Valdemar's key supporters, his foster brother **Bishop Absalon**, became Archbishop of Denmark and was given the village of Havn, strategically located on the **Øresund** – the narrow sea channel that divides Denmark from Sweden, and the main entrance to the Baltic – which was soon to become one of the main trading routes of medieval Europe.

Within a decade, Absalon had built a castle on the small island (today's Slotsholmen) opposite Havn, from where he countered the Wendish pirates, based in eastern Germany, who had previously raided the coast with impunity. Besides being a zealous churchman, Absalon possessed a sharp military mind and came to dominate Valdemar the Great and his successor, Knud IV. In this period, Denmark saw some of its best years, expanding to the south and east, taking advantage of internal strife within Germany. Havn itself developed rapidly following the castle's construction. In 1209, Vor Frue Kirke – later to become the city's cathedral – was consecrated by Bishop Absalon's successor (Absalon had died in 1201), and in 1238, the city's first monastery was established on Gråbrødretorv; by 1254 the town had acquired its modern name, **København** (Merchants' Harbour), a fortified market town with full municipal rights.

Thirty years later, following a German invasion of Jutland, the Danish nobles seized the opportunity to curb the powers of the monarch, forcing Erik V (in 1282) to sign a charter under which he agreed to rule together with the nobles of the **Council of the Danish Realm**, an institution that was to survive as a major influence in Danish government until 1660. Almost a century of civil war followed, as the nobles fought against the king and one another, during which Copenhagen was passed back and forth between the warring factions. In 1369, the city fell to Hanseatic forces, and stonemasons from the city of Lübeck proceeded to dismantle Bishop Absalon's castle brick by brick, with the intention of ending Danish control of the Øresund once and for all.

The Kalmar Union

Despite the temporary loss of its castle, however, Copenhagen's fortunes continued to prosper. Following the death of her son, King Olav – for whom she had reigned as regent for much of his life – **Margrethe I**, one of Denmark's shrewdest rulers, ascended the throne. Her moment of glory came in 1397 when she formed the **Kalmar Union**, an alliance between Denmark, Norway and Sweden aimed at countering the Hanseatic League's influence on regional trade. It became evident that Denmark was to be the dominant partner within the union, however, when Margrethe placed Danish nobles in civic positions in Norway and Sweden but failed to reciprocate with Swedes and Norwegians in Denmark. Margrethe promptly saw to it that her grandnephew, Erik of Pomerania, was crowned king, though, as he was only 15, she continued to play a major role in the affairs of the country till her death in 1412. Under Erik, a new fort to replace Absalon's dismantled castle was completed in 1417, becoming the main residence of the royal family. Erik also ensured Copenhagen's further growth by imposing the **Sound Toll** tax on all vessels passing through the Øresund, an endless source of income that would underpin the city's fortunes for the next four centuries. Revenues from the toll allowed an increasingly self-confident Copenhagen to seize growing amounts of trade from the declining ports of the Hanseatic League and to establish itself as the Baltic's principal harbour.

In 1443, Copenhagen was made the **capital of Denmark** by Erik's nephew, Christoffer III, decisively shifting the national balance of power away from the former capital and ecclesiastical centre of Roskilde. Thirty years later, the first **university** in Scandinavia was founded in Copenhagen by Christian I, helping to establish the city as the nation's cultural as well as administrative hub. At the same time, **Kronborg Slot**, just north of Copenhagen at Helsingør, was built to control the Øresund and enforce payment of the Sound Toll, further entrenching Copenhagen's pre-eminent position in the region.

The Reformation to the Thirty Years' War

At the time of **Frederik I**'s acquisition of the crown in 1522 there was a growing unease with the role of the Catholic Church in Denmark, especially with the power – and wealth – of its bishops. Frederik, though a Catholic, refused to take sides in religious disputes and did nothing to prevent the destruction of churches, being well aware of the groundswell of peasant support for Lutheranism. When he died in 1533 the fate of the Danish **Reformation** hinged on which of his two sons would succeed him. The elder and more obvious choice was Christian, but his open support for Lutheranism set the bishops and nobles against him, while the younger son Hans, just 12 years old, was favoured by the Church and aristocracy. **Civil war** ensued – peasant uprisings spread across the country, and Hanseatic Lübeck sent mercenaries to Copenhagen, where they sided with the city's anti-clerical merchants. A year-long siege of the city followed, and though Copenhagen's defensive ramparts held up, many of its citizens starved to death or died during the epidemics that ravaged the city. The capital finally surrendered in the summer of 1536, signalling the end of the war, and, after the dust had settled, the nobles found themselves back in control, but obliged to accept religious reform. With Christian III on the throne, the new **Danish Lutheran Church** was established, with a constitution placing the king at its head, and Lutheranism became the official state religion.

Following the travails of the Reformation, Copenhagen experienced a period of relative peace and prosperity. The city was now home to the Danish navy – during the fifteenth and sixteenth centuries the largest in northern Europe – and the Sound Toll provided a continuous source of revenue for Danish coffers. It was in this atmosphere of wealth and stability that **Christian IV** became king. Ruling from 1588 (when he was 10) until 1648, he became the Danish monarch who made the most lasting contribution to Copenhagen's skyline, ordering the creation of buildings including the Rundetårn and Rosenborg Slot, along with the district of Nyboder and the fortress of Kastellet. In addition, he almost doubled the city's size by moving the defensive fortifications outwards to include Frederikstad and Nyboder to the north and the newly reclaimed island of Christianshavn to the east.

Unfortunately, Christian IV's architectural vision was not matched by his political skill. As Denmark's arch-rival Sweden became increasingly powerful, Danish military prowess steadily declined. In 1625, Christian IV took Denmark into the disastrous **Thirty Years' War** – Danish defeat was total, and the king was widely condemned for his lack of foresight. The war led to increased taxes, inflation became rampant, and a number of merchants displayed their anger by petitioning the king over tax exemptions and other privileges enjoyed by nobles.

In 1657, during the reign of **Frederik III**, Sweden occupied Jutland, and soon after marched across the frozen sea to Funen island with the intention of continuing to Zealand and the capital. Hostilities ceased with the signing of the **Treaty of Roskilde**, under which Denmark finally lost all Swedish provinces. Sweden, however, was still suspicious of possible Danish involvement in Germany, and broke the terms of the treaty, commencing an advance through Zealand towards Copenhagen. The Dutch, to whom the Swedes had been allied, regarded this as a precursor to total Swedish control of commercial traffic through the Sound and sent a fleet to protect Copenhagen. This, plus a number of local uprisings within Denmark and attacks by Polish and Brandenburg forces on their troops, halted the Swedes' advance and forced them to seek peace. The **Treaty of Copenhagen**, signed in 1660, acknowledged Swedish defeat but allowed the country to retain the Sound provinces acquired under the Treaty of Roskilde, so preventing either country from monopolizing trade through the Sound.

Absolute monarchy

The conflict with Sweden and the loss of former territory left Denmark heavily in debt, and, to make matters worse, the nobles of the Council of the Danish Realm were reluctant to impose the taxes needed to rescue the state's finances. In response, in 1660 Frederik III compelled the nobles to sign a charter reinstating the king as absolute monarch, removing all powers from the Council. The king proceeded to rule, aided by a Privy Council in which seats were drawn mainly from the top posts within the civil service. The aristocracy's influence on royal decision-making had been drastically cut and Copenhagen was made a free city, with commoners accorded the same privileges as nobles. Frederik III started rebuilding the military, and, following three minor wars with Sweden, a peaceful coexistence was finally achieved.

Christian V, king from 1670, instigated a broad system of royal honours, creating a new class of landowners, who enjoyed exemptions from tax, and whose lack of concern for their tenants led Danish peasants into virtual serfdom. In 1699, **Frederik IV** set about creating a Danish militia to make the country less dependent on foreign mercenaries. While Sweden turned its allegiances towards Britain and Holland, Denmark re-established relations with the French, a situation which, in 1709, led to Danish involvement in the **Great Northern War**. The end of the conflict saw the emergence of Russia as a dominant force in the region, while Denmark held a strong position in Schleswig, and Sweden's exemption from paying the Sound Toll was ended.

The two decades of peace that followed saw the arrival of **Pietism**, a form of Lutheranism that strove to renew the devotional ideal. Frederik embraced the doctrine towards the end of his life, and it was adopted in full by his son, **Christian VI**, who took the throne in 1730. He prohibited entertainment on Sunday, closed down the Royal Theatre, and made court life a sombre affair: attendance at church on Sundays became compulsory and confirmation obligatory. Meanwhile, in 1711, bubonic plague wiped out a third of Copenhagen's population, while two devastating **fires** in 1728 and 1795 forced the reconstruction of most of the city, during which the basis of the present-day street plan was established.

The Enlightenment

Despite Christian VI's beliefs, Pietism was never widely popular, and by the 1740s its influence had waned considerably. The reign of **Frederik V** (1746–66), saw a great cultural awakening in Copenhagen, as the new royal district of Frederikstad, with the grand royal palaces of Amalienborg and the Marmorkirken church, were erected (though the latter wasn't finished until 1894), and there was a new flourishing of the arts. The king, perhaps as a reaction to the puritanism of his father, devoted himself to a life of pleasure and allowed control of the nation effectively to pass to the civil service. Political life enjoyed a period of relative stability, and, with their international influence significantly reduced by the ravages of the Great Northern War, the Danes adopted a position of **neutrality** – a decision that saw the economy benefit.

In 1766, **Christian VII** took the crown, but, with his mental state unstable and his moods ranging from deep lethargy to rage and drunkenness, by 1771 he had become incapable of carrying out even the minimum of official duties. Decision-making became dominated by a German court physician, **Johann Friedrich Struensee**, who spoke no Danish (German was the court language) and had no interest in Danish traditions, and was sympathetic to many of the Enlightenment ideas then fashionable elsewhere in Europe – during his short period of power a number of sweeping **reforms** were enacted, including the dissolution of the Privy Council, the abolition of the death penalty and the relaxation of press censorship. However, these reforms invited opposition from several quarters: merchants complained about the freeing of trade, and the burghers of Copenhagen were unhappy about their city losing its autonomy. In addition, there were well-founded rumours about the relationship between Struensee and the queen. Since nothing was known outside the court of the king's mental state, it was assumed that the monarch was being held prisoner, and Struensee was forced to reintroduce censorship of the press as their editorials began to mount attacks on him. Eventually, a coup in 1772 by Frederik V's second wife, Juliane Marie of Brunswick, and her son, Frederik, saw Struensee arrested, tried and, soon afterwards, beheaded, while the dazed king was paraded before his cheering subjects. Anyone who had been appointed to office by Struensee was dismissed, Danish became the language of command in the army – and later the court language – and in 1776 it was declared that no foreigner should be given a position in royal office. In the wider sphere, the country prospered through dealings in the Far East, and Copenhagen consolidated its role as the new centre of Baltic trade.

The Napoleonic Wars

Despite its improving domestic position, Denmark found itself once again embroiled in the mire of international power struggles with the outbreak of the **Napoleonic Wars** (1796–1815). Under the leadership of Crown Prince Frederik (his father, the unstable Christian VII, had been stripped of all authority since 1784), Denmark at first reluctantly sided with the League of Armed Neutrality

– Russia, Sweden and Prussia – in an attempt to stay out of the conflict between expansionist Britain and revolutionary France. However, the British, considering the treaty potentially hostile, sent a fleet under admirals Nelson and Parker to Copenhagen in 1801, damaging the powerful Danish navy and forcing them to withdraw from the agreement. In 1807, the British returned, worried that Napoleon's advancing armies would take over the newly rebuilt Danish fleet if they didn't, and demanded Danish surrender. When Frederik refused, the British blockaded the city, subjecting it to a murderous three-day bombardment that saw many of its finest buildings damaged, before towing away what was left of the Danish fleet. Denmark understandably rejected the subsequent British offer of an alliance, siding instead with France. With the eventual defeat of Napoleon, however, the luckless Danes were left bankrupt and without allies, and Norway had to be handed over to Sweden as payment for war debts.

The Golden Age and the coming of Liberalism

Despite this terrible beginning to the century, by the 1830s Copenhagen had become the centre of the Danish **Golden Age**. For two decades the nation's arts flourished as never before (or since): Hans Christian Andersen charmed the world with his colourful fairy tales, while **Søren Kierkegaard** (see p.91) scandalized it with his philosophical works. At the same time, the nation's visual arts reached new heights under the auspices of sculptor **Bertel Thorvaldsen** (see p.39) and artist **C.W. Eckersberg**, who led the emergence of the first specifically Danish school of painting and gathered around him a circle of pupils whose idealized, patriotic paintings of Danish seascapes and landscapes can be seen in the city's art museums. From this period, too, date many of the city's most notable Neoclassical buildings, many designed by ubiquitous architect **C.F. Hansen**, such as Christiansborg Slotskirke, the Domhus (Law Courts) and Vor Frue Kirke. Social changes were in the air, too. In the early nineteenth century, the theologian **N.F.S. Grundtvig** (see p.108) developed a new form of Christianity that aimed to draw its strength and inspiration from the people.

On the political front, however, there was trouble brewing in the duchies of Danish-speaking **Schleswig** and German-speaking **Holstein**, which, in response to the wave of nationalism in France and Germany, were demanding their independence. The issue became inextricably linked with the call for constitutional reform when a group of scholars in Copenhagen suggested that Schleswig be brought closer to Danish affairs and, to pursue their aim, formed the Liberal Party and began pressing for a new liberal constitution. As the government wavered in its response, the movement grew, and its first newspaper, *Fædrelandet* (*The Fatherland*), appeared in 1834.

In 1839, **Christian VIII** came to the throne. Despite introducing a liberal constitution during his brief tenure in power in Norway during its short transition phase from Danish to Swedish rule, the new king didn't agree to a similar constitution back home. By 1848, when Christian was succeeded by his son **Frederik VII**, the liberals had organized themselves into the **National Liberal Party**, and Frederik signed a **new constitution** that made Denmark the most democratic country in Europe, guaranteeing freedom of speech, freedom of religious worship and many civil liberties. Legislation was to be put in the hands of a Rigsdag elected by popular vote and consisting of two chambers: the lower Folketing and upper

Landsting. The king gave up the powers of an absolute monarch, though he could still select his own ministers, and his signature was required before bills approved by the Rigsdag became law.

Continuing strife over the duchies of Schleswig and Holstein saw a series of small wars; eventually, Denmark ceded both to Germany during the reign of **Christian IX**, leaving the country smaller than it had been for centuries. The blame for this territorial loss was laid firmly on the National Liberals, and the new government, appointed by the king and drawn from the country's affluent landowners, saw its initial task as replacing the constitution with one far less liberal in content. The landowners worked in limited cooperation with the National Liberals and the Centre Party (a more conservative version of the National Liberals). In opposition, a number of interests encompassing everything from leftist radicals to followers of Grundtvig were shortly combined into the **United Left**, which put forward the first political manifesto seen in Denmark. It called for equal taxation, universal suffrage in local elections, more freedom for the farmers, and contained a vague demand for closer links with the other Scandinavian countries. The United Left became the majority within the Folketing in 1872.

The ideas of **revolutionary socialism** had begun percolating through the country in 1871 via a series of pamphlets edited by Louis Pio, who attempted to organize a Danish Internationale. Following a major strike, the government banned the organization, but the workers banded instead into trade unions and workers' associations, while the intellectual left also became active. A series of lectures delivered by Georg Brandes in Copenhagen cited Danish culture, in particular its literature, as dull and lifeless compared to that of other countries. He called for fresh works that questioned and examined society, instigating a bout of literary attacks on institutions such as marriage, chastity and the family, and starting a conservative backlash as groups in the government formed themselves into the **United Right**. The fortunes of the two sides fluctuated until the end of the century, when the left reasserted its dominance.

Meanwhile, the city itself had been undergoing something of a transformation. In 1851, Copenhagen's fortifications were demolished, finally allowing the cramped city to expand beyond its medieval limits and sowing the seeds for the new industrial era. Railways, factories and shipyards began to change the face of the city, and Copenhagen gradually developed into a thriving manufacturing centre, while the new working-class districts of Nørrebro and Vesterbro were flung up, with Copenhagen's workers packed into slum tenements that would subsequently become hotbeds of left-wing politics. The second half of the nineteenth century also saw the establishment of the **Carlsberg Brewery**, the rapid growth of the **Royal Copenhagen Porcelain** factory, and the founding of a number of recreational possibilities for the city's aspiring bourgeoisie, from the city's two main department stores, Magasin du Nord and Illum, to Det Kongelige Teater and the city zoo.

Parliamentary democracy and World War I

The elections of 1901, under the new conditions of a secret ballot, saw the right reduced to the smallest group within the Folketing and heralded the beginning of **parliamentary democracy**.

The government of 1901 was the first real democratic administration, assembled with the intention of balancing differing political tendencies – and it brought in a number of reforms. Income tax was introduced on a sliding scale, and free schooling beyond the primary level began. As the years went by, Social Democrat support increased, while the left, such as it was, became increasingly conservative. In 1905, a breakaway group formed the **Radical Left** (Det Radikale Venstre), politically similar to the English Liberals, calling for the reduction of the armed forces to the status of coastal and border guards, greater social equality and votes for women.

Denmark had enjoyed good trading relations with both Germany and Britain in the years preceding **World War I**, and was keen not to be seen to favour either side when hostilities broke out in 1914. On the announcement of the German mobilization, the now Radical-led cabinet, with the support of all the other parties, issued a **statement of neutrality** and was able to remain clear of direct involvement in the conflict. At the conclusion of the war, under the **Treaty of Versailles**, a new German–Danish border was drawn just north of Flensburg.

In 1920, a change in the electoral system towards greater proportional representation was agreed in the Folketing, but the prime minister, **Carl Theodore Zahle**, whose Radicals stood to lose support through the change, refused to implement it. The king, Christian X, responded by dismissing him and asking **Otto Liebe** to form a caretaker government to oversee the changes. The (technically legal) royal intervention incensed the Social Democrats and the trade unions, who were already facing a national lockout by employers in response to demands for improved pay rates. Perceiving the threat of a right-wing coup, the unions began organizing a general strike to begin after the Easter holiday, and there was a large republican demonstration outside Amalienborg.

On Easter Saturday, urgent negotiations between the king and the existing government concluded with an agreement that a mutually acceptable caretaker government would oversee the electoral change and a fresh election would immediately follow. Employers, fearful of the power the workers had shown, met many of the demands for higher wages.

The next government was dominated by the Radical Left. They fortified existing social policies and increased state contributions to union unemployment funds. But a general economic depression continued, and there was widespread industrial unrest as the krone declined in value and living standards fell. A month-long **general strike** followed, and a workers' demonstration in Randers was subdued by the army.

Venstre (the "Left", though the party was originally Liberal in ideology), formed in 1872 to represent the significant agricultural lobby, and the Social Democrats jostled for position over the next decade, though under the new electoral system no one party could achieve enough power to undertake major reform. The economy did improve, however, and state influence spread further through Danish society than ever before. Enlightened reforms were put on the agenda, too, making a clean break with the moral standpoints of the past – notably on abortion and illegitimacy.

World War II

When **World War II** broke out, Denmark again tried to remain neutral, this time unsuccessfully. At 4am on April 9, 1940, the German ambassador in Copenhagen informed Prime Minister Stauning that German troops were preparing to cross the Danish border, and issued the ultimatum that unless Denmark agreed that the country could be used as a German military base – keeping control of its own affairs – Copenhagen would be bombed. To reject the demand was considered a postponement of the inevitable, and to save Danish bloodshed the government acquiesced at 6am. "They took us by telephone", said a Danish minister. German troops marched up Nordre Frihavnsgade to the royal palaces at Amalienborg and took power the same day. The Danish parliament was left to operate purely as an administrative body, and the economy was geared towards German war needs. At first, the Danes could do little other than comply, but growing resistance made life difficult for the Nazi forces. Passive non-cooperation gradually turned to armed struggle, and by the war's end, thousands of citizens had fought (and many died) for the Danish Resistance, whose crowning moment came with the smuggling of 7000 Jews to Sweden to avoid their deportation to concentration camps (see box, p.42). In Copenhagen, the effect of the war was felt mainly in food and fuel rationing, and, apart from the occasional air raid, the city largely escaped the devastation visited on other European cities – its finest moment came when a British air raid on the Nazi headquarters on Rådhuspladsen allowed most of the captured members of the Danish Resistance to escape.

The modern era

While Copenhagen and the country as a whole had been spared the devastation seen elsewhere in Europe, it still found itself with massive economic problems following World War II, and it soon became apparent that the newly elected liberation government – consisting largely of former leaders of the Resistance – could not function. In the ensuing election there was a swing to the Communists, and a minority Venstre government was formed. Domestic issues soon came to be overshadowed by the **international situation** as the Cold War began. Denmark had unreservedly joined the United Nations in 1945, and had signed up to the IMF and World Bank to gain financial help in restoring its economy. In 1947, Marshall Plan aid from the United States brought further assistance. As world politics became polarized between East and West, the Danish government at first tried to remain impartial, but in 1947 agreed to join NATO – a total break with the established concept of Danish neutrality.

The years after the war were marked by much political manoeuvring among the Radicals, Social Democrats and Conservatives, resulting in many hastily called elections and a number of ineffectual compromise coalitions, notable mainly for their infighting. Working-class support for the Social Democrats steadily eroded, and support for the Communists was largely transferred to the new, more revisionist **Socialist People's Party**.

In spite of political wrangling, Denmark succeeded in creating one of the world's most successful **welfare states**, with a comprehensive programme of cradle-to-grave benefits, and a quality of life that soon ranked among the highest in the world. Social reforms continued apace, not least in the **1960s**, with the abandoning of all forms of censorship and the institution of free abortion on demand. A referendum held in 1972 to determine whether Denmark should join the EC resulted in a substantial majority in favour, making Denmark the first Scandinavian member of the community. Perhaps the biggest change in the 1970s, however, was the foundation – and subsequent influence – of the new **Progress Party** (Fremskridtspartiet), initially headed by Mogens Glistrup, who claimed to have an income of over a million kroner but to be paying no income tax through manipulation of the tax laws. The party stood on a ticket of immigration curbs and drastic tax cuts. Glistrup was eventually imprisoned after an investigation by the Danish tax office; released in 1985, he set himself up as a tax consultant. The success of the Progress Party pointed to dissatisfaction with both the economy and the established parties' strategies for dealing with its problems. In September 1982, **Poul Schlüter** became the country's first **Conservative** prime minister of the twentieth century, leading the widest-ranging coalition yet seen – including Conservatives, the Venstre, Centre Democrats and Christian People's Party. In keeping with the prevailing political climate in the rest of Europe, the prescription for Denmark's economic malaise was seen to be spending cuts and an extension of taxation into areas such as pension funds.

The 1980s and 1990s also saw further huge changes, as attempts were made to clean up the derelict areas of **Nørrebro** and **Vesterbro**. In Nørrebro, the result was disastrous, with blocks of ramshackle but characterful buildings being replaced by concrete housing estates until mass protests forced the city to desist. The remaining buildings in Nørrebro – and most of Vesterbro – were restored rather than demolished, with the result that housing in these areas increased enormously in value, and waves of Copenhagen yuppies took the places of the districts' formerly working-class inhabitants.

Immigrants – the so-called **new Danes**, mainly from Yugoslavia and Turkey – brought in during the boom years of the 1960s to fill the city's menial jobs, became suddenly less welcome in the 1970s, as unemployment rates rose and racism reared its ugly head. Tensions reached boiling point in 1999 with riots in Nørrebro, protesting against the extradition of a second-generation Turkish immigrant. Though nothing along these lines has occurred since, whether the city's ethnic communities – often faced with overweening pressure to conform to the Danish way of life – will succeed in bringing true cultural diversity to the city remains to be seen.

Despite being members of the **European Union** for over thirty years, the Danes frequently rocked the European boat. A 1992 referendum saw them reject the Maastricht Treaty, and it took a second referendum in 1993, backed by massive state propaganda, to establish the necessary majority for the treaty's implementation. This result so inflamed popular opinion in parts of Copenhagen that it led to a riot in Nørrebro during which eleven people were shot and injured. At a third referendum, in late 2000, the Danes again shocked fellow EU member states by choosing to opt out of the third stage of EU monetary union (adopting the euro), as right-wing politicians stirred up nationalist emotions, claiming that giving up the Danish krone was equivalent to relinquishing national sovereignty.

Poul Nyrup Rasmussen's Social Democratic government retained the largest share of the vote in the 1998 elections, and, as the new millennium dawned, the country enjoyed a relatively strong position compared to other European countries, in terms of environmental awareness, healthcare costs and low poverty and unemployment. Meanwhile, as well as significantly enhancing Copenhagen's connections with the rest of Scandinavia, the opening in 2000 of the **Øresunds Bridge** brought the Swedish city of Malmö within thirty minutes of the city centre, adding at a stroke half a million people to Copenhagen's catchment area and establishing it as a major regional hub capable of attracting serious foreign investment.

Copenhagen today

Copenhagen today faces an identity crisis as it struggles to maintain its much-cherished individuality and independence in the face of an ever-expanding Europe and the pull of **European monetary union**. Though, like the UK, Denmark is yet to go the full mile and adopt the euro, the Danish government was fairly swift in ratifying the Lisbon Treaty, though a referendum due to be held in 2006 on the adoption of the full EU constitution would surely have resulted in a no had it not been cancelled in the wake of the French and Dutch "no" results. In the meantime, the city's ties with the rest of Scandinavia, particularly Sweden, are undergoing a period of frenetic activity. The Øresund region, in particular, is booming, with a network of Danish and Swedish universities, cross-border migration and an influx of biotech, medical and food companies employing nearly thirty thousand people.

It's not all positive, though; **immigration and asylum** issues have, over the past decade or so, risen to the forefront of the Danish political agenda. As a result, the general elections of 2001, 2005 and 2007 saw the ousting of the once-dominant Social Democrats in favour of the centre-right party **Venstre**, with its hard-line stance on immigration. Since 2001 the government – a coalition of Venstre and the Conservative People's Party and, in the 2007 election, with parliamentary support from the Danish People's Party (see below) – has passed a series of laws (the most stringent in Europe), aimed at curbing non-EU immigration and severely limiting asylum applications. The government, led by Prime Minister Lars Løkke Rasmussen, answers its numerous critics by asserting Denmark to be at capacity, even though the country, with an ageing population and expensive welfare state to maintain, is in need of the boost to the workforce and young population that immigration can bring. There has also been a rise in popularity of the right-wing, anti-immigration **Danish People's Party** (DFP), which gained almost fourteen percent of the vote (25 seats) in the 2007 election, making it the third party of choice, and it continues to lobby the government into taking an even harder line. In 2005, issues surrounding the integration of sections of the immigrant population were highlighted with the highly controversial printing of twelve **cartoons** featuring the prophet Mohammed (some depicting him as a terrorist) in the daily broadsheet, *Jyllands-Posten*. The cartoons brought condemnation and violent protests from Muslims around the world and death threats to newspaper staff and the cartoonists; in Denmark, five thousand Muslims took to the streets in largely peaceful protest and radical Danish *imams* demanded an apology. However, *Jyllands-Posten* stood firm, backed by the prime minister, defending its democratic right to freedom of expression.

The Danish government has shown itself to be hard-line on many other issues, too: anti-environment (with cuts in energy-saving initiatives); anti-development (cuts in overseas aid); anti-culture (slashing financial support to alternative types of entertainment); and, on a subject dear to Copenhageners' hearts, anti-Christiania (see p.58). In contrast, Copenhagen itself, which can already claim to be the **greenest capital in Europe**, hosted the 2009 United Nations Climate Change Conference, leading to renewed pledges from the city council and government for increased funding for environmental projects and further plans to cut carbon emissions. With an expanding metro system and renovated harbourfront dominated by cultural institutions and prestigious public buildings, the city also seems to be bearing up well in the global recession.

Books

There are relatively few English-language books on Copenhagen and it's especially difficult to find an English history of the city or, for that matter, the country; it's almost as if historians consider the Vikings the only thing worth writing about. The list below represents a fairly comprehensive selection of what's available. All are very readable, but those marked with ✱ are particularly recommended.

History and philosophy

Jane Chamberlain & Jonathan Ree (eds) *The Kirkegaard Reader*. By far the best and most accessible introduction to this notoriously difficult philosopher and writer, with an excellent introduction and plentiful extracts from his most famous works.

Ole Feldbæk *The Battle of Copenhagen 1801*. Accessible examination by the leading Danish authority on the period of the events surrounding the great sea battle that saw Nelson deliberately disobeying his superior in the fight to crush the Danish navy during the Napoleonic Wars.

Joakim Garff *Søren Kirkegaard: A Biography*. The most comprehensive book on Kirkegaard's life to date, this eight-hundred-page tome is surprisingly readable, offering an insight into the tortured world of a great thinker through the minutiae of his life.

Tony Griffiths *Scandinavia: At War with Trolls*. A concise and witty cultural history of Scandinavia and the contributions of its great thinkers, artists and musicians from the eighteenth century to today. One of the best contemporary histories available.

Stig Hornshøj-Møller *A Short History of Denmark*. This 72-page romp through Danish history is the perfect, lightweight companion to sightseeing, giving succinct information on the key periods and figures you'll encounter along the way. Available from the shops of the major historical museums, castles and palaces.

✱ **Knud J.V. Jespersen** *A History of Denmark*. Readable and accessible history of Denmark since the Reformation, examining the way the modern Danish state evolved through its numerous territorial wars and providing interesting insights into the Danish identity and psyche.

✱ **Gwyn Jones** *A History of the Vikings*, 2nd edition. Regularly updated since its publication in the 1960s, this scholarly classic is still the best book on the subject: a superb, thoughtful and thoroughly researched account of the Viking period.

W. Glyn Jones *Denmark: A Modern History*. A valuable account of the twentieth century (up until 1984), with a commendable outline of pre-twentieth-century Danish history, too. Strong on politics, useful on social history and the arts, but disappointingly brief on recent grassroots movements.

Palle Lauring *A History of Denmark*, 3rd edition. Originally published in the 1960s, this was written with English readers in mind. It's a highly readable account of the country's history from the Stone Age to the post-war period, and also explores the historic connections and relationships between England and Denmark.

Søren Kirkegaard *Either/Or*. Kirkegaard's most important work, packed with wry and wise musings on love, life and death in nineteenth-century Danish society, including the (in)famous "Seducer's Diary". His next book,

Fear and Trembling, faces the subject of faith with a discussion of the biblical account of Abraham; *The Sickness Unto Death* focuses on despair and its relationship to weakness and sin.

Else Roesdahl *The Vikings*. A lucid, introductory account of the three-hundred-year reign of Scandinavia's most famous (and most misunderstood) cultural ambassadors, covering all aspects of their society, including religion, dress, language and politics.

Peter Sawyer (ed) *The Oxford Illustrated History of the Vikings*. Highly readable essays on various aspects of Viking culture and history from shipbuilding to the Vikings in England to the Viking legacy, accompanied by wonderful photographs and illustrations.

Emmy E. Werner *A Conspiracy of Decency: The Rescue of the Danish Jews During World War II*. A short, compelling account detailing how the Danish people were able to rescue nearly all of the country's Jews from deportation and death by hiding them and helping them escape to neutral Sweden. The eyewitness accounts make moving reading.

Literature and biography

Hans Christian Andersen *Fairy Tales*. Andersen's fairy tales are so widely translated and read that the full clout of their allegorical content is often overlooked: interestingly, his first collection (published in 1835) was condemned for its "violence and questionable morals". *A Visit to Germany, Italy and Malta, 1840–1841* (o/p) is the most enduring of his travel works, while his autobiography, *The Fairy Tale of My Life*, is a fine alternative to the sycophantic portraits that have appeared since.

Karen Blixen (Isak Dinesen) *Out of Africa*; *Winter's Tales*; *Letters from Africa*; *Seven Gothic Tales*. *Out of Africa*, the account of Blixen's attempts to run a coffee farm in Kenya after her divorce, is a lyrical and moving tale. But it's *Seven Gothic Tales* that sees Blixen's fiction at its zenith: a flawlessly executed, weird, emotive work, full of twists and strange, ambiguous characterization.

Elias Bredsdorff *Hans Christian Andersen: A Biography*. From the acknowledged world expert on the famous storyteller (and descendant of the people who looked after the author on his arrival in Copenhagen), this is the most comprehensive and probably the best of a raft of works on the life and times of the great fairy-tale writer.

Stig Dalager *Journey in Blue: A novel about Hans Christian Andersen*. Dalager, one of the most renowned Scandinavian authors of recent decades, tells the fictional biography of Andersen through a series of flashbacks and recollections, providing insight into what caused the writer's sense of alienation and how this drove him to search for literary validation in the world that shunned him.

Leif Davidsen *The Serbian Dane*. In this pacy thriller a hired assassin (he of the title) is on the loose in Copenhagen charged with the task of carrying out a fatwa on a visiting author. Will he make his target in time or be thwarted by the Danish cop assigned to protect the target?

Tove Ditlevsen *Early Spring*. An autobiographical novel of growing up in Copenhagen's working-class Vesterbro district in the 1930s. A captivating evocation of childhood and early adulthood.

Per Olov Enquist *The Royal Physician's Visit*. Gripping historical novel revolving around a particularly racy episode in Danish history – the power struggles of the various weasly courtiers manipulating the young and mentally unstable Christian VII, including his German doctor, Johann

Struensee, who took the queen, Caroline Mathilde, as his mistress.

Martin A. Hansen *The Liar*. An engaging novel, showing why Hansen was one of Denmark's most perceptive – and popular – postwar authors. Set in the 1950s, the story examines the inner thoughts of a lonely schoolteacher living on a small Danish island.

Peter Høeg *Miss Smilla's Feeling for Snow; A History of Danish Dreams; The Woman and the Ape; Tales of the Night; The Quiet Girl*. Probably Denmark's most famous modern author, with the worldwide bestseller, *Miss Smilla* – a compelling thriller dealing with Danish colonialism in Greenland and the issue of cultural identity. *The Quiet Girl* is a challenging, quirky thriller set in Copenhagen and populated by a cast of surreal characters like circus clowns, nuns and kidnapped children with supernatural abilities.

Christian Jungersen *The Exception*. A real page-turner, this thrilling bestseller follows the fictional lives of four women who receive threatening emails at the Centre for Genocide Studies where they work. It delves deeply into the issues of moral ambiguity as the women confront the ethical dilemmas that face them.

Thomas E. Kennedy *Kerrigan's Copenhagen: A Love Story*. The city co-stars in this witty, Joyce-style tale of an American writer attempting to come to terms with his past with the help of Copenhagen's many bars. Each chapter is devoted to a different bar, with the loveable if frustrating hero meeting a host of characters and musing on life, the city, beer, books, jazz, sex, cigars and architecture, among other things.

Dea Trier Mørch *Winter's Child*. A wonderfully lucid sketch of modern Denmark as seen through the eyes of several women in the maternity ward of a Copenhagen hospital. See also *Evening Star*, which deals with the effect of old age and death on a Danish family.

Martin Andersen Nexø *Pelle the Conqueror*. Made by Bille August into an Academy Award-winning film in 1989, this moving tale about life as an immigrant has been a classic in Denmark for years.

Hans Scherfig *Stolen Spring*. A group of Copenhagen high-school kids studying for their exams feel they're missing out on the most important spring of their lives. A classic novel, mandatory reading for Danish youth.

Judith Thurman *Isak Dinesen: The Life of Karen Blixen*. The most penetrating biography of Blixen, elucidating details of the farm period not found in the two "Africa" books.

Rose Tremain *Music and Silence*. Captivating novel that follows the lives of Christian IV, his consort, his English lutenist and their lovers. Life in the many castles around Copenhagen is brilliantly described, and the novel provides a delightful insight into Danish aspirations and superstitions during the period.

Jackie Wullschlager *Hans Christian Andersen: The Life of a Storyteller*. This finely documented and insightful work examines the misery of Andersen's childhood, his subsequent rapid success and his troubled sexuality, arguing that it was the shock and power of these experiences that fuelled many of his mournful fairy tales.

Architecture and design

Marisa Bartolucci & Raul Cabra *Compact Design Series: Arne Jacobsen*. A very useful primer to the life and works of one of Denmark's most prolific and talented designers.

Christian Datz & C. Kullmann (eds) *Copenhagen: Architecture and Design*. Great little glossy featuring the city's and suburbs' modern architectural masterpieces.

Charlotte Fiell & Peter Fiell *Scandinavian Design*. Beautiful, photo-driven history of Scandinavian design from 1900 to the present day, covering all of the major designers and the whole range of crafts – from glass to furniture to jewellery – with ample coverage of more modern design phenomena such as Ikea and Lego.

Andrew Hollingsworth *Danish Modern*. Great book covering the history of Danish design from its earliest traditions in cabinet making to the present day. There's also a helpful section on what to look for when buying Danish classics, where to find them and how to look after them.

Olaf Lind & Annemarie Lund *Top 50: Copenhagen Architecture*. A pithy rundown of the city's top buildings from historic landmarks to hotels to churches to housing projects, with lots of photos and thumbnail plans.

Noritsugu Oda *Danish Chairs*. If you've been bitten by the bug, this fabulous book will tell you all you need to know about the illustrious history of chair design in Denmark, featuring timeless classics from the likes of Kaare Klint and Arne Jacobsen, as well as more up-to-the-minute designs.

Travel, cooking and film

Stig Bjorkman *Trier on von Trier*. Bjorkman manages to draw out the man behind the *enfant terrible* of contemporary film-making in this series of fascinating interviews. Trier (the "von" is an affectation) opens up about his childhood influences, his long-standing love of cinema and the inspiration behind the Dogme movement.

Tom Cunliffe *Topsail and Battleaxe: A Voyage in the Wake of the Vikings*. The intertwined stories of the tenth-century Vikings who sailed from Norway, past the Faroes and Iceland to North America, and the author's parallel trip in 1983 – made in a 75-year-old pilot cutter. Enthusiastically written, and with good photos.

Richard Kelly *The Name of this Book is Dogme 95*. Offering excellent insights into the Dogme movement, this diary-style account of the making of a documentary on the subject features interviews with the founders, and an in-depth look at some of the films.

John Nielsen & Judith Dern *Danish Food and Cooking*. One of few books on Danish food in English translation and featuring seventy classic Danish recipes, all well illustrated and with background information on the country's cuisine and traditional ingredients.

Ben Nimmo *In Forkbeard's Wake: Coasting Around Scandinavia*. Light and lively account of the author's sailing trip around Scandinavia, brimming with mishaps and encounters with Nordic types – divers, fishermen, archeologists and a drunk Swedish dentist. An all-too-rare modern travel book on the area.

Jack Stevenson *Dogme Uncut: Lars von Trier, Thomas Vinterberg and the Gang That Took On Hollywood*. Accessible, jargon-free and in-depth history of the Dogme movement, focusing on its origins and development and influence on current film-making.

Mary Wollstonecraft *A Short Residence in Sweden*. A searching account of Wollstonecraft's three-month solo journey through southern Scandinavia in 1795. Part travelogue, part history, part love story – a remarkable trip for a woman of that era, albeit from the author of one of the first truly feminist works, *A Vindication of the Rights of Woman*.

Language

Language

Danish

Though similar to German in some respects, **Danish** has significant differences in pronunciation, with Danes tending to swallow the ending of many words and leaving certain letters silent. In general, English is widely understood throughout Denmark, as is German, and young people especially often speak both fluently.

However, even with little need to resort to Danish, learning a few phrases will surprise and delight any Danes you meet. If you can speak Swedish or Norwegian, then you should have little problem making yourself understood – all three languages share the same root.

The section below will equip you with the bare essentials, but if you want something more comprehensive, the *Berlitz Danish–English Dictionary* and *Berlitz Danish Phrase Book* are both good reference guides. If you're planning to really get to grips with the language, the best teach-yourself book on the market is *Colloquial Danish* (W. Glyn Jones and Kirsten Gade). For serious students of the language, the *Danish Dictionary* (Anna Garde and W. Glyn Jones, eds) is excellent; while for grammar, you can't do better than *Danish: A Comprehensive Grammar* (Philip Holmes, Robin Allan and Tom Lundskær-Nielsen).

Words and phrases

Basics

Danish **pronunciation** is a confusing affair, so for the phrases below we've explained in brackets how to pronounce them.

Do you speak English?	Taler de engelsk? (tayla dee ENgellsg?)
Yes	Ja (ya)
No	Nej (nye)
I don't understand	Jeg forstår det ikke (yai fusTO day igge)
Please	Værså venlig (verso venli)
Thank you	Tak (tagg)
Excuse me	Undskyld (unsgul)
Hello/Hi	Hi (hye)
Good morning	Godmorgen (goMORN)
Good afternoon	Goddag (goDA)
Goodnight	Godnat (goNAD)
Goodbye	Farvel (faVELL)
Where is?	Hvor er? (voa ea?)
How much?	Hvor meget? (voa maYETH?)
How much does it cost?	Hvad koster det? (vath kosta day?)
I'd like...	Jeg vil gerne ha... (yai vay GERna ha)
Where are the toilets?	Hvor er toiletterne? (voa ea toaLETTaneh?)
A table for…	Et bord til… (et boa te...)
Can I have the bill/ check, please?	Må jeg bede om regningen? (moah yai beyde uhm RYningan?)
Ticket	Billet (billed)

Numbers

0	Nul	18	Atten
1	En	19	Nitten
2	To	20	Tyve
3	Tre	21	Enogtyve
4	Fire	30	Tredive
5	Fem	40	Fyrre
6	Seks	50	Halvtreds
7	Syv	60	Tres
8	Otte	70	Halvfjerds
9	Ni	80	Firs
10	Ti	90	Halvfems
11	Elleve	100	Hundrede
12	Tolv	101	Hundrede og et
13	Tretten	151	Hundrede og enoghalvtreds
14	Fjorten	200	To hundrede
15	Femten	1000	Tusind
16	Seksten		
17	Sytten		

Days

Monday	Mandag	Friday	Fredag
Tuesday	Tirsdag	Saturday	Lørdag
Wednesday	Onsdag	Sunday	Søndag
Thursday	Torsdag		

Months

January	Januar	July	Juli
February	Februar	August	August
March	Marts	September	September
April	April	October	Oktober
May	Maj	November	November
June	Juni	December	December

Some signs

Entrance	Indgang	Closed	Lukket
Exit	Udgang	Arrival	Ankomst
Push/pull	Skub/træk	Departure	Afgang
Danger	Fare	Police	Politi
Gentlemen	Herrer	No smoking	Rygning forbudt/ Ikke rygere
Ladies	Damer	No entry	Ingen adgang
Open	Åben		

Food and drink

Utensils and tableware

Gaffel	Fork	Kop	Cup
Glas	Glass	Ske	Spoon
Kniv	Knife	Tallerken	Plate

Basics

Bøfsandwich	Hamburger	Pølser	Frankfurters/sausages
Det kolde bord	Help-yourself cold buffet	Ris	Rice
Is	Ice cream	Salt	Salt
Mælk	Milk	Sildebord	A selection of spiced and pickled herring
Nudler	Noodles	Skummetmælk	Skimmed milk
Ostebord	Cheese board	Smør	Butter
Peber	Pepper	Sukker	Sugar

Bread (Brød) and pastries

Brød	Bread	Småkage	Cookie
Fuldkornsbrød	Wholemeal bread	Smørrebrød	Open sandwiches
Kiks	Biscuits	Wienerbrød	"Danish" pastry
Rugbrød	Rye bread		
Rundstykke	Crispy roll baked with seeds and grain		

Egg (Æg) dishes

Kogt æg	Boiled egg	Røræg	Scrambled eggs
Omelet	Omelette	Spejlæg	Fried eggs

Fish (Fisk)

Ål	Eel	Rejer	Shrimp
Forel	Trout	Rogn	Roe
Gedde	Pike	Rødspætte	Plaice
Helleflynder	Halibut	Røget sild	Kipper
Hummer	Lobster	Sardiner	Sardines
Karpe	Carp	Sild	Herring
Klipfisk	Salt cod	Søtunge	Sole
Krabbe	Crab	Stør	Sturgeon
Krebs	Crayfish	Store rejer	Prawns
Laks	Salmon	Torsk	Cod
Makrel	Mackerel		

Meat (Kød)

And(ung)	Duck(ling)
Dyresteg	Venison
Fasan	Pheasant
Gås	Goose
Hare	Hare
Kalkun	Turkey
Kanin	Rabbit
Kylling	Chicken
Lammekød	Lamb
Lever	Liver
Oksekød	Beef
Rensdyr	Reindeer
Skinke	Ham
Svinekød	Pork
Vildt	Venison

Vegetables (Grøntsager)

Ærter	Peas
Agurk	Cucumber
Artiskokker	Artichokes
Asparges	Asparagus
Blomkål	Cauliflower
Bønner	Beans
Brune bønner	Kidney beans
Champignoner	Mushrooms
Grønne bønner	Runner beans
Gulerødder	Carrots
Hvidløg	Garlic
Julesalat	Chicory
Kål	Cabbage
Kartofler	Potatoes
Linser	Lentils
Løg	Onions
Majs	Sweetcorn
Majskolbe	Corn on the cob
Peberfrugt	Peppers
Persille	Parsley
Porrer	Leeks
Rødbeder	Beetroot
Rødkål	Red cabbage
Rosenkål	Brussels sprouts
Salat	Lettuce, salad
Selleri	Celery
Spinat	Spinach
Turnips	Turnips

Fruit (Frugt)

Æbler	Apples
Abrikoser	Apricots
Ananas	Pineapple
Appelsiner	Oranges
Bananer	Bananas
Blåbær	Blueberries
Blommer	Plums
Brombær	Blackberries
Citron	Lemon
Ferskner	Peaches
Grapefrugt	Grapefruit
Hindbær	Raspberries
Hyldebær	Elderberries
Jordbær	Strawberries
Kirsebær	Cherries
Mandariner	Tangerines
Melon	Melon
Pærer	Pears
Rabarber	Rhubarb
Rosiner	Raisins
Solbær	Blackcurrants
Stikkelsbær	Gooseberries
Svesker	Prunes
Vindruer	Grapes

Danish specialities

Æbleflæsk	Smoked bacon with onions and sautéed apple rings
Æggekage	Scrambled eggs with onions, chives, potatoes and bacon pieces

Ålesuppe	Sweet-and-sour eel soup
Biksemad	Diced leftover roast pork fried with onion
Bøf med bløde løg	Thick minced-beef burgers fried with onions
Boller i karry	Meatballs in curry sauce served with rice
Brune kartofler	Small boiled potatoes glazed in buttery sugar
Fiske frikadeller	Fish meatballs
Flæskesteg	A hunk of pork with red cabbage, potatoes and brown sauce
Frikadeller	Pork rissoles
Grillstegt kylling	Grilled chicken
Hakkebøf	Thick minced-beef burgers fried with onions
Kalvebryst i frikasseé	Veal boiled with vegetables and served in a white sauce with peas and carrots
Kogt torsk	Poached cod in mustard sauce with boiled potatoes
Medisterpølse	A spiced pork sausage, usually served with boiled potatoes or stewed vegetables
Røget sild	Smoked herring on rye bread, garnished with a raw egg yolk, radishes and chives
Sild i karry	Herring in curry sauce
Skidne æg	Poached or hard-boiled eggs in a cream sauce, spiced with fish mustard and served with rye bread, garnished with sliced bacon and chives
Skipper labskovs	Danish stew: small squares of beef boiled with potatoes, peppercorns and bay leaves
Stegt flæsk med persille sovs	Thinly sliced fried pork with boiled potatoes and a thick creamy parsley sauce
Stegt ål med stuvede kartofler	Fried eel with diced potatoes and white sauce

Drink (Drikke)

Æblemost	Apple juice
Appelsinjuice	Orange juice
Appelsinvand	Orangeade
Citronvand	Lemonade
Eksport-Øl	Export beer (very strong lager)
Øl	Beer
Fadøl	Draught beer
Guldøl	Strong beer
Vin	Wine
Husets vin	House wine
Hvidvin	White wine
Rødvin	Red wine
Gløgg	Mulled wine
Mineralvand	Soda water
Chokolade (varm)	Chocolate (hot)
Kærnemælk	Buttermilk
Kaffe (med fløde)	Coffee (with cream)
Letmælk	Semi-skimmed milk
Mælk	Milk
Sødmælk	Full-fat milk
Te	Tea
Tomatjuice	Tomato juice
Vand	Water

Glossary

Båd	Boat	**Lufthavn**	Airport
Bakke	Hill	**Museet**	Museum
Banegård	Train station	**Nørre**	Northern
Bro	Bridge	**Ny**	New
By	Town	**Ø**	Island
-et/-en	suffixes denoting "the"	**Øster**	Eastern
Fælled	Common	**Plads**	Square
Færge	Ferry	**Port**	Gate
Folketing	Danish Parliament	**Rådhus**	Town Hall
Gade	Street	**Sankt (Skt)**	Saint
Gammel	Old	**Skov**	Forest, wood
Gård	Yard	**Slot**	Castle
Have	Garden	**Sø**	Lake, sea
Havn	Harbour	**Sønder**	Southern
Hus	House	**Stor**	Big
Kanal	Canal	**Stræde**	Street
Kirke	Church	**Strand**	Beach, shore
Klit	Dune	**Tårn**	Tower
Kongens	King's, royal	**Tog**	Train
Kyst	Coast	**Torv**	Square
Landsby	Village	**Vej**	Road
Lille	Little, small	**Vester**	Western

Small print and

Index

A Rough Guide to Rough Guides

Published in 1982, the first Rough Guide – to Greece – was a student scheme that became a publishing phenomenon. Mark Ellingham, a recent graduate in English from Bristol University, had been travelling in Greece the previous summer and couldn't find the right guidebook. With a small group of friends he wrote his own guide, combining a highly contemporary, journalistic style with a thoroughly practical approach to travellers' needs.

The immediate success of the book spawned a series that rapidly covered dozens of destinations. And, in addition to impecunious backpackers, Rough Guides soon acquired a much broader and older readership that relished the guides' wit and inquisitiveness as much as their enthusiastic, critical approach and value-for-money ethos.

These days, Rough Guides include recommendations from shoestring to luxury and cover more than 200 destinations around the globe, including almost every country in the Americas and Europe, more than half of Africa and most of Asia and Australasia. Our ever-growing team of authors and photographers is spread all over the world, particularly in Europe, the US and Australia.

In the early 1990s, Rough Guides branched out of travel, with the publication of Rough Guides to World Music, Classical Music and the Internet. All three have become benchmark titles in their fields, spearheading the publication of a wide range of books under the Rough Guide name.

Including the travel series, Rough Guides now number more than 350 titles, covering: phrasebooks, waterproof maps, music guides from Opera to Heavy Metal, reference works as diverse as Conspiracy Theories and Shakespeare, and popular culture books from iPods to Poker. Rough Guides also produce a series of more than 120 World Music CDs in partnership with World Music Network.

Visit www.roughguides.com to see our latest publications.

Rough Guide travel images are available for commercial licensing at www.roughguidespictures.com

Rough Guide credits

Text editor: Samantha Cook
Layout: Umesh Aggarwal
Cartography: Swati Handoo
Picture editor: Nicole Newman
Production: Rebecca Short
Proofreader: Wendy Smith
Cover design: Dan May, Chloë Roberts
Photographer: Roger Norum, Helena Smith
Editorial: **London** Ruth Blackmore, Andy Turner, Keith Drew, Edward Aves, Alice Park, Lucy White, Jo Kirby, James Smart, Natasha Foges, Róisín Cameron, James Rice, Lara Kavanagh, Emma Traynor, Emma Gibbs, Kathryn Lane, Monica Woods, Mani Ramaswamy, Harry Wilson, Lucy Cowie, Alison Roberts, Joe Staines, Peter Buckley, Matthew Milton, Tracy Hopkins, Ruth Tidball; **Delhi** Madhavi Singh, Karen D'Souza, Lubna Shaheen
Design & Pictures: **London** Scott Stickland, Diana Jarvis, Mark Thomas, Sarah Cummins, Emily Taylor; **Delhi** Ajay Verma, Jessica Subramanian, Ankur Guha, Pradeep Thapliyal, Sachin Tanwar, Anita Singh, Nikhil Agarwal, Sachin Gupta.
Production: Liz Cherry
Cartography: **London** Ed Wright, Katie Lloyd-Jones; **Delhi** Rajesh Chhibber, Ashutosh Bharti, Rajesh Mishra, Animesh Pathak, Jasbir Sandhu, Karobi Gogoi, Alakananda Bhattacharya, Deshpal Dabas
Online: **London** Faye Hellon, Jeanette Angell, Fergus Day, Justine Bright, Clare Bryson, Aine Fearon, Adrian Low, Ezgi Celebi; **Delhi** Amit Verma, Rahul Kumar, Narender Kumar, Ravi Yadav, Debojit Borah, Rakesh Kumar, Ganesh Sharma, Shisir Basumatari
Marketing & Publicity: **London** Liz Statham, Jess Carter, Vanessa Godden, Vivienne Watton, Anna Paynton, Rachel Sprackett, Laura Vipond; **New York** Katy Ball, Judi Powers; **Delhi** Ragini Govind
Reference Director: Andrew Lockett
Operations Assistant: Becky Doyle
Operations Manager: Helen Atkinson
Publishing Director (Travel): Clare Currie
Commercial Manager: Gino Magnotta
Managing Director: John Duhigg

Publishing information

This fourth edition published May 2010 by
Rough Guides Ltd,
80 Strand, London WC2R 0RL
14 Local Shopping Centre, Panchsheel Park, New Delhi 110017, India
Distributed by the Penguin Group
Penguin Books Ltd,
80 Strand, London WC2R 0RL
Penguin Group (USA)
375 Hudson Street, NY 10014, USA
Penguin Group (Australia)
250 Camberwell Road, Camberwell, Victoria 3124, Australia
Penguin Group (Canada)
195 Harry Walker Parkway N, Newmarket, ON, L3Y 7B3 Canada
Penguin Group (NZ)
67 Apollo Drive, Mairangi Bay, Auckland 1310, New Zealand
Cover concept by Peter Dyer.

Typeset in Bembo and Helvetica to an original design by Henry Iles.

Printed in Singapore

240pp includes index

A catalogue record for this book is available from the British Library

ISBN: 978-1-84836-478-3

1 3 5 7 9 8 6 4 2

Help us update

We've gone to a lot of effort to ensure that the fourth edition of **The Rough Guide to Copenhagen** is accurate and up-to-date. However, things change – places get "discovered", opening hours are notoriously fickle, restaurants and rooms raise prices or lower standards. If you feel we've got it wrong or left something out, we'd like to know, and if you can remember the address, the price, the hours, the phone number, so much the better.

Please send your comments with the subject line "**Rough Guide Copenhagen Update**" to ⓔ mail@roughguides.com. We'll credit all contributions and send a copy of the next edition (or any other Rough Guide if you prefer) for the very best emails.

Have your questions answered and tell others about your trip at ⓦ www.roughguides.com

Acknowledgements

Caroline thanks Henrik Thierlien for his help and advice on all matters Copenhagen; Roy and Lise for being the first to show me their lovely city; Karin and Steen for their wonderful hospitality over the years; Sam for being a great editor and a joy to work with; and last, but not least, Martin, Daisy and Lucy for plenty of laughs, Easter eggs and fairground rides along the way.

Lone would like – once again – to thank Henrik Thierlein of Wonderful Copenhagen for his enthusiastic help. Also huge thanks to Knud og Klara; Merete, Emma og Jan; and Tina for housing me and Pepe, and putting up with our many quirks. We owe you…

Photo credits

All photos © Rough Guides except the following:

Front Cover

The Little Mermaid © Marco Cristofori/Getty

Things not to miss

10 Queen Margrethe and Prince Henrik tapestry © Jorgen Schytte/Visit Denmark

19 Roskilde Viking museum © Marco Cristofori/Alamy

Black and whites

p.197 Swedish band bob hund at the Roskilde Festival © Torben Christensen/Getty

Index

Map entries are in colour.

L

M

N

O

P

R

S

T

U

V

W

Z

Map symbols

maps are listed in the full index using coloured text

Chapter boundary
Expressway
Major road
Minor road
Pedestrianized street
Steps
Railway
Path/cycle route
Coastline/river
Ferry route
Gate/entrance
Bridge
Airport
Metro station
S-Tog station
Bus stop
Windmill
Campsite

Point of interest
Internet access
Information office
Post office
Hospital
Toilets
Museum
Castle/fort
Stately home/palace
Fountain/gardens
Statue
Synagogue
Building
Church
Stadium
Cemetery
Park
Beach

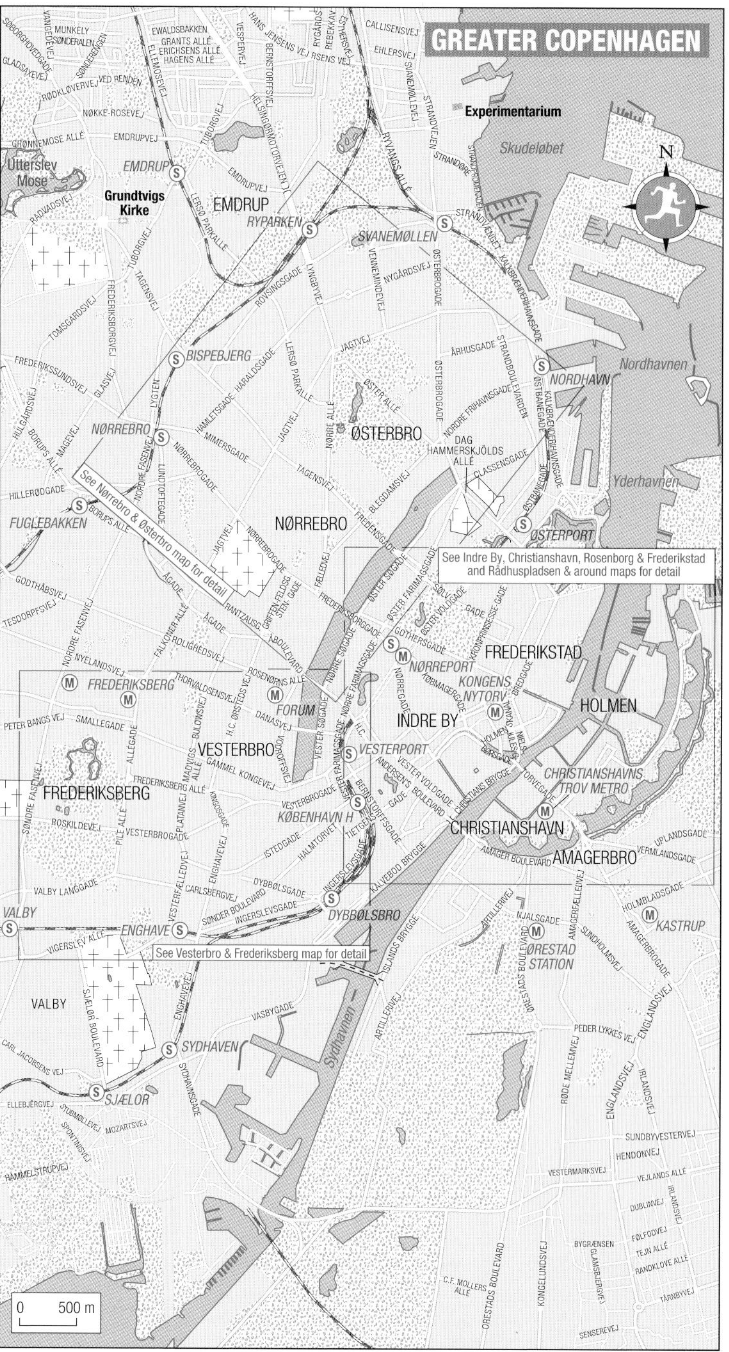

GREATER COPENHAGEN
Experimentarium
Skudeløbet
N
Utterslev Mose
Grundtvigs Kirke
EMDRUP
EMDRUP
RYPARKEN
SVANEMØLLEN
BISPEBJERG
NØRREBRO
ØSTERBRO
NORDHAVN
Nordhavnen
Yderhavnen
FUGLEBAKKEN
NØRREBRO
ØSTERPORT
See Nørrebro & Østerbro map for detail
See Indre By, Christianshavn, Rosenborg & Frederikstad and Rådhuspladsen & around maps for detail
FREDERIKSTAD
NØRREPORT
KONGENS NYTORV
HOLMEN
FREDERIKSBERG
FORUM
INDRE BY
VESTERBRO
VESTERPORT
FREDERIKSBERG
CHRISTIANSHAVNS TROV METRO
KØBENHAVN H
CHRISTIANSHAVN
AMAGERBRO
VALBY
DYBBØLSBRO
KASTRUP
ENGHAVE
See Vesterbro & Frederiksberg map for detail
ØRESTAD STATION
VALBY
SYDHAVEN
Sydhavnen
SJÆLOR
DAG HAMMERSKJÖLDS ALLÉ
0 500 m

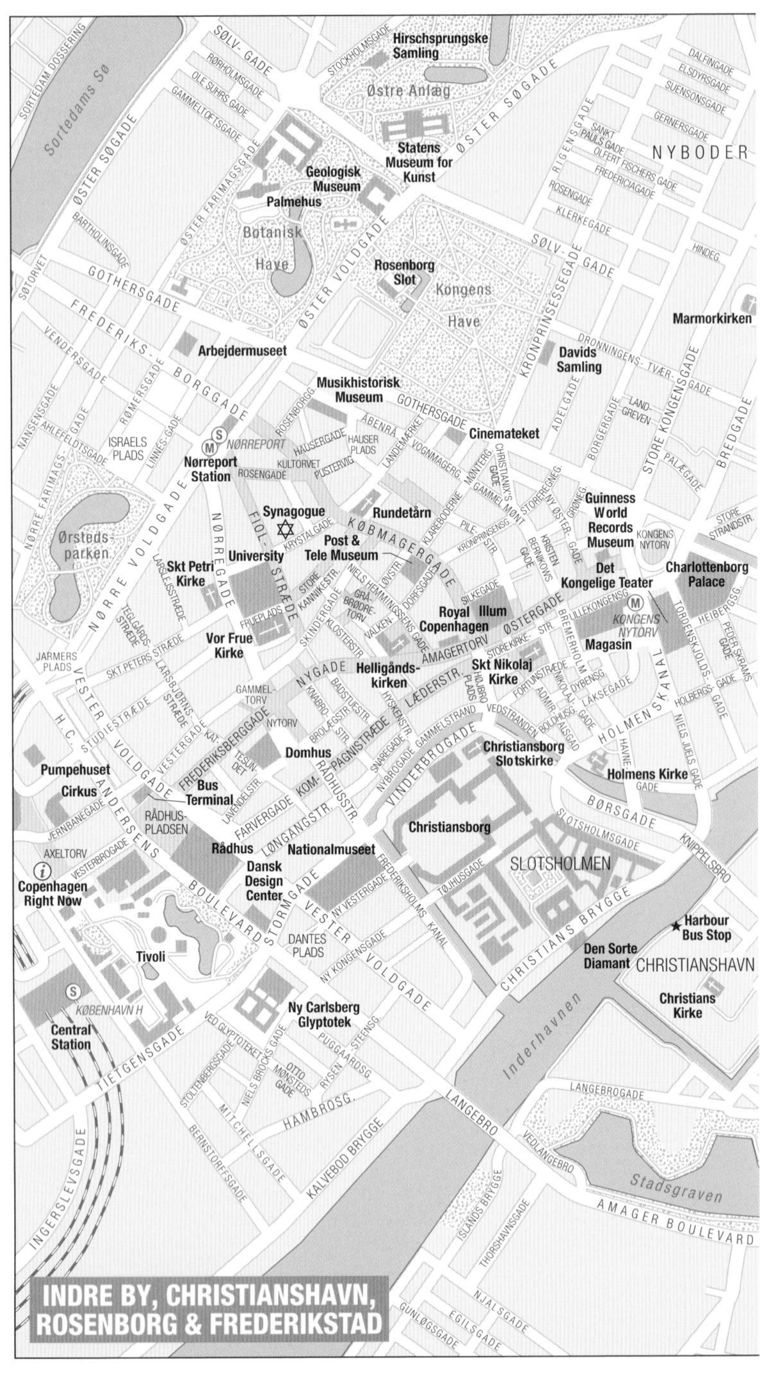
INDRE BY, CHRISTIANSHAVN,
ROSENBORG & FREDERIKSTAD
Hirschsprungske Samling
Østre Anlæg
Statens Museum for Kunst
Geologisk Museum
Palmehus
Botanisk Have
Rosenborg Slot
Kongens Have
NYBODER
Marmorkirken
Arbejdermuseet
Davids Samling
Musikhistorisk Museum
Cinemateket
Nørreport Station
NØRREPORT
ISRAELS PLADS
KULTORVET
HAUSER PLADS
Synagogue
Rundetårn
Guinness World Records Museum
Ørstedsparken
Skt Petri Kirke
University
Post & Tele Museum
KONGENS NYTORV
Charlottenborg Palace
Det Kongelige Teater
Royal Copenhagen
Illum
Magasin
Vor Frue Kirke
JARMERS PLADS
Helligåndskirken
Skt Nikolaj Kirke
GAMMELTORV
NYTORV
AMAGERTORV
Domhus
Christiansborg Slotskirke
Holmens Kirke
Pumpehuset
Cirkus
Bus Terminal
RÅDHUSPLADSEN
Christiansborg
SLOTSHOLMEN
AXELTORV
Rådhus
Nationalmuseet
Copenhagen Right Now
Dansk Design Center
DANTES PLADS
Harbour Bus Stop
Tivoli
Den Sorte Diamant
CHRISTIANSHAVN
Christians Kirke
KØBENHAVN H
Central Station
Ny Carlsberg Glyptotek
Inderhavnen
Stadsgraven
Sortedams Sø
SØLVGADE
ØSTER SØGADE
ØSTER VOLDGADE
GOTHERSGADE
FREDERIKSBORGGADE
KRONPRINSESSEGADE
STORE KONGENSGADE
BREDGADE
NØRRE VOLDGADE
NØRREGADE
FIOLSTRÆDE
KØBMAGERGADE
ØSTERGADE
NYGADE
VESTER VOLDGADE
H.C. ANDERSENS BOULEVARD
STORMGADE
VESTERGADE
FREDERIKSBERGGADE
KOMPAGNISTRÆDE
RÅDHUSSTR.
VINDERBROGADE
HOLMENS KANAL
BØRSGADE
KNIPPELSBRO
CHRISTIANS BRYGGE
LANGEBRO
TIETGENSGADE
INGERSLEVSGADE
KALVEBOD BRYGGE
AMAGER BOULEVARD
LANGEBROGADE
HAMBROSG.
BERNSTORFFSGADE
MITCHELLSGADE
NJALSGADE
EGILSGADE
GUNLØGSGADE
ISLANDS BRYGGE
THORSHAVNSGADE